The Making of a Chicano Militant

José Angel Gutiérrez. Photograph by Richard Avedon. Crystal City, Texas, 1979.

The Making of a Chicano Militant

Lessons from Cristal

José Angel Gutiérrez

THE UNIVERSITY OF WISCONSIN PRESS

Wisconsin Studies in Autobiography

WILLIAM L. ANDREWS
General Editor

The University of Wisconsin Press
2537 Daniels Street
Madison, Wisconsin 53718

3 Henrietta Street
London WC2E 8LU, England

5   4   3   2   1

Printed in the United States of America

Library of Congress Cataloging-in-Publication Data
Gutiérrez, José Angel.
   The making of a Chicano militant : lessons from Cristal / José Angel Gutiérrez.
   352 pp.   cm. — (Wisconsin studies in autobiography)
   Includes index.
   ISBN 0-299-15980-9 (cloth: alk. paper).
   ISBN 0-299-15984-1 (pbk.: alk. paper)
   1. Gutiérrez, José Angel.   2. Mexican Americans—Texas—Crystal City—Biography.
3. Political activists—Texas—Crystal City—Biography.   4. Mexican Americans—
Texas—Crystal City—Politics and government.   5. Crystal City (Tex.)—Ethnic rela-
tions.nt.
I. Title.   II. Series.
F394.C83G88   1998
976.4'437—dc21
[B]   98-13866

Para Adrian, Tozi, Olin, Avina, Lina,
Andrea y Clavel, mis hijos

Contents

Illustrations   ix

Preface   xi

1. Introduction   3
2. Aztlan: The Chicano Homeland   15
3. The Education of a Chicano   45
4. Los Cinco Candidatos   62
5. Texas A & I   78
6. MAYO   97
7. Conditions and Preparations for El "Walkout"   122
8. The Thirty-Ninth MAYO Walkout: A Diary   142
9. The MAYO Plan for Aztlan   177
10. Ciudadanos Unidos: The Base   193
11. Chicano School and City Governance   202
12. El Partido Nacional de La Raza Unida   215
13. Chicano County Governance   242
14. Exile to Oregon   267
15. The Return to Texas   288

Appendix: FBI Documents   307

Index   317

Titles in Wisconsin Studies in Autobiography   333

Illustrations

José Angel Gutiérrez   *frontispiece*

Map of Zavala County   6

Gutiérrez with his mother, grandmother, and aunt   25

Gutiérrez at age 2   26

Gutiérrez in his grammar school photo, 1952   29

Gutiérrez as a junior in Crystal City High School, 1959–1960   32

Albert Fuentes, Jim Ferguson, Senator John Tower, and
José Angel Gutiérrez   82

Luz Bazan Gutiérrez and José Angel Gutiérrez at the 1967
signing of the agreement between Chicano students and
school officials that brought an end to the student protest
in Glendale, Arizona   120

Walkout and demonstration at Crystal City High School, 1969   149

Gutiérrez speaking at the dedication of the Maria Hernandez
Resource Center, 1972   210

La Raza Unida Party poster from the 1970 campaign   216

Mario Compean and Maria Jimenez, 1974   233

Reies Lopez Tijerina and Gutiérrez, 1973   235

Dedication of the Chicano movement mural at the University of
Houston, 1975   238

A meeting at the Casa de Americas during the 1975 trip to Cuba   240

Gutiérrez in his office as county judge   249

Gutiérrez and Riche Diaz putting up political signs for the 1976
elections in Zavala County   263

The tenth anniversary of the Crystal City High School
walkout, 1979   264

Gutiérrez and Ernesto Gomez in the parade celebrating the tenth
anniversary of the 1969 Crystal City High School walkout   265

Gutiérrez family in front of their home in Independence, Oregon   276

Gutiérrez in front of the state capitol in Salem, Oregon, 1984   279

Gutiérrez, Adrian, and Luz, 1986   286

Gutiérrez, Gloria, and Andrea, 1988   294

Gutiérrez and Gloria, 1988   296
Gutiérrez and family at the Activist Reunion, San Antonio,
    1989   296
Activist Reunion: Gutiérrez, Maria Elena Martinez, Maria
    Jimenez, and Frank Shafer-Corona   297
Activist Reunion: Gutiérrez and Olin, and Emma Tenayuca   298
Activist Reunion: Mario Compean and Gutiérrez   299
Activist Reunion: Gutiérrez and Reies Lopez Tijerina   300
Texas Governor Ann Richards and Gutiérrez, 1989   302
Gutiérrez speaking at Crystal City High School, 1989   302
Gutiérrez after taking the oath admitting him to the Texas
    State Bar, May, 1990   303

Preface

Over the years, I often would burn and chafe at reading two types of written material: that written about Chicanos, and that written which ignored the Chicano presence and contribution. I often would ask myself how and why such trash could be printed about us and without us. But, I didn't write.

Later, as the Chicano movement and I became the focus of some of these writings, I not only burned and chafed while reading the material, I also became enraged at the content. I could not believe that it was us or me they were writing about, I did not recognize the social movement or the person. But, I didn't write.

My rationalization was that I was too busy making things happen during the Chicano movement to take time to write. And, it takes a lot of time to write. I did manage to keep a diary and notes from time to time.

On occasion during the 1970s and into the 1980s, I would give a speech or engage in conversation, and the anti-Chicano content of these magazine and newspaper articles, books, and documentaries would come up. My responses to this type of material invariably led someone in the audience, or the partner in conversation, to implore me to "write that up so that other Chicanos can learn the real truth." I recall specifically such early prodding from Hank Lopez, Bill Crane, Lupe Angiano, Rudy Acuña, Armando Gutiérrez, Tatcho Mindiola, Irma Mireles, Reymundo and Maria Marin, Irene Blea, Armando Navarro, Charon D'Aiello, Charlie Cotrell, Elizabeth "Betita" Martinez, my former spouse, Luz Bazan Gutiérrez, my current spouse, Gloria Garza Gutiérrez, and my older children, Adrian, Tozi, and Olin. While visiting Hank Lopez at his home in upstate New York in the early 1970s, I recall outlining with him over many bottles of beer the plot of a novel he and I would write based on my activities in South Texas. He wanted to develop the character of a super Chicano hero in a serial novel who would liberate South Texas. I surmised that I was the prototype for his Chicano hero. Lopez dropped this idea in favor of another contemporary theme involving the takeover of Manhattan by black militants. *Afro 6* is the book he ultimately wrote. Neither he nor I ever got around to writing about the Chicano hero and the takeover of South Texas before he died. During the late 1970s, Tatcho Mindiola and I discussed with the novelist Max Martinez the possibility of having him write my biography. After a heated argument between Max and me about his all-consuming interest with sex and violence in my lifestyle, I declined. Over the years, countless people in Cristal have asked me when I would write THE real story about our struggle in that community. But, I didn't write.

I was still too busy with the Chicano movement, governing Zavala County, Texas, and running La Raza Unida Party in eighteen states and the District of Columbia. I barely managed to keep records and recordings of happenings, meetings, and speeches in the 1970s.

Finally, I was made to write by the demands of seeking promotion and tenure at Western Oregon State College in 1981, and later, in 1993, at the University of Texas at Arlington. I wrote and had published articles in scholarly journals, coauthored a book, written book chapters and reviews, essays, and several newspaper editorials in both English and Spanish. At the beginning of this decade, I began earnestly researching and writing several manuscripts, mostly for academic audiences.

Irene Blea, the prolific scholar and director of Chicano Studies at California State University at Los Angeles, called me shortly after the death of Cesar Chavez in 1993, urging me to think about writing an autobiography. She offered to write my story if I didn't have the time or inclination to undertake it myself. This time, I was ready for the idea and began the labor, thanks to this last prodding by her. Most recently, during the summer of 1996, while embroiled in an employment dispute at my present university over the leadership of the Center for Mexican American Studies that I founded there in 1993, Ricardo Gonzales suggested we collaborate and write a biography of my struggles. This is not that manuscript, but it is a beginning narrative of some aspects of my life.

While attending the National Association for Chicano and Chicana Studies conference in Spokane, Washington in 1995, I met with several editors of academic presses exhibiting their works at the gathering. Rosalie Robertson of the University of Wisconsin Press took particular interest in me and my life story. We discussed the various manuscripts I had under production, she was most interested in this manuscript and suggested I send a copy of the first chapters to Bill Andrews, the editor of this series. I did. Shortly thereafter, I received a letter from him encouraging me to continue the manuscript to completion, along with a contract from Rosalie Robertson. From that moment on, not a day went by that I was not dictating to a microcassette recorder, or word processing on a laptop, home computer, or office computer. Even while camping in northern New Mexico or the rolling hills of Wyoming, or staying in a Motel 6 with the smaller children of the family during the summer months of 1995 and 1996, I kept writing and rewriting. In December, 1996, when the completed manuscript was mailed off, my wife, children, and I celebrated with my favorite pastime, a backyard cookout. On that occasion my two youngest daughters, Clavel Amariz and Andrea Lucia, then ages six and eight, asked if this meant they now could yell and scream while playing in the house and if now I would have time to read them stories instead of admonishing them with "*¡Cayense! ¡Estoy escribiendo!* (Quiet! I'm writing!)"

Bill, Rosalie, and I made the postal service and Kinko's copy service lots of money. The packaged manuscript copies kept coming and going from late 1995 through 1997 from whatever geographic points Bill or I were located at during this period, and to Rosalie in Madison. Not only did Bill, Rosalie, and Brian Bendlin become my writing teachers, they also became my mentors in this writing process. They, together with the constructive criticism of the final manuscript reviewers, one of whom was Genaro M. Padilla, helped me shape this work into a solid manuscript.

There are many people that deserve credit for making this book possible. To the Chicano movement and those within the circle of family, friends, and fellow Chicano activists, thank you for the faith, advice, *compañerismo* (comradeship), encouragement, guidance, and support during the decades of struggle in Cristal. To those who provided the technical help to see this book to fruition, from the transcriber and word processor, Karen McGee, to the countless nameless and faceless people that were participants in the larger Chicano struggle, and to the folks at the University of Wisconsin Press that took the manuscript and made it into the book you now hold I owe my thanks. Finally, to those responsible for the negative character attacks in the media going back at least three decades, thank you for giving rise to the *coraje* (rage) in me that kept the idea of writing this manuscript alive and waiting for the opportune moment. *Mil gracias,* or as some say in Texas, a thousand thanks, y'all!

The Making of a Chicano Militant

1

Introduction

When I was growing up, newspaper and magazine articles, movies, and books written and published in the United States invariably were overwhelmingly concerned and focused on the experience of white people. Occasionally, and now with more frequency, these publications and movies contain at least a reference to the black experience in the United States. I have often bristled while reading such stories because the authors, editors, and publishers have knowingly omitted mention of us, *los Mexicanos*. None of these so-called professionals could have finished high school and graduated from universities without the knowledge of our historic presence in the Americas, particularly the Southwest and Western parts of the United States, yet, still they chose to ignore us. Not only is our history omitted from the public discourse, but our contributions to the social fabric of this country are disconnected from us as a people. Anglos always seem to tell the world what they have "discovered" as the best of our culture, and loudly proclaim their patent.

Scholarship on Chicanos has grown in quantum leaps since the days when I was an activist attempting to read and learn about others like me. This is not to say that the body of existing knowledge is enough; it never is. It is to say only the obvious, that there is more material available now than ever before. We have finally begun writing about ourselves and finding publishers willing to market these products.

There are several students of Chicano politics whose research focus has been *Cristal* (or Crystal City, Texas, as it is now known) and La Raza

Unida Party. Chicano politics has become a serious research interest and subfield in American Government for academics, policy analysts, and leaders of institutions. Richard Santillan (1973), Ignacio Garcia (1989), and Armando Navarro (1998), respectively, have been the first and last to write on La Raza Unida Party. Herb Hirsch and Armando Gutiérrez (1974), Rudolfo de la Garza and F. Chris Garcia (1977), David Montejano (1987), Juan Gomez Quiñones (1990), Carlos Muñoz (1988), and Armando Navarro (1995, 1998) have written articles and books about Cristal and La Raza Unida Party. Dr. Navarro recently published a book with the University of Texas Press on MAYO, the Mexican American Youth Organization, the precursor organization to La Raza Unida Party. His most recent publication is *The Cristal Experiment: A Chicano Struggle for Community Control* (1998). He is also at work on a book on the national Raza Unida Party.

John Shockley (1974) was the first scholar to study the Chicano happenings in Cristal. His book, *Chicano Revolt in a Texas Town* covers two distinct periods in the politics of Cristal. He writes of the first "revolt" of 1963, propelled by Los Cinco Candidatos, and of the second "revolt" in 1969 by MAYO that led to the formation of La Raza Unida Party. To this day, he and Armando Navarro have been the only scholars to write exclusively about Cristal.

John Shockley's work contains several grave omissions and theoretical errors, however. There is no mention of the role of community organizing, for example, or of the creation of the local grassroots organizations that provided the foundation for both Los Cinco Candidatos and later La Raza Unida Party. The community organization and subsequent mobilization of the Chicano population made possible their electoral victories during both periods. Shockley attributes the Chicano electoral success not to the organizing and mobilization of the Chicano community, but to the "charisma" of the two leaders—Juan Cornejo in the first revolt and myself in the second. This analysis is much too shallow and perpetuates certain social science fictions: that a person's charm is a substitute for community organization; that personality is a sufficient motivation for revolt; and that the Chicano people only follow when led by charismatic leaders. Shockley discounts the family-based organizing model utilized in both revolts and relied on his notion of charisma as complete explanation for the leadership skills, grassroots organizing, and community organization developed by Chicanos in Cristal.

Another major flaw with the Shockley book is his use of the "great men/great events" paradigm for the political history of the two periods. His reliance on this notion of why events happen is too simplistic, Shockley's view of history is unequivocally male-centered. He reverses the order of social dynamics—events occur from the top down and flow to the masses. First of all, events seldom are initiated only by male political actors positioned atop the social hierarchy; more often than not, events are initiated by people, both men and women, positioned below the top strata of the elite. Average people in the course of daily life make things happen, and elites react to those happenings. Because of the "great men/great events" view held by Shockley and applied in his study of Chicanos in Cristal, the central role of women in both revolts is never acknowledged. More important, he concludes that both Chicano revolts in Cristal occurred because the community and the two Chicano leaders were unique to the locale, arguing that this electoral success could not be replicated elsewhere. In my view, he is completely wrong. The electoral successes of the second revolt were made possible by the groundwork and experience of the first. And, the Chicano model taken from Cristal was indeed repeated in many Texas communities such as Mathis, Robstown, Cotulla, Pearsall, San Juan, Anthony, and San Antonio's Edgewood area during the 1970s.

Many of the participants in the second revolt in Cristal were leaders in the first as well. And in 1969–70, the youths involved were the sons and daughters of those involved in 1963. His book stops its description of events and analysis at 1973. Perhaps, had he returned to Cristal later in the decade—as Armando Navarro has done in his study of MAYO—Shockley would have noted the shortcomings mentioned here and revised his book. Participant observation is a legitimate research tool, as is the personal interview. The application of theory to practice, of applied research, is a prerequisite for those in the academy. The fine line separating the use of knowledge from the abuse of power is the development of skill in both the application and practice of learned theorems. In other words, it is not enough to know better, we must also *act* better. Because methodology rests on ideology, research and practice methodologies are the main stuff of primary source material needed to present a point of view.

In 1977, the anthropologist Douglas Foley, together with others, wrote *From Peones to Politicos: Ethnic Relations in a South Texas Town 1900–1977.* That book is about relations between Chicanos and Anglos in a small town, Pearsall, within the Winter Garden area of South Texas. (The Winter Garden area forms a rectangle of land just southwest of San Antonio in Bexar County and is comprised of six counties: Uvalde, Medina, Frio, La Salle, Zavala, and Dimmit.) In essence, the book is about the community organization and politics of Chicanos in Pearsall, Frio County, during the 1970s. This effort also occurred during the time of the Chicano movement and the rise of La Raza Unida Party in that

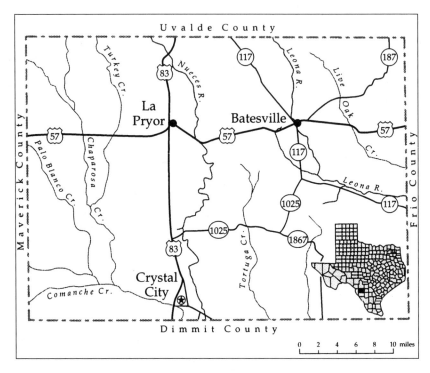

Zavala County, Texas

geographic area. Foley's book radically differs from Shockley's in that it clearly credits the work of average Chicanos in making political change in their environment. Regrettably, though, Foley utilizes the trademark of anthropologists, omitting the real names of people and places in his book. I can tell you, however, that the book is about the political efforts of MAYO and La Raza Unida Party activists in the city of Pearsall and Frio County while the second revolt in Cristal was in the making at the other end of the Winter Garden area.

In 1972, Richard Santillan wrote *El Partido de La Raza Unida*, a book on the organization and rise of this political party in the United States. His focus was primarily on the extensive political activity in California of these party militants, but he also surveyed the activity in other states, including Texas. This was the first book, short and brief, on La Raza Unida Party. Later, in 1989, Ignacio Garcia wrote *United We Win*, the second book on the party. The Garcia book is much more comprehensive simply because many years had passed since the founding of the party in Zavala County (Cristal) in 1970; its spread to California by the following year; the national convention held in El Paso over the Labor Day weekend of 1972; its subsequent expansion to eighteen additional states and the District of Columbia; and its demise toward the end of the decade. Both books cover events in Cristal as part of their description of the development of La Raza Unida Party.

The 1995 book by Armando Navarro, *Mexican American Youth Organization: The Avant-Garde of the Chicano Movement in Texas*, is a contribution not only to the literature on Chicano politics but also to the role Chicano youth held in the Chicano movement. Navarro's book serves as the bridge between events in the early part of the 1960s (with the rise of the Political Association of Spanish Speaking Organizations [PASO] and their involvement with the first revolt in Cristal) and the subsequent youthful generation of Chicanos that engineered a greater political upheaval against the existing social and political order in Texas. His book analyzes MAYO's contribution to the political struggles of the day. Navarro utilizes the many school walkouts that occurred in South Texas to depict the organizing activity of Chicano youth and serves as a case study on the second Cristal revolt in 1968 and on into the 1970s. The politics of MAYO, while engaged in community organizing in the Winter Garden area, are placed within the larger framework of the Chicano movement.

Over the years I have written numerous academic and popular accounts of Chicano politics, among them *A Gringo Manual on How to Handle Mexicans* (1974) and *El Politico: The Mexican American Elected Official* (1968). On occasion, I have written on Cristal and La Raza Unida Party. I have not written, however, about my personal experiences as an actor in Chicano politics. I have placed most of my personal papers, memorabilia, recordings, posters, political buttons, photographs, and government documents indicating the surveillance of my activities and that of other Chicanos in archives at two University of Texas locations, in Austin and San Antonio. The reader is encouraged to visit these archival collections for two reasons: first, to review the supporting primary source material for the interpretations that are the basis of this narrative; and second, to independently reach conclusions on this written material from that primary source material. In some cases in this book, I regret that I am unable to pinpoint specifically the actual box and file that could tie my narrative back to its sources. The material at the University of Texas at San Antonio may not yet be completely inventoried, catalogued, and indexed. Records from my candidacy in the special election for the U. S. Senate in Texas beginning in 1992 and ending in May, 1993 are not written about in this narrative, and remain in my possession. After the Victor Morales race for U.S. Senate in Texas in November of 1996, perhaps this material will make for fruitful comparative data.

Chicano biography and autobiography, as a method of scholarship, is woefully undeveloped. A special issue of the journal *Americas Review* (1988) on the autobiography of Latinos contains several articles on this lack of published material and the state of the field. Genaro M. Padilla has an excellent first chapter, "Recovering Mexican Autobiography," in his 1995 book, *My History, Not Yours: The Formation of Mexican American Autobiography*. In the chapter, Padilla compares Mexican American autobiographical scholarship with that of Native Americans and African Americans. He concludes that Mexican American autobiography from the time of conquest has necessarily been concerned with nostalgia for the past. This nostalgia is a dynamic process; it is the need not to forget or be forgotten. His book is an attempt to reconstruct the historical autobiographical discourse of the people of Mexican ancestry who remained in the United States after 1848. Padilla and others have since been involved with a national project to recover the rich literary tradition of the Spanish speaking peoples, particularly Mexican Americans.

There are some earlier notable autobiographical works: *Barrio Boy*, by the late Ernesto Galarza (1971), comes to mind. Galarza writes of his childhood days in Mexico, of his family's migration to the United States, and of coping with forced assimilation and conformity to Anglo societal norms. Later in the book, Galarza the academician writes of his own farm labor organizing efforts and about the *bracero* program. Oscar "Zeta" Acosta, a Chicano militant and lawyer from Los Angeles wrote two books in succession, *The Autobiography of a Brown Buffalo* in 1968 and *The Revolt of the Cockroach People* in 1973. In both books, Acosta struggles with issues of his cultural identity as a Chicano and as a man. His autobiographical writings make for masterful storytelling.

Another autobiographical form is found in *Hunger of Memory: The Education of Richard Rodriguez* (1981) and *Days of Obligation: An Argument with My Mexican Father* (1992), both by Richard Rodriguez. Rodriguez recounts in essay form his experience of distancing himself from his Mexicanness as he searched for an alternative cultural identity within the Anglo milieu. In the regard of searching for a cultural identity, the Rodriguez works are similar to those of "Zeta" Acosta. Both the Rodriguez and Galarza autobiographies are the subject of Ramon Saldivar's *Chicano Narrative: The Dialectics of Difference* (1990), a cogent piece on this type of narrative by Chicano authors who long for a cultural identity. These works are accounts of shifting and conflicting models of self.

Bettina (Elizabeth) R. Flores, a first-generation Mexican American woman, began writing *Chiquita's Cocoon* at the end of the 1980s as she prepared to approach her fiftieth birthday. Unable to find a publisher for her autobiography at the time, she published the manuscript herself in 1990. The publication is available in both English and Spanish. In 1994, Villard Books, a division of Random House, published a paperback edition. This book, according to her, is about Bettina's "growing up Latina." She has insightful commentary on Chicana life from the married-with-children, female perspective. Her writing, however, is often negative and stereotypical. She does manage to exude confidence and self-esteem in the writing, and every page of the text is a challenge for Latinas to overcome adversity in life as she has.

An example of a commissioned, straightforward biography is Jay Mathews's *Escalante: The Best Teacher in America* (1988). Jaime Escalante is the teacher who made national and international news with his highly successful approach to teaching calculus to Chicanos in an East Los Angeles high school, and whom the film *Stand and Deliver* is based on. Some literary critics surmise that Al Urista, a.k.a. Alurista, actually wrote Rodolfo "Corky" Gonzales's epic autobiographical poem *Yo Soy Joaquin* (1967).

Another autobiography written in the traditional chronological, narrated style is that of Luis J. Rodriguez. His book about his life while in Chicano gangs in East Los Angeles, *Always Running: La Vida Loca, Gang Days in L.A.* (1993) is powerful. Most recently, Mona Ruiz provided a major contribution with her book, *Two Badges: The Lives of Mona Ruiz* (1997). Mona's story details her transformation from gangbanger to police officer in Santa Ana, California. These works are comparable to that of the Puerto Rican barrio experience in New York's Harlem, chronicled by Piri Thomas in *Down These Mean Streets* (1967) and Claude Brown's similar treatment of the African American experience in the Harlem ghetto in *Manchild in the Promised Land* (1965). In 1992 Elaine Brown, the only female to lead the Black Panther Party, wrote her autobiography, *A Taste of Power*, which is rich with details of the internal workings and developments of that political party from her perspective. This book is valuable to me for comparison and contrast with my efforts at building La Raza Unida Party.

Manuel Gamio's *The Mexican Immigrant, His Life Story* (1931), is a unique biography, reporting tales of woe from the lips of recent Mexican immigrants. Gamio's open interview and narrative response style is the model subsequently employed by Studs Turkel in his work among the working class.

In 1993, Mario T. Garcia teamed up with another Chicano militant and activist, Bert Corona, to write a book, *Memories of Chicano History:*

The Life and Narrative of Bert Corona. They used a most unique approach, that of the double voice. Bert Corona dictated to audiotape his memories of certain events of Chicano political history in which he was involved. Garcia transcribed and reworked these select narrated events into an interpretive and discursive manuscript, done much in the tradition of the oral history interview. Together, they wrote and edited the final version to minimize filtering and mediation by the interviewer. The Corona-Garcia technique resembled the approach used by others, such as Elisabeth Burgos-Debray and Rigoberta Menchu, who together created *I, Rigoberta Menchu: An Indian Woman in Guatemala* (1990). The story of Elvia Alvarado, a Honduran woman, was also told in similar fashion by Medea Benjamin in *Don't Be Afraid, Gringo* (1987). Malcolm X and Alex Haley teamed up to produce *The Autobiography of Malcolm X* (1965). In the Malcolm X book, however, Haley never surrendered the authority to write the final draft; he was the scholar and Malcolm was the subject/participant. In the Garcia book on Corona, the project reportedly was more collaborative than dichotomized into a scholar-subject/participant activity. In other joint venture biographies and autobiographies there is a hired coauthor or even a ghostwriter. The division of labor is unidirectional and flows from the subject/participant to the writer/scholar. In oral history interviews and projects, the opposite is in effect, the writer/scholar writes of and not for the subject/participant.

Rosaura Sanchez, in her 1995 work, *Telling Identities,* labels this process of transcription from dictated testimony in the form of a memoir a "mediated narrative" because the dictation is a surrender to the hegemonic influence of the transcriber or mediator. Sanchez believes this surrender is a loss of agency, a loss of power to represent one's self before others. Her work with the *testimonios* (testimonials) of some sixty-two *Californios* gathered under the direction of Hubert Howe Bancroft in the 1870s is a critical text on the distinctions between autobiography, biography, and mediated narratives. *Testimonios,* according to Sanchez, are distinguished from autobiography in five areas: 1.) they are first person narratives; 2.) the narrator is a witness or participant in a significant historical experience; 3.) there is an urgency to the narration; 4.) the perspective is collective and marginalized; and 5.) the testimonial is a production by an informant and a professional interviewer. Autobiography, on the other hand, is self-generated and a discursive construction of "self" within a particular social space.

My effort with this book has another facet, as an autobiography of political lessons. While I am the subject, the writer, the speaker, and the scholar/interpreter, I am also the teacher. The events depicted have special meaning for me. From these events, I learned to become a Chicano militant. I am writing this book with the expectation that it will be received as a treatise on political lessons that made me and others into Chicano militants. Undoubtedly, this has been a different labor.

In this introduction and the next three chapters, I position this book in its place within autobiography; I give my view of the Chicano homeland; and I relate the very earliest political lessons learned during childhood and adolescence. The 1963 electoral victory of *Los Cinco Candidatos* in Cristal, my time at junior college and at Texas A & I University are the stuff of chapters 4 and 5. Together with four others, I began the Mexican American Youth Organization (MAYO) during my graduate school days at St. Mary's University. This story is told in chapter 6. The famous school walkout that occurred in Cristal is detailed in chapter 7. The formation of the grassroots community organization, *Ciudadanos Unidos;* the rise of La Raza Unida Party and the governing of the Crystal City School District and the county of Zavala are the middle chapters, 8 through 13. The last chapters, 14 and 15, cover my self-imposed exile from Texas to Oregon in 1980, and my return to Texas in April 1986 through to 1990. I end the manuscript at this year because it is when I opened my own law practice and returned to teaching at the University of Texas at Arlington. Perhaps, in a full-bodied autobiography at a later date, I will be more current.

I do not write from the perspective of a victim. Rather, I write as a protagonist. My generation of Chicano activists made events happen. We were determined, motivated, political actors in the Chicano movement. As proud militants and ready activists, we had resolve. In our Chicano world, we sought group ascendancy; we wanted to uplift our people, *la raza,* as a group. As Chicanos in that world, we were in solidarity with one another. As Chicanos before the world, we asserted our right to a homeland, Aztlan. My generation began the struggle to make a reality of Aztlan, building community in a serious way. Nation building begins at the neighborhood level, and we were the epitome of community development. To date, our generational struggle and creativity is manifest in the numerous Chicano institutions we created while making community. We took the Chicano movement from sporadic unrest to social protest to social movement to political party to governance and left Chicano institutions in place to keep vigil and shepherd over our gains.

We created more organizations and programs for all Chicanos than any previous generation of activists. Our record as builders of the Chicano community remains unmatched and unchallenged by the present-day generation of Hispanics. The contribution of the Hispanic generation so far has been to change the name of existing organizations and programs from "Chicano" and "Mexican American" to "Hispanic" or "Latino." They have yet to build and organize new entities, and may never. Hispanics, as a generation, are into neither group ascendancy nor solidarity with one another. They are primarily into individual aggrandizement and achievement. The Hispanic notion of solidarity with others is the exchange of business cards at after hours gatherings and the sending of e-mail to faceless persons on the Internet. Rather than promote ethnic identification and cultural nationalism for persons of Mexican ancestry, as *mestizos,* Hispanics seek inclusion with other non-*raza* groups; some want to be identified with the Caucasian peoples and regarded as "white Europeans." Nothing much has been created or built by the subsequent Hispanic generation. Our Chicano contribution stands alone.

How I became a Chicano and why I never became a Hispanic is what this book is about. Most assuredly there will be critics who will dismiss this work as a highly partisan, subjective, biased, and personal polemic. Maybe they will see little academic validity in this narrative. There are people like that.

Let me anticipate a few concerns. I have no need to set the record straight about my doings, if there is such a thing as a straight record. I have no compulsion to tell my side of the story. There are always many, many sides to any story. And, finally, I do not claim that this labor is the ultimate "truth." Truth is relative. Most often, truth is faith or belief, and blind in both cases. This work is my truth about Chicano militancy.

I have simply written of what I saw and recalled both as an observer and a participant during my childhood years and into mature adulthood, roughly 1950 to 1990. I was always involved back then; still today I am involved with some organizations within La Raza Unida's umbrella of groups and continue doing some home-base organizing. More directly related to this endeavor, I am writing to be sufficiently, intellectually, detached from my past and current activities in order to glean from those events subjective lessons on Chicano politics. I want to write and I want to teach with my writing; I strive to become good at both. My purpose in writing now is to teach about our Chicano perspective. Over the years I have been busy *doing* politics and not *writing about* politics. Now, I am making the time to write.

This book relies heavily on two sources: my personal recollections, notes, diaries, recordings (both audio and video); and documentary materials I have collected over the years. Awhile back my records and documents were intact and in my possession. On three occasions I placed archival materials at the University of Texas at Austin and at San Antonio. The first donation of material occurred in 1976 when some of the MAYO and La Raza Unida Party activists interested in the legal defense of Ramsey Muñiz made an initial deposit at the University of Texas at Austin; this contribution was paltry. Later, when I returned briefly to Texas from Oregon in 1984, I made a second deposit of material, again at the University of Texas at Austin. This contribution was substantial. Most recently, in late May 1994, the last deposit of material was made at the University of Texas at San Antonio. This contribution is final; I have no other material from that era.

In these pages the reader will find a retrospective interpretation of events that mark my evolution into a Chicano militant. This book is neither a straight autobiography nor a political history—although it reads, in part, like one or the other—but can best be categorized as an extension of the Ernesto Galarza model of the activist/organizer/scholar as writer.

This book is written in an anecdotal style and from a chronological perspective. It would have been most awkward for me to write in the third person about detail, events, and happenings that I caused, was involved in, indirectly made happen, or witnessed firsthand. I have rejected the third person approach and ask for the reader's indulgence in my frequent use of "I." It is most difficult to avoid its overuse under the circumstances.

This book is about the power relations between Mexicans and Anglos in South Texas generally, and Cristal, in particular. In many ways, it is a sequel to a work I started in 1974, *A Gringo Manual on How To Handle Mexicans.* In that book, I listed 141 "tricks" that the powerful gringos used against the less powerful Mexicans in and around South Texas. That book was an adaptation of an appendix to my doctoral dissertation of 1974. The appendix was a listing of miniature case studies of power relations between Anglos and Mexicans during the Chicano movement days. That earlier book focused on the mechanics of specific tactics utilized in the power relationship between gringos and Chicanos. No academic press was interested in this type of material at that time, and the popular press thought it too anti-Anglo and also declined its publication. I finally had it published in Piedras Negras, Coahuila, Mexico. The customs authorities at the border with Eagle Pass, Texas, twice refused to allow me to import the books without duty, though books were not then or now subject to an import tax. I arranged to smuggle them across and subsequently twenty thousand copies were sold. The book went out of print, but a year after my mother's funeral in September of 1986, while going through personal effects in her Crystal City home, I found another three hundred copies stashed away in a closet. My children remaining at home peddle these copies at Chicano conferences from time to time for their extra spending money.

In 1984, with John Hammerback and Richard Jensen, I coauthored *A War of Words* in which we discuss and analyze Chicano political rhetoric and ideology. Many of the speeches they utilized and the ideas I traced in that book had to do with the Chicano movement in which I was centrally involved. These publications are not exhaustive of what I have written over the years, but are the closest material to this work.

This book is a patchwork of events that make for me a political history of the rise of the Chicano movement, particularly the role of MAYO and La Raza Unida Party from the events I saw develop, and ultimately from how our group efforts began and how some of these efforts ended. On occasion in the book I protect a source and provide some anonymity by omitting real names and ascribing fictitious names to persons, places, and events. The omission of real names is simply to protect individuals currently involved in the business of living out their lives. There is no ax to grind or finger to point. I am sure that the most curious and the most learned among the readers will be able, with minor effort, to identify the names, the places, and the events, if it is that important to them. This is my recollection of significant political lessons learned from the people involved.

The record is clear, to me at least, that without my actions combined with those of other Chicanos, there would not have been a *movimiento, causa,* or *lucha.* Without the actions of Chicano militants there would have been no legacy for others to study, research, write, analyze, discuss, criticize, or with which to memorialize the Chicano movement.

I hope that the words on these pages will contribute to the body of knowledge on Chicano politics in general, and specifically, on Cristal, La Raza Unida Party, and MAYO.

2

Aztlan

The Chicano Homeland

Nearly two centuries back, my ancestors claimed Aztlan, the land area known today as the southwestern portion of the United States, as their homeland. Then, my ancestors, the *indio* and the *español* (Native American and Spanish) permitted—involuntarily in the case of the *indios* and grudgingly in the case of the Spanish—the immigration of a set number of Anglo families, led by Moses Austin, into Texas (then part of the state of Coahuila, Mexico). The newly born Mexico of the 1820s also gave more land to other Anglo immigrants in order that they may settle Texas. The Mexican government imposed three conditions on the Anglo settlers: do *not* own any slaves; become Catholic; pledge *loyalty* to the government of Mexico. The Anglos, however, lied when making their pledge to abide by these conditions in exchange for acres and acres of land.

Before the ink was dry on the deeds granting them land, there were more African slaves and illegal alien Anglos in Texas than there were Mexicans. Shortly thereafter, all the lands of Texas were stolen by these illegal alien Anglos who neither became Catholic nor remained loyal to Mexico. To steal our land, and enslave black people, became the "patriotic" things to do. They likened "freedom" to thievery. By 1850, when the first census was taken in Texas after it became a part of the United

States, there were 58,558 black slaves in the state. That figure represented 27.5 percent of the entire population, according to John Sharp's *The Changing Face of Texas* (1993).

The First Illegal Aliens

By 1850 the Anglo population rose to 154,034, representing some 72.5 percent of all Texans. These "white" Anglo people also began to reverse the definition of "illegal aliens." Illegal aliens now became the Anglo term to refer to Mexicans who ventured into "their" lands without their permission. They made us, as Mexicans, foreigners; they made my ancestors illegal in their own homeland. The power of definition is awesome.

Anglos, other Latinos, and some Mexican Americans refuse to believe that the land of the West and Southwest, beginning with Texas, was stolen from Mexicans. If they were to read any basic history book—such as Carey McWilliams's *North From Mexico: The Spanish-Speaking People of the United States* (1968), Leonard Pitt's *The Decline of the Californios* (1966), Rodolfo Acuña's second edition of *Occupied America* (1986), Arnoldo de Leon's *They Called Them Greasers* (1983), Albert Camarillo's *Chicanos in a Changing Society* (1979), Robert J. Rosenbaum's *Mexicano Resistance in the Southwest* (1981), or David Montejano's *Anglos and Mexicans In the Making of Texas, 1836–1986* (1987)—they would find additional support for my statements here. Nevertheless, the traditional texts used to teach Texas history during my childhood, such as Ralph W. Steen and Frances Donecker's *Texas: Our Heritage* (1962), which was the most frequently used in Texas school classrooms, contain erroneous information. *Texas: Our Heritage* was, of course, not written by Chicanos.

The Steen and Donecker book makes heroes of illegal alien Anglos such as James Long of Natchez, Mississippi who invaded the area in the summer of 1819 and after taking Nacogdoches proclaimed the territory to be the Republic of Texas. Long was repelled by the Spanish troops; he tried again in 1821, and occupied Goliad from a base at Point Bolivar, near Galveston Island. This time he was captured, jailed in Mexico City, and then killed by a Mexican soldier.

To this day, the school children of Texas are taught that Jane Long is the "Mother of Texas." As a grade-schooler, I couldn't begin to understand how this white woman could be the mother of my state, and I recall asking my father and mother for an explanation. Both of them told me that white persons are forever claiming not only to "discover" what has already been discovered by our people, but also that they always claim to be the "father" or "mother" of everything. That answer satisfied me, at the time, because I had already had years of memorizing that George Washington was the "father" of my country. Yet I always felt awkward uttering these words.

Anglo History, Not Mine

The textbooks on Texas that I had to study as a boy, including Steen's earlier edition of *The Texas Story* (1958), were all written by Anglos. These authors proclaimed Stephen Fuller Austin to be the "Father of Texas." As a college student I had to read the infamous book *The Texas Rangers: A Century of Frontier Defense* by Walter Prescott Webb (1935). The title is all wrong. The period of 1835 to 1935 was a century of frontier *offense* that included murders of hundreds of thousands of innocent Mexican children, women, and men in the ancient homeland; this century of butchery parallels the Jewish holocaust. The lynching of blacks in the South pales in comparison to the wanton murder of Mexicans in the Southwest at the hands of gringo racists and bigots. The "good" reputation of the Texas Rangers was built on atrocities committed upon innocent, unarmed Mexican people, not on bravery in the face of organized and effective armed Mexican resistance.

In the early 1920s, the United States Attorney General, A. Mitchell Palmer, began his infamous Palmer Raids; his assistant in charge of the General Intelligence Division, appointed in 1919, was none other than the young J. Edgar Hoover. These attacks were aimed at breaking the incipient organized labor union movement of the era. Many laborers of Mexican ancestry were then caught up in the push-and-pull of labor— lawful and unlawful—between U.S. agricultural interests and unorganized Mexican workers looking for employment, which led to the running of a "rent-a-slave" operation.

Ernesto Galarza has written extensively on this subject. I recall in my college years reading his books *Merchants of Labor, Tragedy at Chulamar,* and *Spiders in the House, Workers in the Field* about this cheap labor program and the subsequent international transfer of cash payments. I call this a "rent-a-slave" operation because the men had no rights, nor any recourse for grievances. The Mexican government went along with the program because the *braceros* (laborers) would send dollars home. The government of Mexico, at all levels, has to this day profited greatly from the bracero program and the continued migration to the Chicano homeland in the United States, because Mexican laborers in the U.S. weekly send money orders, cashier checks, and cash in U.S. dollars to their families in hundreds of Mexican cities, villages, and *ejidos* (communal farms). Today, estimates of this international transfer of money range from three to five billion dollars annually. Present-day immigrants from other countries in Central and South America also send U.S. dollars home to their country of origin; thus, the receiving countries continue to make money off of these legal, and illegal, labor arrangements.

The contract a bracero signed was a three-party contract, which means the person he signed with was not going to be the person he ultimately worked for. A contemporary analogy might be the purchase of an automobile or major appliance via a finance program: after the equipment is sold to you by a dealer, his obligation to you is finished. The dealer is not interested in any further relationship with you, except another sale. You, as purchaser, have no recourse if a problem arises. At best, you can make demands of the seller and the finance company, even enlist the assistance of lawyers to aid you with the problem, but each level you may acquire one thing—an increased frustration level, but still no solution.

The bracero program worked the same way. It was an international agreement signed between the United States government's Department of Agriculture and the United States of Mexico's Department of Foreign Relations. The countries negotiated the terms of the agreement and signed it without any input from Mexican labor or the individuals being recruited. The U.S. agricultural interests, however, were well represented in the negotiations.

The program worked this way: individual braceros signed a third-party contract in Mexico to work, usually for thirty cents an hour, in U.S. agriculture. They reported to an employer, who might have been a grower, a rancher, or the operator of a fishery, lumber mill, or food processing plant, or even a railroad company. Both the labor contractor and the employer were certified, approved, and designated by the U.S. Departments of Labor and Agriculture. An employer did not know his braceros, nor cared to know them, individually or collectively; he was only interested in getting as much work out of "his" Mexicans for as little money as possible. Growers, as did all employers, would deduct from the wages of the bracero all meals provided, up to $1.50 a day. Basically, the first five hours of the paid work day, at thirty cents an hour, went for the meals; the remaining hours of pay would cover incidentals. Employers would charge for all work-related supplies, equipment, and personal items, including soap, toothpaste, underwear, coats, shoes, rubber boots, gloves, pants, hoes, pruning tools, hats, and aspirin. Housing and transportation costs from Mexico to the labor site were passed on to the worker. If the bracero wanted to go into town from the farm for a haircut or for his day off, that charge was extra. U.S. taxes, including federal income tax and social security, were deducted in the later years of the program. These taxes remain in the U.S. treasury and are largely unclaimed, but it is likely that they have been absorbed into the general fund by now, and thus spent.

The imbalance in the relationship became apparent the first week that there was rain or injury or lack of work for whatever reason, because the bracero still had to pay for food, housing, supplies, medicines, and doctor's bills, regardless of earned income. In other words, braceros only got paid for the hours worked during the week but had to pay for all the costs and living expenses of a seven-day week.

Any complaints by the *bracero* to the employer were referred to the Department of Labor, which in turn advised the bracero that its agreement was with the Mexican government, and to call or write the Secretaria de Relaciones Exteriores, his Secretary of Foreign Relations, about his grievance. There were no telephones for braceros at the camps, only mail service handled by the employer. Too many braceros ended up owing money to their employers for living expenses, as the cost to the bracero for the privilege of working for a gringo was outrageous. Many braceros refused to tolerate the injustices and broke the contract. They fled the farms, ranches, timber stands, fisheries, factories, nurseries, and canneries for the cities, where they sought refuge within the Chicano community; these were the first Mexicans without proper immigration documents in the United States. Back then, the Immigration and Naturalization Service (INS) and its border patrol did not go hunting for "illegal" Mexicans, they simply recruited more workers into the bracero program.

Mexico initially ignored the pleas for help from the braceros. Occasionally, a press conference and press release was held by a Mexican government official to protest the treatment of their nationals under the agreement. Only until the outrageous acts by growers and other gringos against the individual braceros reached epidemic proportions in many states did the Mexican government act on behalf of its citizens. The Mexican authorities knew from past experience of the brutality and racist aggression of Anglo Texans toward Mexican people and banned the importation of braceros into Texas from 1942 until October, 1947. The bracero program then continued on a smaller scale until December 31, 1964.

The bracero program became the first major inconsistency in U.S. immigration policy: one set of immigration rules applied to Mexico, different rules applied to nationals from other countries. As always, foreign policy overrode all other policy in the country, including immigration policy. Agricultural profits and the war effort were more important than the rights of labor and human rights.

My Bracero Labor Camp Experience

I had first-hand experience with this program as a child. During my early adolescent years, 1954 and 1955, I worked as a dishwasher and tortilla maker at a bracero labor camp at the California Packing Corporation (later Del Monte) farm near Crystal City. My father thought it was a good idea for me to learn manual labor and work "like a man" for the summers, since I was approaching manhood. To him, manhood began at twelve, and I was then ten, nearing eleven. He offered me to our neighbor, Armandina Galvan, who had a subcontract from the agribusiness conglomerate to cook and feed the braceros at the camp. Armandina was a first rate entrepreneur who operated a corner grocery in Cristal, lent money for bail bonds, and subsidized her husband's efforts at ranching. At first I thought working was a great idea because I was going to keep all of my hard-earned money. The twenty cents an hour I was paid was less than the minimum wage for braceros, but I was a kid with no expenses or deductions.

The kitchen crew was taken out in a pickup truck to the labor camp at four each morning by Pedro Galvan, husband of Armandina, seven days a week. I always got to ride in the cab of the pickup because I lived across the street from the Galvans and was among the first to arrive for the twenty-minute ride to the labor camp. The late arrivals had to ride in the windy and cold bed of the pickup truck. I only worked the morning shift, which ended just after the lunch hour. Upon my arrival I would fire up the tortilla making machine, while another person made the dough balls, *testales* that were pressed flat into the round, *masa* (cornmeal) pancakes we call tortillas. While southern Mexicans only eat corn tortillas, and sometimes a French-style bread called a *bolillo*, those of us born in northern Mexico and north into the Chicano homeland Aztlan eat bleached white, wheat-flour tortillas. The braceros only got corn tortillas and sliced white bread, which they hated. As the corn tortillas began cooking and rolled past me on the tortilla machine, I would stack them and deliver them to the serving line. As soon as we had made enough tortillas for the breakfast that ran from six to seven, I had to help either with making hundreds of sandwiches or stuffing the paper sacks for lunch, which the men would pick up on their way out from breakfast. The workers usually got a sandwich consisting of a thin slice of bologna or processed cheese, one green *serrano chile*, an apple, a banana or an orange, a paper napkin, and a half-pint carton of milk. Sometimes, we would add two vanilla wafer cookies.

After the meal, my job was to help wash the serving trays and utensils in hot soapy water, then rinse them with even hotter water mixed with bleach; this was a horrible task, especially after the lunch hour. For lunch, we prepared a regular Mexican *guiso* of some sort, usually a stew-like mixture of meat and vegetables, for the one hundred or so men who were trucked in to the mess hall or who worked in the camp itself—the mechanics, tractor operators, irrigation crews, maintenance workers, and drivers.

I always wondered, during my work on the lunch line, how the men in the fields could drink their milk warm and eat a soggy white bread sandwich. I have always been a cold milk person and to this day hate white bread. For dinner, the routine was the same, except without me— I never worked a dinner.

There were hundreds of men who tended the crops to be harvested for the food processing plant in Crystal City belonging to the same company. They lived at the labor camp, which was located in the middle of thousands of acres of farmland owned by the company. There were four long rows of barrack-like huts with tin roofs, and each row had about sixteen huts. There was another large single barrack farther down the road from the mess hall that also housed men, but I never went there to see inside. The "windows" of these huts were made of entire plywood sections, four feet by eight feet, that opened up and away from the wall to reveal a screened opening. Each barrack had eight to ten U.S. Army cots inside, and nails on the wall served to hang clothes. One bare light bulb was in the center, hanging from the open ceiling; there was no other electrical outlet.

Between every two barracks was a single faucet for water. That was the only place where grass grew in the entire camp. To spice up their food and the bland sandwiches, some men planted *yerba buena* (mint) and *cilantro* (coriander, or Chinese parsley) by the faucet. They would eat the cilantro with their meals, and when Armandina Galvan would let them get boiling water from the kitchen, they would make tea from the mint leaves. In the back of each row of barracks was a makeshift stall with a shower head. In the summer the water was hot and in the winter the water was very cold. The toilets were outdoor privies, some ten yards from the shower stalls behind the barrack row. There was one privy per barrack row, each serving about forty men.

I saw the injustices firsthand, but did not fully comprehend what I was seeing because I was so young. For example, I saw the men charged fifty cents each to ride in the backs of trucks into town. I assumed they also paid to get back, or walked the fifteen miles to the labor camp from Cristal. The braceros were not welcome at the local Catholic church for mass or at other religious services in town. I never saw a bracero at either the Spanish or English masses; instead, the priest came to them at the camp. I know about this because I also was an altar boy and went a couple of times to assist the priest.

I saw the cooks put rotten meat in vinegar, or sometimes in milk, to remove the smell prior to cooking. Sometimes I had to take sandwiches and a soda pop to sick and injured men who lay in their cots unable to work or go to the doctor for treatment. My father was a medical doctor, but he was never asked to go to the camp and treat the men; nor were they brought to him in town. I saw the INS border patrol regularly come by and take men away from the camp. I assume they were deported. The reasons for these removals escaped me then, but today I guess that it was for insubordination, grievance filing, protesting, organizing, injuries, sickness and the like.

On Saturdays and Sundays, local entrepreneurs from Cristal would bring their wares, such as clothing, soda pop, cigarettes and tobacco, illegal booze, personal items, other sundries, and even prostitutes, out near the camp. Their pickups, closed panel trucks, and vans would park on the side of the highway, and the men would walk over there for their transactions. We would see the business going on as we drove by in our truck.

The Beginning of Chicanismo

During these years of the 1950s, my generation began calling themselves Chicanos, as we didn't like the term Latin American. Hardly anybody, except the braceros, called themselves Mexican. The Mexicans called us *Pochos*, meaning Mexicans who are trying to be Anglos and not succeeding very well. Success at being a Pocho meant you spoke good English, without a trace of an accent, and dressed like a gringo, with loafers or Hush Puppies, button-down collars, Levi's jeans, and no hats, much less a cowboy hat. You denied being Mexican as best you could and tried to hang around with Anglos. If you could cover up your Mexicanness, then you were called *agavachado*.

For the Anglos we also had various names, such as gringo, *gavacho*, *bolillo*, *blanco*, *pan blanco*, *huero*, *americano*, and *norte americano*. There are many explanations for the meaning of these names. Gringo, some say, comes from the lyrics of a song that the invading U.S. Army often sang in the campaign against Mexico in 1846: "*Green grows the laurel. . . .*" The French-style bread, which is white on the inside, is called a *bolillo*. Napoleon III's invasion of Mexico and subsequent occupation for a limited time had introduced French bread into the Mexican cuisine. *Blanco* and *pan blanco* refer to the color white and to white bread. These names refer not only to the whiteness of the Anglos' skin but also to what was perceived as their sour body smell; white bread has that color, and a sour smell from the yeast and preservatives. *Huero* is used for any light-skinned person, Anglo, Mexican, or of any nationality, and means, simply, "light skinned." The words *americano* and *norte americano* are used as both literal and exclusive descriptors of Anglos. Sometimes, Mexicans and Mexican Americans will also call themselves *americanos* because these lands, the North and South continents are both "American." People recognize the political and social reality, however. The Anglos have monopolized the term "American" or *americano* for their exclusive, but erroneous, use. *Norte americano* is used to further drive home the point that the user is describing or referring to a gringo. *Gavacho* is a term that escapes me—its origins are sketchy, the term meaning "from the Pyrénées," or "French-like"—but I have heard it used all my life. I know it is not derogatory, as when Chicanos use the word "gringo," which usually refers to a racist Anglo who has an anti-Mexican attitude, is open about his prejudice, has airs of racial superiority, and acts out those feelings, beliefs, attitudes, and opinions against Mexican people.

The name calling helped keep the groups apart. It defined who "us" and "them" were. Chicanos occupied, often side by side, the same general physical space as that of Anglos. We definitely were not, however, a part of their reality. We existed, but did not matter to them. I learned very early that there are several reasons for this. Anglos historically have learned how to dominate Mexicans without a large police force; psychological violence, fear, physical harm, and economic reprisals were their methods. The police and Texas Rangers were effectively employed against us from 1826 to the present time. In addition, economic dependence on whites has been the formal arrangement. With our lands stolen and now in their hands, the whites have the ability to profit from our land, our labor, our consumption of goods, our tax payments, and our presence as "illegals." *We* have to work for *them*, by and large, and we work for them on their own terms. Any attempt to organize or rebel has historically met with immediate retaliation. By making some of us "illegal," they pit us against each other, and all of them against all of us, legal or otherwise. The tag of "illegal" also lowers the wage-earning capacity to whatever the worker must accept, not what the economic system will bear. The Anglo legal system was and remains oppressive. It was used, along with the armed thugs, the Texas Rangers, the INS border patrol, and local police not only to legally steal our lands but also—and more importantly—to keep them. Laws were passed aimed directly at subordinating us. Any of the history books mentioned earlier, including Alfredo Mirande's *Gringo Justice* (1987), detail this process.

As the "underclass" of that era, we did not count or matter. We existed
to serve exclusively the interests of the Anglos.

The Segregation of Chicanos in Cristal

At the public schools, we still are segregated. The grammar school I attended in the 1950s was predominantly Anglo, and the De Zavala school
was predominantly Mexican, as was *el campo*, near the airport. Today,
the migrant program, bilingual education, compensatory (remedial)
education, special education, and many vocational classrooms are filled
with only children of Mexican ancestry. Those of us who did ultimately
enter a "white" school, such as the grammar school in "Cristal," were
further segregated within the school building by "grade." There was a
fifth year grade-one class, a fifth year grade-two class, and a fifth year
grade-three class; the "one" was all Anglo, the "two" mostly Mexican
students with a few Anglos, and the "three" was all Mexican. This practice continued into the junior high grades, and in another modified
fashion, into high school.

At the end of the school day, as at the end of the work day, the Anglos
went to their side of town and the Mexicans retreated to their side of
town, primarily across the railroad tracks. The Anglos stayed among
themselves; their white world was exclusive. We were not invited to
their social functions. In fact, it was illegal for a Mexican to join the Crystal City Country Club, to swim at the city pool on the Anglo swim days,
to be buried in the Anglo cemetery, to join the service clubs like the Lions
Club or Chamber of Commerce, or to join an Anglo Boy Scout troop. The
only time some Anglos and Mexicans came together was at the Catholic
church. Even there, the priest had a separate service for Anglos billed as
the "English language" mass, even though in those years all mass services were said in Latin. The other religious rituals were also segregated; protestant Mexicans such as the Methodists, the Pentecostal
groups (*los alleluias* we called them, because they yelled and screamed
during their services), and the Baptists had their own churches, for Anglos only. Later came the Mormons and the Jehovah's Witnesses, and
they sought out Mexicans for conversion. The Mormons never built a
church, they just came to do missionary work among the Chicano "natives." The Jehovah's Witnesses built churches for Mexicans and most
of us hate them because they tell our people not to vote, not to get involved in civic affairs or protest bad conditions because the end of the
world is near. The Jehovah's Witnesses don't have any time to spare in
getting ready for Armageddon. The Chicano members of these other
churches did not practice their faith with Anglos in their buildings, ei-

José Angel Gutiérrez with his mother, Concepcion *(left)*, grandmother Refugio Fuentes *(center)*, and aunt, Lucia Fuentes *(left)*.

ther. Apartheid of Mexican people by Anglos in South Texas extended beyond the political, economic, and social realm into religious practice.

The Three Destinies of Chicanos

My world was comprised of three spheres: the parental Mexican world, the Anglo school world, and my Chicano peer world. I've often thought of writing a book about my three destinies and, perhaps I will, after this book. As a child, it was not difficult to move between these worlds. This is so because children are largely ignored, have no civil rights to assert, and are not usually subjected to direct attack for being Mexican, though their parents are. Also, as a child, I had not yet learned of the prejudice against Mexicans that the Anglo world held. I was naive and uninformed about history, economics, politics, and culture. I once wrote a poem entitled "22 Miles," which I began with "at 22 miles, I could see my first 8 weren't," meaning that I didn't realize much about me, about being a Mexican, about Anglos, and, like most children, about my environment and life in general until the age of eight.

As I got older, I found it increasingly more difficult to move with ease

The author at age 2, watering the grass at the family home in Crystal City.

in and out of my three spheres. The classroom curriculum, particularly with regard to the history and contribution of Mexican people, did not jibe with my home version; I found with more frequency it becoming necessary to choose between historical versions. Daily, I faced obstacles because I was Mexican or Chicano and had to make choices having to do with my culture: do I eat in the school cafeteria with most of the Anglos and hardly any of the Mexican kids? (The Mexican kids had no money and there was no school lunch program, then.) Even if I take a lunch to school to be with my Chicano kind, will it be a sandwich of white bread or tortilla tacos? Which kind of tortillas—corn or white flour, real Mexican or Chicano tortillas? Do I sit or play with Chicanos or Anglos? Do I talk with the pretty *gringita* girl or the pretty Chicana? If I ask gringo kids to play after school, will it be at my house or theirs? And will they say, "I'm sorry! Noooooo! You are Mexican!"? Should I continue to pronounce "ch" words with a Chicano accent, like "sh," after the teacher corrects me in front of everybody for saying things like "shurch," "shicken" and "share" for church, chicken and chair? Should I say "Meese" when I can say "Miss," in order to sound like the other Chicanos? Am I related to George Washington, the father of my country and Davy Crockett, the hero of the Alamo? Am I to be as proud of my biological father, Angel Gutierréz Crespo, the medical doctor for the Mexican people of Cristal, esteemed by many of them as their "hero" for saving a life? Is Santa Ana a traitor for fighting to keep Texas a part of Mexico and trading his life for that land, unlike Lorenzo de Zavala, who conspired to take Texas and destroy the government of Mexico? Which of these two men is a *vendido* (sellout)? Why should I be taught to feel shame for the fact that the Mexicans won at the Alamo? Besides, none of the gringos in the Alamo were from Texas or legal residents. They were all illegal aliens who had crossed into Mexican Texas from Kentucky, Tennessee, and other places.

It is always easier to retreat within a familiar world. As Chicanos we are constantly choosing one from among the three options. There is no pervasive Chicano culture for us yet, but we are working on it. Ilan Stavans attempts to describe the assimilation process for all Latinos in the United States in *The Hispanic Condition* (1995). He confuses the condition of Chicanos, a people who have always been here, with those recent immigrants from Central and South America, including himself. In many respects, these Latinos are not unlike the European immigrants that came, in yesteryear, voluntarily to assimilate into the "Anglo" culture of the United States. Some persons of Mexican ancestry totally deceive themselves while attempting to deceive others, by claiming to be "American," just like an Anglo. Invariably this is the subject, over drinks at cocktail parties and in arguments between Chicano militants and members of the right-wing, hawkish American G.I. Forum. Persons of Mexican ancestry can claim to be "Hispanic" today, when they opt for being more Spanish than Mexican. This Hispanic identity is not Mexican, to be sure, and is also geographically and historically impossible for those of us with a Mexican ancestry in the Southwest that spans generations.

The Cure-All "I'm Sorry!"

When we state our names in Spanish, invariably some Anglo will tell us, "I am sorry, but I don't speak Spanish." They feign embarrassment when told that we are not speaking Spanish, simply telling them our names! Anglos also love to use the "I'm sorry" as an all-purpose excuse. Sometimes they add "I'm *soooo* sorry!" on a second try to cool down the situation, in case we didn't get their intonation and emphasis right the first time. Regardless of how severe the personal transgression is, they always think that an "I'm sorry" will soothe it away. Chicanos hear countless "I'm sorry's" in a lifetime and we don't believe any of them to be genuine. An "I'm sorry" said *en español* from one Spanish speaking person to another certainly is not going to soothe the hurt; after a serious personal transgression that a Chicano commits against another Chicano, the wrong-doer best get ready, make a stand, and fight like an angry devil, for all hell will usually break loose shortly from the offended party.

The new Hispanic identity as a generic term for la raza (the race), all Spanish-speaking peoples, was born with the 1980 census, and the term was kept in use for the subsequent 1990 census. In the previous four enumerations, from 1940 to 1970, the U.S. Bureau of the Census had been unable to fix a label on this diverse and complex ethnic group. In Spanish, each subgroup of la raza has no problem with the question "What are you?" The group members of each subgroup will answer with a nationality, such as "*Soy Panameño!*" "*Soy Cubano!*" "*Soy Mexicano!*" and the like. In response to the same question in English, we trip mentally over the acceptable term for the ethnic group: "I'm Chicano! I'm an American! I'm a Puerto Rican! I'm a Cuban American!" According to the Census, however, we are not in charge of our self-description. We have lost our primordial right of agency, to represent ourselves to the world with an identity of our choice.

There are Spanish-speaking children today who have, in their lifetime, not heard of a descriptive ethnic group label other than Hispanic. The Census Bureau and the mainstream media are busy instilling in all

The author in his grammar school photo, 1952.

that the proper term for Spanish-speaking people and their progeny, even if the latter be English-speaking monolingual, is Hispanic. In order to reject the Hispanic label on a census form, an employment application, a questionnaire, or other similar survey instrument, a Chicano must skip "Hispanic," mark "Other," and then fill in the blank with "Chicano" or another word choice. Reluctantly, however, most Chicanos mark "Hispanic" because it is currently so imposing and all-pervasive.

We are also confronted with a forced choice of race in the Census designations. Prior to 1940 we were racially unclassified. We were neither "Mongoloid" (Red Indian or Yellow Asian), "Caucasoid" (White Anglo), or "Negroid" (Negro, then Black, now African American); we were classified as "Other Race." Then, the League of United Latin American Citizens, LULAC, a civil rights organization of middle-class Mexican Americans formed in the 1920s, begin to press for the racial designation of persons of Mexican ancestry to be white, and prevailed. After the 1940 census, Mexican Americans have been racially classified as Caucasian, or white. Beginning with the 1980 census, and the switch to the label Hispanic, the Census Bureau now requests of Hispanics only to pick a racial designation among four choices: White; Black; American Indian, Eskimo, and Aleut; or, Asian and Pacific Islander. This is a neat trick on us. We are now further divided among ourselves and from others on the issue of race; the concept of la raza is no longer a common denominator of culture, as it once was.

The Trauma of My Father's Death

My informal education in the streets of my barrio and Cristal taught me many political lessons, which I later employed in the formal education setting and in life situations. One of these lessons came when my father died in 1957, when I was almost thirteen. My father was the medical doctor who practiced exclusively among the Mexican community. Because of his standing and role in the community, my mother and I were treated very well by all the Mexican people. They all thought we were very rich. Even in the Anglo establishments, restaurants, and by the Anglos themselves, we were treated very well, with great respect and deference, particularly in my father's presence.

Upon his death, the funeral and burial were held in Piedras Negras, Coahuila, Mexico, to comply with his wishes, as my dad had made my half brother, Horacio, promise to bury him in Mexico and not the United States when he died. The burial was well attended by many people, Mexicans and Anglos from both sides of the border. After his death, however—within a matter of days—the Anglo social doors in Cristal shut tightly on us. The annual Christmas baskets of fruit from Anglo employers whose laborers my Dad had cured stopped coming; the occasional boxes of chocolates from the local pharmacist and the pharmaceutical salesmen stopped altogether; and the local "high tone" restaurant, The Tavern, refused our reservations.

Our economic world also turned upside down. The local banker refused to lend my mother any money, even for the remaining funeral and medical expenses related to his death. No job was available for my mother, as she had no high school diploma, and had been an eighth grade "push-out" from the local school. She did have some twenty years of experience as a physician's assistant, nurse, midwife, X-ray technician, and medical office manager: she had actually run my father's office and business while he did the doctoring.

The suggestions many Anglos made to her, all of whom had an interest in buying us out cheaply, were to sell the medical equipment, supplies, X-ray machine, laboratory appliances, the accounts receivable, the car, and the house. "Take what you can get as cash money and move to San Antonio where your sister, Antonia, can help you and the boy out," I recall a "friendly" Anglo medical supplies salesman saying to my mother. He suggested that she could get a job in a hospital as a nurse's aide. These aides turn over patients, empty bed pans, and make beds, primarily. The local Anglo doctors, area hospital owners, and administrators did not want her to get any crazy ideas of recruiting another Mexican doctor to take over my father's practice in Cristal and pay her rent for the fully equipped, outpatient clinic she now owned. You don't need a license to own a clinic, you just need a licensed doctor.

It was not so subtle, the way the Anglo community shunned my mother, and they also told her with their actions to return to her Mexican world or leave town if she didn't like the new treatment. She didn't like it and neither did I, but she suffered quietly. She never complained to me about the Anglos and what they did to us when I was growing up; she buried her feelings inside her heart and took them with her to her death in September, 1986.

I only found out indirectly about the tactics employed to take our assets and run my mother out of town. Shortly after the death of my father, the pharmacist at the local Rexall drugstore, Dave Howard, took me aside one day when I was in the store. He offered to send me to pharmacy school if I would agree to work only for him after I graduated. I guess he meant for life, though I never really found out because I was too young to even understand the implications of what he was saying.

The author as a junior in Crystal City High School, 1959–1960.

The other pharmacist, Joe Prestage, stopped me cold a few days after the burial with a comment. He told me in front of my Chicano student friends and many Anglo people in the drugstore that from now on there would be no more signing my name to tickets for food, counter drinks, or items for my mother. He said, in a harsh tone, "You, from now on, must pay cash!" as he slapped one hand into the palm of his other. I still remember the sound that gesture made.

I began to learn firsthand the hate held by gringos toward me shortly after my father died. I also began to understand from those hateful experiences why I in turn learned to despise them. The choices I had to make about loyalties and group identity caused one reaction in me and another among my immediate friends. My Chicano friends started to call me *agavachado*—trying to be white—and the Anglo reaction was one of rejection because I was now, without the doctor father, just another Mexican. I was not to get out of my "social place" or try to narrow the social distance between myself and Anglos. Since it was important to be liked, as a Chicano I had to choose which group to be liked by first and foremost. Which is preferred, groups of other Chicanos or groups of Anglos? Anglos liked me only when I was identical to them. That is to say, I had to learn how to stop being my Chicano self and acquire a new posture, identity, attitude, and traits, all of which were anti-Mexican! I had to learn to dislike myself enough to reject my bilingual being and become a clone of Anglos as a rite of cultural passage into *gringolandia*. Anglos did not let me be both, even if I was able to and could. My experience with bilingual education is proof. Anglos didn't want me to speak Spanish, only English, even if it meant I would fail in school trying to learn English first. Yet everybody knows that learning around the world occurs in any language, not just English. In other words, two plus two in Chinese or German or Spanish still equals four. Anglo educators are not interested in the real learning of math, only that learning take place solely in English. Chicanos aren't the first to feel this language policy bias and anti-Mexican attitude. The Texan Anglos outlawed the speaking of German and closed down the Lutheran schools in the 1920s. Today, the descendents of these Germans and other Anglos are busy attempting to pass "English only" legislation once again.

Cristal vs. Crystal City: Two Worlds

Chicanos always referred to our town as Cristal. The Anglos always dropped the word "City" and simply said "Crystal." I never think of my life as a Chicano in "Cristal" without almost simultaneously thinking of the gringos there. The social distance between the two groups was, and

remains today, enormous. Yet we were tied inextricably to each other.
The gringos owned almost everything and controlled everybody, especially those associated with the Del Monte plant. Mexicans lived physically apart from Anglos, and the two groups did not mix socially. Mixing was limited to economic relations. Anglos *worked* Mexicans, but no
Anglo *worked for* a Mexican. During the early morning before the beginning of the workday, the cars driven by the working Anglo women
would cruise into the barrios and pick up their Mexican housekeepers.
The *Mexicana* women, by day, would take care of the housekeeping,
cooking, and babysitting for the Anglo women. These so-called liber-
ated Anglo females owe their independence to Mexican American
women. It is on the sweat and backs of brown sisters that the white
women could work beside their Anglo male counterparts.

Race over Class

Many of my classmates, like Carmen Contreras, would work part-time
in Anglo homes doing washing, ironing, and general housecleaning
after school and on weekends. I always wondered how Carmen felt, seeing the product of her ironing on Charles Schaief, a classmate, and how
Charles may have felt when he saw Carmen. Charles was the son of a
postal clerk and Carmen the daughter of a migrant family, but the level
of jobs that Anglos held didn't matter as much as the fact that they were
Anglo. There were many Chicano kids, like Jesse Rodriguez Jr., Pete
Galvan Jr., and myself, whose parents had occupations or businesses of
more prestige and status than the Anglos, but we were still Mexicans.
In social standing Anglo came before occupation, race before class, and
that racial fact was more central to relationships than the wealth or status of any person. Mexicans were considered inferior in all respects by
Anglos. These notions of Mexican inferiority were not muted: I grew up
hearing racial slurs and calumny about Mexicans uttered regularly by
gringos. It mattered not that Mexicans heard the epithets. Often, that
was the point of the public derision, to say what they felt about us in
front of us. These anti-Mexican statements were windows into the atti-
tudinal makeup of Anglos: they had only contempt in their hearts for
us. If only they could live life without us, I often felt, they would be hap-
pier. And the gringo children who were my age perhaps just mouthed
the feelings expressed by their parents, and did not really believe what
they said. Yet still they said the ugly anti-Mexican words, such as "Meskin," "wetback," "beaner," and "greaser." I don't think they liked us,
or living in Cristal, much.

At first chance, many Anglo classmates left town, never to return to

Cristal. A few remained, though, or returned after college. Joe Taylor, for example, came back to run his father's law firm, largely an abstract company that prepares title policies and deeds, and handles real estate transactions. Jim and Pat Byrd never went on to finish college; they stayed to run their family farm and onion processing plant. After a brief stint as a lawyer in Austin, Ronnie Carr returned home to become a justice of the peace and later a political judicial careerist. Jon Taylor became a veterinarian and relocated down the road in Carrizo Springs. Sylvia Bookout stayed and ended up working at the bank. Gladys Crawford worked in a few bars, disappeared from Cristal in the late 1970s, resurfaced in Uvalde in the 1980s, and then left the area again in the early 1990s.

One other person, Lynn Pegues, married several times and stayed in the area before finally moving on to San Antonio. It was hers that was the only gringo home I was ever invited into as a child in Crystal City. Lynn's father was the county judge for Zavala County in the mid-1950s. As a seven- or eight-year-old, I thought Lynn was the most beautiful girl I had ever seen: blonde, blue-eyed, long-legged, and white. Lynn had a younger sister, Bonita, the name in Spanish for "beautiful," and a younger brother, Johnny. As a very young child, while we both were in kindergarten and the elementary grades, I played occasionally with Lynn and Jon Taylor, her neighbor. We usually played at school and sometimes in the street or in their garages. Lynn's house was across the street and down the block from the Buick dealer and Sinclair gas station where my father would take his car for regular maintenance and service or gas fill-up. On those occasions, I insisted on going with him because I could see Lynn. I would cross the street and go find her or Jon to play. When I entered her house at her invitation it was usually without parental consent. Mostly though, Jon and I played with her in the garage of her house.

Political Activism: The Beginnings of Chicano Power

It was in the summer of 1962 when I first heard rumblings of organizing in the Mexican community in Cristal by members of PASO, the Political Association of Spanish Speaking Organizations. This was a new organization from San Antonio. By the fall of 1962, political rallies and voter registration drives began to take place in Cristal. These events attracted my friends and me. The well-dressed speakers from San Antonio in their suits and shiny shoes thrilled us most. They spoke of gringo injustice and implored us as Chicanos to do something about it. Not being of voting age, which was twenty-one years old at that time, we were relegated to supporting roles by the PASO leadership. We didn't mind. This was the most exciting thing happening in Cristal and we were eager to be a part of it. More important, we had access, even if it was peripheral, to the important men in suits from San Antonio. Access, however, was not being able to speak to them one on one; rather, it was limited to being within earshot of conversations and watching them dialogue with our local leaders.

The rumor in the barrio was that five Mexican Americans were going to run for all five seats on the city council. My friends and I knew it was more than a rumor, as we had heard it said by the PASO leaders from San Antonio to our local leaders more than once. Chicanos were going to have Cinco Candidatos, five city council candidates in the upcoming election. During that time, a person interested in voting had to pay cash for the $1.75 poll tax in order to register to vote, had to be of voting age, and, of course, had to be a citizen. Most eligible Mexicans that I knew did not eagerly seek to pay the poll tax in order to qualify to vote. My mother was no exception: she, like many others, simply saw no gain or benefit in voting in a primary election of the Democratic Party, as it was always a contest between two middle-aged white men. The Democratic party was basically the only political party that had contested races throughout the state, from precinct chair, constable, justice of the peace, county commissioner all the way up to the governor, U. S. representative, senator, and president. Texas, since Reconstruction, was a one political party state controlled by white male Democrats. Later, it continued to be controlled by white males—some Democrats, some Republicans. Only recently, with the election of Raul Gonzalez to the Texas Supreme Court in 1986, Ann Richards as governor and Dan Morales as attorney general in 1990, and Kay Bailey Hutchison to the U.S. Senate in 1993, has the white male dominance been broken.

The Poll Tax

The process of participating in elections was a nightmare for most Mexicans. You could lose your job by voting for the wrong person—such as another Mexican—if there was one running for office; you could also lose your job for not voting when the *patron*, the employer, took you to vote. But the nightmare really began upon registration: the window of opportunity to pay the poll tax occurred only during a three-month period that began in the year *preceding* the election. If a person wanted to vote in the city council election of 1963 in Cristal, he or she had to pay the poll tax for voter registration between October 1, 1962, and January 31, 1963, in order to be eligible to vote. People generally had no real knowledge of which candidates were running, since the filing deadline for candidates was not until the beginning of February, after registration had closed. In 1962–63, all Chicanos had to go on was the rumor that Mexicans would be contesting all five seats in the upcoming city council election.

The partisan elections at the county level had primary and run-off elections on the first Saturday in May of even-numbered years. The city, school board, and junior college elections were held on the first Tuesday in April (unless it fell on April 1; in that case the election was held a week later). Each election was held in a separate location, so it was never easy to vote. The restrictive time frame for eligibility (by paying the poll tax) was also most discouraging. After identifying those potentially eligible candidates, an interested voter had to find a way to get to the courthouse during business hours to pay the poll tax or find a registrar of voters. No Chicano that I knew of had ever been designated registrar of voters. The first two, la señora Cumpian and la señora Perales, were employed by gringos in early 1963 to blunt the efforts of PASO in the city council election. Their job was to get the Mexicans registered and voted early during the absentee balloting period, which nowadays is called early voting.

The supporters of Los Cinco Candidatos went after voter registration by going to Chicanos who were thought to be ineligible to vote or unable to register for lack of the poll tax. It was the young Chicanos (such as my friends and I) and the older women who did the actual walking and knocking on doors, looking for persons eligible to register. What we were doing was not legal since we were not officially designated as registrars, but we merely identified the potential voter or passed on the completed poll tax receipt to the registrar. It was also mostly the women who baked the cakes, sold tickets, cleaned up the meeting areas, made the coffee, served the *pan dulce* (Mexican sweet bread), and generally did all the work associated with a campaign. Neither the women nor the young people made decisions or set policy for the campaigns; only the men did that. Throughout the era when I was first involved in politics in Crystal City and even before, older women and young Chicanos (both male and female) had been the backbone of the campaigns of la raza Democrats Cleto Lopez and Jesus Rodriguez, both of whom ran for the position of Zavala County commissioner, Henry B. Gonzalez, who ran for governor, and Joe Kennard, who ran for U.S. representative.

In retrospect, it seems crazy that we were forced to buy the right to vote by collecting $1.75 from poor, migrant, seasonal farmworker families who felt they had better uses for the money, such as buying one hundred pounds of potatoes or a case of Southern Select or Jax beer. A dollar seventy-five seemed simply too much to pay for the privilege of voting, so we developed alternative incentives for potential voters. The favorite tactic was to sell a dozen tamales made by women volunteers, from goods donated by the local Mexican grocery stores: Serna's, Ruiz's, Gomez's in Barrio Grande. My friends and I would accompany the local PASO leaders on visits to these merchants, carry the donated merchandise to the cars, and unload the goods at specified homes for preparation.

Jesus Rodriguez, who had the larger downtown grocery store, usually declined to contribute. He usually was in political opposition to us despite the fact that his customers were Mexicans—not one Anglo shopped in his store. He was the only non-Anglo member of the Crystal City Chamber of Commerce, but he sided with the gringos. They always named him to the Grand Jury and to one board or another because he would vote as instructed by the Anglos. Ultimately, he was appointed as the first Mexican American county commissioner for Zavala County, in 1964. We did not rely on him for donations, just pestered him regularly. My friends and I occasionally would, as an act of protest, vandalize his store by ruining merchandise on the shelf and pinching the fruit. The other stores in the Mexico Chico neighborhood, Estrada's, Peña's, and Blanquita Gamez's, were the ones who would help from time to time with donations of materials to use in making tamales.

Women would volunteer to make the tamales and another crew, usually my friends and I, the youth, would volunteer to go door to door taking advance orders or actually selling outright a dozen tamales for $1.75. We would take the money and give them not only the tamales but also the poll tax receipt of voter registration for one person. If they bought more than one dozen tamales, we would give them another receipt of registration for their wife, an uncle, grandfather, son, or whoever was living in the house.

Another device we used to encourage paying the poll tax for voter registration was the cake walks, a fundraising technique we borrowed from the Catholic Church. Tickets were sold to earn a chance to walk in a circle that contained numbered squares, up to twenty-five or fifty. Those wanting a chance to win the raffle presented their ticket and stepped on a number in the circle. The music began, and the participants would walk clockwise in the circle. When the music stopped a number was drawn. The person standing on that number in the circle won a cake. We would sell tickets, ten for $1.75, and people would get ten walks around the ring, and invariably somebody would win a cake. In addition to the cake, the winner would get the poll tax receipt of voter registration. The material to make the cakes, like the tamales, was donated. Women would bake the cakes and a crew would sell tickets, while another crew would conduct the cake walk.

But my favorite of all of the tactics employed to pay for the poll tax was the dances. We would have a dance with an entry fee of $1.75 per person or $3.50 for *la pareja* (the couple). The ticket money would go toward the purchase of their poll tax. We would also use this money for Spanish language radio advertising, printing of sample ballots, and gasoline to run voters to the polls. These dances were the opportunity for us boys to socialize with the girls.

Gringo Intimidation at the Polls

Another nightmare of local politics began once Chicanos registered to vote. Mexican Americans presenting themselves to vote either absentee or in person at the polling place were subjected to intimidation by the clerks and precinct judges. The first questions out of a clerk or election judge usually were framed in a loud, angry tone of voice, in English: "What is your name?" "Are you a citizen?" "Can you speak English?" "Where do you live?" Rather than being helpful, hospitable and supportive of the voter, their demeanor was one of contempt and suspicion that the voter was up to no good. Usually, the clerk or election judge would fire off several more questions in that same ugly tone: "Where is your voter registration card?" "Where is your poll tax receipt?" "What proof of eligibility do you have?" "Where do you work?" This last question was most ominous, as your job could be on the line if the clerks spoke to your employer about you.

If the voter forgot the poll tax receipt or voter registration card, the inquisition ended and the person was told to go home. Never did the clerks offer to look for the name in the voter roster for eligibility, unless the voter demanded that the clerk look. Similarly, the offer of language assistance in Spanish was never made to voters so that they could understand the clerk's questions, nor did the clerks or election judge offer an alternative to a missing voter card, by giving them the right to sign a sworn affidavit stating that they were eligible to vote. Many a time a Spanish-speaking poll watcher was reprimanded and threatened with expulsion from the polling place for attempting to assist a voter with the English language questions.

For the longest time, Texas used paper ballots in rural areas. At times the ballots were so large they resembled pillowcases and were hard to handle and mark. Any mark made on the ballot other than precisely where indicated meant starting again on a new ballot, but it was a hassle to convince the election judge to provide another one. Usually the voter tried to erase the marks made and hoped the ballot was counted and not disposed of as a mutilated ballot. In Texas, you could also mark a big X by the political party label at the top of the General Election paper ballot and vote a "straight ticket." In order to split the vote for choices among candidates of different political parties, a voter had to mark little Xs by the name of each individual. Many Mexican American voters would either make the big X at the top of the Democratic Party label or mark the little Xs for candidates in the top offices such as president and governor and then skip way down on the paper ballot to the local precinct races to find the names of the few Mexican Americans running. The very bottom of the paper ballot was usually reserved for constitutional amendments or similar propositions. Texas to this day still has no referendum or initiative process; hence the constitutional amendment is the only avenue for change.

The First Political Organizations

When I was a teenager, PASO, a statewide organization of Mexican American Democrats, was very active in Cristal. PASO was a Phoenix-like structure that emerged from the 1960s Viva Kennedy Clubs: rather than disband a "club" as usual after that year's campaign, the Mexican American Democratic leaders charted an independent course of action to politically empower the Chicano communities in South Texas. The national margin of victory for John F. Kennedy had been so slim that Chicano Democrats readily could see the pivotal importance of their vote in a close contest. PASO was significant for many reasons. The name itself was controversial in that it stated up front that the group was political. The names of the traditional organizations that Mexican Americans rallied around in the 1960s were in English, avoided reference to being Mexican, and gave no hint of the civil rights nature of the organization. For example, the name of the first major organization founded in 1929 was the League of United Latin American Citizens (LULAC). The next major organization founded in 1948 was the American G.I. Forum, which was established to promote the interests of returning Chicano war veterans. It was founded when the city of Three Rivers, Texas, refused to permit a wake and burial of Felix Longoria, a Mexican American soldier from that community who had seen action and died in combat in Europe, in the Anglo funeral home and Anglo cemetery. In spite of the outpouring of hate and protest, the soldier was not buried in Three Rivers; rather, then Congressman Lyndon Baines Johnson saw to it that he was given an honorable ceremony and buried in Arlington National Cemetery in Virginia.

The PASO name also created a new ethnic label, that of "Spanish-speaking," and the organization was sometimes referred to as PASSO as a result. In California, the Viva Kennedy Clubs also evolved into a political organization similar to PASO. The name taken in California was Mexican American Political Association (MAPA). The California group was up front about being political and Mexican. This group is still in existence today. There was no consensus between Chicanos in Texas and California to merge the two organization into one because of the name. The Texas group wanted to distance themselves from being Mexican. The California group wanted to embrace their Mexicanness.

PASO had support from Anglo liberals and from organized labor in the San Antonio area, namely the Teamsters Union. The leadership of PASO was comprised of Democratic Party stalwarts from across the state but predominantly from South Texas. PASO sought to take power in areas where Mexican Americans were a majority.

PASO in Cristal

Cristal was such a place. There were a lot of people coming to Cristal under the direction of Bexar County Commissioner Albert Peña Jr., from San Antonio. Men like Albert Fuentes, Martin Garcia, Carlos Moore, Johnny Alaniz, and later on, other people like Emmett Tuggle, an architect, and Ray Schaefer from the Teamsters Union, all came from San Antonio to help the organizing efforts of PASO in Cristal. These individuals, particularly Carlos Moore and Martin Garcia, provided election law expertise, campaign technical assistance, and leadership, to our fledgling local PASO chapter. These men were mistaken for attorneys by the Anglo county clerk and the tax assessor for Zavala County, who were in charge of the registering of voters and the certification of voter registrars. Had they investigated and found out that these men were not in fact attorneys but simply Chicano activists wearing suits, well versed in English and the requirements of the Texas Election Code, PASO's efforts in Cristal would have been stymied.

Moore and Garcia were able to get some Chicanos certified as voter registrars. This was a tremendous boost to our registration efforts because Chicanos did not want to go to the courthouse. The courthouse traditionally has been viewed by la raza as a bad place: you go to the courthouse when you are arrested and jailed; to pay taxes; to go to court; to bail someone out of jail; or to get your license plates. Each of these experiences cost money and many were often dangerous. In fact, most older Mexicanos to this day will tell you that you can check on their good record by going over to the courthouse and asking about them. In other words, if they haven't been to the courthouse there was no record—they haven't been bad!

La Placita en Mexico Chico

The election campaigns in Cristal centered around public rallies. Days before a rally, the local sound truck that advertised the Mexican movies at *el teatro* Luna (the Luna theater) would give notice of the upcoming event. The day of the rally, the loudspeaker would remind the folks of the meeting and give the names of the featured speakers. People would gather during the rally around the speakers' area and a musical group and listen to the speeches. Our rallies were held at a neighborhood park, *La Placita,* in the Mexico Chico neighborhood. Mexico Chico was the most impoverished and segregated barrio in Cristal. To date, it still remains the most impoverished neighborhood in Crystal City. La Placita was no more than a large circular slab of concrete surrounded by a dilapidated picket fence in the middle of the block. The surrounding land was bare except for rocks, broken glass, weeds, an outhouse, and assorted garbage thrown onto the vacant lot. There were boards and plywood for the makeshift stage, but it was not elevated. This is where we Mexicans had our outdoor dances and where we celebrated the Cinco de Mayo and the Diez y Seis de Septiembre (the two major holidays celebrated in Mexico in honor of the defeat of the French, on May 5, 1860, and of Mexican independence from Spain, on September 16, 1810, respectively) and where we held our Chicano rallies. To me, the rallies were tremendous explosions of enthusiasm by la raza. Hundreds, if not thousands, would gather at these rallies to hear the speeches. Speaker after speaker would talk about the need for unity, the need for bravery and courage, the need for participation through voter registration by paying the poll tax, and would generally encourage the people to rise and protest the discrimination leveled against Mexicans by Anglos. I loved these rallies! At rallies, la raza felt comfortable and safe with the large numbers of people who would turn out in this location deep in the barrio of Mexico Chico; this was basically the foundation of group solidarity fused by the rhetoric of the campaign of Los Cinco Candidatos.

The campaign activity escalated through the spring of 1963. The violence against Chicanos began to emerge in the persons of the Texas Ranger Captain A. Y. Allee, Sheriff C. L. Sweeten, and City Marshal J. P. English. The Justice of the Peace housed in the courthouse was always willing to find Mexicans guilty of any charge brought to him. His name was Stormy Davis; "Stormy" was a nickname, but I never really knew him by any other name.

El Pinche Rinche: A. Y. Allee

During the spring of 1963 is when I also began to have my first brushes of violence with the Texas Rangers, particularity with Captain A. Y. Allee.

Ranger Captain Allee caught up with me and a group of my friends one night after a political rally, half a city block from my home. He was trying to intimidate me and the other young guys involved in helping Los Cinco Candidatos by getting la raza registered to vote. Allee's car was followed by a carload of Sheriff's deputies, who were always more dangerous in groups: they would concoct any story and serve as witnesses for each other. On that particular night they pulled over in front of us as we walked home; Chicanos walked everywhere in town then, as few of us, especially the teenagers, had cars. The deputies let Allee step forward toward us as they ambled to the rear of the car and poised themselves for whatever was to happen. Allee was short, heavy, and potbellied. He was mean and he was gruff, and his white, pearl-handled six-gun was enormous.

He asked me if we were involved with that "PASO Communist bunch." Without waiting for an answer, he then asked if I was that "smart-ass Goo-Tee-Air-S kid that made those speeches." I denied we were doing voter registration, saying we weren't old enough to be eligible to vote and that we weren't county registrars. I didn't have to answer his second question directly: by speaking up, I not only confirmed who I was but also that I was a "smart ass." He knew I had been the one making speeches because the Rangers, the city marshall, the sheriff, his deputies and constables had circled La Placita in their distinctive cars during each rally we had. They would stare at us hatefully, making surly, inaudible comments. Their mouths moved over clenched teeth holding unlit cigars, so we knew they were saying something to somebody, perhaps only to the others in their cars. At those times, if I was speaking, I would turn up the rhetoric and point to them, exhorting the crowd to realize that the Rangers and sheriffs were intimidated by our solidarity and impending Chicano victory. I often used the Spanish-language term *pinches rinches* when referring to them because it rhymed well and was particularly offensive to the Rangers. (*Pinches* translates as "mean, gauche, or bad," and *rinches* as "rangers.") Allee said we were lying to him and making him "goddamn mad"; he told us that night what he wanted from us, and especially what he expected of me. He told us to stop registering voters and going to these rallies, and he advised us of the dangers of walking across town late at night (La Placita, in Mexico Chico, was clear across the other side of Cristal, some five miles from where we lived in Barrio Grande). Coming from Allee, these words sounded more like a threat, not advice. He also ordered me to stop making inflammatory speeches, because, he said, I was most effective at "making the Meskins act crazy." I again denied doing anything like that, and he got very upset and slapped me. As I flinched and turned away from what I thought would surely be the next blow, he kicked me in the behind with his pointed boot.

Unbeknownst to me, my friends, or the police, my mother had noticed the Rangers and deputies stopping us. She loaded our double-barreled shotgun and walked toward the site of the confrontation. In a firm and loud voice, my mother raised her shotgun, and pointing it at the cops, said, "Hey, Allee! You want something with my boy? You talk to me now!" To me and my friends she said, *"vayanse para sus casas, y tu pa' la tuya, andale"* (Go to your homes, and you to yours). I could believe neither my eyes or ears: my mother was "packing," and she was facing down the pinches rinches! Allee admonished her to put the gun down and get inside the house, but he did not move toward her. The other cops were dumbfounded. My mother just kept pointing the shotgun at them and walked backward toward the house. Once inside, she told me to turn off the lights and look out the windows to see if they were gone. They did leave, and no sooner were they gone that she lit into me about what I had said or done at the rally to get the rinches on my ass. Rather than answer her questions, I told her the story of the confrontation and how Allee had slapped and kicked me. She shut me up by telling me she had seen all of that. "From now on," she said in Spanish, "we are going to the rallies together." She kept her promise: I was the only teenager whose mother walked with him across town to and from the rallies.

3

The Education of a Chicano

I graduated from high school in May, 1962, just as PASO was beginning to organize in Cristal, and there was talk of Los Cinco Candidatos for the 1963 election. I welcomed the possibility of social change that PASO seemed to be trying to bring about because I was frustrated with my inability to understand why there were two worlds during the school day, one of privilege for Anglos and another of exclusion and discrimination for Chicanos. My feelings were jumbled with regard to who *could* be my friends, who *should* be my friends, and who *were* my friends after school while in the barrio. As a Chicano I felt proud that we as a community would rise and take from the Anglos what had been rightfully ours to begin with, our self-respect and equality. My thoughts about these concepts had evolved during my high school years. I became the declamation champion for medium size schools in the state of Texas in 1961. No prior champion had been a Mexican American. In track and field events, another classmate, Richard Gallegos, also won the mile run state championship in 1961, another first for Mexican Americans in our school and in the entire state of Texas. At a school assembly where all athletes and interscholastic league forensic winners for the year who had "lettered" were given their varsity jackets, Richard and I, among others, were honored by the administration and student body. His trophy and my plaque for those honors were not displayed in the awards case of our high school in any prominent fashion; however, our awards were placed away in the lower rear shelf of the case, nearly hidden. There have been no other state champions for Cristal in either of these two categories since.

My winning state championship speech, ironically, was on the meaning of democracy. For demonstration I used a copper penny. With the coin I would elaborate on the contributions made by President Lincoln and on the meaning of the engraved words, *E Pluribus Unum*. The speech was very moving and emotional, and I bowled the audience over with both the message and my delivery. Here was this young Chicano kid from some dinky little school in South Texas who spoke English without an accent, was very poised and natural, and declaimed better than Anglos. The use of the penny was also most effective: I had studied the coin and found a unique feature not found in other coins. The profile of the personality on the nickel, dime, and quarter all face left, while Lincoln's profile on the penny looks toward the right. I found symbolism in this pattern: only Lincoln looked forward into the future of the nation as one people while the others turned away from that reality. Everyone could relate to the coin and speech. While today, you cannot buy anything for a penny, it was the most frequently used coin by the poor during my youth.

White Girls and Speech

I actually got interested in public speaking because of my budding interest in girls. As I passed the auditorium in the high school during my freshman year one afternoon, practice for interscholastic league activities was underway. On stage reciting were some of the school's prettiest white girls and only a white boy or two. I gawked at the white girls through an open window until the speech teacher, Aston Pegues, yelled at me. "Keep moving or come in and recite. You're a distraction to the girls." I am not one to play the coward before authority, then or now, so I walked into the auditorium and up to him. Mr. Pegues was a slight, small man with a big greasy nose and thinning hair who was effeminate in his gestures. He gave me the once over and pushed a mimeographed sheet into my hand, saying, "Read it. Be ready to read aloud in a few minutes. We're practicing for interscholastic league forensic competition." I didn't comprehend the big words he uttered but did begin reading the words on the sheet. And then I did exactly what he told me to do, I read it aloud. He loved my voice projection, poise, and delivery, and said so. (Little did Aston Pegues know that I had learned my oratory in Spanish in kindergarten with Suse Salazar, the barrio teacher my family had sent me to when I was five years old, and who had trained me very well.) I knew I was going to be in "speech" from then on. It was easy, and I was right there next to the prettiest white girls in the school—all of them.

This was a turning point for me because Chicanos did not try out for speech as an extracurricular activity. Chicanos took the speech class in high school because it was an easy elective course, but we didn't take this stuff seriously, much less try out for competition. For the Chicano boys, however, the speech class gave us access to the Anglo girls, some of whom liked to be with Chicano boys after dark.

In my time Chicanos didn't read poems, give speeches, partner in a debate team or act in plays. Chicanos also didn't hang around with Anglos, and Anglos avoided Chicanos as study partners, social friends, and dates. One's own Chicano group of friends would also apply severe peer pressure not to become white-acting, or agavachado. The only one who I knew of who did become agavachado by always hanging out with Anglos and entering the speech competitions was a boy named Hector, who was a year or two ahead of me. Chicanos called him *joto* (queer) because of his effeminate ways, and because he hung around during school hours with two other Anglo classmates of his who were considered "queer" looking. He also became our first Chicano drum major, which was a big no-no for any male Chicano. In our teenage view of the world, girls, not boys, became twirlers and drum majors!

I had tried out for the football team my freshman year but the coach used the big Chicano kids like me as practice dummies for the scrawny, puny Anglo kids. The coach would place us to be tackled by them over and over. We never got to practice tackling them. Chicanos were placed mostly on the B team, not the varsity A team. All the Anglo punies, however, made the varsity squad, along with a few Chicanos. The average Chicano player like me never seemed good enough to make the varsity or traveling team, though we were always good enough to take hits from the Anglos every afternoon. Given the alternative of the Anglo girls in the auditorium for speech practice, I lost interest in football very quickly.

Risking all of the accusations and ridicule that was sure to come from my Chicano peers, I gave up football and tried out for the forensics team. After brief practice sessions of poetry reading and extemporaneous declamation, I was good enough to travel with the group to out-of-town competitions.

Most of the time, I would bring home the first- or second-place ribbons; I was getting really good at public speaking. I was often given a motel room to myself on these trips. I thought the special treatment was because I was a winner, a "star"; little did I know that my speech teacher was only following the local rules against Anglos mixing with Mexicans, let alone sleeping in the same room together. The good side

of this segregation eventually was that I could have female company—
from either our group or from a rival team—during the night. No one
knew of these escapades except me and my female companion.

Speeches about the Conditions of La Raza

The next year at the first Chicano political rallies at La Placita for Los
Cinco Candidatos, I honed my speaking ability not in English but in
Spanish. I would rail against the discrimination in Cristal that was obvious to me. Chicano barrios had unpaved and unlit streets, no sidewalks, no sewers, and no parks. My block on West Edwards between
West Zavala and North Avenue A was the only one in my barrio with
pavement, sidewalks, and a street light, and only because my father and
the Galvan family across the street had paid for these improvements.
The De Zavala elementary school, like the county, was named after the
first Vice President of the Republic of Texas, Lorenzo de Zavala. The
school was across the street from my house and occupied an entire block
of its own. That block had street lights on two sides only, but no sidewalks. The playground, where the Martinez boys and I played baseball,
had no grass. What it *did* have was broken glass, plain dirt, rocks, and a
rickety backstop made of chicken wire mesh nailed to a wood (two by
four frame). This was our "athletic field." The classroom buildings were
old Army barracks, except for one that had been removed from a Japanese internment camp that had been located in Cristal from 1941 to 1947.
It had held mostly Japanese Americans forcibly brought from California and the West Coast, and a few German and Italian prisoners of war,
and was located over in another barrio, *el Avispero en el Campo*, the "hor-
net's nest by the camp." I don't know why Chicanos called the neighborhood that. Sometimes the camp area was also called *"el* airport" because the municipal airport was adjacent to it. The Army barracks near
the airport location had also been made into a junior high school for
"migrants," meaning Mexicans.

The Anglo elementary school, on the other hand, had lights on each
corner, sidewalks, green grass, real backstops and a baseball diamond,
and extensive playground equipment such as merry-go-rounds, see-
saws, monkey bars, and many sets of swings. I don't think it had a name
other than "the grammar school"—at least that is the name that Chicanos gave it—and it was nothing like the Mexican schools. This school
was a two-story monument made of red brick with two gleaming metal
slides for fire escapes attached from the top of the second floor. My
neighborhood buddies and I would sneak over without permission
from our parents to that school at night because we loved to climb up

the slides and come down. The school authorities tried to keep us out with their "KEEP OFF" signs, chains across the top and bottom of the slides, and even with lights shining on the tops of the slide platforms. But to no avail: this was our Chicano amusement park at night.

The dilapidated conditions of the schools, streets, and La Placita; the social distance between whites and browns in Crystal City, specifically, and South Texas generally; the presence of the Texas Rangers and their intimidation tactics; and the increased wages and price per piece work offered to Chicano labor during election times were the themes in my early political speeches. The democracy I spoke of in my state championship speech with the penny as the symbol of all that was good and right with my country was long forgotten because of its irrelevance to Chicano reality. My Chicano friends and I would always mock the ending of the Pledge of Allegiance, reciting ". . . with liberty and justice for some." Democracy didn't exist for Mexicans in Cristal, only for gringos. This is so because the *gringos* thought democracy was reserved only for white people, that they "fought" for it at the Alamo, and they would tell you so in school. I said this repeatedly in public at La Placita. I would also admonish la raza who would rather earn money than pay money for the poll tax in order to go vote. Then, I did not understand why Chicanos turned away from the poll tax. Later on I learned that Chicanos had very limited choices on the ballot: with the poll tax and voter registration certificate, the only choice was still to vote for or against the only white Democrat on each ballot for all local, and most statewide, contests.

Candidate Recruitment

April of 1963 was the first time that la raza could vote for Mexicans. In essence, it was the first time they could vote for themselves. No organized slate of Mexican Americans had run previously and the few individual efforts in the past had all failed. But in the fall of 1962, prior to the elections of the next spring, Chicanos did not know that: we were just getting people enthused about the idea that there would be a possibility of a slate of Chicano candidates. Leaders from PASO in San Antonio kept exhorting Chicano adults in Cristal to organize a PASO chapter, and then to find Mexican American candidates willing to run for local offices. I remember how shocked I was at the first PASO chapter meetings to hear grown men say in public upon nomination that they couldn't run because they were afraid. They were afraid of losing their jobs and of other economic reprisals; they were afraid of the Texas Rangers; they were afraid of not knowing what to do if elected. The favorite phrase used by Chicanos as a euphemism for declining was that

they were "not qualified." We had learned to harbor feelings of inade-
quacy, and Anglos seemed to be the only ones who were qualified. In
fact, I thought then how curious it was that being Anglo meant axiomatically that you were qualified. Being Chicano you had to prove
your qualifications time and again. Our local PASO leaders faced a
dilemma in finding "qualified candidates" and who were also unafraid
to run, but after months of searching and pleading with potential candidates they finally did.

The Anglo Model of Organizing Failed

During the fall of 1962, however, it was kind of futile to talk about individual candidacies and what was going to be happening in the spring
1963 election. The organizing was very hard going, and there were several reasons for this. First, the PASO organizational structure was mod-
eled after other Anglo political clubs. To join one had to be male and
over the age of 21; these two qualifications for membership alone eliminated more than two-thirds of all Chicanos in Cristal. Second, even
though women and youths like myself were not members, we were the
ones doing the political work out in the barrios. The older male Chicanos, however, did not listen to us, as we were not members and we
were women and youngsters. Third, PASO had been born after the parent organization, the Viva Kennedy Club of the 1960 presidential campaign organization, had disbanded. Because the campaign organization always disbands after an election, partisan electoral organizing
does not ever empower a community, it only empowers the candidate.
PASO, as a Viva Kennedy club, had asked Mexican Americans in
Cristal and across Texas to vote a straight Democratic ticket, beginning
with John Fitzgerald Kennedy at the top, to the bottom of the ballot
which still included local gringo racists. Now, PASO was asking the
people to vote against some of the same gringo racists and their cronies.
La raza is not apathetic when it comes to voting, but it is cynical because
of the lack of consistency among its leaders. Even in 1960 the people
knew the score and had refused to play this hypocritical game.

Chicano Rhetoric

By the early spring of 1963, I improved my public-speaking ability in
Spanish with every rally. I learned to use my ability to convince people
at these rallies. I learned which themes got la raza excited and made
people applaud. I learned how to make the audience hang on to my
every word just by changing the pace and volume of my voice: going

from a fast and loud voice to a slower, more quiet speech makes people listen more intently. Gesturing with agitation and sounding angry in a speech would get the audience in a near frenzy. Chanting *"¡Viva La Raza!"* or *"¡Vivan Los Cinco Candidatos!"* would elicit *"¡Viva!"* back from the crowd time and time again. The audience would feel involved, as if they, too, were helping me give the speech. If you were tough and direct, people attributed great courage and ability to you.

Most Mexican American people think that public speaking is a *don*, a gift from God. They also say *"tiene labia"* (he has a way with words). But like leadership, organizing, intellectual prowess, or personality, these abilities and skills are learned and improved upon with practice. And I was given plenty of practice by the local PASO leaders who recommended me for the public speaking role to the PASO organizers from San Antonio.

Spoken and Printed Rhetoric Draws Reaction

My speeches began to attract the attention of more than just the PASO organizers and my own Chicano people, as had been evidenced by my run-in with Captain Allee and the Texas Rangers in the spring of 1963, and numerous other incidents. Neither my Chicano audiences nor my mother ever seemed shocked by the content or manner of my speeches, except for a profane word or two like *cabrones* (motherfuckers), *pendejos* (imbeciles), *babosos* (idiots), or *culeros* (assholes). She would tell me on those occasions that only uneducated people needed obscene words to make a point. She was largely correct, but I didn't listen. Back then, I'd use an offensive phrase or obscenity for effect; the message is etched into the memory of the audience because of those words, even if people are turned off by their use. Portions of these speeches that irritated Texas Ranger Allee and inspired la raza are recorded in the *Texas Observer* of the day. People active in the 1963 Cristal election still have fond memories of that era because I was a very aggressive public speaker in Spanish. I still am.

A small group of us enrolled at the local two-year college, Southwest Texas Junior College, some forty miles north in Uvalde, Texas. Juan Patlan from Carrizo Springs, and Hector Alva, Francisco Rodriguez, Mike Delgado, Rudy Palomo, Esequiel Romero, and Eddie Avila from Cristal were among those who went to junior college with me. There were others, but these in particular were the ones who collaborated on the printing of a little newsletter in English that we called *In Fact or Fiction*. This was a scurrilous piece of anonymous literature: we attacked every Anglo sacred cow and described them in more glaring and elaborate detail than I could in my brief public speeches in La Placita. These were topics I couldn't deal with in speeches because they involved complex details or were events largely unknown to the Mexican American people. For example, we unmasked the taboo of sexual relations between Anglo women and Mexican men by identifying the locations, dates, and times of their rendezvous, printing only the first names of the parties. We counted liquor bottles in the trash cans of prominent Anglos and accused them by name of being alcoholics. We compared the conditions of streets in the Mexican barrios to that of the Anglo side of town and demanded parity of services and repairs.

The campaign organizers for Los Cinco Candidatos would probably have censured me and my collaborators on these topics as not entirely relevant to the issues at hand for the election. We hid our identities as editors for fear of Anglo retaliation, but we only fooled ourselves. Everybody, Anglo and Mexican, would quickly surmise that we, the "young Chicano militants," were behind the newsletter.

Cristal is a one-newspaper town belonging to the *Zavala County Sentinel.* Newspapers are the propaganda arm of the white power structure in every city: while Anglos love to proclaim these publications as evidence of a free press, they are more akin to the mouthpiece of big business and other powerful Anglo interests. Chicanos seldom get accurate reporting from these editors and their writers. The content of local English language newspapers has always been strictly for gringo consumption. In 1963 (as it still is in 1998), the gringo voice of Cristal was that of Dale Barker, the local editor and publisher of *The Zavala County Sentinel.* Named *el Barker* by the Chicano population, he had a section called "The Barker" in which he would blast Los Cinco Candidatos or some other Mexican American in every issue.

That spring we managed to print three or four issues of our newsletter, *In Fact or Fiction,* before violence erupted. In the midnight hours, we would drop off copies of our newsletter at strategic locations in town, and people would read it the following morning. With every issue, there was greater alarm among the whites. Chicanos and Anglos both wanted to find out who was printing this outrageous paper. We were hot in our attacks and critical in our comments regarding community issues including taxes, contracts, employment, conflicts of interest, and the romantic liaisons between Mexicans and Anglos.

The publication of the newsletter brought about my second brush with the law. I was kidnapped as I got off the junior college bus coming home from Uvalde one afternoon by Raul Tapia, a local Gulf station operator.

The college bus dropped us off at the Dairy Queen, at the intersection of East Crockett and East Zavala streets. As my friends and I walked across the street from the Dairy Queen and were in front of the ice plant, Tapia drove up alongside us. He called out my name: *"¡Angel, subete!"* He pointed a handgun in our direction as he ordered me to get into his car. Tapia was a big man, about six feet tall, who easily weighed 250 pounds, and had a thick neck, muscular arms and big strong hands. I got very scared. The barrel of his gun looked like a cannon at that moment. I reluctantly walked in front of his car to the passenger side, opened the door, and got in. I looked at my friends for help as I sunk into the seat. My friends had panic in their eyes and were frozen in their steps. Tapia had switched the gun from his right hand to his left and held it across his lap, aimed in my direction.

He made a snappy U-turn and sped off in the direction the college bus had just come from. He drove toward the Highland Circle subdivision, a one-street development in Cristal where the middle-class Mexicans lived, and where Tapia himself lived. I was convinced that he was going to kill me; I thought I would never see my friends or family again. Through a dry, parched mouth and with a scared voice, I asked him where we were going. He just sneered at me with bloodshot eyes, reeking of alcohol, and mumbled in broken English, "You gonna pay!" I had no idea what he meant by that. My mind was racing in panic but my eyes were riveted on the gun he kept in his left hand. It remained pointed at me under his right elbow. I could not say anything else to him, I was so scared. In silence, he drove me to his home. A lot of cars were parked along the street by his driveway, some I recognized to be cop cars. I knew I was in real trouble then. He ordered me out of the car and into his house.

Round Two with Captain Allee

There waiting for me were five other men: County Commissioner Jesus Rodriguez, the only Mexican American member of the Commissioner's Court, Justice of the Peace Stormy Davis, County Commissioner Tom Allee (cousin of A. Y.), Sheriff C. L. Sweeten, and Texas Ranger Captain A. Y. Allee. As we entered the front door I was told by Sheriff Sweeten to sit at the breakfast table in the kitchen. On the table were paper, a pencil, and a bulky tape recorder. They all joined me at the table, except for Rodriguez and Tapia. Tapia had disappeared somewhere into the recesses of his house, and I didn't seen him again for hours; Rodriguez remained seated on the sofa at the entrance to the living room. Ranger Allee sat to my right, Davis to my left and Sweeten stood, leaning against the wall, facing me.

Commissioner Allee sat at the table directly across from me and pressed buttons on the tape recorder. Allee the Ranger immediately started talking to me. He said, "Nothing is going to happen to you, boy, if you cooperate with us. We just want to talk to you about your doings." That assurance had the opposite effect on me: I was sure then that I was going to die. Why else would he bring up something happening to me if it wasn't on his mind? He told me he wanted me to admit that I had been trained by PASO and the Teamsters Union. "Tell us about your communist training by that PASO bunch. And the union communists," he said in what sounded more like a statement than a question. But I knew he meant the meetings Chicano leaders from San Antonio had held with local folks to organize a PASO chapter and recruit candidates. The Teamsters Union had a local representative at the Del Monte plant in Cristal, and Juan Cornejo, a member of the slate of Los Cinco Candidatos was the local business manager for the union. There was also Ray Schaefer, the Teamster boss from San Antonio. I knew who he was and had seen him but had never really talked or even met him formally.

I said to Allee, "I don't know any communists." For some reason, he didn't press this issue; rather, he said, "I want you to tell us who told you what to say at the rallies. Who wrote the speeches for you?" Nervously looking down at the table, I said, "Nobody, sir. I just talk about what I feel. What I see." I glanced quickly at him sideways to see Allee bite down hard on his cigar and take it out furiously with his hand. He nearly touched my face with his nose as he leaned into my direction and with the most horrible breath I have ever smelled, I heard him say into my face, "Recant every speech you have made, boy! Tell this tape recorder you didn't mean what you said at those rallies!"

A. Y. Allee also wanted me to admit in writing that I was being paid for my voter registration work and speechmaking. He grabbed my right hand from my lap and thrust the pencil from the table into my palm, telling me, "Write down, here on this paper, that you are being paid to do this by PASO." He made other statements I was to write but I couldn't hear out of fear. I just recall staring at his horrible mouth inches from my face and hearing something about, "not being coerced into writing this statement. You are doing it out of free will and your own volition." I was in panic because I did not know what the word "volition" meant. "What do you mean?" I asked. "I don't know what you want from me. I am not writing anything I don't know about."

I was there for about four hours, very nervous and shaking badly. Ranger Allee and Sheriff Sweeten took turns egging me on—sometimes softly, other times roughly—into making these declarations. I bloodied my left thumb with my index finger by nervously picking on the cuticle. I thought I was going to die. Most of the time I simply looked at them while I shook my head saying, "No!" again and again. Complete sentences wouldn't come out of my throat. I wondered at whose hands I would die—Allee's or Sweeten's? I covered my ears with my hands, trying to keep their words out, only to have them jerked away by either the pinche rinche Allee or Stormy Davis. To keep from shaking, trembling, bloodying my thumb, and covering my ears, I sat on my hands.

The presence of Stormy Davis, the justice of the peace, unnerved me each time I looked at him when he yanked at my hands. He was also the coroner. He would be the one to determine that I had died by accidental means or suicide. I was convinced that is why he was there. The fact that both Ranger Allee and Sheriff Sweeten had often made public declarations to the press about the men that they had killed, not counting Mexicans, was very scary to me, to say the least. I believed that I was going to join that list of the Mexicans not counted—the "disappeared." From time to time that afternoon and into the early evening, as they got weary of my refusal to recant either in print or into the tape recorder, they would leave the table and go over to where Rodriguez was and caucus. One time they all went outside and I was left alone, but I was too scared to run for the kitchen door. I had heard the stories of how Allee and Sweeten both had shot Mexicans in the back "while attempting to escape." I just knew they were trying to get me to do something like that, as an excuse to shoot me.

I never recanted, nor did I die. There was a little fly that was bothering us that day in the hot, airless kitchen as we sat around that table. This little fly, as much as they tried to swat it away, continued being a pest. I noticed that any one of them could have decided, at any given time, to kill that fly, yet none of them did. They simply wanted to intimidate the fly or scare it into going off to bother someone else. I reasoned in my fear that I was like that pesky fly: they really didn't want to kill me, they just wanted to scare me big time, to stop me from organizing. I focused on that fly as best I could to hold my sanity. It saved my life.

I grew into full manhood that long afternoon and evening. Somehow, political courage found me even though I was not looking for it. Slowly, as the minutes turned to hours and the afternoon became night, I began to realize the extent to which these men would go to keep things in Cristal as they were. Their job was to keep Mexicans in their place using fear, intimidation, and outright physical harm. Clearly, it was a defining and transformational moment in my life. I went from naive Chicano to militant Chicano. Fear of gringos in me was replaced by rage at their repression of Chicanos. I realized how afraid they were of independent and fearless Chicanos; this Chicano attitude was most threatening to them. It was the beginning of the end of their political control over our lives.

My Fearless Reputation

I don't know what ultimately caused them to give up on me or why, when they finally all left the house. They didn't order Tapia to beat me up either. If they did, he didn't touch me. After the gringos left his house, Tapia was most impressed with my valor and said, *"Tienes muchos huevos, Gutiérrez."* (Basically, he said that I had a lot of balls.) *"Vamanos,"* he said as he escorted me back into his car and took me to the Oasis Drive-In at the edge of town. He ordered two dinners and Lone Star beer. I ate and drank quietly. I still did not know where this situation was ultimately headed. I was still in his car and while the gun was not present my fear kept me very much under his control. Slowly the beer and food took effect and I regained my composure and nerve enough to ask him why he had taken me to the gringos. He wouldn't answer directly except to say, *"Tu no sabes nada. Estos de PASO son unos pendejos y nos van a joder. No puenden contra los gringos. Por ellos tenemos todo. Asi es. Come, ya no te voy a decir mas."* His words were typical of sell-out Mexicans who ally themselves with the powerful gringos. He felt that PASO would fail and Chicanos would ultimately lose out because the gringos were too powerful. Chicanos owed their future to the gringos and that was the way things were. He didn't want to talk, and ordered me to eat.

My friends, who had been looking for me all afternoon, discovered that I had been sequestered in the Tapia home. They drove straight to Tapia's house and saw the police cars there. They also knew that no law enforcement person would come to my aid because they were the ones who held me there, were accomplices in this conspiracy to harm me. When my friends saw me at the Oasis Drive-In, they were relieved to see that I was not in any apparent danger. I was eating and drinking beer with Tapia. I smiled at them, indicated that everything was okay. Tapia then took me home. This time my mother was not at home waiting. During my first year at the junior college she had taken work as a nurse's aide in Chicago and lived there with Consuelo, her sister.

What I found out after this incident was that Tapia had earlier in the day, been going from bar to bar in the Mexican side of town with a loaded 30–30 Winchester rifle, saying that he was going to kill me. No one had stopped him; no one had alerted me or anyone else who knew me; no one ever said to me later that they had called the police for help (not that it would have done any good). Most people were simply afraid to get involved with such an incident. Tapia went around all day with his bravado, in the bars, boasting that he was going to get me off that bus and kill me. After that he had a lot of explaining to do because he didn't do it. All he could say was that young Gutiérrez was one brave son of a bitch for not backing down. Tapia never used my first name again; he called me "Gutiérrez" from that point on. He never really became my friend, but he did afford me great respect thereafter. He even told others—right in front of me—the story of my bravery in facing up to Captain Allee and the Sheriff.

Junior College

Doing political work at the community college in Uvalde was much harder than in Cristal. The story of my kidnapping was spread by my friends and I was looked at with awe by other Chicano students. The area Chicano students attending this commuter school were mostly reluctant to put up a challenge, let alone a fight. The odds seemed impossible: the whites outnumbered us by about four to one. I soon learned that the Chicano students on the campus were easily divided and controlled by contacts with their former, hometown Anglo classmates. The Anglos knew each other, even across the region, because their families socialized together. We, as Chicanos, did not know each other from one town to the next. The Anglos have always been in solidarity with each other because they have lived with a siege mentality among us forever, since their ancestors took our land. Anglos were a minority in most of the South Texas towns, so they had to stick together to keep us under control. And to maximize their strength they had to keep us divided. I learned early that when divided, the many become few.

Other Chicanos viewed those of us from Cristal as being too radical. They believed all of the negative press coverage of PASO, the Teamsters, Los Cinco Candidatos, and the general Chicano struggle in Crystal City. Because of this persistent and extremely negative press, most Chicanos avoided affiliation with Cristal. An Anglo had only to ask of a Chicano, "Do you want another Crystal City here?" to get a resounding "No!" Chicanos actually learned to become ashamed of us having taken power in Cristal, and they felt compelled to apologize for that exercise in democracy. Their colonial mentality was more pervasive than I wanted to admit at that time.

The battle of the Alamo of Mexican-era San Antonio is negatively treated in the press and in both high school and college courses in much the same way. So much so that to this very day, most Chicanos will shun identification with General Antonio Lopez de Santa Ana and the

Mexican troops in that battle. The extremely sad irony is that Chicanos *did* win in Cristal, as their ancestors had won at the Alamo. And we were *entitled* to win.

At the junior college the relations between Chicanos and Anglos were not much better than they had been in my earlier years. I had decided to seek the office of student body president, and met with a lot of resistance, to say the least. There were very few Mexicans attending the junior college—I dare say a little under two hundred—and most of them were terribly intimidated by the all-Anglo administration and teaching staff (except for the Spanish teacher, Dr. Roberto Galvan) and the overwhelmingly Anglo student body. Needless to say, I lost the election. Additionally, I was rebuked by the dean of students, Jerald Underwood for having run a very "anti-Anglo" campaign. This was another extremely sad irony that I encountered. Here I was championing a Chicano cause: open admissions, more Chicano faculty, more Chicano scholarship money, and the right to run for office. I knew I couldn't win—that was not the point! The educational campaign, the organizational effort, and the challenge to Anglo dominance were what drove me. Rather than interpret these actions as pro-Chicano, I was accused of being anti-Anglo. I refused then, as I do now, to accept that twisted, illogical, self-serving gringo trick, that our only option is to be pro-Anglo. To be pro-Chicano is *not* axiomatically or automatically to be anti-Anglo.

During the campaign I was called a communist, atheist, radical, and militant Chicano. These words were scrawled on my posters. Dean Underwood dismissed the name calling and defacing of my campaign posters. He said they were my own doing, a reaction to my negative campaign. I reminded him of how I was kept from campaigning in the dormitories by racist gringo students. He somehow did not recall my complaint that these *busca burros* (burro seekers), as we called the storefront cowboys, had chased me on one occasion in an attempt to beat me with their wide-strap belts and big buckles. The students who wore the cowboy garb back then were only the white kids; we Chicanos hated the cowboy look because it reminded us of the dress code of the pinches rinches and of most of the police. Today the *Tejano* look is to dress in that garb of an earlier time; we have a right to reclaim all of our cultural trappings, including this type of dress and country style.

Bloc Voting

During the 1963 spring semester college election, I put into practice the concept of bloc voting that I had first learned from the Anglos in high school. The way they would win an open, at-large election was to bloc vote, that is to say, get all their voters to cast only a vote for their candidate regardless of how many others are running. Invariably, in high school, there would be an Anglo or two running along with three or four Chicanos for the same race. All the Anglos would vote *only* for the Anglos, while we would vote for our favorite candidates, both Chicano and Anglo. Since some of the Anglo candidates got some of the Chicano votes, and they voted only for themselves, invariably they would win. It never happened the other way around until I figured it out and organized my Chicano voters in high school to only vote for me. I was the first Chicano to win my junior class presidency, and—the next year— both the senior class presidency and the student body presidency at the same time. I had not only learned how to win but also how to control.

At the community college I received 206 votes on election day. There were only 198 Mexican American students registered at Uvalde. Every Chicano voted for me, except for the two or three absent that day, and in addition I won the votes of a few Anglos, including some women, and Tracy Allee, the nephew of Ranger Allee. At that time, the colleges used paper identification cards that bore only a name and address, and no photograph of the student. I realized that by gathering identification cards we could have voted on behalf of the entire Chicano student body if we had only tried. Anglos cannot tell one Chicano from another; they work at making us invisible. A mental block is built up over time in the Anglo mind that says we shouldn't count, hence we aren't seen and don't exist.

While I lost the election, I did not lose the desire to make change happen nor the desire to take on the Anglo power structure. In fact, I grew stronger in my resolve to press the challenge. Politics weren't the only concern, however: there were classes, grades, and women.

Social Contacts and Dating

There were a few Anglo girls who favored Mexicans, but this had to be on the sly, just as it had in my high school. I saw that this is the way it was between Anglo girls and Chicano boys: you met after sundown and kept the relations top secret. I had learned by then that relations with white girls were taboo. The only difference at the junior college in Uvalde was that it was easier to conceal the relationships because Anglos only knew each other, not the Mexicans from other cities. And, unlike high school in Cristal, where people were known by the car they drove, a person's car at the commuter college was not recognizable, many cars were alike. The nearby hill country offered a private retreat; cabins could be rented in many spots within thirty miles of the campus.

Even San Antonio, a very large city, was but an hour's drive away from Uvalde. During this era the legal speed limit was seventy miles per hour, and a person could zip over the miles quickly.

George Ozuna, the Cristal city manager, on occasions lent me his car to enjoy female companionship. Aside from a couple of Anglo girls, I had my eye on Ernestina Rodriguez, a beauty from Uvalde. She was the most beautiful Mexican American girl I had ever seen and she liked me. The problem was that she did have a local boyfriend and I had competition from another local boy, Rafael Tovar Jr. Hence it was not easy to drive off with Ernestina to Garner State Park, twenty miles away. It was easier to hit on the Anglo girls and trip out to San Antonio, or to any number of camping areas with cabins near Uvalde, any morning or afternoon in a borrowed car.

It was still, however, very dangerous for a Chicano to be seen alone with an Anglo girl in a car. Schoolmates of mine in high school found this out the hard way. They were almost killed by irate Anglo fathers and their friends because they were dating Anglo girls. The usual technique, then, was to get some of the gay Anglo guys to supposedly call on the Anglo girl for a date, take her out away from the home, and deliver her to the waiting Chicanos. The Chicanos reciprocated by getting someone to do favors for the gay Anglos. Some of these girls got pregnant by Chicanos and had abortions, which was unheard of at that time.

The Big Yellow Bus as Cafeteria and Student Center

Chicanos (and some Anglos) who had neither cars nor gas money for the eighty-five-mile trek from Cristal to Uvalde and back rode the big yellow school bus. I was one of those. At the junior college we met Chicanos riding the yellow buses from all over the region, not only Uvalde, but also from Del Rio and Eagle Pass near the Mexican border, Leakey, Sabinal, Hondo, and Devine toward San Antonio, and south from Asherton and Carrizo Springs to Crystal City and La Pryor.

Our lunch and books often remained on the hot, sun-drenched bus, serving as our locker while we scurried back and forth to classes during the day. The Anglos, who had money to spare, ate in the cafeteria and rented lockers from the college. Chicanos congregated at the bus for socializing or napping. One vicious game played by Chicanos was to steal or eat part of someone's lunch, usually that belonging to another Chicano. We knew that Esequiel Romero brought the best *chile* (hot sauce) in his lunch, that Eddie Avila's lunch always contained a thermos with some *guiso*, tasty and warm, and that Rudy Palomo always had great *chorizo y frijoles* (sausage and bean) flour tortilla tacos.

Another game was to lure girls, Mexican or Anglo, to the bus for light petting and propositioning for greater adventures. If a Chicano was able to talk an Anglo girl into the bus, she would not sit on the same seat, but on the opposite side or in the next seat to the front so that it would appear to anyone looking from the outside as if they were not together. With Chicanas as guests, we would sit together and sink down on the bench seat as far as we could to kiss and pet. Occasionally, those of us from Cristal would scout the other buses to see which girls, Anglo or Chicana, would accept a quick date on the bus so we could then hit them up ourselves to visit our bus.

Our most frequent contact was with those that rode our bus, the Asherton to Uvalde route on Highway 83. There was a lot of tension on that bus: Anglos sat in front and Chicanos sat in the back. Never did I see an Anglo girl share a seat with a Mexican boy—the barrier was ever-present. And because we sat in the back, we had to pass by the front seats in order to get on or off the bus.

On one occasion, Eddie Avila stroked a white girl's head and hair as he exited the bus in front of the Catholic church in our hometown. Richard Tumlinson, a white kid, took it upon himself to defend the white man's "property" and honor. He leapt on Avila's back from the bus and knocked him to the ground. Eddie was as skinny as a bean pole and very nearsighted. His glasses flew in one direction, his books in another, and Tumlinson proceeded to beat him severely about his head, back, and ears as he lay pinned face down on the ground. The Chicanos who tried to come to Eddie's defense were blocked from the only bus exit by the Anglos sitting in front. Only when the rear emergency door was opened and Chicanos flew out the back to pull Tumlinson off did the beating stop. Eddie never knew what had hit him. For the next few days, the taunts and the name-calling back and forth was heavy. Another bus was added and another route created because of this, and we were segregated from then on.

4

Los Cinco Candidatos

The election of Los Cinco Candidatos in Cristal turned out better than mine did at the junior college: the Mexican American candidates won in Crystal City in April, 1963. That came as no surprise to those of us working closely with the campaign. At the end of January 31st of that year the voter registration period had ended, before most of the candidates had filed to be included on the ballot. Yet, due to a few candidates filing early, rumors had surfaced about the potential for Chicano candidates, and when the local PASO leaders in charge of getting Mexicanos to pay their poll tax added up the number of registered voters—first the Anglos and then the Chicanos—they found that more Mexican Americans had paid the poll tax than Anglos. The obvious campaign strategy was now simply to organize and mobilize to get the Chicano vote out for Los Cinco Candidatos. Through inaction, the election was ours to lose. But with the proper mobilization, we had the potential to win!

Our five Mexican American candidates were Juan Cornejo, Manuel Maldonado, Antonio Cardenas, Reynaldo Mendoza, and Mario Hernandez, the only persons willing to run. Juan Cornejo was the best of the candidates in that he was single, employed by the Teamsters Union, and was experienced with confrontation and negotiation as the union representative at the Del Monte food processing plant. He was very active in representing the interests of the cannery workers; they knew him and liked him. Manuel Maldonado, a ranch foreman, had a large family and was the elder of the group. He was very quiet, serene, and down-to-earth. He was tall, soft-spoken, and very direct, and his analytical skills were tremendous. The most complex problems or issues were like soft butter to his knife-sharp mind. When he spoke, he commanded attention and enjoyed support from many quarters in the Mexican community. Antonio Cardenas and Reynaldo Mendoza, both married and with young families, were migrant laborers. Cardenas was a migrant labor contractor and Mendoza also had a beginning business as a photographer. The youngest and most quick-tempered was Mario Hernandez. He dressed very sharp and drew much attention with his loud and boisterous manner, living up to the stereotype of the used car salesman that he was.

The election was marred by the violence of the Texas Rangers. No sooner had the voter registration results been released to the public that the infamous rinches showed up in town. They began patrolling the streets where the candidates lived and monitoring the political rallies we had. The campaign workers for Los Cinco Candidatos, seeking voters who needed absentee ballots, were trailed by the *rinches.*

To qualify for the absentee vote (later known as "early voting"), a voter had to prove illness, as verified by a medical provider's statement, or absence from the county on election day due to one of three reasons: employment elsewhere, service in the military, or the attending of college. I learned from the women working the campaign how to get the vote out among the elderly, the sick, the military, and those who were going to be working or studying outside the county on election day.

Getting votes cast as absentee ballots was an art form and became a second career for many retired persons and housewives in Cristal. Our first get-out-the-vote experts were Enriqueta Palacios, Virginia Muzquiz, Pura Mendoza, and Rita Yanas. I learned from them, during the 1963 election in Cristal, that the campaign that obtains the majority of the absentee vote will invariably win the election. The reason is simple: rather than organize and mobilize all get-out-the-vote efforts on election day, a successful campaign gets votes cast every day of the absentee voting period, and then again on election day. Trying to mobilize all Mexican American resources on election day was often too taxing on the volunteers and underfunded campaign staffs. It was both foolish and unsophisticated to wait for election day to try to get hundreds or thousands to the polls, as there is no room for error. Why not target neighborhoods, categories of people, age groups, worksites, and students, and get 200 or so of them to vote each day of the early voting period?

We built our margin of victory one day at a time, one block of votes at a time, by adjusting our get-out-the-vote strategy as needed. The voter tally was posted daily in the office conducting the election. We

Table 1. Election Results

Crystal City Election Results			
1963		1970	
Manuel Maldonado	864	Ventura Gonzales	1,341
Juan Cornejo	818	Pablo Puente	1,306
Mario Hernandez	799		
Antonio Cardenas	799	Emmett Sevilla	835
Reynaldo Mendoza	796	Charlie Crawford	820
Ed Ritchie	754		
W. P. Brennan	717		
Bruce Holsomback	716		
J. C. Bookout	694		
S. G. Galvan	664		
Dr. Henry Daly	164		
Rev. Arnold Lopez	146		

Crystal City School Board Election Results			
1963		1970	
Dr. S. S. Peters	888	Miguel Perez	1,397
R. E. Boyer	873	Arturo Gonzales	1,344
		José Angel Gutiérrez	1,344
Jesus Maldonado	789		
Lorenzo Olivares	782	E. W. Ritchie	1,119
		Rafael Tovar	1,090
		Luz Arcos	1,081

would boost morale by announcing that we were getting a margin of victory before election day. We sought out voters who often presented a problem on election day or took too much time to vote such as the elderly, the timid, the sick, the physically impaired, the non-English speaker, the agricultural migrant workers, and those slow to remember all the designated candidates or ballot measures. And of course we were careful to only seek out voters favorable to our slate.

When the election of April, 1963, was over, the candidates met at my father's ranch house at the edge of Mexico Chico to hammer out a deal on who was going to be mayor. It was always assumed by la raza that Juan Cornejo would be the mayor. As a bachelor, he had no family obligations as did the other four newly elected councilmen. Moreover, he had the backing of the Teamster's Union and PASO. He had brought them to Cristal. But no sooner had the returns been made official that schisms and problems began to develop. Power can cause divisions as well as unity; it causes people to become addicted to its use, for better or for worse. Power itself is disloyal and promiscuous. It goes with anyone willing to have it and use it. As such, rivalries began to emerge among the five right after the election.

Manuel Maldonado, the ranch hand, had the highest number of votes of all the candidates. He worked as a ranch foreman for the Keller family. Gringos immediately began pushing for his election as mayor because, they argued, tradition had it that the candidate with the most votes was chosen mayor. But the Chicano community knew that he was the most vulnerable of the five. Maldonado was the only one who worked directly for a gringo rancher. Juan Cornejo was eventually able to prevail, obtaining the votes of the others to become the first Chicano mayor of Cristal.

The Anglo community did not accept their defeat. The Anglos do not believe in fairness. To Anglos, being fair means always winning. The defeated Anglo politicians, the Anglo businessmen and the local newspaper editor did not rest after the election. The losing Anglo slate started attacking Los Cinco the night of the election victory. The Anglos first had the ballot boxes impounded and filed a court petition to have the votes recounted. The winning totals remained unchanged. Next, the Anglos sought to contest the election in district court. They alleged fraud and voting irregularities. Their legal strategy was not based on any evidence; it was based on economics and psychology. We did not have money to defend these lawsuits and even our own people were not convinced that Los Cinco had won outright, since no Mexican candidate ever had before.

Dissension and Harassment

The Anglos immediately began to seek ways to discredit the winners. Mario Hernandez was charged with the criminal offense of bouncing a check a year prior and the statute of limitations had not run out for this offense. He was vulnerable to prosecution and, of course, had to plea bargain. Anglos demanded he switch sides, turning him against the other four. Reynaldo Mendoza and Manuel Maldonado were accused of not paying utility bills owed the city. The City Charter required the elected councilmen to be current in their tax and utility payments, so the Anglos sought their disqualification for office on these grounds. Antonio Cardenas was attacked on residency status. As a migrant labor contractor he regularly left Cristal for long periods at a time. The Anglos recruited middle-class Mexican Americans into a coalition that began circulating a recall petition and another petition to amend the City Charter to provide for staggered terms for the council members.

Regardless of the escalating controversies surrounding the election, Cornejo, as the elected mayor, began making personnel changes, and George Ozuna was brought in immediately as the city manager. Ozuna's selection soon caused a power struggle between them: he wanted to run the city in a professional manner without undue interference from the mayor or individual council members. He was under the impression that he had been hired to do just that. The City Charter placed all the power over administrative, fiscal, and personnel matters with the city manager, not the mayor. But Juan Cornejo had other ideas. He wanted to run the city as a strong mayor in a big city in contravention of the City Charter. Cornejo wanted to use the power of the office of mayor, with a majority on the council. He was not afraid of using his newly obtained power for la raza.

Reform or Patronage?

Cornejo knew he had to deliver for la raza. Our people had been waiting for so long for such an opportunity. Many a Chicano politician and appointee had run from this responsibility because they could not handle this pressure well. Many a new appointee or elected official felt that la raza should not ask for anything, much less make political demands of them. They thought that we should give them time to act and not expect immediate or great things from them; we never expected or demanded that from their gringo counterparts, so why should we now? We expected better because we had elected them for that very reason. We were tired of being ignored, lost, omitted, forgotten, refused, denied, and short-changed. It was *our* turn at the table.

Cornejo wanted to be able to afford patronage to his supporters, to get his team of supporters into positions of power over budget and policy. There was no civil service in Cristal. The mayor could remove individuals from city positions who had been and would continue to be obstacles to the reforms about to be implemented by Los Cinco, but only upon the city manager's recommendation. The City Charter gave the exclusive right of hiring and firing to the city manager.

Cornejo felt that J. P. English, the city marshall, R. A. Taylor, the city attorney, and others in critical departments, such as the English-only–speaking clerks who provided services to la raza, had to go immediately. Ozuna won out over Cornejo because of the City Charter regulations on these personnel changes. That set the stage for a total rupture within the newly elected government. Cornejo wanted immediate and total change in personnel. Ozuna wanted to go slow, document the need for change, study the options, and hire the best people for any vacancies. Ozuna did not want any lawsuits; ironically, neither did the new Chicano council. They already had their hands full with election lawsuits and the continuing bad press. Cornejo couldn't push Ozuna too far, but he was also not about to fire the first Chicano to be hired.

A Double Set of Books

One of the most remarkable things that occurred when George Ozuna took office and settled into the routine of governance was the discovery of the existence of a dual set of accounting books for the collection of utilities. There was a book for "American water" and a book for "Mexican water." These books were the accounts of water service from which monthly billings were made. Ozuna also found out that the Anglo country club and golf course was on city property, and under lease to them for a dollar per year. And Mexicans were not allowed to join the country club or play golf on the links. Another issue that came to light was that the Anglo cemetery had full utility services—running water, maintenance, security, and regular landscaping. The Mexican cemetery didn't even have water, much less any attention from city crews. All residents of Cristal paid a minimal monthly fee for cemetery maintenance, but it went only toward the Anglo cemetery maintenance. The adjacent neighborhood of El Campo Santo did not have water, but the Del Monte plant nearby to both the neighborhood and the Mexican cemetery had all utility services.

The streets of El Campo Santo, like all other Mexican barrios, were without paved streets or sidewalks. Anglos had sewer lines, Mexicans enjoyed outdoor privies. It was clearly a divided city, where services were given to the Anglos and denied to the Mexicans. George Ozuna set about correcting that deprivation of services and the imbalance in funding of improvements favoring only the Anglos. Ozuna conceded to Cornejo the right to make recommendations about who to hire for what position, and the appointments usually reflected Cornejo's choice. They had begun to work out a relationship to determine whose turn it was to be first among equals, and when.

City Hall at that time was an old WPA-built building from the 1940s. It was decrepit and almost totally nonfunctional most of the time. If the roof wasn't leaking, the plumbing was running over, the plaster from the walls was peeling, the ceiling tiles were always falling off, and the floor was cracked. Soon after the election, plans were laid by the Chicano council to pass a bond issue and build a new city hall. Listening to

this discussion at a city council meeting was my introduction to investment banking and the world of municipal bonds and high finance. I
have not forgotten the earlier total exclusion of Mexican Americans
from that type of business. And, to this day, Mexican Americans are
woefully underrepresented and totally inconspicuous as owners of investment banking firms and high finance entities of other types. Usually
an Anglo investment firm will now hire a Mexican or two as token employees; they send them before governmental bodies containing Mexican American officeholders to make a pitch for contracting their services. In bond issues, our people as voters do not get to place items on
the bond plan or have access to the process of decision-making. We only
get to vote for or against the bond issue. Then, we help pay the taxes for
a generation or two. In some cases involving a facility or service, if we
pay a user fee, we might derive benefit from the improvement. Invariably, we get involved in a bond issue to ensure its passage, because
among the many other line items totaling millions of dollars there is one
line item that we, as Chicanos, need to have addressed, such as a neighborhood center, a cultural center, a swimming pool, a park, a flood levy
or a health clinic. This process is tantamount to eating porridge with
your finger: Chicanos call it *comiendo atole con el dedo*.

My Political Reward

The summer of 1963 was particularly trying for me. My patronage re-
ward for having assisted Cornejo and Los Cinco was to become the director of parks and recreation, a big title for one sorry job—lifeguard at
the city pool. The pool had been segregated for years, as far back as I can
remember. It was not segregated by areas or sections of the pool, but by
use on days of the week. There were days when Mexicans were allowed
to swim, after the Anglos had been swimming in fresh water for a couple of days. Before the dirty water was drained out, the Mexicans were
let in. The water was flushed out twice a week and the pool refilled; this
was before the wonderful filtration systems of today.
   It was terrifying for me to work the city pool because of the constant
interaction with Anglos. Crystal City loses about half of its population
when the Mexican migrants leave for work in the northern states. Many
Anglos leave in the summer for vacation, as well. The remaining Anglo
strength in the city is magnified during the summertime. Anglos would
come to spend time at the city pool, particularly in the evening when it
was cooler. My job was to watch over the swimmers, maintain order
and evict the disorderly, which was no small task. I was challenged
with regularity and subjected to threats and potential violence nightly

by Anglo rednecks. At that time, I also lived alone in my home. My mother had gone, as always during the summer, to work elsewhere like the other migrants. I learned to hate the gringos who challenged me every night. The new Chicano cops had to come to my rescue regularly. I never felt so alone, vulnerable or powerless as when la raza finally had power. They had the power on the city council, but I didn't. I began to think of getting power myself because I needed it every night. As a life-guard, with many layers of authority to go through before any real power could be had—the police, the councilmen, the city manager, Juan Cornejo—my hopes for instant social change died that summer. I began to realize that it would take years to change the way things were, even if we had political power.

The Split on the City Council

I particularly disliked the deep divisions beginning to emerge among Los Cinco, and also Mayor Cornejo and City Manager Ozuna. Regardless of how much Ozuna tried to please Cornejo, he couldn't. Cornejo's thirst for power was unquenchable. Cornejo also wanted to build a political machine, while Ozuna wanted to maintain a nonpartisan posture. Rumors fueled by the local and San Antonio Anglo press ate into our group's solidarity. Cornejo was linked romantically with every woman who worked the elections, the same women who formed the formal grassroots network and were the backbone of the PASO organization. This network included the wives of the other councilmen and union leaders. Mario Hernandez, in order to save himself from criminal indictment, prosecution, and possible jail time for check bouncing, constantly attacked the other four of Los Cinco. The legal bills for defense mounted, as individuals could only afford to donate so much. The media attacks were incessant. PASO itself was undergoing internal dissension over the role it played in Cristal. Many PASO members and other influential Democrats criticized the leadership of Albert Peña Jr., Albert Fuentes, and Johnny Alaniz specifically for the direct action tactics employed in Cristal. PASO, as an organization across Texas, ended shortly after the victory in Cristal.

I decided to go to Los Angeles and run away from the job of lifeguard and the problems it presented. Conveniently, Cornejo had sent me as an advance man to Los Angeles shortly after the election at the beginning of the summer. I was 18 years old. Los Cinco had received invitations from many places, including Mexico. I've never forgotten how a small victory can become larger: the symbolic value of a victory to la raza anywhere, including Mexico, is most important. Los Cinco had become celebrities. They met the Mexican President, Gustavo Diaz Ordaz, in Piedras Negras, Coahuila across from Eagle Pass on the Texas border. They had been invited to visit Southern California as guests of MAPA, the Mexican American Political Association of California. MAPA, headed by Eduardo Quevedo, was like PASO in purpose and goals. And like PASO, it was a remnant of the Viva Kennedy clubs. In this regard PASO and MAPA differed from the older and more traditional Mexican American organizations, such as the League of United Latin American Citizens and the American G.I. Forum, which were neither political nor interested in contesting elections with Mexican American candidates.

While acting as advance man for Los Cinco in Los Angeles, I had met other individuals associated with MAPA, such as Bert Corona, Juan Acevedo, and Frank Casado. The MAPA office was on Second Street in the downtown area, and Quevedo and Casado were always there. Bert Corona would drop in from time to time to present some new strategy or scheme to old man Quevedo, who never bought into Corona's suggestions. Quevedo always seemed skeptical of Corona's latest ploy for reasons that escaped me then.

MAPA, the Southern California two-week tour, old man Quevedo, and observing the other MAPA leaders was intoxicating for me: I was drunk with happiness over so many Chicanos pouring admiration and affection over us. I was so impressed with their wisdom and scope of vision, and Cristal seemed so small from this vantage point. Our differences back home seemed so petty upon comparison with MAPA and their efforts in southern California. When the tour ended and I returned to the swimming pool and the politics of Cristal, I passed my time conjuring fantasies of my life in Los Angeles.

I acted on those fantasies and quit my post as director of parks and recreation in late August, 1963, and took the train from San Antonio back to Los Angeles. Upon arrival I lived in the train station for a couple of weeks, out of a locker. I did not immediately seek out the MAPA leaders I previously had met. I was going to make it on my own, then go see them. I thought they would think less of us in Cristal if I suddenly reappeared and asked for personal favors from them.

The Streets of Los Angeles

A prostitute of mixed Chinese and Mexican ancestry who was working the train station befriended me. She helped me got a job with the *Los Angeles Times* newspaper as a copy runner. A copy runner rides a bicycle from building to building in downtown L.A., picking up ad copy and running it to and from the newspaper office. I got to know the downtown streets fairly well. This was one of the most dangerous experiences I have ever lived through, the supposed assassination attempt at the hands of Raul Tapia notwithstanding. Dodging cars, buses, and other large, moving machines on downtown streets every second I was on the bicycle was extremely dangerous. Several hours each day I was risking my life for this job and developed a reckless side to my nature because of this. I met a lot of people in the advertising-related departments of major companies. I became a familiar face in their art and photography studios, as well as some of the modeling agencies and film production companies with downtown studios. Additionally, I had access to various other offices of major corporations doing business in downtown LA. And through these various contacts, I finally met people at the gas company.

The gas company people offered me an opportunity to work in their print shop. I had no idea how to do any printing, but I lied. I had learned earlier to mask the truth and exaggerate on application forms because of my experience with the University of Texas at Austin. I had applied for admission there in the beginning of 1962 and listed my mother's address in Chicago, where she was living at the time of my application. The university classified me as eligible but as an out-of-state resident. I couldn't afford the escalated tuition cost and ended up at Southwest Texas Junior College instead. On my application to the gas company, I stated not only that I had junior college credits, but also that I knew the printing business. I had never seen a multilith machine in my life, other than from a distance. I got the job, and this sent me scurrying to the downtown library for books on printing. Fortunately, my first few days were spent as apprentice to Ann Dougherty, a multilith operator. She did not let me touch the machine until she decided I was ready. In those first few days of observation, I learned how to operate the machine like a professional.

The job paid very well for a kid my age and relative inexperience. I had been a migrant worker and had done assorted jobs in the past, and the longest tenure I'd ever had was as assistant manager at the Eagle gas station in Crystal City. I had worked at the J. C. Penney store in Cristal as a stock clerk and part-time sales person. At Bowman Farms in Carrizo Springs, I was simply a field hand on weekends. But this, now, was a regular full-time job with the largest utility in the *Los Angeles* metroplex.

I was working there at the time of the Kennedy assassination in 1963. The picture of John Kennedy was hung in many window displays in downtown L.A. after that and the news media continued on the subject for days. Kennedy's assassination was shocking to me: gringos had instilled in my mind that assassinations happened only in Latin America.

More shocking was the implication that because I was from Texas, I was somehow indirectly responsible for his death; people actually asked me how Texans could do such a thing, as if all of us in the state were responsible. Hell, I had never even been to Dallas! I was very happy to learn that the assassin charged was a white man and that he himself was killed by another white man. Like millions of others, I saw Ruby's assassination of Oswald on the television. In the future I learned to look for the usual Anglo reaction to this type of violence, which was to blame nonwhites, as if to say that they themselves are not capable of such ultimate, drastic action.

While working at the gas company I also spent considerable time with an older man who ran the photography department, someone I had met while running ad copy for the newspaper. It was he who had actually suggested I apply for the printing job. The photography department was not a regular studio such as those found at a modeling agency or department store. Rather, it was the office that photographed architectural plans of the gas lines beneath Los Angeles, as well as the other major transmission lines and tunnels for water, sewer, electricity, and the like. Architectural planners for new buildings or renovations would always come and check the files at the archives of the gas company, which were located in this man's department. His work was fascinating to me: he operated a huge camera that could accommodate a large blueprint or drawing pinned on the wall. He could take its picture then reduce it to a small photograph, microfiche, or any kind of negative film. Then, on another huge machine called the plotter, he would print up a gigantic picture of the image.

I used to go there during my lunch hour and have fun with the machines. He would show me things in the files and tell me stories of blunders with ripped transmission pipes and collapsed tunnels. He showed me the underground maps that reveal the whole city sitting atop this web of utility lines. We thought that anyone with knowledge of this underground grid could paralyze the city. Together, he and I would fantasize about all kinds of conspiracies and sabotage as a script for a Hollywood movie. I guess out of eagerness to have a young learner, which he had not had in some twenty-odd years as head of that department, he made my visits interesting with lessons on this type of industrial photocopying and map storage.

When I wasn't with him, I was trying to hustle the young ladies who worked at the gas company. In those days, customer service was staffed 100 percent with young, white women, and most of the secretaries I saw in buildings as an ad copy runner also were white women. The gas company was no different: It was a very white world, a white female world.

About 70 percent of the staff was female on the floors I had access to. This gender division of labor shocked me because I thought that women were the ones who did most of the work in the home. How could these women not be at home?

Later, I realized that the executives were white males, but I rarely saw them. My world was that of young, white females in the cafeteria, customer service, the typing pool, and the print shop. I was glad to be there, in that refuge. It was heaven compared to the mean streets of downtown L.A. and the streets of rural, hot, dusty, migrant, and segregated   Cristal.

Shortly after the Kennedy assassination, the older man who ran the photography department died. Everyone who relied on access to the information contained in that department was in a tizzy. They could not find what they needed. I offered and assisted with many requests for information. Soon, I got the attention of the higher-ups, who realized that I was the only person who knew what was what and where it was within the department. I was made the acting department head at nineteen years of age. My salary doubled overnight to almost eight hundred dollars a month. In 1963, that was a lot of money for me, single, with not a care in the world, and with some tenuous political ambitions connected to Crystal City and to MAPA. But with money in my pocket and so many available women at the gas company, there was not much free time for politics.

While I was in heaven, my subconscious never let me stray too far from thoughts of returning to college. I began looking at the possibility of attending one of Los Angeles' colleges or universities and finally enrolled at Los Angeles City College. It was the best choice in terms of proximity and access from my living area, since I had no car and relied on public transportation to get around. The thought of having to go to night school, however, was not particularly attractive to me. Although I was admitted and enrolled in the college, I never made it to classes. Eventually I decided that this lifestyle of bounteous pleasures was too much. It was not for me; I couldn't fully digest the white environment.

I yearned for a return to Texas. I was homesick for Chicano life and I still wanted to go to college. Besides, my local draft board was reminding me that I was now classified 1-A, which meant that I was ready for induction into the military. They may have been ready for me, but I certainly was not ready for them. Sometime in mid-spring, I returned to Texas. Needless to say, I couldn't enroll into college in the middle of the semester, and ended up doing odd jobs in Cristal to make ends meet.

Out of necessity, I migrated to the north in the summer and worked at a subsidiary of the Ford Motor Company in Waterford, Wisconsin, near the Illinois border. I also worked there as a lifeguard at the municipal pool. At the Ford Motor Company, Rudy Palomo and I were on the on-call night shift, and we always volunteered for the extra work. Rudy Palomo was one of my best friends from junior high and high school, and we had started at the community college together. After a few weeks, we knew our way around the town. I started to hang around with the local young people working at the pool and also at the plant.

Originally, Rudy and I had started working at a flower farm that the Patlan family from Carrizo Springs had worked at for years. The elder Patlan was able to arrange for us to join the flower work crew that he took up north annually to this farm. The Patlan family consisted of our friend, Juan, three teenage girls, and the parents. Juan lived with his family in a regular house, but Rudy and I had to live in a makeshift apartment of a sorts. We sectioned off a corner within a barn and made that our home. At that particular time, Rudy wanted to get married to Odilia Villareal, also from Cristal. He traveled from Waterford to Fargo, North Dakota, over the Fourth of July weekend to see his girlfriend. Meanwhile, I traveled to Chicago to see my mother.

The Chicago Connection

My mother's family started going to the Chicago and the Detroit areas during the Depression and through the early 1940s. In fact, my grandfather, Ignacio Fuentes, died in the race riots of the 1940s in Detroit while working at the Ford Motor Company. That was the story told in my mother's family of my granddad's death, though no further details were ever forthcoming. My mother's older brothers had stayed in Michigan, but two younger brothers, Jesus and Salvador, ultimately moved to Chicago. Salvador moved to Chicago because he had run over a local influential gringo, Sterling Fly, in Cristal. (Fly was an open racist, and as superintendent of schools had kept segregation in force.) While it had been an accident, the family thought it best for him to leave the area. Salvador remained in the Chicago area, mostly South Chicago, until his murder, a death which remains an unsolved homicide. He was not the most mentally balanced relative I had; according to the family, he was schizophrenic and an alcoholic. When he did come to Cristal he would go on a drinking binge with his former friends from *el swiche* ("the switch," an unincorporated Mexican American community near Cristal—so named for a railroad switching break there), and eventually he'd end up in jail for assaults, drunkenness, or both.

On one of those occasions in January 1967, I went to see him at the county jail in Cristal to please my grandmother. Sheriff C. L. Sweeten locked me in the cell with my uncle rather than let me visit from the hallway, as was the custom. My uncle was out of his mind at that time and I narrowly avoided serious injury. The gringo sheriff and deputies thought that it was the funniest thing they had ever seen, me jumping over bunks and running around a twelve-foot cell screaming to my uncle to stop and to the cops to let me out. Perhaps the sheriff took perverse pleasure in witnessing this attack on my person having missed this opportunity when he, Raul Tapia, and others had me at their mercy.

My uncle Jesus finally settled in Monterrey, Mexico, after leaving Chicago and a stint in military service in the Korean War with the Marines. He left the U.S. a bitter and dejected citizen, because he had sought admission to college only to be denied. He ultimately earned a professional degree in Mexico and became a dentist, able to practice only in Mexico. More recently, Jesus and his wife Carolina came back to the states, to the Galveston area, where he opened an import store specializing in Mexican furniture. They regularly travel back to Monterrey, to keep in contact with their five children: Jesus Jr., and Ulysis, both doctors; Ignacio, a restaurateur, Laura, a homemaker, and Carlo, who is presently an accounting student at the University of Houston. While all five children were born in the U.S., they live primarily in Mexico. My mother's sisters, Consuelo, Antonia, Susan, and Lucia all moved to South Chicago at one time or another. Antonia later moved back to Crystal City and then finally to San Antonio, where she presently lives. She and her sons José Luis Jr. and Mario are my only remaining relatives in Texas; a third son, David, committed suicide in 1984. My aunt Susan has a son, Roberto; my aunt Lucia has one son, Stanley, and four daughters, Loretta, Cynthia, Yvonne, and Suzanne; I also have an uncle in Michigan, Ignacio Fuentes, who has nine grown children.

My mother alternated between migrant work and work in nursing homes in South Chicago area hospitals. My grandmother, Refugio Casas Fuentes, lived to ninety-one years of age, outliving my mother who was her oldest child. Like my father, *abuelita Cuca* refused to become a U.S. citizen. Both insisted in their last years that they were to be buried in Mexico. This phenomenon is generational. Most Mexicans who migrated north of the Mexican border during the Mexican Revolution of 1910 to avoid death and destruction believed that their stay would be brief. To their dying days, both my father and grandmother believed they would return to Mexico as soon as the revolution subsided. They never did. Mexico, for the next twenty years, continued to work at establishing a stable democracy in a one party nation-state. The children born of these parents that were "going back to Mexico, *mañana"* grew up not only listening to that refrain but also witnessing their parents' total noninvolvement in community issues. What for? They were going back to Mexico, mañana!

The Muzquiz Campaign

Earlier in the spring of 1964, when I had returned from California, Virginia Muzquiz had decided to run for state representative from our hometown. I believe she was the first Chicana to do so. I became her campaign manager, and we traveled the width and breadth of the district, up into Sabinal and D'Hanis, Hondo, Devine, Uvalde, Carrizo Springs, La Pryor, Batesville, and Cristal. The district consisted of Zavala, Uvalde, and Medina counties, about half of the Winter Garden area. She did not win the election but the experience was fascinating for me. I had never thought of public office beyond the confines of Cristal. Mrs. Muzquiz showed me the obvious, that Mexican voters were everywhere and Chicanos had to contest all types of elections. More importantly, she often repeated to me while campaigning, "Our people have to get used to voting for all Mexicanos and Mexicanas that appear on the ballot."

Trying to get people to pay the poll tax, to have the courage to organize themselves into the campaign, to represent us in their respected communities and neighborhoods, and to hold public rallies on our behalf was sheer hell. What struck me the most was the fear that people had of going public with their politics. The fear of politics must have been a legacy from the Mexican Revolution and the pinches rinches. The revolution was costly in one sense for those who died in that fight, and also for those who fled into exile in the U.S., into the hands of the gringos once again. This second Chicano diaspora was a mere three decades before my current political generation in 1964. The fear Chicanos had of the Texas Rangers and the Anglo establishment was very real.

The second thing that struck me most in that campaign for state representative was our total lack of resources. It became commonplace for Mrs. Muzquiz to appear before a group and there would not be a hall in which to meet, much less a microphone to use, printed literature to hand out, or money with which to place ads on the radio or in print media. We just simply did not have resources. What we had was our wits, moral support for each other, and some gasoline whenever she or I could borrow a car, which I would drive. I didn't have a car and neither did her husband; he didn't believe in owning one. We made a comical pair, the older woman and the young man hustling for votes which were nonexistent, campaigning without money.

We had to encourage people to pay their poll tax in order to register to vote at the same time, which was counterproductive to the election at hand, as the voter registration period had already passed! We ended up only targeting those who had already paid their poll tax, were registered and therefore eligible to vote. We tried to convince those select Mexican American voters to vote for the sole Mexican American woman on the ballot. The last obstacle to overcome was the bias among both male and female voters against a female candidate. Although Mrs. Muzquiz was very capable and the community responded to her appeal for support, her leadership abilities were overshadowed and crippled by the gender bias of most Mexican Americans. Fortunately, the anti-woman attitude among Mexican Americans in the district, the state, and the nation has largely disappeared in contemporary Chicano politics. Today, Chicanas can get elected to any position. Where most of the current gender bias occurs now is when women try to hold onto power once they've been elected over their male peers.

5

Texas A & I

After Virginia Muzquiz's defeat in the state race and the summer employment up north that had made me some cash, I arrived at my new college, Texas A & I University in Kingsville, in time for the fall semester of 1964. I thought of myself by then as a worldly man. I would be twenty years old in October and had been through the organizing and electoral success of the Cristal revolt. My community had organized itself and taken the reins of power from the powerful gringos for the first time since they had ripped Texas away from Mexico. I had helped them win by selling poll taxes for voter registration and through public speaking. I had learned a lot because I had seen a lot and had been involved with Chicano politics both in Texas and Los Angeles. The politics in South Texas and Los Angeles and in the leadership of PASO and MAPA fascinated me. Besides, I had made it alone in L.A. If I could do that, I could do anything. I had even run someone's campaign for the state legislature!

With the money earned from the summer work in Waterford, I bought a car. My aunt Lucia's husband, Leonard, an auto mechanic, helped me obtain the car at a great price. My two buddies from the community college in Uvalde—Gabe Tafolla and Greg Gutiérrez—and I had made a pact to live together when we met at A & I. While I began to search the city for them, I ran across ads for boarding house rooms, apartments, and house rentals. I also noticed the many announcements of parties for clubs and organizations.

Chicanos and Chicanas

A & I was going to be a wonderland for me: I had not seen as many beautiful Chicanas in one place as in Kingsville. Since the later high school years and in Los Angeles at the gas company, I had been on a white female binge. A sexual experience with a white girl was easier to get and quicker to move away from before going on to the next one. White girls were comfortable having sex with Chicanos because, like us, they weren't seeking a lasting commitment. They could move on to the next as well. They lusted after us as much as we lusted after them. And, because our relationships with gringas were "forbidden love," we had intercourse in the privacy of night out in the countryside—brown/white sexual liaisons were never public. One could easily deny any accusation as sheer rumor, and it was often safer to do just that. The Chicanas, in contrast, would generally hold on to their virginity or abstain from sex until a young man promised marriage. Besides, I never could lie very well when face to face with a girl and say "I love you" just for sex.

And then I met Luz Bazan. I had arrived at Texas A & I from Waterford, Wisconsin, barely two days prior to registration for the fall semester, had met some girls while looking for an apartment or house to rent, and had begun dating. Luz first caught my eye when I went to pick up a date that lived in the same rooming house—she was the one who came to the door. Within that same week I saw her again at the weekly singles dance at Texas A & I. I discovered then that she was—and still is today—a fabulous dancer, vivacious and long-legged. I had to be quick in getting to her for a dance that night because her reputation was quickly established as a good dancer, the kind that makes even the worst guy look great twirling her around the dance floor. I liked her instantly, and we hit it off right away. During the next few weeks, we met regularly at the student lounge; Luz soon learned of my political activities from others.

The number of Chicanos at A & I was about 1,030, or 25 percent of the total student body in 1964. There was no unity among us except at parties. We came from towns all across South Texas. The larger blocks were from the Rio Grande Valley and Laredo. Only the latter had an organization, the exclusive Laredo Club. Its members were very elitist, almost snobbish, and admitted only students from Laredo. These students, and as many from the Rio Grande Valley, denied that there was rampant discrimination by Anglos against la raza. They would deny the problem, as they still do today, by stating that Mexican Americans controlled the politics of their communities and that they owned the majority of businesses in their towns. Neither was or is true. The problem

is that they still believe it; consequently, they will argue anytime against
you on this issue. Inadvertently, they are divisive in public and this is
used by the gringo to turn Chicano against Chicano. Laredo students
thought that we who called ourselves Chicanos were anti-white. Border
residents from other towns, I found, had no concept of being Chicano.
The border makes for more intense nationalism, even against one's own
in culture and heritage. I always loved to ask the Laredo students why
no Chicanos had ever been elected to represent George and Martha
Washington in their annual celebration. The same question can be
asked today of those from San Antonio who proclaim to be "in control
and in charge" as to why "King Antonio" of their Battle of Flowers fiesta is always a rich gringo. Even to this day in Mission, Texas, the community holds a parade in honor of King Citrus, an Anglo grower. No
Mexican has ever been so honored, and yet, the Mexican laborers are
the real ones who make the citrus grow, not the so-called grower. In San
Antonio, as in Mission, the festivities during these events are attended
by the white rich and are held at exclusive locations, such as country
clubs and hotels, while the working class Mexican American community is entertained by a parade and a carnival located near the barrio
and away from the center of the *fiesta*.

Within a month of my arrival I quickly set about trying to organize
the Chicanos of Texas A & I but couldn't find a way. I joined the Young
Democrats (YDs) and soon was very frustrated with their choice of discussion topics and issues. Democrats were always praising the federal
administration or the party ticket and forgetting to work at empower-
ing the grassroots. Any new idea or organizing strategy or proposals of
reform that I raised within the political party were opposed with the
question, "Do you want to lose to the Republicans?" The substance or
merit of my issues went undiscussed. Besides, the Democrats in Texas
just used the Mexican vote; they never wanted to give us any leadership
position or access to money. The few Chicano officeholders we had, primarily in the Rio Grande Valley, got caught up in the idea that they represented the main bloc of voters statewide and therefore they were the
spokesmen for all Mexican Americans. These Mexican Americans used
this argument with Anglo Democrats and it worked against Chicano
leadership that lived and worked for the party in other parts of the state
beyond the Rio Grande Valley. For years, white Democratic Party leaders from Austin called upon and negotiated appointments, campaign
finances, candidate recruitment, and public appearances of national
Democrats only with the Valley group of Mexican Americans instead of
with others across the state who were just as significant. Statewide issues of concern to Chicanos never got aired because the Valley leader-

ship simply thought locally, occasionally regionally, but that, too, was limited to the Valley.

Meanwhile, my housemate Gabe Tafolla had gotten us pledged into the Alpha Phi Omega fraternity, the only Greek organization—male or female—that admitted Mexicans, and which was comprised of former Boy Scouts. We really were not interested in becoming part of the Greek scene, but the idea that we were generally not welcome simply made it a greater challenge to take on. Often segregation and discrimination have this reverse effect: while many people will accommodate and even change their cultural ways to assimilate, most people will just get enraged and organize alternative structures. This is good. It is the beginning of group consciousness and a community of interest, even if the compelling reason to organize was initially negative in nature.

The First Campus PASO Organization

These campus clubs, including the YDs, didn't do anything political for Chicanos. I got the idea of repeating the Cristal model on the campus and began to organize a student chapter of PASO. The membership age for PASO was twenty-one, and I was about to turn twenty. My communications with Albert Peña in San Antonio, the state PASO leader, were not encouraging for recognition of our college chapter. He said it couldn't be done without a major change in the Constitution of PASO and that would require a two-thirds vote. The college administration also did not want to certify us as a legitimate campus organization. They required a charter as proof of official affiliation with a state or national entity, so I was caught in a trap from both sides. I still marvel at how stupid we are sometimes in following gringo models for our Chicano needs, such as this PASO age requirement and the gender discrimination against women. The overwhelming majority of Chicanos has always been youth and women.

I organized the A & I PASO chapter around the issue of age discrimination and pledged to go to San Antonio and fight for the change. I blunted the criticism of those who argued of the futility of such an effort by pointing out that we had to show interest by having dues-paying members first and then take the fight to them. I also promised a great, party! party! party! time in San Antonio. Mixing the social enticements with the political goals as an organizing tool has always worked for me.

The time came for the PASO state convention to be held in San Antonio. The A & I PASO chapter members traveled in a large group to the site. At the registration desk we were stopped cold. We were not members, they said, and even if it were so, we had not paid our dues some

From left to right, Albert Fuentes, chairman of PASO, Jim Ferguson, of the Young Republicans chapter at Texas A & I, U.S. Senator John Tower, a Texas Republican, and José Angel Gutiérrez.

thirty days prior nor submitted the membership list for review by the PASO credentials committee. I gathered my group and marched onto the convention floor, without nametags or registration badges, demanding the right to join. We called for a vote on the very issue of giving us the right to join and on lower the voting age within PASO to eighteen. I recall hearing "out of order" shouted in my direction. I ignored it. I was already busy giving a very moving speech to the assembly on how shortsighted it was for them to constantly talk of youth being the leaders of the future and then not teaching us leadership until we turned twenty-one. I brought up Vietnam and our military enlistment age, that for some of us this was to be a premature death. Surely we should be able to vote if we were old enough to die for our country! I brought up the victories PASO had accomplished with the help of young Chicanos, many of whom were present, in Cristal with Los Cinco Candidatos, and the many confrontations they had had with the pinches rinches. All the while I was standing directly in the faces of Al-

bert Peña, Johnny Alaniz, Albert Fuentes, and Martin Garcia. They recognized me as the young speech maker from Cristal. I walked closer to
the head table where they sat and asked rhetorically why I and other
young males under eighteen, always in the company of *mujeres* over
twenty-one, were good enough to be PASO's grassroots army in Cristal
but not good enough now, after victory, to become members. I asked
how it was to be possible, for those interested in furthering the work of
PASO, to make other Crystal Cities without such young blood.

Virginia Muzquiz, Enriqueta Palacios, Elvirita de la Fuente, and
other women from Cristal attending the convention helped us get access to the convention floor and the right to speak. At the end of my
speech they stood, starting a standing ovation by the delegates. They
made the motion to suspend the rules and change the bylaws right then
and there. Not only did the issue get placed before the assembly, but we
voted on the measure without a challenge and our votes were counted
along with those of the regular delegates. It passed. Thereafter, two
other chapters of PASO were formed at campuses in Texas. Soon, other
youth organizations took over from the dying PASO organization. As a
PASO chapter, even without campus recognition, we began to prove
the existence of residential housing segregation and discrimination in
Kingsville against Mexicans and blacks.

The Henry B. Gonzalez Rebuff

I remember writing once to Henry B. Gonzalez, the congressman from
San Antonio, to invite him to address the A & I student body, generally,
and our PASO group in particular. He was the first Mexican American
from Texas elected to the U.S. House of Representatives. He had come
to Cristal a couple of times to campaign for himself when running for
Governor and U.S. Senator. A reply from him arrived several weeks
later with the terse note that Kingsville was not in his district; therefore,
he could not help me. His reply upset me. How could a Mexican American leader not see that as Mexican Americans we had problems with
Anglos, regardless of the districts we lived in? He was our leader, our
only leader. He was rejecting our plea for help. At Texas A & I, the overt
and heavy-handed prejudice and discrimination against Mexican-
American students ran rampant. Little did I know then that Henry B.
Gonzales was the arch rival of Albert Peña Jr., the state Chairman of
PASO.

I began to understand more about rivalries between leaders of the
same ethnic group. The fight between Cornejo and Ozuna was different
from this schism between Gonzalez and Peña. The Cornejo-Ozuna fight

was over the City Charter and their respective notions of managing political power. They were not competing with one another for leadership of the ethnic group. They were negotiating the exercise of power, concerning who was going to do what. Congressman Gonzalez, on the other hand, was practicing the politics of being the token "Mexican." Henry B. had made it a lifetime goal to nip incipient Mexican American leadership in the bud. He was against PASO and against lowering the voting age to eighteen. Later in the decade he would be against the formation of the Mexican American Legal Defense and Educational Fund (MALDEF), against extension of the Voting Rights Act to cover Texas, against MAYO, against our school walkouts, against everything that was to empower us during the Chicano Movement. Henry B. made it safe for the gringo racist to be against us. He was their couch to sit on. If Henry B. was against us, so were they. Now the gringo racists did not have to be overtly racist; they could simply state that they were supporting Henry B. Gonzalez. His congressional district was primarily comprised of Anglo voters. I did not know that. I assumed he was elected by Mexican Americans. Beginning with that total rebuff from Henry B. Gonzalez, I learned of other intra-ethnic rivalries that existed across the state. I was not prepared, however, for the competition for leadership among the Mexican American leaders of the community; it was that intense and fierce. Henry B. Gonzales was my second lesson in this area; the experience with Los Cinco Candidatos after they took power had been first. Leaders will always fight to remain leaders.

The Stereotype of Chicanos as Divisive

The bitter divisions between Los Cinco Candidatos and other factions in Cristal have always been attributed to innate and inherent deficiencies of the Mexican American personality. It never was seen as the dynamics of the struggle, the pursuit of power by competing individuals, and the different group goals. It was never seen as the shortcomings of an individual person. Chicanos as a group are always blamed.

Women, particularly, are singled out as the carriers of some defective gene. The blood in all Mexicans is bad, according to the myth of La Malinche, the Indian woman. She was given in 1525 to Hernan Cortez as booty in his first encounter with the Taino and Carib natives in the Caribbean who had originally enslaved her. Her tribe, with her mother's permission, had given her to these other natives. To take revenge both on her captors and those who delivered her into slavery, she sided with Cortez. That was her ticket to freedom. Reportedly, she bore Cortez several sons and daughters. These, then, were the first *mestizos*, the first progeny of a mixed marriage between a European and a Native American. Every one of us—male or female, Chicano, white, black, yellow, or red—would do as she did under the circumstances. Yet, because she sought escape and bedded down with Cortez, all of us are branded as self-hating, white wanna-bes. I don't think La Malinche hated herself. She hated her condition and her betrayal. She sought freedom and she sought revenge by punishing those who enslaved her. Cortez offered her the opportunity for both. La Malinche is the mother of la raza.

I soon began to realize that the notions of bad blood and Chicano divisiveness are media stereotypes and also used by the Anglo academic community as reality. They believe that about us. Because this myth comes from the mouths of those in the media and the academy, Chicanos learned the same thing about themselves as "truth." We repeated the falsehoods, even among ourselves, to ourselves. But we can combat the stereotype. We can simply be the exception to the "stereotype." Instead of telling them they are wrong, we *show* them to be wrong. Bigots don't think, they react. They alone can persuade themselves to get rid of stereotypes by finding the error in their ways. To unlearn the stereotype they must reteach themselves by observing us. We can help the process. First, they may say something like "You're different," or, "I don't think of you as Meskin" or "You are just like me"; and the clincher: "Some of my best friends are Meskins." We must resist the temptation to succumb to that seduction of becoming "Joe, the different Mexican." Second, they will challenge our Mexicanness by turning the tables on us with "Why don't you go back to Mexico?" or "Why do you hate white people?" or "Why are you people reverse racists?" Again, we must resist the temptation to answer, as there is no sufficient answer to these loaded questions. These are not real questions, but linguistic tricks designed to use our strength against us, like verbal *jujitsu*. Being proud Chicanos and championing the interests of la raza does not make us antiwhite or reverse racist. Each position is different. We must be for ourselves, beginning with each of us. If we are not pro-Chicano, why should anyone else be? We can be antiwhite, and we should be antiwhite when they are against la raza because we are different from them. We must fight for our own group interests when challenged or threatened. Always.

Discrimination in Kingsville and at A & I

The fight against discrimination brought forth unity and challenge among Mexican Americans students at A & I. This discrimination consisted of various kinds of behavior. On the one hand, we were not allowed to reside in the dorms in any integrated fashion. The few Mexican Americans who could afford to pay for dormitory housing were segregated. Most of us lived in boarding houses or apartments owned by Mexican Americans near the campus, of which there were only a few.

The real barrio in Kingsville was across town. In the case of my friends and myself, we rented a home in the barrio which was far away from campus, across the tracks, some twenty blocks away on Henrietta Street. We were the first Chicano students to rent a whole house. Just like the Greek fraternity houses, our house permitted us to live among those who would perpetuate our interests and culture.

Another kind of discrimination that existed at A & I was the denial of information and of support services for Chicanos that would enable us to excel in academics. Chicanos were then and still are today the smallest minority on most campuses. We don't get recruited or have enough programs to help the few who remain on campus through graduation. In 1964, tutorial assistance with problem courses simply did not exist. The only program that I recall being available was federal work study, and I found that out by accident. A political science professor, William Hobbs, took note of me in class because I sat in front and asked questions. He asked one day what my major was. I told him "prelaw," and he suggested I apply for work study so that I could work with him. Most of the Mexican American students, like me, did not know much about scholarships, financial aid, loans, or grants. I had never met a counselor in my high school, junior college, or university life who talked to me about these kinds of opportunities.

The other form of discrimination at A & I was the rigid barrier to communication between Anglo and Mexican students. In classes, we Chicanos sat in the back. We did not join nor were we invited to join certain organizations and clubs; we did not star in sports or serve student affairs; we were segregated in the dorms; we were not selected to be cheerleaders, twirlers, drum majors, or any other prominent positions in student life. There was little mixing and dating between us and the Anglos. The Chicanas did date Anglos, but mostly they were servicemen from the local naval station. In the student union building, in the Tejas Room, Mexican American students would sit together in an area by the jukebox, though the jukebox did not play Mexican music. There were a few blacks and they sat together or mingled occasionally with us. The cafeteria personnel served only Anglo food. The cashiers were all matronly Anglo women, and the only Mexican helpers were in the kitchen or on the serving line. The subject matter in the courses and the class discussions was always on topics of white interest, and campus student life placed heavy emphasis on Greek activity, the fraternities and sororities. There simply was not a significant Chicano presence at the campus although we were about 25 percent of the entire student body. We only paid tuition and occupied classroom space.

This campus had more Mexican American students than I had ever seen anywhere, so I set out with the help of my housemates to organize them all. Texas A & I's identification card, like that of my junior college, was photoless, bearing only a name and address. When I received my identification card on the first day of registration I knew then that a few of us could bloc vote the entire group of Chicanos in an election—just as we had done in Uvalde—and the white students at A & I would never know what happened. This would be as easy because A & I, like the junior college, was also a commuter college; almost all Mexican American students and many Anglos deserted the campus on the weekends. The Anglo students on campus organized their life around the Saturday football games and outings to the beach near Riviera, Corpus Christi, or South Padre Island. Chicano students went home to their families—if they could afford it.

The Politics of Parties and Beer: The Hen House

We devised an organizing strategy for Chicano students at A & I that was both chauvinist and sexist, but successful. We noticed that all students, ourselves included, would spend a considerable amount of money and time partying on weekends. We found that the way to maximize this activity was to pool our money and purchase liquor in quantity. We rediscovered the wonderful world of beer kegs. To get Chicanos hyped up to vote for a gringo candidate everywhere in Texas, Democrats would sponsor a *pachanga*, a party with plenty of keg beer, tamales or tacos, and maybe music. We did the same thing, only with smaller beer kegs called pony kegs which were eight gallon containers of beer that we could purchase through someone who was of age (twenty-one) at the Apple House in the barrio of Kingsville. We realized that everyone at A & I was trying to establish a physical and romantic relationship with someone else of the opposite sex, ourselves included. Parties were the intersection for these sex interests. We knew that college girls loved to dance; we wanted women, so we became good dancers. We practiced our dancing steps by watching both American Bandstand and the Domingo Peña Show on television. We traveled every Monday night to Corpus Christi to the Galvan Ballroom for the ninety-nine-cent dance promoted by Domingo Peña. On Thursdays we went to the dateless dance held on campus. The Chicanas loved us because we danced, *and* we danced with as many of them as we could, not just the pretty ones.

We began organizing parties at our house on Henrietta Street. For our weekly parties, we began mid-Friday afternoon. We would pool our money, buy a pony keg, and then cook up a supersaturated sugar and Kool-Aid concoction, either grape or strawberry, to which we would add Everclear—a 190-proof alcohol—usually bought in Mexico for ninety cents a liter. A couple of drinks of supersaturated sugared, Kool-Aid mixed with Everclear was enough to zonk anyone unconscious. The Kool-Aid mixture was placed in a washtub containing a block of ice and a bag of crushed ice, and water was added to half fill the tub. The drink was unusually sweet and smooth but extremely potent, so I usually stuck to the beer. The women who came to our parties learned three things: there was plenty to drink; we were the best dancers; and, they would be "safe" with us because we did not overtly attempt seduction. Rather, we offered protection for them from the regular pests found at every party. They frequently used us as the excuse for turning down an obnoxious suitor. They enjoyed our parties at the Hen House, as it became known on campus because of the large numbers of women visiting us.

Women could always be found at the Hen House. Within a few weeks of socializing in this fashion, they began to stay the night feeling completely safe. They could drink more than they should, stay later than they should, and end up sleeping over. They would wake up in a private bedroom, with their clothes on, unmolested. Unless, of course, they let someone know that they had other interests.

The use of the pony keg to kick off the event on Friday afternoon led to more collections of money during the evening. A repeat performance on Saturdays was often combined with a cookout. In front of our women guests, we would begin to clean the house, wash dishes and clothes, and offer to cook for them. We had a second rule among the housemates: we did not ask the women to do housework. We made them feel guilty by doing it ourselves in front of them, and within minutes, the women would be doing our work, which was the idea all along.

Basically, what we were doing was a "potluck." People would bring beer, drinks, ice, snacks and other food to our parties. Later in the evening we would take up collections of money for more items and beer. In planning a meal, be it breakfast, brunch, lunch, or dinner, we would take up a collection for hamburger patties, wieners and chicken. We even barbecued bologna and salami sometimes.

The Hen House crowd became my core group of people with whom to organize. By now I was regularly dating Luz Bazan, who was a regular at the Hen House and quickly becoming an activist herself. I began recruiting people, particularly the pretty girls, to get involved in organizing a political group on campus. The focus on the pretty women was simple: everyone gravitated toward them and only the smarter suitors that followed the political line were successful in getting their attention. Soon, everyone was political and on the *onda Chicana* (Chicano wave). I especially wanted to form a voting bloc to influence elections on campus and to begin pressuring for certain reforms. We used our association with Alpha Phi Omega fraternity to recruit Anglo friends into our activities. Soon, we had two Anglo housemates at the Hen House as well, Pat Lawrence from the Young Democrats and Braden Rawlins from Alpha Phi Omega, and all of us were interested in politics.

Our central focus at A & I was on discrimination. Later, we expanded our organizing to reach the Chicano employees on the campus at the cafeteria, in maintenance, and in the landscape department. This fight on behalf of Chicano labor continued long after I left A & I, into the 1980s. We also began to organize political campaigns to contest student elections for the *South Texan* newspaper, the *El Rancho* yearbook editorship, the student government and student activities governing board, and the beauty contests such as Lantana Queen and Court, Homecoming Queen, and the campus Who's Who. We began to change the makeup of these bodies by adding seats, such as seats for the off-campus students, dorm students, and other clubs. This reform was augmented by our constitutional challenge to the method of elections, from requiring a majority vote to a plurality of the vote. The move to a plurality was finally accomplished by the next generation of Chicano student leaders, led by Carlos Guerra, the year following my graduation. These seats and positions were the ones that regulated the use of money for the student union building, student activities, speakers, and beauty queen ceremonies and pageantry. We began bloc voting and winning. Our core group of cadre leadership from the Hen House would vote on behalf of all the Chicano students whose identification cards we could get. A & I had separate polling places across the campus, which made our effort easier to disguise.

Meeting Anglo Liberals

Although PASO accepted us as members, we were not allowed to have a PASO chapter on the A & I campus without a charter and faculty sponsors. The faculty and administration at A & I were mostly racist gringos, though there were two or three "Latin" professors, mostly Spanish or Cuban. I was befriended at A & I by a host of liberal professors, the most notable of whom was Charlie Cotrell, the youngest and newest professor in the Political Science department. Charlie had been a former student of Bill Crane, professor of Government and department head at St. Mary's University in San Antonio. During the 1963 Cristal takeover, Bill Crane visited Crystal City repeatedly at the behest of Jesse Gamez and Ambrosio Melendez. Both were attending law school at St. Mary's University. Other professors from various departments at Texas A & I who were liberals were William E. "Bill" Renfro and his wife, Billie in Art; the Palmer brothers, Paul and Dewey, and George O. Coalson in History; Wayne Johnson, Robert "Bob" Rogers and his wife, Carole, in Government; Dimas Steinbaugh in Education; Stanley Bittinger and Ron G. Barding in Sociology; and Light German in English, all of whom were supportive and sympathetic toward the Mexican American student. Often they would counsel and provide mentorship to some individual students. We usually drank beer and laid out the campus underground paper at the Renfros'; heavy political discussions and partying went on at the Rogers' and Steinbaughs' homes; Professors Bittinger and Barding did not drink but were always good for a fun evening and a free meal.

Dimas Steinbaugh was a legend in his own time. He easily weighed 350 pounds and was over six feet tall. He was very large, with rolling fat that began at his jaw and continued down to below his knees, bushy eyebrows that hid cold blue eyes, and grossly thick fingers. He made a loud rushing noise just to breathe and waddled when he walked to and from the classrooms. Some Chicano and black students considered him a racist because he attacked and provoked us in class. It was a most unorthodox teaching method. I took his class during my first summer session in 1965, when I roomed in a boarding house along with William Leon "Bill" Richey. Steinbaugh usually would begin his course on the foundations of education with the observation that Chicanos and blacks were genetically inferior to Anglos. Those of us accused would cringe at the words while the white students would smile smugly and beam with racial pride. He challenged anyone in class to disprove his hypothesis, given the low rates of educational attainment and scores on standardized testing by Chicanos and blacks compared to Anglos. None of us ever did that I know of, although many of us did immediately argue with him from personal experience. At times he would wear an actual Nazi helmet to class and proclaim Germanic superiority; at other times he would physically harass Chicano students with chalk and erasers. This last trick was my introduction to Steinbaugh.

No sooner had I sat down in my front row chair the first day of class that he stared at me for what seemed an eternity. Slowly, in his best drawl, he asked me to close the door behind me. I got up quickly, did as he asked, and sat down quickly again. Then, he stared at me for another eternal minute and asked me to open the door. I did. After a few minutes, he asked me to close the door. By this time the rest of the class was giggling, smirking at me, and nervously eyeing us both. He asked me again to open the door. He did not say please or thank you, just a straight monotone instruction from his mouth. I got the courage to say "No sir." He instantly grabbed a piece of chalk from the blackboard behind his chair and with his left hand flung it in my direction. He missed. This could not be happening to me! He yelled for me to open the door. I said "No sir! Open it yourself!" He grabbed an eraser, transferred it to his right hand and threw it at my head. I caught it and threw it right back at him and hit his ample belly; how could I miss? He gave me an evil look and barked at me to see him after class. He then turned to a black kid sitting in the back and pointed at him, saying, "You, go open the door. It is hot in here!" The student nervously looked around, figured he was being singled out and meekly went and closed the door then returned to his seat. Steinbaugh went on with his course introductions, explanations of the syllabus and the readings to the end of class. He reminded me to stay. When all were gone, he ambled over to me and while towering over me, said, "You're the first Chicano student with balls I have ever had. I'm going to teach you a lot and become your friend, if you let me."

The professor I hung around with most often was Charlie Cotrell, and through him and his wife Glenda, I met other professors and liberal Anglo students. Bill Richey, who later was to serve in a pivotal organizing role of La Raza Unida Party, both in Crystal City and Cotulla, was also a student of Charlie's. The relationship between professors and students is always difficult and somewhat strained given the obvious disparity in power and in the role each must play. In Charlie's case, however, he made short shrift of the power issue and befriended students regularly. Charlie and I got to be good friends, drinking buddies, almost brothers, I would say, and when I later married I made him a *padrino* (best man) at my wedding to Luz.

The Issues

We began by protesting the housing discrimination and segregation at the dorms and also in the community. We conducted a couple of field surveys on housing discrimination. If Anglos would call inquiring about a listed rental property for student housing, they would usually be told that it was available and what the rent price would be. Then, Mexicans or blacks would show up and the property all of a sudden would not be available. It had just "been rented" or the rent price would double or triple over the previously stated amount. An Anglo ally would call again to verify its availability, and it was always available again. The test for black discrimination involved both the phone call and a personal appearance. As South Texas blacks have Anglo-sounding surnames and do not have the same discernible accent as their urban counterparts, it was hard for a racist landlord to identify the caller as black; it was therefore necessary to send black students to confront landlords, followed later by Anglo students. For discrimination against Mexicans we would just follow up an Anglo telephone call with a heavily accented Chicano call. If the ethnicity was not obvious to the landlord over the telephone, the surname was a dead give away. We documented all of these encounters, compiled the statistics, named the landlords, and took our concerns and demands to the dean of men, J. E. Turner, and the dean of women, Carrie Lee Bishop, who was also in charge of the dormitories. Dean Bishop had publicly stated and made it personally known to white girls in the dorm that she frowned upon and totally disapproved of courtship between Mexican American males and Anglo females. She actually called parents to inquire if it was all right for their daughter to date a Mexican.

The administration did not respond when we presented them with our survey data providing evidence of discrimination in housing. But to my surprise, the local Chamber of Commerce became aware of our survey and began a campaign to encourage landlords to rent to all students and to standardize the rents. I learned then the value of pitching a Chicano cause in terms of an economic benefit to the Anglo business community. Student spending in Kingsville was big business. We utilized the results of the housing discrimination study to press for an amendment to the student governance code that would permit the election of off-campus representatives to the student government. That amendment ultimately would give us control of the student government in the years to come.

One of the many issues that we tackled at Texas A & I was the grading discrimination affecting Mexican American students. Chicanos would flunk orientation and flunk the remedial reading classes. I should not say we flunked, because we did get passing grades, but that we *were* flunked so as to repeat and repay for the course. I remember that during my junior year we were required to take a written English exam, to see if we were proficient in writing, reading and spelling in the language. The overwhelming number of Chicano students and blacks would fail that exam. We began questioning the validity of the exam, the obvious bias in its format and questions, and the subjective grading by faculty of our exam responses. We questioned the validity and the cultural relevance of some of the composition, language use, and vocabulary portions of this exam after we had already passed college entrance exams. We were already in college; if we were good enough to get admitted and pass our courses, why couldn't we be good enough to be graduated without this exam? Some of us had already even taken and placed well in the Graduate Record Examination (GRE) and the Law School Admissions Test (LSAT). Not many Chicanos know or had familiarity with words such as "galoshes," "ornament" and "parasol." Although the word parasol (for umbrella) is a combination from Spanish, we knew it as *paraguas* (*para aguas,* or "stop water") instead of *parasol* (*para sol,* or "stop sun").

First Direct Action

We did not succeed in establishing a PASO chapter recognized by A & I's administration during my years there, 1964 to 1966. We succeeded neither in reforming the methods of testing, nor eliminating the segregation in housing on and off campus, but vowed to escalate the fight with collective, direct action. This method was new to me. Reading about the tactics and strategies of direct action of Saul Alinsky, the famous radical organizer from Chicago, of the farmworkers, and of the antiwar protesters was one thing; now we were going to try it ourselves. I find it most curious to read now that we were heavily influenced by the activities of blacks in our pursuit of civil rights. Except for *Look* and *Life* magazines in the library that ran photos of blacks in the civil rights struggle, we seldom saw or read about them in our area newspapers. Blacks at A & I were not active as black militant activists as there weren't any organizations for them. Rather, they integrated into our Chicano effort on campus; they followed our lead.

We combined all our groups—those interested in the campus electoral reform, those interested in the fight against housing discrimination, those into radical antiwar politics, and those of us, who were militant Chicanos—under one umbrella for our next efforts. We began to organize small, quick, public demonstrations on campus against the President and his administration on each of these issues. We would call for a gathering at a symbolic location via campus leaflets. The *RAG,* our underground campus newspaper, would lay the groundwork with articles, cartoons and the call for action. At the gathering, we would have a speaker or two and some of our supporting faculty in very public view so as to give the appearance of sanction and support. Initially, the gatherings were small and produced no results. These were the first demonstrations ever seen at A & I. A few years prior, another Chicano who had simply sought to become the student body president, Juan Rocha, provoked a demonstration by gringos. They even hung him in effigy from a window of a dorm that faced the student center.

Bill Richey, Pat Lawrence, the fraternity brothers from Alpha Phi Omega, the art students like Gary Bigger and Amado Peña (the famous artist), the sociology students from Bittinger and Barding's classes, the Young Democrats, the Hen House cadre, and I, among others, were involved as organizers in building these protest movements. We used all kinds of tactics: we tried to physically take over the offices of the school publications, the newspaper and the yearbook, though our choice of editor in the general student body election was refused the position by the administration on some technicality. We made excursions into the dormitories under the guise of "panty raids" but it was basically to protest the issues of free speech, student qualifications for elections, and discrimination. We were joined by hundreds and hundreds of students over time. The gatherings reached larger proportions and became marches. Both marches and rallies were successful simply in terms of attendance. We even began weekly printings of The *RAG*, now my second venture with a newsletter, with the power of the press, since my days in Cristal.

The Lessons Learned

The university president, James C. Jernigan, and other administrators began to acknowledge our effectiveness by speaking out against us and even meeting with us. We got some concessions and on some issues won outright victories. I learned to negotiate with authority figures and how to give and take without compromising principles. I also learned that by working in coalition with others Chicanos could accomplish some of our goals, but not all of them. A coalition seldom is organized for support of a single group. It can be built around a single issue that transcends those of individual groups. Anglos and blacks are willing to join collective efforts to push their agenda but do not often join a strictly Chicano cause. Yet, Chicanos will join collective efforts on behalf of someone else. I learned that the reason for this seemingly contradictory behavior is due to our lack of a comprehensive ethnic group agenda or work program. We really did not know in 1965 and 1966 what was in our best interests because these group interests had not been previously defined by our elder generation of Chicano activists in PASO, the G.I. Forum or LULAC. Chicanos back then had neither an agenda nor a set of leaders. We could not be in solidarity with each other on any larger issues or interests, only those locally, on the campus or in the community.

On many occasions I burned with frustration at meetings with other non-Chicano student leaders from other groups. My inability to prevail and win over these sympathetic and liberal peers to a more pointed and stronger Chicano position on issues taught me to push as far as possible toward that position but not so far as to break with the group. Chicanos acting alone on the campus could not prevail. We needed to stay in coalition. Rather than make me a good politician, moderate and eager to work out a compromise, these experiences made me long for organizing a larger group of Chicanos and pushing only for a Chicano agenda without compromise, from a position of numerical strength, not needing anyone else.

I learned to bloc vote the entire Chicano student population and in so doing began to take control of key student government positions and committees. We elected Gloria Garza as editor of the yearbook, the first Chicana to hold that position. We elected some Chicanas as members to the prestigious Lantana Court, the elite event of the year, for the first time in the history of A & I. And we began preparing the next generation of student leaders. Campus organizing demands a constant and sustained recruitment effort not just for members but also for secondary and tertiary leadership. Students drop out, transfer, sit out a semester or two, and, of course, graduate. Campus organizations, like athletic teams, are always at the risk of losing their best leaders and members with the end of each semester. Chicano campus organizations are the most susceptible to this turnover because their members not only face the same academic pressures all other students face but also additional burdens such as family economic needs, dropping out in favor of a younger brother or sister attending college, and marriage or unplanned pregnancy.

Professors Renfro, Cotrell, Bittinger, and others were very helpful with advice. While teaching us to silk-screen posters for use in the demonstrations and marches on campus in the late night hours, we talked about our personal dreams and goals with these professors. I had never had the opportunity to talk with someone more experienced than I about such things. My dad had died before I had formulated such thoughts, and my mother would often begin that type of conversation, but only as a way to learn about my goals for the future; she was not able to aid me with her advice from personal experience. She had not gone to school beyond the eighth grade and had been married by age sixteen.

Just by being supportive of our right to engage in these kinds of protests and causes, these professors taught me the difference between paternalism and mentoring. My relationship with these Anglo liberal professors was personally quite rewarding. Getting to know them as persons, not just as professors in the classroom, began to enlighten and awaken me to the world of Anglo liberals and radicals who were supportive of social change. They were genuine in their empathy for our Chicano cause and issues from which they stood to gain nothing. In fact some of them, like Charlie Cotrell and Bob Rogers, risked not getting tenure in the future by supporting us. They not only understood the trials and tribulations that we had endured as a people over time but also stood in solidarity with us when times got rough on campus. At first I wouldn't allow myself to simply judge them by their behavior; I held on to suspicion about their motives. Over time and after repeated demonstrations of their support, I embraced them.

These academicians certainly were more learned than I. Often I was enthralled by their analysis and the depth of their commitment to the causes important to me. They could explain to me much of how the world worked. I learned from them how little I actually knew without feeling inadequate. I regretted graduating in May, 1966, because their friendship was made stronger by the many shared experiences in the various struggles at A & I. But above all, professors instilled in me a hunger for additional knowledge.

6

MAYO

The next step was deciding what to do after my graduation from Texas A & I. I had always said, parroting my mother, that I wanted to become a lawyer, but in truth I wasn't quite sure what I wanted to do with my life. My self-doubt regarding my abilities and intellect had somewhat been quieted by my mentors, the liberal Anglo college professors at Texas A & I, but the lack of information about law school was very disconcerting. My vision of the future did not include becoming a college professor at that period in my life. Graduate school remained in the recesses of my mind. I didn't know what to do, much less know if I could do it. I knew I had to do something to further my education, to reach a professional degree.

My parents had instilled that goal firmly in my mind since early childhood. My dad always spoke to me and to his friends, saying that I would surely follow in his footsteps. That idea never took hold in me; I did not want to become a medical doctor. My mother, on the other hand, always spoke to me about how smart and articulate I was and that I would make a great lawyer. I had no idea what that was, never having met a lawyer during my formative years. More important, however, was pressure from another quarter in 1966: I had to avoid the clutches of Ruth Webb at my local draft board. At the end of each semester, she would reclassify me as 1-A, first choice for the military draft. Vietnam was not where I wanted to go—my fight was here. I always considered furthering my education and that helped avoid the draft.

Law School in Houston

My girlfriend, Luz, had a year to go before her graduation from Texas A & I, but upon my own graduation from college, I relocated to Houston, found a full-time job as a credit manager with the local gas company, and immediately enrolled in law courses during the first summer session. I took the Contracts course from the famous professor W. White at the Bates College of Law of the University of Houston for the first six weeks. My scores on the law entrance exam, the LSAT, were solid, though my scores on the Graduate Record Examination were not so terrific. Supposedly, the LSAT score was an indicator that I held promise as a student of the law and had the aptitude to become an attorney. Conversely, the GRE score indicated a lack of probability of success in graduate studies. In my case, it did not mean that at all: years later, when all was said and done, I did better with graduate school than law school, obtaining a doctoral degree from the University of Texas at Austin before obtaining my law degree.

The University of Houston Law School was a nightmare, compared to my years at A & I. I was one of only three Chicanos enrolled in the entering class. There were no women, no blacks, only white boys, predominantly from East Texas, and the three of us. Every time I opened my mouth, both students and faculty attacked my positions. I had to prepare extra hard for class discussion because I knew that everyone would attack my view. The study of law is not an intellectual challenge. I wish someone had explained that to me early my college years. That advice would have saved me many a night of anxiety and days of worry over the nagging questions I suppose all young people have about themselves, which is whether you have the intellectual ability to compete with others in the pursuit of your professional goals.

In the study of law, I found out that you simply memorize the material and organize it in order to succeed. The trick is to spot the issues and have prompt recall of the appropriate and applicable law for that issue. Most questions I had regarding "the law" were answered with a terse, "Because of six hundred years of Anglo-Saxon common law!" I found out that Anglo-Saxon law was based on the two hundred years of Anglo presence in this country plus the four hundred years of Anglo-Saxon jurisprudence from Britain, with the colonists and settlers making up the law to suit their interests as they went along destroying other cultures. In law school there were few discussions of public policy, new areas of law, judicial law-making, or the economic bias against poor people. There were no studies or suggestions on how to start and run a legal practice, other than the admonition to get a job with a big law firm. The big firms, however, did not hire Chicanos in the 1960s. There were no legal aid clinics, much less legal defense funds for Mexican Americans in 1966. I felt completely out of place and alone at the law school. They were not ready for me and my Chicano views, and I certainly was not ready for them and their redneck views. By the end of the fall semester, after eighteen hours of course work, I had had enough and dropped the study of law for graduate studies in government at St. Mary's University in San Antonio. One additional benefit here was that I now lived closer to Luz and we were able to see more of each other. Later, upon her graduation from Texas A & I in May of 1967, she would find a teaching job in San Antonio and we would be reunited.

Graduate Studies in San Antonio

While at St. Mary's University, Willie Velasquez and I met. We were both enrolled in graduate studies programs, he in economics and I in government. Willie and I, from our first meeting, began discussing the need for a statewide student organization. I told him everything that had been going on at Texas A & I, he was fascinated and wanted to know more about the organizing of such public demonstrations. I had heard from friends back home that Juan Patlan from Carrizo Springs, my former classmate and campaign manager at the Uvalde junior college was also in San Antonio so I began to seek him out. Through the activities of the Government department at St. Mary's University I also met Mario Compean, then a freshman, who was from San Antonio's west side barrio. Ignacio "Nacho" Perez also joined us, though he was not a student at St. Mary's. Willie had met Nacho through his work with the Bishop's Committee on the Spanish Speaking, an agency under the direction of the local Catholic bishop that advocated on behalf of Mexican Americans. At that time, the phrase "Spanish-speaking" as a euphemism for Chicano or Mexican was commonly used. Nacho was organizing support for the striking farmworkers in the Rio Grande Valley and dropped in the offices of the Bishop's Committee from time to time. Willie invited him to meet us and share his experiences.

The five of us, Mario, Willie, Nacho, Juan, and I, began to meet as a group. We would meet every week, usually after work or school on Fridays, at the local watering hole, The Fountain Room, for rounds of beer and talk. Our talk, however, focused almost exclusively on politics and was frequently centered around the issues of lack of leadership in our Mexican American community and the low political efficacy of organizations such as LULAC, the American G.I. Forum, and PASO. We lamented that there were no organizations available for youth mem-

bership, except the Catholic Youth Organization (CYO), which we saw
as a generational experience for Catholic preteen altar boys, not young
men such as ourselves. Both LULAC and the American G.I. Forum held
themselves to be nonpolitical, and we thought that posture was absurd;
the impact of politics on Chicano life was everywhere.

At our weekly gathering the five of us would criticize these organizations for relegating young men and all women into minor support
roles to their older, all-male leadership. In our opinion these Mexican
American middle-class leaders not only had their heads in the sand but
also did not want to identify with their Mexican indigenous roots. We
saw them as wanting to become assimilated into the Anglo world, thus
leaving behind their Mexican roots and culture. The thought of these
organizations dividing our community on the basis of assimilation, culture, citizenship and class status in addition to age and gender for membership was abhorrent to us.

A Brief History of LULAC, The G.I. Forum, and PASO

LULAC was open for membership only to male U.S. citizens over the
age of eighteen. Women members became part of the Ladies Auxiliary.
The American G.I. Forum was open for membership only to veterans.
These two organizations date back to 1929 and 1948, respectively, both
were nonpartisan and nonpolitical organizations. PASO, the only orga-
nization that engaged in community political development, did poll tax
drives for voter registration and openly demanded political power for
Mexican Americans, but the organization was practically dead by 1967.
Because of their direct action strategies in communities like Cristal and
Mathis, near Corpus Christi, PASO had been targeted in the media as
subversives and trouble makers. The conservative elements within the
Democratic Party literally shunned them. Texas had been a one-party
Democratic state since Reconstruction. The white Democratic party
leaders wanted Mexican Americans in the political party's fold, but not
as officeholders or party leaders. PASO did manage to marshal enough
support to help eliminate the poll tax as a prerequisite to voter registration, so voting no longer would be a privilege, but a right.

We longed for a return to the days of PASO activism and realized
that our group of five had to become the catalyst for the emergence of
an activist organization. We could envision obstacles and dangers in
that pursuit, however; at that time, there was no legal defense fund, like
the Mexican American Legal Defense and Education Fund of today,
and no Southwest Voter Registration and Education Project. The National Association of Latino Elected and Appointed Officials (NALEO),

Involved Mexican American Government Employees (IMAGE), and Project SER (Service, Education, and Rehabilitation) and many of the current institutions we have now grown accustomed to did not exist then.

Once you arrive at a consensus, action must follow. Our group would be radically different from the organizations of the past. We decided that an organization of organizers was what was needed; we also decided that this organization should be comprised of youths and engage in direct action. Each one of us had a constituency of sorts in various regions of the state. For example, Willie and Mario, each being from San Antonio, had access to Catholic private school youths and to toughies from the West side barrio, respectively. Ignacio Perez, also from San Antonio, had been most recently involved in assisting the farm workers in striking the melon crop in Rio Grande City, deep in South Texas. He had been working with others, including college students at the University of Texas and St. Edward's University in Austin to provide emergency food and medical relief to these strikers. Juan and I had constituencies in our respective communities of Carrizo Springs and Crystal City, and more important, at the community college in Uvalde and Texas A & I University. Not more than a year prior, I had left the fledgling PASO student group at A & I. From that group, future MAYO organizers and leaders such as Carlos Guerra and Efrain Fernandez would emerge. The most extensive contacts in the San Antonio area belonged to Mario, Nacho, and Willie. Willie was well-connected with the Catholic church hierarchy and programs, namely the aforementioned Bishop's Committee on the Spanish Speaking. It was from that office that we were able to obtain supplies with which to copy materials, make long distance phone calls, and meet at their location in the International Building on West Houston Street. Mario introduced us to many small business owners in the West Side barrio, as his family had been there for generations. Juan and I had gotten part-time employment with a federally funded program.

The MAYO Name

Once we formally decided to form an organization, we argued endlessly for weeks about the name for our group. Some of the proposals were YA for Youth Association, SAS for Sociedad de la Aguila y la Serpiente (The Society of the Eagle and the Serpent), LEON for Liga de Estudiantes y Obreros Nacionalistas (League of Nationalist Students and Workers), and La Raza Unida. The name Mexican American Youth Organization (MAYO) emerged as a deliberate attempt on our part to postpone the media controversy that was surely to erupt. We figured that choosing an innocuous name such as the Mexican American Youth Organization would buy us time from criticism. We knew that once we achieved notoriety for our direct action tactics and strategies, our pronouncements would be targeted by the media. With negative press accounts we would then have a harder time organizing more chapters around the state. We figured the name was safe sounding enough so as to not attract as much attention as the more sinister SAS, LEON, or even La Raza Unida. Nacho Perez was the main proponent of the name La Raza Unida. It was an attractive name because it encompassed a goal of ethnic unity as well as the vision of a united people in struggle. Ultimately, though, we decided to use this name as a slogan rather than a name. We decided to put it in our political button together with the acronym MAYO.

The internal debate among the five of us centered around the image that we wanted to project to capture the imagination of potential recruits. We wanted organizers, young people with a hunger for social justice who would be willing to risk much while engaging in direct action tactics. We wanted a forceful name, we wanted a nationalistic logo, something that would identify us with the indigenous side of our heritage. We finally decided on an Aztec symbol. The Aztec motif however was that of Huitzilopotchtli, the war god of the Aztec nation. We wanted a warrior much like Huitzilopotchtli with a club used in battle. The logo of the Aztec warrior with a club was borrowed from the now defunct Mexican airline, Aeronaves de Mexico.

All of us at one time or another had experience in publishing a leaflet or underground newspaper. My experience was with the *RAG* newspaper at A & I and before that with *In Fact or Fiction* in Cristal. We began to look around for someone to help us with the newspaper. We found a young man on the west side of San Antonio that was very pro-Chicano, Tom Cahill, who was publishing a newspaper already, the *Inferno*. Together, we began publishing a newspaper aimed at the Chicano market, and two other items: an internal newsletter called *MAYO Times* and our own MAYO newspaper called *El Deguello* (The Beheading). Many such publications were also beginning to emerge and proliferate across the Southwest under an umbrella group called the Chicano Press Association. Cities such as Milwaukee, Chicago, and New York also had these types of publications. In Lubbock, Texas a MAYO activist, Bidal Aguero, began to publish *El Editor;* to this day he still does, and the paper now has circulation into most of West Texas.

During the early months of organizing MAYO, Willie and I, as St. Mary's graduate students and Mario as an undergraduate, had access to the reading lists of many professors. These syllabi usually included the latest written material on politics of the day, and many professors provided additional information to us for use in our study circles. As MAYO members and leaders, we sought to be well read and informed. We would discuss and argue the content of the readings. Someone from the study circle invariably would bring additional material on Chicanos or social change. These discussions sharpened our views and honed our articulation of these ideas. Dr. Charlie Cotrell, my former teacher at A & I, had transferred to St. Mary's in 1966, and now frequently attended the MAYO study circles held in various parks or homes around the city. The group sat for hours on end discussing articles in the various Chicano newspapers on Chicanismo, reading Franz Fanon, Saul Alinsky, Ricardo Flores Magon, Stokely Carmichael and Charles Hamilton's *Black Power*, and the early material on Chicanos, such as Ernesto Galarza's *Barrio Boy*, Leonard Pitt's *The Decline of the Californios*, George I. Sanchez's *Forgotten People: A Study of New Mexicans*, Raul Morin's *Among the Valiant*, a book on Chicano war heroes in World War II, and the first books about Cesar Chavez, *Delano: The Story of the California Grape Strike*, by John Gregory Dunne (1967), and *Huelga: The First Hundred Days of the Great California Grape Strike*, by Eugene Nelson (1966). We would review articles and books, such as Walter Prescott Webb's *The Texas Rangers* (1965), and the reports on Mexican Americans issued by the Bishop's Committee on the Spanish Speaking, and later those of the U.S. Commission on Civil Rights. We read exhaustively the writings of Antonio Gramsci, Che Guevara, and Regis DeBray. We then would write our own material for the various MAYO publications from this shared and collaborative information gathering and the ideas gleaned from study circle participants.

During these formative months we also traveled widely. We not only traveled within Texas to the Rio Grande Valley, Austin, Houston, and the Winter Garden area, but we also reached out further into the Southwest and the Southeast. Some or all of us, depending on the availability of space, money, and time, traveled to Albuquerque, Denver, Los Angeles, El Paso, Tucson, Phoenix, Chicago, Atlanta, and New York. Our purpose was threefold: we wanted to meet face to face and talk to those persons whom we had read about and whose politics we liked; we wanted to establish a formal relationship of dialogue, collaboration, exchange of information and form a network of activists; and, we wanted to improve on our own organization's capability by borrowing the best ideas and programs from other organizations. We learned, for example, that many organizations infiltrated President Lyndon Johnson's War on Poverty programs and used those structures and resources to expand their organizing. The plethora of federal funded programs such as the Peace Corps, VISTA (Volunteers in Service to America), and the Legal Services Corporation (or Legal Aid), for example, were principally aimed at serving blacks and had not quite reached into the Mexican community of the Southwest in 1967. The Community Action Agencies (CAA), usually called the "CAP" agencies (for Community Action Program), were just being established in our region of the country. This was going to be my introduction to Johnson's War on Poverty.

As graduate students at St. Mary's, neither Willie Velasquez nor I had any financial assistance. I was an exam proctor and grader for my Government professor and now old friend, Charlie Cotrell. When at the beginning of 1967 I traded the study of law for graduate school, Charlie had offered me a job in the Government department at the university and a rent-free stay at his home for a few weeks.

For additional money to finance my graduate studies, I worked at the San Antonio Neighborhood Youth Organization (SANYO), a War on Poverty program for youth. A Catholic priest by the name of John Yanta ran the program. His top lieutenants were Belvin Stewart, Romy Vela, John Williams, and Paul Edwards. Paul was from Uvalde, and had married Heather, who was one of my classmates at the junior college. I was a counselor in a SANYO component, the Neighborhood Youth Corps (NYC). The NYC student enrollees were teenagers who had been pushed out of the public schools of San Antonio. The usual term for these kids is "dropouts," as if to say that they *chose* to leave school, but most Chicano dropouts I met had been pushed out of the school system by the poor curriculum and the personnel. The public schools I went to were for educating Anglo kids, and if Mexicans happened to enroll, the educational mission still remained the same: educate them into becoming Anglo kids.

The enrollees at the NYC center on Castroville Road where I worked were dropouts from the public schools on the West Side of San Antonio, where the majority of Mexican Americans resided, though there were other NYC centers located across the city. During the course of counseling these students I recruited these students into the Mexican American Youth Organization. Many future organizers for MAYO came from these NYC programs, among them Irma Mireles. She confirmed my hypothesis, as did many other students, that in the public schools, often the problem affecting Chicano kids is teachers who can't teach rather than students who can't learn. Irma, bright as could be, became one of the best organizers and leaders within MAYO. Years later she was the successful candidate for La Raza Unida Party, winning election to the San Antonio River Authority with a mere seventy-six dollars spent on her campaign. This was a very powerful position, as she became one of those in charge of the area's water regulation. Years later Irma told me, "I was the only one on the board with all those old gringos who never fell asleep during a meeting—the entire six-year term I served."

In time, I became the first state spokesman for MAYO. Together we contacted our individual networks of activists in the state and got them affiliated, and overnight we had MAYO chapters across the state. We began experimenting with several strategies. To show support for the farmworker's strike at La Casita Farms in the Valley, we joined their picket lines at the site of the strike in Rio Grande. While on the picket line we taunted the Texas Rangers and dared them to attack us, though we only displayed this bravado when the television cameras were there—their presence was our insurance that the Rangers would not attack. We urged and encouraged school protests by Chicano youth, we initiated issues conferences and began electoral activity in the barrios of San Antonio and other cities. During my tenure as head of MAYO we focused on these type of strategies and built the statewide mechanism of governance for the organization. As groups were recruited to join us or sought affiliation on their own, they were instructed on the rules of the organization.

Each MAYO group was autonomous and could continue to do as it wished in local matters, and their leadership was their choice. The only officers we recommended they have were a corresponding secretary and a spokesman. Though MAYO initially had an all-male membership, Chicanas were recruited and selected to leadership roles within the first six months of organizational existence. Luz and I had married on July 15, 1967. We had a typical Chicano wedding in her hometown of Falfurrias, with a best man and groomsmen (*padrinos*), a maid of honor and court (*madrinas*), a Mass celebrated with the traditional ritual of the passing of coins (*arraz*), kneeling cushions (*cojines*), figure-eight rope (*lasso*), and, of course, the rings (*anillos*), followed by a reception and dance that lasted past midnight. It was quite a memorable evening in all, though our honeymoon didn't amount to much because I was in the middle of my graduate school summer session.

The first months of marriage were sheer hell because we had no money; like most young people, the economic reality of marriage had never entered our minds prior to taking the vows. We ate potatoes, beans, and eggs most of the time; sometimes friends from Cristal would give us deer meat, and sometimes I would steal cans of sardines from the grocery store. Luckily, I won $550 from a contest on KTSA radio, and that helped us make it through these first few months. Luz became pregnant before the summer was out.

Juan had married too, and our new wives, Elena and Luz, became principal architects of MAYO, along with Nacho, Willie, Mario, and myself. While the MAYO leadership was all male, the women were equals in making suggestions, comments, and critiques, in planning, and in supporting the group's decisions.

Mario often was in the company of Alicia "Licha" Mayorga at these meetings, and she was very vocal. Nacho married shortly after the founding of MAYO, and his wife, Orcilia, often attended meetings but did not speak out as did these other women. I think it was because she had only recently come from Mexico and did not fully understand Chicano politics at this point.

We did stress that each local MAYO group would join all others semi-annually at a meeting, during which the representatives from each group would make policy and establish goals for the statewide organization. Each MAYO group was allocated two positions on the board of directors for the statewide governing structure. We began to meet in June during the first year or two, then added a second meeting in December or January. The May or June meeting was held for two purposes: to establish our organizing goals for the year and to elect a statewide spokesman and support staff to carry out that mission.

From among the original five organizers of MAYO, only Mario Compean and I ever served as statewide chair and spokesman. Willie Velasquez and Juan Patlan were tapped to lead the nonprofit organizations that we formed in order to hire staff to aid with our program goals. MAYO always sought funds to pay staff to do the organizing. Nacho Perez never sought to lead, choosing instead to remain among the second or third tier leadership of support staff. MAYO was adamant about not charging membership dues or electing officers by popular vote every year. We had seen how debilitating to organizational and personal resources those two practices were to the traditional Mexican American organizations that had come before us. It seemed to us that these other organizations spend too much of their time preparing to elect the next slate of officers and collecting dues. Worse yet, they sought to carry out organizational programs with dues money, and we knew that an organization cannot carry out programs on those meager funds, even with an all-volunteer staff.

Usually we operated our meetings informally utilizing a combination of *Robert's Rules of Order* and a rotating dialogue. Each person was called by name to make a comment on an agenda item. Basically, we attempted to reach consensus on each point. Once we reached these decisions by either consensus or vote, all delegates would return to their groups around the state and ensure compliance with the statewide organizing goals—that was a rule and we demanded discipline. The need for a December or January meeting came about because of our individual chapters' autonomous activities. At this meeting we would review the progress or lack thereof made toward the statewide goals, learn of other issues developing across the state, and make adjustments in the operations, "fine tuning" the work, if you will. Our MAYO newsletter carried the official word to the rank and file and contained information of the doings of the various MAYO groups. The press conferences we held had three purposes: first, to get publicity in the Anglo media, even if it was negative; second, to utilize the media to galvanize opinion by polarizing the media audience; and third, to show defiance toward the Anglo system and its institutions. Our public speeches were covered extensively by the Anglo media, both print and electronic.

The Issues Conferences

The idea for a conference centering on issues was first articulated and conceptualized by Willie Velasquez. The five of us mulled it over and agreed with him on the need for such an organizing and politicizing tool. We adopted the strategy and implemented the first of several beginning in the early autumn of 1967 under the name La Raza Unida.

The idea was very simple: issue a call to la raza to come on a Saturday to discuss topics of concern and draft an action agenda. Previously, only the traditional organizations such as LULAC and the G.I. Forum had called conferences. When they did, the location was at an expensive hotel, and only dues-paying members could gain admission and vote on resolutions. At these conferences not everybody could afford to attended for the entire weekend, so there was definitely an economic bias built into participation; in contrast, MAYO held its issues conferences in auditoriums and halls in or near the barrio. At the traditional conferences, typically some Anglo politician would come and address the membership on the problems of Mexican Americans. With this public ritual the Mexican Americans in attendance acted as if they didn't know what these problems were and applauded loudly the Anglo's words. Oftentimes, the Mexican American organizational leadership would honor the Anglo with some sort of award and proclaim him an *amigo* of the Mexican people. At the issues conferences, by contrast, the people would do the talking, voting, and doing. The only guest speakers were either MAYO members or local raza leaders—not one gringo ever spoke at an official MAYO meeting.

More importantly, the only thing the traditional organizations did with the resolutions passed at conferences was to have a press conference and report them; there was consensus without action. No one ever took them seriously, not even their own membership. It was a feel-good ritual of middle class, hyphenated, "Mexican-Americans." These organizations were perceived by the Anglo politicians and influentials as paper tigers with lots of roar and no attack. We held the same views of these organizations and sought to remedy this inactivity by engaging in direct action on our own resolutions.

By the summer of 1967 we had also expanded our organizing base tremendously to many of the communities, junior colleges, senior colleges and universities across the state. The first La Raza Unida Issues Conference was held in Kingsville, Texas, in response to the call from MAYO members at Kingsville to protest the lack of hiring, promotion, and retention of Mexican Americans within the Humble Oil Company. It was important to us that we begin with this conference strategy on behalf of middle-class Chicano workers against a very visible international megacorporation located in the heart of the King Ranch empire (the largest privately held ranch in the U.S., whose land was allegedly stolen from Mexicans in 1836 and 1848). We surmised that the Chicano middle class would not be supportive of future MAYO activities unless we began to be supportive of their interests as well. Of supreme importance to us was to show individual MAYO members the meaning of being in solidarity with one another. If one MAYO group called for help, all MAYO chapters had to respond with people, to *hacer esquina* (literally, "to make corner"—to show solidarity), especially if the strategy had been previously approved by the statewide group at the June meeting. And, if MAYO came to the defense of a Chicano or an organization or group, we expected support from them in the future.

The Kingsville Issues Conference was well attended. The speakers and the sessions concentrated on the topic of Chicano labor and our relative status to other workers. As the general assembly came into session toward the close of the conference, one tactic proposed for the action agenda caught the attention of every person. People in the audience were asked to break their Humble Oil credit cards in half, and those not in attendance were requested to mail us their credit cards already cut in half so we could cancel their accounts. We promised to mail them to Humble Oil with a letter of demand on behalf of Chicano workers. The participants did not hesitate—hundreds of credit cards were torn up that very moment and were gathered, and we mailed those cards out promptly. The media loved the stunt, and carried the story. More cut credit cards arrived at MAYO offices in San Antonio, and others mailed their own cards directly to Humble Oil, which responded immediately through the media promising to investigate all complaints of discrimination, and if warranted to implement a new and improved hiring program. Oil company representatives wrote to each person identified on the torn credit cards. The tremendous energy of raza labor and consumer power had been harnessed for that occasion. This was the first consumer boycott of Humble Oil, which later became known to the world as Exxon.

At the second issues conference held at the John F. Kennedy High School in San Antonio, we again targeted two middle-class pressure points: the local municipal utility and Kelly Field, the military airbase. The high utility rates, shutoffs for nonpayment, and the hostile attitude of the City Public Service Board's (CPSB) clerical personnel toward Chicano customer job discrimination at Kelly Air Force Base were the issues. The utility company (CPSB) did not have a humane shutoff policy for tardy or delinquent payments. Without notice or chance for partial payment, utility service was cut off. Only after full payment was made was reconnection possible, and it was very costly. The Anglo Customer Service representatives of CPSB wouldn't—or probably couldn't—speak Spanish and were extremely rude to Chicanos. They used their clerical power as a weapon against us when they wrote out the shutoff orders.

We took on CPSB with some ingenious tactics. We voted to overpay each utility bill by one penny to cause bookkeeping and accounting problems in debiting and crediting each payment. CPSB had to notify each customer of overpayment, which forced the bureaucracy to do double work first to debit the account and balance, then credit the account with an overpayment by a penny. The next month the customer was encouraged to underpay the account by two pennies. First, the utility had to debit the credit balance of one cent, debit and balance the general account for the amount sent in, then adjust the account against the two penny underpayment. Three transactions for each account. They also had to notify the customer of the charge off and a deficit of one penny. The underpayment by a penny was not sufficient enough to warrant a shut off or issuance of a check. This tactic had not even begun to take hold when CPSB began hiring Spanish-speaking clerks and the City Council appointed the first Chicano member to the Board of Directors. We interpreted these first steps by CPSB as concessions to our public statements about the anti-Mexican attitudes held by personnel at the municipal utility.

Students interested in MAYO attending this issues conference from other colleges and universities improvised similar tactics to these for their own use. At the University of Texas at Austin boycotting Chicano students protesting the lack of a Mexican American Studies program applied political pressure by targeting the many libraries on campus. Demanding a Chicano Studies program, increased recruitment, and retention of Mexican American students, Chicano students simply threatened to rearrange the books in the library. When one goes to a library one is specifically asked not to reshelve books for fear that they may become misshelved and thus lost to other users—unless (or until) a staff person or other do-gooder locates and properly reshelves the books. A rearranged library might take years to fix if hundreds of books are misshelved. The threat of this tactic was enough to settle the situation, and the Mexican American Studies program got underway with funding as a result of this initiative.

Seeking Out the Mexican Government

At the Laredo and then the John F. Kennedy High School issues conferences we started talking about joining with social protest movements in Mexico. We publicly stated that we would seek out the Mexican president and demand that this government protect Mexicans and Mexican Americans in the United States. Jorge Bustamante, then a doctoral student at Notre Dame University, attended the San Antonio conference. He interviewed, dialogued, and questioned many of us on this subject at that particular time. Later, he emerged as the premier Chicanologist for the Mexican government. He was instrumental in assisting us with making the first contact with then Mexican president Luis Echeverria Alvarez. We wanted an accountability session with the Mexican president, to ask him what he intended to do to ensure that Mexicans in Mexico would begin to see Chicanos as their progeny and the land mass north of the Rio Grande as Mexican territory. We were searching for an alternative to assimilation with Anglos that was either Aztlan—a Chicano homeland independent of the Mexican nation state—or Mexican *irredenta*, a rejoining of Mexico as it was in 1820.

Mexicans in Mexico know that the land in the southwestern U.S. belongs to Mexicans, not Anglos. They study it that way in school. We Chicanos know from reading and looking at the names of places and things in the world around us—San Antonio, El Paso, Albuquerque, Los Angeles, Colorado, and the Sangre de Cristo mountain ranges, for example—that this was Mexican territory at one time, is still, to us, Mexican today and will remain our homeland. Something stolen can never be made lawful; the Southwest is occupied Mexican territory. The names of the rivers, mountains, cities, counties, and states—particularly those names that match our own—remind us of that fact every day. The Anglo teachers, administrators, school boards and many of our own people who work and study under them all work diligently, daily, to keep that theft from our minds, work at keeping the record erased. They live a lie. Because they have the power over curriculum and personnel they can and do excise from the books, myths, arts, and history those items indicating a Mexican presence, thus laying claim to Texas and the Southwest. They redefine themselves as heroes and freedom fighters. At the same time, Chicanos are given the opposite images, those of illegal aliens.

Young Chicanos in the late 1960s were the generation that decided to fight these kinds of issues, which date as far back as the 1820s. But we will not be the last generation; most assuredly, future Chicano generations will continue to press for political sovereignty over our Aztlan homeland, or will seek union with Mexico. This is not to say that no struggle occurred prior to MAYO; it is to say instead that we struggled in a more direct way. We took to the streets; we walked out of school; we picketed and engaged in overt manifestations of disgust and rage at the goings-on in many small Texas towns. There were many protests across Texas, across the Southwest, and across the nation organized by Chicanos: I participated in thirty-nine of them between 1967 and 1969.

A Protest at the White House

Right after the first school walkouts in San Antonio's Lanier and Fox Technical High Schools and the issues conferences, I got involved organizing a protest against the White House Cabinet Committee Hearings on Mexican American Affairs which were slated to be held in El Paso. I called key contacts in other states to poll them on their views regarding this event and recruit those not in agreement with White House policy initiatives toward the Chicano community to join our protest. Several of our MAYO leaders—Juan, Willie, and Mario—attended the El Paso conference in the fall of 1967. They were not invited as participants to the conference, but they proceeded to speak up about the MAYO perspective on issues. They pushed for a boycott of the proceedings because no grassroots Chicano leaders or organizations had been invited as participants, and because of the virtual exclusion of Chicanos in the developing War on Poverty programs. The cabinet officials reportedly attending had no Chicanos on their staff in any capacity. The first Chicano appointed to a newly created quasi-cabinet position on the Interagency Committee on Mexican American Affairs, Vicente Ximenes, was the former Chicano appointee to the Equal Employment Opportunity Commission. MAYO opposed this latest White House creation of an agency without power—neither cabinet nor independent agency—for Chicanos. The appointment was seen as continuing tokenism by many Chicanos: Ximenes seemed to be the Chicano destined for all appointments.

Upon arrival in El Paso, MAYO leaders helped organize a rump conference, the name for a meeting following a walkout. They were joined by other Chicano luminaries such as Ernesto Galarza, "Corky" Gonzales, Reies Lopez Tijerina, and many other leaders we had heard of and followed over the years. Now they were working together and meeting with MAYO leadership for the first time. The rump conference idea was not unique to MAYO, others had it on their agenda also, so it was organized readily. During the course of the rump conference several priests that had joined the boycott, such as Miguel Barragan, Henry Casso, and Roberto Peña began calling for an association of Chicano priests to be formed. They felt that the personnel of the Catholic Church, particularly priest and nuns, needed to stand with their Chicano parishioners not only while they were in church but also when they were engaged in social protest. As Chicano priests they had the first obligation to send out the call to organize.

The conference proved to be terribly embarrassing to President Lyndon Johnson, a Texan himself. The Mexican Americans that rejected the call to meet with us in a rump conference and remained in the official proceedings were accused of selling out and working toward getting token positions at the White House at our expense. A walkout by Mexican Americans in Albuquerque the prior year over federal government employment discrimination had first dramatized the issue of the absence of Chicanos in high positions within the Johnson administration.

The rump conference prompted the White House to make changes in their employment practices, to expand the War on Poverty program into our barrios. The War on Poverty, based on eradicating hunger in America, was basically aimed at and geared towards blacks. The rhetoric from Washington was that the war was for all poor people, but they thought poverty was to be found only among blacks in the South, and some whites in Kentucky, Tennessee, and perhaps Arkansas.

Nobody in Anglo America knew about us, the Mexican American people of the Southwest, West, and Midwest regions of the country. Lyndon Johnson knew about Mexican Americans but he had done little to incorporate our national community into his domestic policies. Congressman Henry B. Gonzalez was a frequent passenger on Air Force One when it flew from Washington, D.C., carrying the president to his Texas ranch near San Antonio. He knew of Chicano poverty and the many other problems of Mexican Americans but refused the opportunity to lobby the president for Chicano causes. To this day Gonzalez loudly proclaims he is a congressman for all Americans, not solely for

Mexican Americans, and for years, he has refused to become a member of the Hispanic Congressional Caucus on these grounds.

The University of California at Los Angeles conducted a study, and published *The Mexican American People* in 1964. No policy recommendations came from that book, only the grim statistics of deprivation, discrimination, and institutional neglect. In many ways, the publication of such a book on Mexican Americans was comparable to the publication of Gunnar Myrdal's *An American Dilemma*, published some twenty years earlier. Myrdal's book dealt with many of the same racial issues, but strictly on a black/white basis. The UCLA study was the first of its type in that it addressed brown/white relations.

Both books document graphically the institutional neglect by government, education, foundations, religious orders, and labor of the black and brown peoples. The Ford Foundation knew of the problems faced by Mexican Americans but did little other than fund the UCLA study. White poverty in Appalachia, however, was dramatized and memorialized in film and with photos in the print media, while our poverty in the Southwest was ignored. Congressmen Henry B. Gonzalez, Eulogio "Kika" de la Garza, Manuel Lujan, Edward Roybal, and U.S. Senator Joseph Montoya all knew about our problems but also did little. They didn't even speak out for our special needs, namely the inclusion of Chicanos in the higher echelons of policy making within the War on Poverty. These politicians were all Democrats, except for Lujan, and at this time the White House and both houses of Congress were controlled by white members of the Democratic party. Together, they did nothing; individually, they did nothing. This is abuse of power and abuse of knowledge.

In 1968 I began to finish up my course of study at St. Mary's and wrote my thesis on the conditions for revolution in four South Texas counties. Luz, as pregnant as she was, typed the entire manuscript more than once. I studied the land ownership patterns in these four counties and found the clear makings of a colonial empire. I found Chicanos stratified and segmented in a reserve labor pool, purposely kept illiterate and without schooling. I predicted revolt. Intellectually, I grew even more resentful of the gringo power structure. Somehow, I finished my course work and thesis at St. Mary's in May of 1968, and we moved to Austin, Texas, so I could begin a doctoral program at the University of Texas.

But the army was even more interested in me now. My nemesis, Selective Service Board Secretary Ruth Webb, from Uvalde, had always worked hard at trying to draft me: at the end of each school term, she would reclassify me 1-A, which was the most eligible draft status, and she did this again in May of 1968. In the days of the Selective Service one had to notify the draft board of school and marital status, which I had, but my family status did not matter to Ruth Webb. She kept my draft status at 1-A. I appealed the classification since I was again in school at the University of Texas at Austin, was married, and had a child on the way. I made a personal appearance before the draft board, with my wife in tow, but lost on both counts. The only Chicano on the draftboard was Agustin Estrada, who worked for the Texas Employment Commission. Estrada did not have the guts to point out to the other Selective Service Board members that my grounds for deferments were solid and verifiable; he did not, in fact, say one word. He waited for others to raise their hands in favor of the denial of exemptions, then voted with the majority to deny my request for continued deferment. The American G.I. Forum had for years demanded that Chicanos be appointed to draft boards. Ironically, Estrada's appointment was of no help to me.

In the summer of 1968, I worked as an administrative assistant to State Senator Joe Bernal from San Antonio. When I lost my draft appeal, it was going to be a matter of days before I was drafted. I had to leave the Ph.D. program in the study of government at Austin. My choices were to wait for the draft notice into the regular army, to try to find a reserve unit to join, or to flee to Canada where many others had gone before because they could not, from there, be extradited to the U.S. for draft evasion. I had made up my mind not to go to Canada or to Vietnam. I chose to become a "weekend warrior" as a reservist in the United States Army. After searching for an opening in many units in Corpus Christi, Uvalde, Hondo, Del Rio, and Austin, I found two openings which kept me closer to home. One unit was with the Airborne Ranger paratroopers in Austin and the other in San Antonio with the Combat Engineers. I chose Combat Engineers rather than risk jumping out of airplanes. Reserve training was to consist of approximately four months in active duty at a regular military base somewhere in the United States.

Back to San Antonio

On July 30, 1968, Luz and I had our first child, a boy named Adrian. Around that same time we moved our family back to San Antonio after I dropped out of the Ph.D. program, waiting to be called up. Luz got a teaching job at an elementary school with the San Antonio Independent School District. I got a job as an investigator with the newly established Mexican American Legal Defense and Education Fund (MALDEF). Pete Tijerina, a San Antonio lawyer who had for years helped promote our particular causes, had gotten the funding from the Ford Foundation for the establishment of MALDEF. Mario Obledo was the general counsel and I reported to him with my findings from civil rights investigations across the Southwest.

In October, 1968, I was called to report for active duty at "Little Korea," which is Fort Leonard Wood, Missouri, in the Ozark Mountains. I stayed there for basic training as well my advanced infantry training, spending all of my four months of active military duty with the U.S. Army in the Ozarks in the dead of winter—an experience I will never forget. My unit, the 277th Engineering Company, was based on the west side of San Antonio, off Culebra and Hillcrest streets. My Master Sergeant and later Warrant Officer was Eliseo Garza and my First Sergeant was John "Top" Gutierrez (no relation). I had several company commanders, but one that remains in my mind is Hugo Heldenfelds, from Corpus Christi. He resented my political involvement with MAYO and my notoriety in the press. At times, he would try to get the noncommissioned officers such as the sergeants to discipline me for one thing or another that he would conjure up. They generally refused or ignored him. I know this because they would tell me to stay clear of him and avoid contact. Once, for the obligatory two-week summer camp at Camp Bullis in Texas, Captain Heldenfelds objected to military higher-ups when Senator Edward Kennedy requested I be excused from duty for two or three days in order to attend, as a witness, a hearing he was holding on Mexican Americans and civil rights. He was overruled and I attended the hearing.

Upon my return, I was given kitchen patrol (KP) duty which is a dreaded experience. My revenge came during pay call when I set up a coffee can for donations to MAYO near the area where the soldiers were being paid. I raised a lot of money because every Chicano soldier knew of Heldenfelds' feelings toward me and my MAYO activities and believed in what I was doing.

The First Electoral Attempt with La Raza Unida, and Further Chicano Organizing

During the time that I was in the military, MAYO grew phenomenally. There were more school walkouts in Texas, and MAYO began actively promoting school strikes and boycotts everywhere. Mario Compean had taken over the reins of MAYO after me. He and others decided to electorally take the city council positions in San Antonio. During 1968, we toyed with the idea of turning La Raza Unida into a political party. In the law school at St. Mary's I had personally researched how to build such a party in Texas at the local level. We mimeographed the "how to" material and mailed it out to various persons such as the Valley strikers, Juan Cornejo in Crystal City, and Manuel Chavez in Mathis, though none responded. George Wallace also went the route of an alternative party in 1968 and his American Party did field candidates in Texas. Juan Cornejo turned us down but did sign up as candidate for sheriff of Zavala County on the American Party ticket, the only Mexican American who opted for a campaign for public office through a political party other than the Democratic Party.

Mario Compean and Nacho Perez began organizing the Barrio Betterment League, whose name was a take off on the Good Government League (GGL). Walter McAllister, head of the San Antonio Savings and Loan Company, was mayor of San Antonio at the time. He also was the titular head of the GGL, the dominant political machine of the Anglo business interests in San Antonio. The GGL had controlled San Antonio politics for decades without any meaningful participation by Mexican Americans. The last time Mexicans had been in local public office in San Antonio was when Henry B. Gonzalez won election to the city council in the 1950s. Prior to that lone victory, Mexicans had last been in the city government in the early 1800s, when Texas was a Mexican state. The first and last statewide Mexican office holder was Lorenzo de Zavala, the vice president of the Republic of Texas. For the next 125 years or so, not one Mexican served in statewide government until Roy Barrera was appointed secretary of state by Governor John Connally in the 1960s.

Mario Compean, Candelario Alejos, and Dario Chapa ran as a slate under the symbol of La Raza Unida/MAYO. They came very close to winning. MAYO and the other candidates ran a typical barrio campaign. By that I mean they used all the ethnic symbols; they campaigned in Spanish; they went barhopping, shaking hands and encouraging people to vote in the key Chicano precincts; they leafleted on corners, made tamales for fund raising, campaigned on Spanish radio. On Sundays, after attending several Catholic masses, they went to Mission County Park, Casiano Park, Woodlawn Lake, all the Chicano parks in the city asking for votes. They went door to door with voter registration; the poll tax, just recently been removed as an obstacle, permitted greater participation by poor people. The MAYO candidates laid plans for getting out the vote and precinct canvassing up to election time.

Mario Compean missed getting the incumbent mayor into a runoff by fewer than 230 votes. San Antonio was not the same after that election because attention had been lavished on MAYO/La Raza Unida and our style of politics. The Mexican precincts voted for Mario and his slate rather than the GGL candidates. Had Mario had a bit more support from the black community or even the middle class Mexicans of the northwest side, perhaps we would have seen a different election outcome. The GGL continued in power for many elections thereafter, until the rise in 1975 of Henry Cisneros, who later served President Bill Clinton as Secretary of Housing and Urban Development.

Cisneros was recruited to blunt the growing militancy on the part of the Mexican American electorate and blunt it he did. Young Henry was always a handy person to use in situations requiring a Mexican to step forward, very much in the fashion of Henry B. Gonzalez. During the rise of MAYO, Gonzalez took it upon himself to attack and vilify those of us involved. From the floor of Congress, he openly denounced MAYO leaders as "Brown Bilbos," as hate mongers in the tradition of the racist U.S. senator from Mississippi (1936–1946) by the name of Theodore Bilbo. Gonzalez was not acting out of character at this particular time, as many people thought. He was completely in character, always taking the low road in attempting to destroy incipient Chicano leadership from any quarter.

At about the same time that we were forming MAYO across the state, Pete Tijerina and others in Southwest Texas—such as Mike Gonzales from Uvalde, Warren Burnet from Odessa, Abel Ochoa from El Paso— would meet in the hill country at Wimberly for planning, strategy, and coordinating sessions, organizing the Mexican American Legal Defense and Education Fund (MALDEF). We attended these sessions as MAYO members and gave our opinions on MALDEF's goals, purpose, mission, staffing, objectives, and the like. We wanted to make sure that the focus of MALDEF included a political agenda that would protect us as activists and community organizers while engaged in civil rights work. As MAYO members who faced arrest and jail with each protest and each direct action, we wanted activist lawyers employed at MALDEF to come to our defense at a moment's notice. We wanted to make sure there were lawyers who would take over from our political work and press our issues in the courtroom—we were eager to be plaintiffs.

At first MALDEF agreed; this was when they hired me as field investigator. Over the years, however, Chicanos have lost the battle of accountability with MALDEF. In the 1980s and 1990s MALDEF grew more concerned about precedent setting cases that generate money for their fundraising than with protection of civil rights. Legal work on behalf of Mexican undocumented migrant workers, children with birth defects, exploited farm workers, displaced workers or renters, Chicano faculty in higher education, and voting rights litigation has been largely ignored. MALDEF did file and win a voting rights case in Los Angeles County that created a new county district (where Gloria Molina became the first Mexican American county supervisor), and did some voting rights work in Texas during the early 1980s. Today, the potential settlement value of a case goes hand in hand with the kind of cases that MALDEF accepts. In the 1990s, MALDEF's San Antonio office has filed fewer cases than ever before, has long gaps without adequate legal staff, and has had no budget increase in years despite the dramatic rise in legal costs—a sad irony considering that it was there that MALDEF first began.

Another of the institutions created in the late sixties was the Southwest Council of La Raza, now known as the National Council of La Raza (NCLR). The MAYO founders had early on consulted with the representatives of the Ford Foundation on the creation of such an entity in the Southwest. Our members provided program ideas, a model of urban community development (the Mexican American Unity Council), and personnel. MAYO wanted to make sure that our vision of creating the institutions with which to build Aztlan, the Chicano homeland, would be located in our base area of operations and not in some distant area lacking in Chicano activism. In order to do this we needed MALDEF for civil rights protection and the Southwest Council for community development.

Both MALDEF and the Southwest Council initially relied heavily on external and exclusive funding from the Ford Foundation. This type of sole source reliance cannot be avoided when starting a new entity. Maintaining that posture over the years, however, made both MALDEF and NCLR less accountable and accessible to the Chicano militants, activists, and community that they purported to represent. Together with other promoters of such new institutions, we kept the principal offices of both MALDEF and the Southwest Council of La Raza in San Antonio for a few months. Congressman Henry B. Gonzalez began to pressure the Ford Foundation to cut the funding to MALDEF and the Southwest Council, and to press his colleagues into an investigation of the Ford Foundation. His voice, added to those of others, caused Congress to begin to reexamine the tax exemptions for foundations.

Congress ultimately passed the Tax Reform Act of 1969. Word reached us from the Ford Foundation that Congressman Gonzalez wanted MAYO and the Mexican American Unity Council, our program organizational affiliate, to be defunded. He also wanted MALDEF and the Southwest Council out of the San Antonio area or the Ford Foundation would face greater scrutiny. Internal fights between Texas Chicano leaders and California Chicano leaders over where to locate these new programs resurfaced, leading to the relocation of the Southwest Council to Phoenix and MALDEF to California. Juan Patlan headed the Mex-

ican American Unity Council and Willie Velasquez was working with
the Southwest Council in San Antonio and only briefly working in
Phoenix to aid in the transition to Miguel Barragan, the new executive
director of the Southwest Council.

The First School Boycotts

We had not been around as MAYO for too long before we had affiliates
across the state. The first walkout school protests occurred—almost simultaneously—in San Antonio and in Los Angeles. If there was ever a
sign of the times, it was this congruence of school blowouts by angry
Chicano students. Chicano rage was beginning to emerge. Through the
ability of Mario Compean to identify key players among students at
Edgewood and Fox Tech schools in San Antonio, we connected with
these youthful protesters.

Through Willie Velasquez we were able to get access to support from
such priests as Sherrill Smith, Henry Casso, Lonnie Reyes, Roberto Peña,
and Miguel Barragan. These priests had also stood with us in the El
Paso rump conference. Willie, via telephone at the Bishop's Committee
and at the U.S. Commission on Civil Rights headed by Richard Avena,
was able to connect with people who had direct channels of information
to the leaders, both students and teachers, of the walkouts in Garfield
and Lincoln high schools in Los Angeles, such as Sal Castro and David
Martinez of the new youth organization, the Brown Berets.

The prospect of the school walkouts in San Antonio was imminent.
We observed the developments at Edgewood and Fox Tech high
schools. The students, like those in Los Angeles, were complaining
about the very same things we in MAYO leadership had complained
about when we were in high school only four or five years earlier. The
litany of complaints included such things as not being able to speak
Spanish in school, the social distance between Chicano kids and Anglos, the prohibition against dating between Mexicans and Anglos, the
treatment of Mexicans in the history books, the lack of recognition of
the contributions made in Texas and the United States by persons of
Mexican ancestry, and the lack of cultural activities. All of this soon led
to the first MAYO-organized school walkouts in Texas. These coincided
with the Los Angeles walkouts and made the Chicano Movement appear to have national dimensions. These walkouts by Mexican Americans in two distant cities shared the same strategy, the same complaints,
the same demands, and occurred in similar metropolitan school districts. While the events in these two distinct geographic locations may
have appeared to be directed by one organization, in fact they were not.

Luz Bazan Gutiérrez and the author at the 1967 signing of the agreement between Chicano students and school officials that brought an end to the student protest in Glendale, Arizona. José Angel Gutiérrez was an investigator for the Mexican American Legal Defense Fund (MALDEF).

It was the beginning, however, of a national social movement among Chicanos in the United States, and MAYO was centrally involved in bringing that tide of social protest about in Texas.

The Need for Single-Member Districts

During MAYO study circles in 1967 and 1968 we had analyzed the demographics for the state and the Southwest. We knew that in two or three decades from 1970 Mexican Americans would be a voting majority in many Texas cities, counties, and regions, and that we would likely be able to win all seats in the at-large elections. But for the time being, and the next thirty years, we needed representation in local government. The only alternative available was single-member districts made possible by extending the Voting Rights Act of 1965 to cover Texas and Mexican Americans.

Texas in 1968 did not have single-member districts from which to elect officeholders of our choice—Chicanos and Chicanas. In the at-large elections of the time, the same Anglo electoral majority won all positions up for election, election after election, partisan or nonpartisan. This method of election was tantamount to a dictatorship by what was barely a majority. As a majority vote is 50 percent plus one additional vote, the losing side could win as much as 49.99 percent of the vote and still remain unrepresented. MAYO demanded coverage of the Voting Rights Act to include Mexican Americans, and not just blacks, in the South, so that we could begin to place our candidates in the many local governments across the state.

Typically, Anglo congressmen with districts that included parts of San Antonio and Bexar county, such as Robert Krueger from nearby New Braunfels and O. C. Fisher from San Angelo, were opposed to such a reform. They wanted to keep the Voting Rights Act out of Texas, or in the alternative, keep the act limited to protection for blacks. Support by Congressman Henry B. Gonzalez in favor of keeping the act out of Texas was totally unexpected. He offered his electoral successes of years past as proof that without the act and with the at-large election method, he had repeatedly been elected to public office in San Antonio since the 1950s. Henry B.'s opposition came as a surprise and shock to many Mexican Americans. He came out of right field on this issue and remained consistent in opposition to the issues we raised and reforms we sought. The old politico Henry B. was once again the couch for racist gringos to sit on and proclaim, "I'm with Henry B. on this one!"

Only through the tremendous efforts of U.S. Representative Barbara Jordan from Houston, the lone black woman member of the Texas congressional delegation, were San Antonio and Mexican Americans included in the coverage of the act. She lobbied enough votes for extension and coverage of Mexican Americans to overcome the opposition of these politicians from Texas. With that change came single-member districts and the first Mexican Americans to get elected to the City Council by district. In the years since then, San Antonio and other cities that adopted single-member districts have seen a number of Mexican American politicos emerge from these districts.

MAYO, in a brief three years, had gained wide notoriety and a reputation for being the new champions of la raza.

7

Conditions and Preparations for El "Walkout"

Conditions for the education of Chicanos seldom improved in Texas without massive confrontation and protest, and still don't today. The public schools in Uvalde, for example, continue to be controlled by Anglo personnel: the school board, administration, teaching staff, curriculum, and social climate are still overwhelmingly Anglo. In 1970, 91 percent of the teaching staff was Anglo and 61 percent of the students were Mexican Americans, and Chicanos have been a majority of students in the Uvalde schools since the late 1960s. Chicano students attempted a student walkout on April 14, 1970, to protest various issues, including the termination of a Chicano teacher, Josue Garza. They failed in that initial effort because they protested too near to the end of the school year. Student leaders in Uvalde did not listen to (MAYO's) advice against their timing.

In 1995, a quarter of a century after that ill-fated walkout, Anglo teaching staff still held 271 of the 363 positions, a 75 percent stranglehold. There were 4,133 Chicano students in the Uvalde schools during 1995, making up 79 percent of the 5,263 student total. Anglo kids were a mere 21 percent of the student body.

In urban school districts such as Houston and Dallas, the statistical phenomenon remains the same. Whites continue to control policy, personnel, curriculum, program and environment for the ethnic majority student population, which is Mexican American. Together, Mexican American and African American students comprise an overwhelming ethnic student population over whites, approximately 85 percent compared to 13 percent white, and 2 percent Asian and Native American. The educational system in Texas as in all other states, has been designed to benefit only Anglo students and no one else.

The Anglo Education of Chicanos

The evils of segregated schools were first protested by Chicanos in the 1920s and again in the 1930s across the Southwest. Prior to 1940, the classification of Mexican children as "Other Race" permitted racial segregation and exclusion, as was the practice for persons racially classified as "Negroid" or "Mongoloid," but the public schools soon faced law suits across the Southwest that forced the allowing of Mexican children into schools filled only with Anglo children. The institutional response to that edict was to begin segregation within the school building itself, by grade and by subject matter.

The public schools insisted on the speaking of English for both learning and teaching. A Chicano student who came from a Spanish-speaking home was at a loss entering the English-only, white school. But the educational system placed the emphasis on student success with the curriculum at the wrong end, and still does today. With English-only they have built an entrance gate that locks out all non-English–speaking children from learning; instead, the emphasis ought to be at the exit of the educational process. Rather than say, "Learn English first in order to learn," the school system should say, "Use your Spanish to learn English and master both languages before you graduate."

The faculty I encountered as a student in the public schools of Cristal from 1950 to 1962 was overwhelmingly white. I finally met two Mexican American teachers in junior high, and two in high school; there were no Mexican American administrators, only a few maintenance workers and cafeteria personnel. At the high school the Chicano teachers were the assistant football coach, Juan Rivera, and the Spanish teacher, Diamantina Rodriguez. At the community college in Uvalde, the token Chicano instructor, Dr. Roberto Galvan, was teaching Spanish, and the token Latinos at Texas A & I were one Chicano and two Cubans, one a graduate student, Rodolfo Cortina, teaching Spanish. At law school there were none; at St. Mary's University there were none; and at the University of Texas at Austin there were a handful of Chicano professors among the several hundred faculty members, though in the Government and History departments there were none. The current statistics for Chicano faculty at these institutions, both public and private, remain dismal: in 1996 I was the only Chicano professor in the University of Texas at Arlington's various departments of social sciences except for those in the Spanish department.

The governing bodies of these public entities—be they local school districts, community colleges, teachers' colleges or universities—are also comprised primarily of Anglos. The elected officials hire Anglo professionals to administer the governmental entity, and the Anglo administrators hire Anglo support staff to manage and provide services to the students of the institution. Given the failure of these institutions to recruit and retain Mexican American students, I believe we are simply an economic necessity to the overall program. Our attendance as students, apart from our ultimate success with graduation, justifies state-funded dollars to the individual entity.

Passage of the Voting Rights Act, through its extension to cover Texas requires single-member districts for the elected officials, but has not really improved the numbers of Chicano elected officials on those bodies. There are two main reasons: many governmental entities have refused to change to single-member districts and wait to be sued for compliance with the federal mandate; and running for office is still a rich person's prerogative. Many school districts still conduct elections at large, which dilute the voting strength of Chicanos. And, of course, the college and university boards of regents are appointed by the governors from among those who have contributed to their campaigns. There have been a few token Chicanos appointed to seats on the governing bodies of the large systems of higher education in Texas, but never more than one at any given time.

Few local school districts outside the Rio Grande Valley of Texas, and no college or university system, have a majority of Chicano members on the Board of Regents—the whites control them all.

The curriculum offerings of the public schools were geared to reinforce the Anglo culture and denigrate the Chicano culture. In literature, we read and studied only European and Anglo-American authors; the grammar and language we had to learned was English and the language we had to forget or ignore was Spanish. Schools did not add a language for Chicanos, they merely took one away. In Social Science or History, for example, we learned of the great American heroes—all white males. The few teaching segments about Mexicans were either in the context of the Alamo and the Mexican War, or of our being agricultural, seasonal labor. In Geography, together with History, we learned that the United States began with the thirteen white colonies. I was never taught of the Spanish exploration, subsequent colonization and nation-building, of the Mexican inheritance of all lands West and East of the Mississippi, nor of the settlements in Florida years prior to the whites' arrival in the Northeast. I never learned because I was never taught that eighty years prior to the founding of Jamestown, San Miguel de Guadalupe had been founded in that same general area; that San Agustin, Florida (St. Augustine, today), founded by the Spanish, is the oldest city in the United States; and that Santa Fe, Nuevo (New) Mexico, is the oldest state capital in the nation. That whole era of history was quickly dismissed by my teachers with a brief mention of the early Spanish explorers and Mexican settlers. To this day, I do not recall learning the first names of such men as Magellan, Balboa, Cabeza de Vaca, or Father Serra. I still Anglicize their surnames as I learned them from Anglo teachers when I refer to "May-Jell-Ann," "Bell-Bow-Ah," "Kah-Bay-Sah Day Bah-Kah," and "Father Say-Rah." Even though these Spanish explorers are far removed from actual Chicano lives today, they remain part of our ancestral claim to this land; they are the legacy of these ancestors made in the Americas.

The Louisiana Purchase was discussed simply as a purchase from the French, without an explanation of the causes for the sale to France of this huge expanse of land owned by Spain, or its immediate resale to the United States. "Manifest Destiny" was presented as divine inspiration for the white peoples' taking of our land; another explanation was that the people on the land were not suited to occupy it and were wasting its resources.

I do not recall ever meeting with a counselor about preparing to attend college. The assumption made by the school board, administration, teaching faculty, and support staff was that the Anglo kids would be prepared to go on to college and that Mexicans—especially the males—would enter the local labor force soon after leaving school at the legal "dropout" age of sixteen; we were seen as not needing preparation for college. The girls, Anglo and Mexican, were seen as needing to learn to iron, cook, budget for meals, and care for babies in Home Economics, and perhaps to learn typing and shorthand. As a result of these biases, courses such as Home Economics and Shop had an overrepresentation of Mexican American students.

I recall the surprise of teachers when several of us Chicanos signed up for Geometry and Physics rather than Bookkeeping or General Math. They were more surprised at semester's end to realize we had done as well, if not better, than the Anglo students.

Policy and control over educational budget was and is firmly in the hands of the white community, yet since my childhood their children have not been the majority of the students in school at the local level.

The Anglo student majority is found in college and professional schools. This is even more true today than yesterday. How, then, can the schools change to meet our needs, if the parents of the white student minority control the policy, budget, administration, instruction, operation, and climate of the public schools from prekindergarten through to the professional schools?

The social climate between Chicanos and Anglos in the public schools reflected the society in Texas. Every aspect of student life is Anglo dominated and directed. The school cafeteria, for example, only served Anglo food; the only two items served and billed as Mexican food were Spanish rice and Frito pie. The former consisted of boiled white rice with tomato sauce poured over it, a horrible concoction. The latter was hamburger meat in spicy tomato sauce, mixed with Frito corn chips, which was occasionally edible. Sour smelling white bread, pork and beans, sauerkraut with wieners, and pasty meat loaf with peas were regular, standard fare.

The school yearbook featured the Anglo kids. Chicanos did appear in yearbook photos, but mainly in those of the individual classes, whereas the school clubs and student leadership—and hence, their photos— were predominantly white. There was no interethnic group mixing, much less dating; the prom and other social events were segregated and policed by teachers or chaperones to enforce this informal rule. The Anglo male kids made the varsity football, basketball and baseball teams, the first string, regardless of ability. Their fathers and mothers were involved with the respective adult booster clubs for these sports, and saw to it that they were chosen. Our parents were not made to feel welcome as members in these booster clubs, except as paying patrons to their activities. Chicanos made the second string, to be sure, and sometimes the varsity squad if they were extremely talented. Anglo athletes got by with mediocrity, Chicanos had to achieve excellence.

The Anglo females became the cheerleaders, twirlers, and homecoming and tournament queens for the various sports, and the overall class and school favorites, such as most beautiful, most popular, most representative, and the like. Their selection was made for us by our teachers or by adult white "outside judges" from nearby communities. This happened in my high school beginning in 1959, to coincide with the switch in student population from majority Anglo to majority Mexican American. I always suspected that the Anglos from our town would trade their votes with those of Anglos from other towns, judging our contests and only voting for Anglo children.

The combination of white administrative and instructional personnel, English only, an Anglo-centered curriculum, and a preferential social setting dominated by Anglos for Anglos in the public schools made for systematic discrimination and exclusion of Chicanos. Against this backdrop of systematic discrimination and exclusion, I managed to get out of high school, into community college and ultimately college at Texas A & I. But few Chicanos can broker the public school system as well as I did.

I had the benefit of two tremendous parents who saw to it that I was bilingual before entering the public school. I also had a firm, ultimate goal of completing college on the road to becoming a professional; I do not recall a day in my life which finishing high school or not going to college was an option with my parents. My Chicano friends did not have that kind of familial support or goal, though my Anglo acquaintances all did. Since the middle school years, I recall hearing them talk of going to a college that their parents or some older sibling had attended earlier, and they looked forward to attending the same school themselves. Their parents planned for that eventuality; they had a complete picture of a future life that involved a college education, while Chicano kids did not. Their picture of a future life was incomplete, without college, and perhaps without even a high school diploma. Most Chicano kids began by getting pushed out of school by the system even before a picture of college or a professional degree could be formulated in their minds. They accepted being pushed out because it didn't interrupt any dream, goal, or plan, since one wasn't there to begin with.

Early MAYO Analysis of the Chicano Educational Experience

During the early MAYO organizing days, we found that conditions in the public schools for Chicanos, regardless of rural or urban setting, still excluded and discriminated against us systematically. More importantly, we found Chicano students now eager to challenge the structure of public education at their local level. We studied their complaints and found the problems not to be much different from what ours once were, during our days as students in the same schools. Nothing much had changed: the kids complained of being called names by teachers, of selective and arbitrary punishments, of not being able to speak Spanish without severe sanction, and of the white bias against them in all facets of the school system.

The Chicano students wanted to protest such treatment, to end it, and that was music to our ears. As the Chicano generation that immediately preceded them, we were the ones closest to their reality and welcomed the opportunity to come to their aid and defense. As such, MAYO began encouraging school protests among Chicanos. The mistakes we made early on with the first school walkouts in San Antonio repeated themselves: we did not involve the parents in the deliberation and analysis of the student complaints, and we did not organize them into support units. Had we done so, the parents would have also seen that not much had changed from the days they attended the very same schools, and would have joined us in the protest.

Eluterio Escobar and Maria Hernandez, for example, faced the same organizational problems in their battle against segregation in the 1930s. They sought to organize school protests against those injustices and took to the streets of San Antonio in protest, but Chicano parents were reluctant to join them. Initially, Escobar and Hernandez faced the local school authorities and state officials with only a few Mexican American children in tow. Only after they recruited parents in house meetings and explained the need for the protests did support grow among the adult population. Their organizing effort, particularly the home visits, were made easier because both Escobar and Hernandez were adults themselves.

In the late 1960s the members of MAYO were barely out of our teen years and had difficulty getting invitations into a home. Our physical appearance—long hair, combat boots and U.S. Army field jackets, MAYO buttons on our lapels, and occasionally with berets or bandanas across our foreheads—was not appreciated by the parents. The use of the self-identifier "Chicano" as a group label and the fiery rhetoric reported in the Anglo press did not meet with parental approval either. We were making a statement with our dress and making ourselves an "issue" unnecessarily.

When we did not include the parents during the early stages of organizing a school boycott, much less organize them into a support unit for the walkout, they were among the first to oppose our protests and tactics during the school walkouts. Later, after we learned from our mistakes, MAYO required the inclusion of parents and the formation of support organizations before engaging in the school walkouts. Timing of the protests was perfected to avoid the six-week exam periods, the end-of-semester finals, and the end of the school year. MAYO also avoided organizing during months when migrant parents pulled their kids out for the journey to the northern states in search of work.

MAYO organizers were still susceptible to Anglo charges of being outside agitators and troublemakers, even after we had compromised somewhat on our appearance. The hair was not as long and our combat boots were worn only during marches and demonstrations. We did little else to dispel the media attacks and stereotypes held of MAYO members until the later, final walkouts in 1968 and early 1969. By then, we also had learned that even when we "won" a school walkout by obtaining commitments from the school board and administration to reform, the Chicano students, together with their parents, could not keep the decision makers accountable. The reforms lasted as long as the goodwill on the part of the school officials and personnel existed. Written negotiated agreements ended school protests, but like many an Anglo treaty, were not complied with and even flagrantly violated when the kids returned to school and faced the same system and personnel.

MAYO organizers across the state got involved with the school protest agenda during 1968. And they all voiced and reported the same difficulties in organizing without parental involvement and support at the year end MAYO meeting.

The Beginnings of the Winter Garden Project

At the regular June, 1969, meeting of MAYO to set the annual agenda, we discussed an area-wide organizing effort designed to take over school boards and cities. MAYO had learned that in order to guarantee the reforms promised, the Chicano community had to take political control of the school board. If MAYO was to expand the organizing project and engage in local electoral activity, why limit ourselves to only the school board, when the city council and perhaps the county public offices were on the same or similar ballots we were going contesting? More importantly, the political takeover of local areas in the building of Aztlan was imperative. Many MAYO members had attended the National Youth Conferences held in Denver in the spring of 1969 and had returned more culturally nationalistic than when they had left. The task of organizing and building community for the Chicano homeland was the overarching ideology within MAYO.

There were five sites across the state that we considered for the comprehensive organizing effort that would begin the building of Aztlan. Cristal and the Winter Garden area was one of these sites. After the aborted spring 1969 walkout in that community, Juan Patlan and I had promised the students we would return to Cristal to help them organize a school boycott if the school situation did not improve by the fall, and it hadn't. MAYO was still in the business of "doing walkouts," as the kids from Cristal had coined the phrase. The place seemed ideal for trying out the grand strategy of taking control of a school board and other local government. Ultimately this was the site approved because this area met the criteria we sought: a high concentration of Mexican Americans in the population; a history of electoral activity; it was small and rural, but within a hundred miles of a large city; students there

sought to protest the educational system; and MAYO wanted local organizers for this project who were native to the area. Luz and I were not
"outsiders" to the Crystal City area of Winter Garden.

MAYO, in choosing this site, had looked for a community with some
history of Chicano activism. The area had to have a sufficiently large
Chicano population to sustain an electoral effort. In other words, we
knew that our population was generally younger, less educated, and
poorer than the Anglo population. And large numbers of our population were seasonal agricultural workers, migrants in small and rural
towns. MAYO needed this foundation to build upon—one that consisted of a larger Chicano population than Anglo to overcome the obvious handicaps inherent in a younger, less educated, poor and migrant
Chicano community.

The Chicano median age in 1960 was seventeen. The voting age requirement was twenty-one at that time. This meant that one half of our
Chicano population in 1960 was seventeen or *younger*! By 1990, however, the median age for Mexican Americans had risen to twenty-three,
and the voting age requirement had dropped to eighteen. But again,
half of the people of Mexican ancestry were twenty-three years of age or
younger. We have simply been too young a population to vote! Chicanos,
as a group, are the youngest of ethnic minorities, both in the United
States and among other "Hispanics." Older Chicanos, like my father
and grandmother, more often than not are not citizens, still waiting for
the call to "go back to Mexico." This segment of the Mexican American
population over the age of fifty-five comprises 25 percent of our total.
In other words, half of us can't vote because we are too young and one
quarter of us can't vote because we are not citizens. This leaves a mere
25 percent of all Chicanos that are eligible to vote.

On the Anglo side of the equation, comparing similar statistics, we
found them to be much older, more educated, and wealthier. We found
that their median age in 1960 was thirty-one years. Only 22 percent of
Anglos in the Winter Garden area were under the age of 21. In other
words, 78 percent of all whites were eligible to vote. All of them were
citizens, born that way, and all of them usually voted. They had—and
still have—an entire system of their own to protect and preserve; they
must keep us out of their system.

Chicanos are too smart and cynical to vote for those persons on the
ballot who are usually the only candidates. We just don't vote; why
should we? When Chicanos do vote, we vote in smaller numbers than
our population statistics indicate. Chicanos have no reason to vote: no
Chicano candidate campaigns on a platform of taking over the system
to make it work only for us, though Anglo candidates run on that plat-

form every election. No Chicano candidate campaigns on a promise of taking the land back and making the Anglos the illegal aliens. Anglo candidates run on those campaign promises during every election and use racist rhetoric against us, disguised as informed public discourse. There is a serious and monumental gap between what individual Anglos say about their commitment to social change and what collectively Anglos do to keep the social system as it is. Slow change is the preferred method of evolution; rapid change forced upon them is perceived to be a revolution. They believe that such lofty ideals as freedom, civic participation, liberty, equality, majority rule, democracy, and multiculturalism are made a reality by merely talking about them as goals, wishing them into a pseudo-reality for themselves alone. When Chicanos attempt to apply these ideals and derive benefit from them, disharmony between Anglos and Chicanos sets in. This is when we are accused of being troublemakers and, invariably, subversive outside agitators. When MAYO came into the Winter Garden area, Chicanos, with our prompting, began to talk about these discrepancies and contradictions.

I was designated the lead organizer for the Winter Garden Project. I was from Cristal and Luz wasn't, but as my wife we knew she would be accepted by the Chicano families in town by my extension. Upon relocating to my hometown toward the middle of summer Luz and I found the organizing easier, since migrants were returning from work up north, one family at a time, just before school would start.

Luz had a teaching certificate and could probably get a job with the public schools to support the three of us, including our baby boy Adrian, during the early efforts. I had a Master's degree and would also seek a teaching job, if necessary. We both soon found out when we applied to the area school districts that she and I were not the type of teachers they wanted. We were considered troublemakers because of the negative publicity in the press. At preliminary interviews our application or letters of interest were in files along with the clippings from news articles about MAYO. The school administrators made no effort to hide the clippings from us.

Juan Patlan and his wife, Elena, were to relocate to Carrizo Springs, the county seat for Dimmit County, which is adjacent to Zavala County. Both were originally from there. In La Salle County, we relocated William Leon "Bill" Richey and Linda Harrison, his wife, both of whom were Anglos. She was from Amarillo in the Texas panhandle and he was from Harlingen in the Rio Grande Valley. Bill and I had been classmates at Texas A & I, and we had attended St. Mary's University together. They had been MAYO supporters and were interested in assisting in the early organizing that would take place in the Winter Garden area. Bill and Linda moved to Cotulla and Luz and I began work in Cristal. Once the local Chicanos in Cotulla responded to Bill and Linda's organizing efforts and they felt the local Chicano community leaders could work by themselves on the plan for the Winter Garden, they relocated to Crystal City. Bill became the office and grant manager and proposal writer for the Winter Garden Project, as well as my political advisor and top lieutenant through the balance of 1969. Ultimately, though, the Patlans did not relocate to Carrizo Springs.

The numbers of Chicanos residing in Cristal were sufficient to take over the school board and city governments electorally; we already knew this from the earlier Chicano victories in 1963. These Chicanos were not afraid of saying that they wanted power or of being accused of plotting a takeover. On the contrary, they boldly proclaimed it as their political agenda.

After we moved to Cristal in late June, Luz and I began to make the rounds of the neighborhoods among the families I knew, to introduce them to her, my wife, and to our son Adrian. Slowly we began to organize around the issues Chicano students had raised the previous spring. With every family visit I was energized because of the warm and cooperative spirit with which we were received. Each family had a story to tell my wife of my roles in the 1963 campaign of Los Cinco Candidatos and in PASO. They recalled what a fearless and motivational public speaker I was. Often during these home visits, individual members would pledge to support me in any organizing or political campaign I would now initiate as an educated young adult. They volunteered information on the problems Chicano students had with the schools. They felt disorganized, powerless, and expressed cynicism to us about participating in electoral activity since the defeat of Los Cinco in the subsequent elections of 1965.

Luz and I did not take advantage of these very personal encounters and conversations to mention the goals of the Winter Garden Project at this early juncture. We merely introduced ourselves to the community, projected the image of a young, professional couple that had come home to begin their adult life among friends. Time was on our side: there would be other opportunities to organize and protest against the schools after we integrated and fit into the Chicano community as one of them.

We made friends with the relatives of the student protesters from the spring semester. Parents began to trust us around them and their children. After I was reminded of the MAYO pledge to assist them with a protest during several home visits, Luz and I begin to hold meetings with these parents and students to discuss issues of importance in

Cristal and around the state. Since we were in constant telephone conversation with MAYO headquarters in San Antonio and with other MAYO leaders across the state, Luz and I were always informed of the happenings in the state, the nation, and the world. Older Chicanos began to respect our informed opinion; students wanted to be with us constantly and even volunteered to baby-sit Adrian without pay.

During the home visits that summer I was reminded of the events the previous school semester, shortly before the end of school, when the school administration of the Crystal City schools had approved the selection of an Anglo queen by the teachers, not the students, for a baseball tournament. The students wanted the right to vote and elect their own choice as queen. The result of such an election was obvious to all, since the Chicano majority of the student body would probably select a queen from among themselves, not an Anglo. The school authorities refused the demand for democratic elections and offered a compromise to majority rule. Instead of just one Anglo queen they created another slot for a Chicano queen. "Separate but equal" had reared its doctrinal head in Cristal. The Chicano students began to talk and organize for a walkout.

MAYO leaders in San Antonio sent Juan Patlan and me to Cristal to talk the students out of a school walkout for fear that the teachers would fail these students for missing class and final exams. A walkout that late in the school year was doomed to fail from the start. The administration would not have to react to the walkout. They could simply do nothing until the year ended and then fail all the protesters. In order to convince the students to calm down and accept the compromise of a dual set of queens for the time being, we had to commit MAYO resources and organizers to helping them with a walkout in the upcoming fall of 1969. Now that time had come and my wife and I were the organizers.

Luz and I joined a large group of MAYO protesters in Austin and took along some Chicano students from Cristal. We were going up to support the workers of Economy Furniture, who were on strike. Management had simply ignored their demands for increased wages, elimination of split shifts, and collective bargaining. These Chicano workers were in their eighth month of strike, and they needed outside help and support, but organized labor had refused their call for help. Unions never had supported nonunion Chicano workers with their struggles to improve working conditions. In their pursuit of union goals and power over the relationship of labor to management, organized labor only worked with their own affiliates. Regardless of this being a union/nonunion issue as well, Chicanos had to support Chicanos.

During the drive to and from Austin, the students and I discussed not only the Economy Furniture strike but also the pros and cons of a possible walkout in Cristal during the fall. The students that made the trip were cashing in their chips: they were still upset with Juan Patlan and me for having canceled the plans for a walkout in the spring. During our visit they kept reminding me of MAYO's commitment to return and help organize a protest the next fall. Luz and I couldn't tell them we already were organizing a plan for the entire Winter Garden area; we had learned from past experience that organizers don't impose a plan on a community. Instead, the individuals in that community have to originate the thought, take ownership of the idea, create consensus around the issue or issues, and then mobilize. There are some shortcuts, however; the more astute organizers will plant the seed of an issue, idea, or plan among those in a group they seek to organize into supporters and followers. Then, the organizer will graciously accept the very same idea as an original proposal from the group when it is voiced by someone. The idea has thus become that of the group and not the organizer. Another shortcut to building rapport and solidarity with potential recruits for an organizing effort is to simply voice agreement with and repeat the propositions or complaints made to the organizer as one's own views. I learned this by listening that summer and fall of 1969 to student and parent complaints about the administrators and teachers in the public schools. I didn't just repeat their complaints to them as if they were mine merely to express empathy. I repeated them to emphasize my understanding of the problem, because I also had experienced them myself, and to drive home the need for Chicano group solidarity in order to end the injustices once and for all.

As we made the four-hundred-mile round trip to Austin, I detailed to the students in the car who pressed me to organize a walkout all the hassles that Chicano students and parents would go through if a walkout were to occur in the fall. "Parental support is crucial to the success of a walkout," I said to them with the intent of teaching them their first lesson in obtaining resources for the organizing effort. I asked each of the students if they could count on *both* parents to stand with them. Luz and I asked each of them about their relatives and the support they could enjoy among them. We asked each of them if their parents had been involved with the earlier walkout effort in the spring. I recall discussing the need not only for a walkout but also for a complete takeover of the school board in the upcoming election in the spring of 1970. The students looked at me in the rearview mirror of the car as if I was from another planet. They had no concept of elections or how we could do that. They were only interested in fighting back against gringo oppression. They had no plan, but, they all knew that MAYO knew how to plan. They had read the many newspaper stories about MAYO walk-outs in other school districts.

The system in Cristal was not changing. The number of Chicanos being pushed out of the school system was outrageous, nearing the 87 percent mark. Corporal punishment was administered to Chicanos liberally along with expulsions from class and even the school. Speaking Spanish was prohibited, and the entire curriculum was Anglo-centered. The Anglo interpretation of the Battle of the Alamo depicted the white outside agitators from Kentucky and Tennessee as heroes, while the lawful Mexicans were labeled "blood thirsty," dictatorial, and brutal. This whitewashed version of history was regularly pushed down the students' craws, just as in my day and that of Luz's. She had grown up in Falfurrias, but it was not any different: the cafeteria food was made exclusively for the Anglo diet, and the personnel in the entire system was almost completely white, save a bus driver, janitor, a teacher or two. Students, both white and brown, were taught the prejudices of the Anglo community. We had learned to keep our place and they learned how to tell us what place that was.

Our community was divided into a white area and several Mexican areas. The town itself was physically divided and racially segregated by railroad tracks running through the center of the community. Our schools had been, and continued to be in 1969, segregated by schools and within the individual buildings by grades, curriculum, and pro-grams. The result is that, as Chicanos, we learn to hate ourselves for not being able to become Anglo, which is tough for a seven year old. The purpose of education was, and still is, to make us into non-Chicanos as quickly as possible; the irony here is that Anglos don't really want us to become Anglos. The prevailing notion among Anglo "educators" at the same time was that Chicanos couldn't learn, not that white teachers couldn't teach.

Our job as organizers was to get the kids and their parents from A to Z on MAYO's Winter Garden Project. By channeling the students' anger and frustration, together with the parental concern for a remedy to the escalating problems in the school district, Luz and I began to set up situations in which steps would be taken by the Chicano community toward the MAYO plan. We already knew from prior experience that organizing among adult Chicanos is done at three levels simultaneously. First, one appeals to their ethnic consciousness as Chicanos—"The gringos hate the Chicanos." Second, you appeal to them as a working class of poor people, as they were—"The *rich* gringos hate the *poor* Chicanos." And, third, you appeal to them as an interest group, as migrant workers, hospital aides, cooks, barbers, mechanics, butchers, truckers, masons, domestics, field hands, painters, housewives, and the like— "The *rich, land-owning* gringos hate *poor, migrant* Chicano farm workers." This rhetorical approach covers all the possible ideological appeals to join an organization, such as cultural nationalism, class consciousness, and personal economic motives.

Getting students to walk out was easy. Carrying forward the plan to achieve lasting power to effect the student demands was very tough. MAYO had not been able to take control of any school district in all of our previous walkouts, so we wanted an opportunity to develop and implement a different organizing strategy. In earlier efforts we mistakenly took on the building principal, the superintendent and the school board. We had not yet learned that the school system is but a small part of the entire Anglo structure.

Taking On the System at the *Coyunturas*

All component parts of the system, or as many as possible and feasible, need to be engaged as targets of a collective action from the beginning of a protest, the reason being that the structure is so large, that seldom does one part know what another part is doing, much less agree with what and how they are responding to each action. The South Texas Anglo hierarchy was not a monolith and not homogeneous: it could be divided, and pitted against itself. The system was multileveled and interlocking. This setup made for many breaks and *coyunturas* (joints) of opportunity that could become windows to enter and engage the system and be used as pressure points.

The Anglo personnel within the system have always had conflicting loyalties and pressures. For example, a local teacher or school board that commits a travesty against a Chicano can be reported to both higher state and federal education authorities and to both state and federal civil rights agencies—not to mention private entities—and made the target of public protests. The institutional response from each of these levels then gets directed at the teacher and school board. These institutional responses usually consist of an inquiry or investigation directed at local persons, and local officials then have to respond to the agency making the inquiry or initiating the investigation. The organizers of the protest can choose to dramatize this development or imply wrongdoing on the part of the school board that warranted such an investigation. Each inquiry or response can be used to further intensify the issue and aggravate the differences of opinion between these segments of the system: they are pitted against each other. The organizer is in charge in this type of scenario, not the system. An Anglo school administrator acting in the role of system supporter will behave in one predictable way, as the culture of the system demands, but as an individual will vary and act another way, as values and morality dictate. In other words, most Anglos if left to their own conscience will act as a decent human being. Unfortunately, Anglos work with and for other Anglos in the system and in an institutional culture that demands team cooperation and is hierarchical. They will do as they must, to preserve the system, at all costs to themselves and others.

We realized, then, that if we could successfully carry out this overall organizing attack on the system we would present our own educational curriculum for Chicanos in the schools and also achieve control over the allocation of resources from City Hall to the citizens of Cristal. We felt we had to show Chicanos across the Southwest and Midwest how to organize into a political party, which the Chicano movement did not have in the late 1960s.

The walkout strategy would prove most effective and fruitful if done in the fall of 1969. We could easily move the Chicano community from step A to step Z in the overall plan for the Winter Garden if we could win the walkout and take control of the school districts, then take the city governments and in the process build a political party for contesting partisan elections in the three-county area.

It sure helped that I was from Cristal, and that I took time to make home visits and introduce my wife and son. In other walkouts, MAYO organizers had been susceptible to the "outside agitator" charge, but not this time. The aborted spring 1969 student walkout over the selection of sweethearts for the baseball tournament had been an excellent, preliminary training exercise for the students on how to engage the school authorities. The parents and students recalled the experience with us, and we took that as an opportunity to have them analyze the event from the perspective of how to win in the next round of confrontation and protest. We felt that the "enemy" had been scouted and tested for us the previous spring by these students and their parents.

The superintendent, the high school principal, the assistant high school principal (who was now a Mexican American), and the school board had during the previous confrontation with Chicano students predictably utilized the various "gringo tricks" I had anticipated and predicted to Juan Patlan when we had first observed and analyzed the situation. With every walkout I had participated in I had been able to add to a list of techniques and maneuvers that Anglos with authority, and working in the system as persons-in-charge, would utilize to thwart the efforts of those seeking change. I referred to these as gringo tricks, but in reality they are the tactics of all who are in power, and are used against all who are powerless. This list of tricks that I compiled is a menu of power relations, if you will, one that I later had published as a monograph entitled *The Gringo Manual on How to Handle Mexicans.*

The parents had learned some of these tricks firsthand in the earlier, aborted walkout; they also learned from that prior exercise to trust the judgment of their children and to follow their leadership. (This aspect had been the most difficult step in prior walkouts organized by MAYO in other cities: parents, Chicano parents notwithstanding, always assume they know better.) And, this was Cristal, not just any South Texas community. The Chicanos in this town knew about organizing, struggle, confrontation, and pressure from gringos. The parents also knew about participating in electoral activity, having been involved with Los Cinco and PASO in 1963.

Actually, though, the 1963 effort was seen as a fiasco, not a first victory, by some Chicanos in 1969, and that attitude was difficult to overcome. Some of the families Luz and I visited during that summer were cynical because of the ultimate defeat of Los Cinco after a single term of office in 1965. They felt that the gringo power structure was too powerful for Chicanos to overthrow. Some Chicano families repeated—in the confidence of their own homes—as potentially true the stereotypes held by Anglos that Mexican Americans as a people were incapable of ethnic unity. Some repeated to us that, like the proverbial crabs attempting to climb out of the fisherman's pail, we would pull each other down. The Chicano community in Cristal, and certainly many Chicanos across the state, had internalized the negative media portrayal of that effort as a fiasco.

The first Chicano effort of Los Cinco Candidatos had been dismissed by the Anglo media, by the white-controlled Democratic Party, and by local Anglo influentials as an aberration of extreme racial politics fomented by outside radicals—both labor and Chicano—from San Antonio. Local Anglos boasted of how harmonious the relations had always been between them and the Mexican people of Cristal and South Texas. When Chicanos accept the status quo and are meek, relations are harmonious. The Anglos pick out and legitimize the Chicano leaders of their choice for the Chicano community. When Chicanos challenge the system and become active in that pursuit, relations become strained. And, when Chicanos pick out and legitimize their own leaders, the Anglos label these Chicano leaders as "radicals" and actively seek to discredit them and find methods to sanction or silence them.

Los Cinco Candidatos, as city council members, had been ousted from office in an April 1965 election by a coalition of middle-class agavachado Mexican Americans and by more sophisticated Anglos who knew how to mask their prejudices toward us. This coalition named itself Citizens Association Serving all Americans (CASAA). But a true coalition involves equals and the parties to this association were anything but equals. CASAA had as members every white wanna-be, sellout, agavachado Mexican American residing in Cristal along with every Mexican American who was economically dependent on Anglos. CASAA held power from 1965 to 1970, when the second resurgence of Chicano power came to fruition. While some Chicanos were cynical of the first outcome in 1963, they were not apathetic in our renewed effort in 1969.

Relocation to Cristal

When we relocated to Cristal, Luz, Adrian, and I settled into my mother's house with her. The other home that my Dad had left the family, which was located at the edge of barrio Mexico Chico, had been burned to the ground a few months prior. I had made the mistake, during my Christmas furlough from the army, of announcing that Luz and I would be returning to Cristal as organizers upon my release from the military. According to the closest neighbors, a block from the house, they saw a couple of young Anglo kids drive by their house on a motorcycle and head toward my dad's house. Minutes later—shortly after they sped by on their return—the neighbors saw the beginnings of a fire in the vicinity of the house. The neighbors had no phone service but walked over to someone who did and called the fire department. By then a blaze was going up one side of the two-story house. The fire department took its time to respond and upon arrival decided it was too late to put it out, according to the neighbors who had reported the fire. The firemen, and our neighbors, watched it burn to the ground. When I learned of this incident I requested the report from the fire department, and discovered that it did not attribute the fire to arson, though the house had no electricity or tenants.

There was no further investigation, despite the allegations from the neighbors concerning two kids on a motorcycle. They described both the kids and the bike to the fire marshall. One kid was a redhead who matched the appearance of a boy I knew, but no arrests were ever made. My mother had been unable to obtain insurance for the property because it was vacant, so my family suffered a terrible loss with the burning of this house. After my rage at this event—and with those involved with the arson cover-up—had subsided I took a positive direction.

I Sought the Challenge

I had sought out from the MAYO Board of Directors the Cristal assignment. It was payback time! All the years of discrimination toward la raza and my family that I had witnessed firsthand and personally felt could now be avenged. My *coraje*, my rage, could find outlet in action, not just talk and angry emotion. The Winter Garden Project was to be under my direction, in my hands. I felt as if the entire weight of righting all the transgressions and wrongs leveled against la raza in Cristal and the three-county area was to be my responsibility.

The mechanics of preparation for the Cristal walkout were handled much like all the other school boycotts. MAYO headquarters alerted all chapters that the Cristal walkout was imminent. The newly organized and now operational MALDEF was put on notice of upcoming events and given a history of the attempted spring walkout. The local Chicano parents were recruited to attend school board meetings and witness firsthand the contempt with which the Anglo-controlled board treated their children. The students were coached on how to avoid the "gringo tricks" when meeting with the local high school principal, superintendent, or school board.

We had a process now for keeping the enemy engaged: we simply polarized the situation initially by making demands of the school board for reform. After clearly articulating what we wanted in the form of a written demand, we also defined the solution that would satisfy our demand. In other words, we first told people what the issue was in our own words by defining the problem, then defined the best response or reform that would constitute victory.

We would depict the opposition as our "enemy," responsible for the existing situation. We made them the problem because they resisted social change. Next, we would force their hand into revealing their true makeup or character: get them angry enough to be careless, ruthless, shameless, racist or violent in public. If our demands did not create that public anger, we would call them names to their faces. That anger, manifested as a public display of gringo prejudice or discrimination we could then transfer away from us, individually, as prejudice against la raza. That would be "their mistake." It would become our justification for action, them against us. That final step usually polarized them into our initial definition of them as being the enemy, a strategy as a self-fulfilling prophecy.

In this walkout we had more available resources than in others. The Chicano people in Cristal had had experience with community fundraising for political causes during the first revolt led by Juan Cornejo and PASO. They not only gave money from their own pockets but regularly held community-wide fundraisers for political causes. We knew before the walkout began that we could again count on their support. We knew that during the walkout we would send our student leaders from Cristal to appear before any audience to get the word out and bring pressure to bear on the state and local education officials.

As part of the preparation for the Winter Garden project we also had obtained financial support from foundations for the area-wide organizing effort. We now had money for salaries that would hold out for many months. We had the lawyers ready now that MALDEF had been formed. We had the Chicano newspapers across the state, as well as the MAYO publications, ready to report on our project. We had the commitment from a local merchant, Victoriano "Nano" Serna, to help us begin our own Spanish-language newspaper in Cristal, *La Verdad* (The Truth). We had made contact with some Chicano teachers in San Antonio who were ready to come and teach our Chicano kids during weekends if a walkout occurred. We had the Chicano community very politicized; we had money; and we had built a semblance of organization during the summer. At the beginning of the school year we were very well poised with enough student and parental support in Cristal to take on the schools and begin the Winter Garden project to create Aztlan, and it was my firm belief that Luz and I would begin the process to recapture our Chicano homeland.

8

The Thirty-Ninth MAYO Walkout

A Diary

When Chicano students in Texas in the late 1960s began protesting un-
equal educational opportunity by walking out of school, these protests
were called walkouts. In California, however, they were called
blowouts. In other places, a walkout might be called a school strike,
huelga (Spanish for strike), or class boycott. As a member of MAYO, I did
not keep a diary on every walkout that I was involved with, but I did on
the last one I organized, in Cristal. By 1969 I had participated in Texas
walkouts in Plainview, Lubbock, San Antonio, Kingsville, Uvalde,
Hondo, Edcouch-Elsa, Alice, El Paso, Del Rio, San Marcos, and Houston
to name a few locations. I had also been involved to some degree in a few
walkouts in other states, such as Glendale, Arizona; Kalamazoo, Flint,
and East Lansing, Michigan; Denver, Colorado, and Los Angeles and
San Jose, California. The state MAYO office kept track of our activity
and I recall the staff there listing the 1969 school walkout in Crystal City
as number thirty-nine.

In Cristal, we sought and obtained community support and leadership before urging the students to escalate their protests to a walkout.
The principal leaders of the fall 1969 walkout were the younger siblings
and classmates of the seniors who had just graduated in May. The top

leadership was Severita Lara, Mario Treviño, and Diana Serna, a junior and two freshmen, respectively.

The first contact with the school administrators in the fall was between Severita and the high school principal, John B. Lair. She presented him with a list of grievances that Chicano students wanted addressed or remedied immediately. He gave her the runaround and ultimately referred her to the superintendent, John Billings, who passed the buck to the school board, saying, "I can't give you these things. I have no power. Only the school board can do this because many items on the list require board approval." These maneuvers by the school authorities played into my hands. I had been holding educational sessions with the student leaders on the power relations between Chicanos and Anglos, and showing them my list of "gringo tricks." The Chicano response to these tricks was to not fall into their traps, or better yet, to pull our own tricks on them.

Severita attempted to get a place on the school board agenda and was unsuccessful. We advised her to print up the grievances on a leaflet and pass it out at the high school. She did and was promptly suspended from school for refusing to give up the leaflets to the assistant principal, Paulino Mata, and for not promising to cease her activity.

We immediately called the press protesting the suspension, and also called MALDEF, where we obtained the services of Gerald "Jerry" Lopez, a staff attorney. By utilizing basic legal maneuvers, he had Severita reinstated in no time. The principal and his assistant, in their haste to rid themselves of Severita and her leaflets, had suspended her without a hearing, no due process, and all persons, young and old, citizens or not, rich or poor, are entitled to due process as a constitutional right.

Severita returned to the high school a heroine. Students interested in her leaflet and its content eagerly sought her out in the halls and between classes to offer support and encouragement. She now began referring to the list of student grievances as *demands*. The school board then agreed to place her list of grievances on the agenda for their next meeting. We got busy mobilizing the parents that we had organized in support of the students.

We knew that the board would not accede to the student demands. Instead they would rebuff them and ask that their parents attend the meeting. As anticipated, the school board did not even pretend to listen to Severita or Armando Treviño, brother of Mario and a recent graduate. The students were dismissed and admonished to bring parents to talk with the principal or superintendent about individual complaints each student had.

In typical fashion, the school board made the same mistake in dealing with these students as they had in dealing with the students in the spring. A group of Anglo alumni had approached the school board and requested that the Homecoming Queen for 1969–70 be selected from among girl students whose parents had graduated from Crystal City High School, and had offered to organize and sponsor the Homecoming events. Without regard for how many girls had parents that had graduated from the high school, the school board approved the plan. Chicana students were outraged at being disfranchised simply because their parents had quit and not graduated from the high school; only six of 280 Chicanas were eligible. The school board had also ignored the student demand that the cheerleading squad be comprised of more than one token Chicana and the rest Anglos.

We approached the fathers of the students, particularly those with daughters, and said to them that the white administrators and school board thought their daughters were ugly for having brown legs and being Mexican. This got the fathers raving mad, since no father wants to think his daughter is ugly. Chicano males knew then and know now that they are powerless and impotent before Anglo authority, and impotence, even in politics, is taboo among Chicano males. In order to save face, the fathers told us to talk to the mothers because if they themselves got involved and went to confront the principal or school board violence was sure to ensue. It was an empty threat, but we conveniently took their advice and recruited the mothers as the front-line of support for the students. At the next school board meeting we took the students, accompanied by their mothers, but again, the board refused to consider the list of demands. The board president, Ed Mayer, a Del Monte plant administrator, explained that the list contained items best addressed by the principals, and that the parents and students should go see them.

I had begun my diary of events. The following pages are what I wrote during those days; they can best tell the story of the walkout:

December 6, 1969
Several nights before the meeting with the Board, we had the students rehearse their presentations. The examples, substantiating and defending every demand, were gone over and over with the students. Our evening included role-playing with Bill Richey (he and his wife, Linda, had been the initial organizers in Cotulla) and me playing the devil's advocate. My wife, Luz, and the students were highly amused. As the night progressed, our confidence in the students' ability to take on the school board was reaffirmed. I left the final touching up on minor points to Luz, Richey and Linda. I went for a beer.

Since our arrival in Cristal one of the most difficult tasks had been to transfer the opinions and beliefs of my companions into action, particularly when discussion centered around the students' problems. Male Chicano parents, for some reason, do not want to understand the issue or even hear of the problem. They will shift the responsibility for action to their *viejas,* their women, "my old lady." A typical response was, "Don't talk to me about that, talk to my wife. She'll go see the principal." Female Chicano parents reacted in opposite fashion. They were eager, if not anxious, to confront whomever necessary on behalf of their children. I won't wait for my intellectual capacity to reason out this strange behavior; I will rely on my understanding of the psychology of a beer joint crowd to overcome this *macho* perversion.

On several occasions, Julian Salas, an elected Justice of the Peace without an office or salary, Victoriano "Nano" Serna, the owner of the Oasis Drive-in, advertising sponsor of *La Verdad* and my local mentor, and I would drink beer together at several bars. At each and every one of the bars, we'd raise the issue of the impending Board meeting. We'd talk about the specific issues. We talked about the guts of the students. We talked about the general conditions in which Chicanos found themselves. Eventually, others within hearing range would echo our remarks. At some point, the predominant conversation in the bar was the school trouble. With that accomplishment, we would leave for another bar. The scenario would repeat itself.

Every night our agenda was the same. Nano, Julian and I made our rounds again and again. The crowd would still be busy telling jokes, talking about women, complaining about their jobs, and drinking beer. Excepting a few newcomers, the school issue was old hat and immediately would be picked up by the drinkers, once we initiated the discussion. I notice a qualitative difference in their remarks, depending on the time we visited. The detachment, objectivity and reflection on the issues that is demonstrated in the early evening when the first beers are downed is gone by 9 or 10 P.M. The beer loosens their inhibitions and with that, their tongues.

Beertalk after 10 P.M. escalates to confronting teachers, principals, the Superintendent, the School Board and anybody connected to their kids' problems. Commitments are made in loud voices for all to hear. There are boasts and personal arrogance in making of commitments to take on all the gringos. Invariably, the beertalk gets to threats of violence and *macho* bravado.

Nano, Julian and I have developed a plan. They are going to make the rounds of the beer joints early the following evening. They will enlist the assistance of most members of *Ciudadanos Unidos* so that each bar would have at least two of our "plants" two hours or so before the school board meeting on December 8th. The idea is to remind the now sober and somewhat apprehensive beer drinkers of their boasts, threats, and commitments made in front of their friends, co-workers and compadres, the night before. Chicanos highly prize the ethic of having *palabra*, integrity of your word. We think we can shame them for not keeping their word, their palabra, by going to the meeting instead of saying, "talk to my *vieja* about that!"

December 8, 1969

The day of the meeting, Bill, Luz and I couldn't get a thing done around the office. By mid-afternoon, as the school let out, the students started coming in. Estimations were made of the crowd size we think will go to the meeting. Copies of the demands were made and collated, and the final dress rehearsal was held. Luz left early to make sure the women were coming. Bill stayed with the students. I checked with Nano to see if the men were ready to hit the bars beginning around 6 P.M.

All being ready, the students, some parents, and I arrived into the parking lot of the Superintendent's office early at seven. As the minutes ticked by, the crowd, mostly students and mothers, began to gather. We knocked on the door several times for admission. Nothing. The doors had been locked since the close of business at five. Only upon the arrival of the first member of the Board was the door opened from the inside. Someone was inside all the time and knew when we knocked and when the member knocked. They must have been watching us from inside.

The air was tense. The time was eight o'clock. Nothing had moved inside. Outside, the students were there by the hundreds. The women were huddled in groups of threes and fours. Smaller children were running around. Others, a few men, were sitting in cars around the area. An occasional lighting of a cigarette flashed the male silhouettes, some with hats, inside the cars. But, they wouldn't get out! A few men were present. The main body of men was missing, but not for long. Suddenly, a long line of cars was driving up the street in our direction. Parking where they could, the men, some led by Nano and others by Julian, got out of their cars and joined the crowd at the periphery. Nano and Julian did a good job! They flashed me proud smiles from the rear of the crowd. I was inaccessible to them being way up front by the doors.

The front doors opened shortly after 8 P.M. and the crowd surged forward. As best we could, we made our way through the front office and narrow hallway leading to the usual meeting room; we were shocked. There were no chairs. Those in front, leading the walk-in immediately stood at the back of the room. These were the students and the women. Those in the back of the crowd—the men—had to stand in front of the school board members, by their sides, and around behind them as they crowded in. I loved it! The men, the machos, were front and center.

We started opening windows for those still outside who were not able to come in or arrived late so they could see and hear. By half past eight, the president, Ed Mayer, called the meeting to order. As he proceeded through the roll call and reading of minutes of the previous meeting, the crowd smiled and giggled. The Board Secretary had read the section dealing with the previous confrontation which canceled the coronation of the Homecoming Queen by Board action. Suddenly, the crowd was shocked. The Secretary read that Urbano Esquivel, one of two Mexican Americans on the School Board, had made a motion to introduce a course into the Social Studies curriculum on Mexican Americans and their contributions. Nobody knew about that. We never heard that said at the last meeting. Somebody had added that motion after the fact! Puzzled faces turned to Severita, Armando and Bill, then to me. The crowd, especially the student leaders, got very nervous. That was one of our demands for tonight. The Secretary finished the reading. The President called for discussion and there being none, called for the vote. They were accepted as read.

The President stopped trembling long enough to look up and around at the crowd. He noticed they were completely surrounded by Chicanos. They should have had chairs! Their tactic of making us feel uncomfortable by standing backfired. Armando and Severita seized the opportunity. She addressed the President and told him they had something to say and had asked to be on the agenda. She and Armando began to pass out copies of the petition for all members. As she walked up to the front to face them at the table, Ed Mayer, the President, mumbled something about already knowing what it was all about. He proceeded to raise his voice and say that this matter had been discussed and they had nothing to say. "This Board has done all it's going to do," he admonished Severita and instructed her to talk to her Principal. Armando bolted forward next to Severita and accused Mayer of giving the people the run-around. That did it. Mayer, in gringo fashion said, "You're out of order, boy. This meeting is adjourned. Is there a motion?" I don't know if somebody made a motion, much less voted. Pandemonium reigned. The gringo board members all rose together with Esquivel and started for the door. Only Eddie Treviño lagged behind and told Severita and Armando in a low voice to keep fighting. He gave me an eye wink and smile as he also made for the door. As the school board members tumbled and pushed themselves out of the room, the crowd came outside. Confusion ran wild. Cussing in Spanish and questions were yelled at them from inside and outside the room.

Severita and I immediately made our way out the door onto the front lawn. She began calling the crowd to listen to her. I started clapping loudly to command attention. She spoke in a commanding voice amidst the pandemonium. Eventually, the crowd rallied around Severita and the other student leaders. She began exhorting the crowd with questions in Spanish, as I remember, "*¿Ven como nos tratan?* See how they treat us? *¿Ven como nos tratan a todos, nuestros padres y madres?* See how they treat all of you, our parents and mothers? *¿Se fijaron en el Mayer, temblando? ¿Seria miedo o coraje?* Did you notice Mayer, shaking? Was it fear or rage? *¿Ven como no les importa de nosotros?* See how they don't care about us? *!Los gringos no les importa de nosotros! ¡No nos quieren en las escuelas!* Gringos don't care about us! They don't want us in school!" The crowd didn't need much prodding nor a verbal replay of the action. They wanted to take action. The students knew all about this type of board behavior; we had practiced this very possibility. They already had been ignored and ejected from board meetings before. The mothers knew that they had not been listened to by the board members before when they came with their children, either. The fathers, who had told us to talk to their wives about this problem, now knew that the time called for bold action. The school board had not listened to them tonight, either. We had cornered both the school board and the macho men with one tactic. This feels real good!

The other students then took turns speaking. The analysis by the students began taking on the rhetoric of denunciations and diatribes. They were applauded repeatedly and egged on by the crowd. Finally, the words came out in English: "Let's walkout! Walkout! Walkout!" The crowd roared back in English, "Walkout! Walkout! Walkout!"

History is going to be made in Cristal daily from this night on.

December 9, 1969
Around 7:30 A.M. parents and students began congregating across the street from the high school. As cars drove up to unload students, our people would urge them to join them across the street. Several parents were at the sides of their children across the street. Some mothers brought hot chocolate, pan dulce, and cookies to the protesting students. Bill Richey and I watched the action from half a block down the street. By 10:00 A.M. over 500 people were across the street. As the day went on, many students were intentionally persuaded to leave our ranks and go into the school. This part of our plan is based on the idea that our boycott should increase in numbers, not decrease. Usually, the

Walkout and demonstration at Crystal City High School, 1969.

target of a protest will just wait out the demonstration. Usually, they prevail just because the protesters cannot sustain the initial enthusiasm. The protests are evaluated in terms of numbers present the first day and then the second day, etc. We must plan carefully. Stage it so the gringos think this is the second Mexican Revolution coming. There were too many outside protesting, too soon. We should not peak too early. More importantly, we need spies inside to tell us what was going on in the building and over the intercom.

Shortly before lunch, Severita, Mario, Diana, Richard Espinoza, Ester Ynosencio and others went as a delegation into the school to see the Principal, John B. Lair. Since the Board at last night's meeting had said to see the Principal, they went in to talk petition demands. He wasn't there, according to the Assistant Principal, Paulino Mata, and he graciously offered to talk with them about the petition.

The students ignored him. Mata was instructed to tell both the Principal and the Superintendent to be available at 3:00 P.M. and they left. They walked out of the office and began lining up the boycotters, according to the plan of things to do, into a column of twos. Before the 3 o'clock appointment, a march from the high school through the downtown and back, about 25 blocks, seemed like a good idea with which to occupy their time. Empty time is the enemy of a protest. People get bored, scared, anxious, depressed, and the like. You must stay busy. Keep them focused on tactics and you on the grand strategy. You must prepare many things to do for as many people as you can. Marches and rallies are perfect examples. So is a newsletter and voter registration.

It was a beautiful march. Cars honked; fists clenched in a power salute shot up everywhere as the students responded in kind. Pictures were taken. And, everyone marching or looking at the marchers, had a good time. It was a fun march. This is the first political march in Cristal. It sure wasn't a parade.

Mario Treviño, the only male student leader, had armed himself with a cassette tape recorder. Others had cameras and more tape recorders. The students had learned from us how lethal the use of cameras and recorders as weapons against the police could be. Mario, to practice with the recorder, proceeded to reach out into spectators lining East Crockett, East and West Zavala Streets for comments on the students walkout, march, and victory. He liked playing television reporter. These are some comments I got from the tape:

Pura Mendoza (housewife): *Vamos a ganar . . . si todos nos proponemos, seguro que si venceremos.* We are going to win . . . if all of us are determined, of course, we will prevail.

Irma Benavides (housewife): I think that if the school board had listened to these students in the first place, they wouldn't have this situation on their hands. They had plenty of time. In fact, this goes back about 10 years, they have known about it.

Elva Castillo (welfare mother): *Yo pienso que es muy bueno que se acaben las injusticias porque siempre han estado, por toda la vida. Haci de esta manera, todos unidos, se acabaran.* I think it is good for injustice to end because there has always been [injustice], all through life. In this way, all of us united, they will end.

Juanita Santos (grandmother of boycotter): *¡Esta muy bien! ¡y adelante! ¡todos unidos! ¡No se dejen!* This is real good! and forward! all united! Don't be taken advantage of!

Ester Mandujano (mother of boycotter): *Todo esto que andamos haciendo es una cosa razonable. Lo que queremos es igualdad para todo los Mexicanos en este pueblo de Crystal City . . .* All this that we are doing is a reasonable thing. What we want is equality for all Mexicans in this town of Crystal City. . . .

Ben Perez (father of boycotter): *Es una cosa buena. Pido que muera la descriminacion y viva el bienestar entre la raza. Si es que es un derecho que le corresponde a todo Mexicano no lease que sea nativo o emigrante en los Estados Unidos, tiene derecho a la leyes que nos respete la ley del los Estados Unidos dentro la ley y la justicia.* This is a good thing. I ask that discrimination die and the welfare of our people live. If it is a right in the United States to be protected by the law that also belongs to all Mexicans, regardless of being native born or immigrant, then the law must respect and protect us also within the law and for justice.

Reynaldo Maldonado (father of boycotter): *Todo esto esta bien hecho. Tengo gusto que no haya habido ninguna violencia y todo eso. Todo va bien en orden. Creo que los estudiantes estan bien . . . siempre todos unidos. Nos hizo falta mas padres aqui con los estudiantes para que ellos mismos tambien tengan confianza en uno, se sientan ellos con mas confianza tambien.* All of this is very well done. I am proud that there has been no violence and all of that. Everything is in order. I believe that the students are right . . . always be united. We are short of parents here with the students so that they also have confidence in them, so they feel confidence themselves, also.

The marchers got back to their picket posture by two in the afternoon. The student leaders again gathered their documents. I saw them as they nervously shuffled papers back and forth. It is not easy to confront authority or your superiors when you are vulnerable. Young people, children, are the most vulnerable. They have no rights anywhere, in any culture. The students paced the sidewalk. When the crowd got too quiet, someone would pierce the silence with a *"Viva la Raza."* The echo was deafening, especially to the news reporters from San Antonio who by now were at hand. The drive from San Antonio takes nearly 2 hours. As the students got restless, Armando, Mario's older brother, who was attending the local junior college in Uvalde, got a brilliant idea. He urged a handful of the students to cross the street with him onto the yard and up the steps of the entrance to the high school. This was not in the plan. I wondered what the hell he was up to. Acts of individual enterprise always are bound to happen and usually they all end up costing us plenty! Everyone thought the students were going en masse to the meeting. That most certainly was not the plan! Armando, however, stopped the group short of the doors and began a prayer. Only Armando's voice was heard above the huge silent body of students. When he finished, it went over very big with the parents and onlookers. Mario, Severita, and Diana then marched up the steps and into the door. Armando's performance made it seem that God himself was going up the steps with them to the negotiating session. I'll never forget the impact of that prayer.

Once inside, the students said to me they turned on the tape recorder and got down to business. The general content of the demands [was] gone over by Severita. Billings, the Superintendent, objected to being recorded. Mario said he turned it off and on again in the same motion as he apologized to the man. I can just see that fool gringo being suckered by Mario. Learning, training, practice pay off handsome rewards! The three men present, Billings, Lair, and Mata, didn't particularly care to follow the student demands in the order written.

The Superintendent got on the question of the counselor. Perhaps, it caught his eye, listed next to the last demand. The superintendent asked what was wrong with the present counselor, Mr. Moore.

Mario: He doesn't encourage the students to take the courses they really need.
Superintendent John Billings: Well, what do you mean?
Mario: Let me tell you. There are some persons, you know, don't make good grades. But, that doesn't mean they can't pass a course. Like art or shop, he says to take or take anything. Will they learn anything there?
Severita: We need sufficient things on loans, scholarships, courses and opportunities.
Superintendent Billings: This is the first year Mr. Moore operated. He has many other administrative duties he can't handle.
Severita: Is he not qualified?
Mario: Yes! Is he not qualified?
Superintendent Billings: Now, he will have the time.
Severita and Mario: Is he not qualified? He should be qualified.
Superintendent Billings: He is qualified.
Principal John B. Lair: Severita, some of these, we had even the experts to come down and explain some of these. No students showed up. There was no one to accept the scholarships. Not one. One of them right now is in the Navy ROTC and Army ROTC. We explained that to all our seniors last year and none of them accepted it. It was explained to them that they received books, tuition, clothes and $150 dollars a month. That was explained by the ROTC and no one accepted it. And, they get four years of education.
Mario: We don't want to go to the army. We want to go to school.
(Getting frustrated with the direction the conversation was going over the counselor, the Superintendent reportedly started over, with demand number 1.)
Superintendent Billings: Now Severita, you asked about election of cheerleaders. The school board policy on the method of election of cheerleaders is set. There is a policy. I have no authority to change that.
Severita: But Mr. Billings, they sent us to you and Mr. Lair. They said you . . .
Superintendent Billings: I said the most I could do were administrative problems.
Severita: How come they didn't discuss this with us when we were here?
Mario: Are you going to have us go back and forth?
Superintendent Billings: The way I read their motion, that was turned down. That's my interpretation of it.
Diana Serna: You mean you didn't look at all we asked for? These incidents and all that? Why?
Assistant Principal Paulino Mata: What we read is from the Minutes. It is difficult for me, us, to act. There is a ruling by the Board and that's what I have to go by.
Mario: We want a special meeting with the School Board and Principals. All the Principals. We want all the Principals, so we won't go back and forth.

Superintendent Billings: If the School Board would like to do that, it's fine. I can't tell the School Board what to do.

Severita: So you aren't giving us the election of students' class representative, cheerleaders, twirlers, most handsome, most beautiful, and most popular?

Superintendent Billings: The student body elects the most handsome and most beautiful.

All students at once: No we don't!

Principal Lair: Severita, we explained to you sometime ago that the teachers were told by the Board to select some of those.

(End of transcription of tape for this entry.)

The students sized up the situation. They were getting nowhere. The tricks we had studied in our training sessions had come up over and over, they said. When briefed on what had happened and I listened to the tape, I agreed. Instinctively, they banded closer together as Severita announced to the Administrative trio that they were going to stay away from school until they got what they wanted. Warning Lair that they were coming back to get their books from their lockers and didn't want "no" trouble, they stormed out. Other students quickly huddled with their leaders as they came out the door and across the street. I could see them shaking their heads in my direction where I was supposed to be parked.

Severita informed them of what happened. Someone gave her a bull-horn. She began relating their conversation to all in the area. Mario tried to re-play the tape over the bullhorn but it didn't work. She demanded unity and individual commitment to staying out as long as it took to get what they wanted. Everybody was told to go inside and get their books. She then invited them to regroup over at the Salon Campestre, the dance hall at the edge of town, for an informal meeting to make plans and have a record hop. She announced this was to be a public meeting, for all to come, mainly parents.

That night's rally was enthusiastic. Severita carefully and slowly read the student demands in Spanish. She gave examples of each and every demand in the revised petition. The parents were being educated. They had never heard of some of these things. Soon Severita's voice gave out. She had been yelling, arguing, directing, and constantly talking all day. Mario Treviño jumped in as the next speaker. He reviewed the topic of the Youth Association. "YA!" he called it. In Spanish, the word *Ya* means NOW! He introduced the Officers: Pete Villegas, Vice-President; Cecilia Guerrero, Secretary; Yolanda Avila, Treasurer; Diana Avalos, Reporter; and Andy Faz, Sergeant at Arms. The crowd guessed correctly, Mario was the President. An outline of the organizational structure, voting power, and meeting schedule was run down. Mario stressed the importance of their solidarity, as in this case. He argued that in this boycott situation they needed all the support they could get.

The remaining items on the agenda were covered by Diana Serna and Armando Treviño, Mario's older brother. They stated the need for more parents at the picket line in front of the school. Armando sternly lectured the students, out of school but not on the picket line, regarding loitering in the downtown area during school hours. He told them to be either at the picket line, at home, or back in school with the enemy. They helped the enemy by giving them issues to use against us, he reasoned. Following this line of reasoning he discussed how easy it was to give way to emotional outbursts and violent acts, especially when you are on the receiving end. He shocked the audience by announcing that he had learned the Texas Rangers were coming into town once again, like in 1963. He was not far off in his prophecy.

Armando then tried to tell the group that some students should stay in school. Some were needed to check out what was going on inside. The crowd would have none of that. Finally, he tried once again, this time on the subject of quotas. Pointing out the need for sustained and growing movement, he suggested the group pull out only 100 students per day. The group shouted him down. They wanted all the kids out, now!

Severita took the mike from Armando and changed the subject to that of a march. She reminded the audience that action was necessary but only if aimed at the target. A permit for a parade was going to be requested, and then all this crowd with their gritos, their shouts, could be heard all over Cristal. *¡Vamos a darle animo a Cristal!* she shouted herself. Let's give spirit to Cristal!

December 10, 1969
Chicano students at East Lansing High School in Michigan formed a committee to investigate their demands on this same day in December. Our MAYO contacts had relayed the news. The Marinez family in Cristal verified that also. That gesture averted a walkout there. In Cristal this same morning, some 500 students were now out of school and across the street on strike. The School Board still refused to listen to the student demands. They had called the Texas Education Agency (TEA) for investigators. Juan Ibarra and Gilbert Conolly, the investigators, had arrived. They have begun making the rounds in the community. Our people gave them an earful.

The *Zavala County Sentinel* came off the press and on the newsstands early this morning. The headlines read, "School Walk Out Continues."

Reading the article, our students got apprehensive. In the middle of the article was a paragraph that read: "Under school policy, students missing classes to participate in the demonstration will receive unexcused absences and two points off their grades for each day's absence." The school board was playing hardball and keeping itself aloof from our protest. Local gringos were getting very concerned, but not with our welfare. Some drove their cars as close to the curb as possible to intimidate our pickets. Students are reporting verbal threats, spitting, obscene gestures, and other incidents against them to the police. Nothing ever happens when the oppressed seek protection from the police.

More marches and rallies are planned for the week. The growing number of students in the walkout are beginning to cause some problems for the student leaders in terms of discipline and control. The kids are growing restless; there isn't much to do.

December 11, 1969
The three student leaders held a press conference in San Antonio this morning. The press was vicious. Grown gringos were trying to trip the students with loaded and leading questions. The kids were too sharp. They stayed on familiar ground and never took the bait. Richey has done an excellent job with them.

In Cristal this afternoon, while we were in San Antonio, another march was organized through downtown and over to the City Park on the Chicano side of town. No incidents were reported.

After the press conference we contacted some well known Chicano activists. Albert Peña Jr., Senator Joe Bernal, Rev. Henry Casso, John Alaniz, and Erasmo Andrade were eager to meet the students. They were full of praise for these young Chicanitos. We brought them up to date on events and discussed needs we had. They promised to generate "friendly" publicity, if necessary, from outside the state. Financially, they pledged some contributions. We didn't hit them up for money. Diana and Severita asked Peña and Casso to come the following Sunday to Cristal for the rally. They accepted. Mario asked the Senator for an investigation of the schools and to find out what the nature of the present TEA investigation was. Bernal agreed to try. The students came back to Peña and asked him to call Senator Edward Kennedy on their behalf. They wanted Kennedy to call someone connected with the Office of Civil Rights within Health, Education and Welfare (HEW) to help us. Peña said he'd call that day.

We went over to the Mexican American Unity Council. Juan Patlan, a co-founder of MAYO, was there. He was happy to see the students. After the congratulations, we talked about our meeting with Bexar

County Commissioner Albert Peña Jr. and the others. We asked Juan for some money for three round-trip plane tickets to Washington, D.C., for the students. Between the visit at Peña's office and Juan's we decided not to talk to Kennedy on the phone, but in person. It would be good publicity and a good tactic.

Juan promised to pick up half the cost. We agreed to raise the rest among our people at the right time. We agreed to keep the trip between us until confirmation was obtained of a meeting with Kennedy. Patlan will get the appointment in Washington.

December 12, 1969

The TEA investigators wanted the students to tell them under what conditions negotiations could begin. The students told them the unexcused absences and two points off per day policy of the Board had to be repealed for them to even think about conditions for negotiations. The TEA investigators went back to Austin.

On this day two additional major issues have developed. First, this afternoon a downtown march was held. When the demonstrators passed Speer's Mini-Max food store, the owner, J. L. Speer, ran out of his store toward the marchers. He grabbed two young men and pulled them out of the ranks. From his grocer's apron, he drew some dollar bills and threw them in their direction. He could barely be heard amidst the *"Viva's"* and other yells, but, the two students heard him clearly. He was firing them from their after school job at his store. He didn't like this Chicano power business.

Not many people noticed it happening, but, when the march reached its destination, Severita told everyone the details. Adding fuel to the fire was a rumor that Cleofas Tamez had been arrested by the Sheriff's police. Cleo was a freshman and alternate for Diana as a freshman student leader. Cleo arrived in time and told his story of harassment and fear to the group. The leaders decided to have Cleo and the other two boys relate their experiences to all the people that night at the meeting. I asked Richey to get Cleo to give us an affidavit of the harassment. Severita and the others found me this afternoon planning their Washington trip on the telephone. They told me of the incidents with the police and J. L. Speer. Then they showed me a statement from the Board President and Superintendent. It read:

The administration and School Board's main concern is that all students be in class. The School Board would like to meet in a unofficial meeting with from ten to fifteen parents to discuss the grievances as presented by the students being in school. It is parents that we want to talk with. These parents should be selected in any way the parents desire. However, let us stress that this is an unofficial meeting and cannot be conducted with large crowds of people and we want to discuss this situation with a representative group of parents. We will request a moderator from the Texas Education Agency. This meeting would be at 8:00 P.M. Wednesday, December 17, in the Administration Building. This meeting will only be held if students are back in normal classes on Monday, December 15. Please advise the Administration Office Monday if the parents will meet with us.

The students rehearsed their speeches for that night. Mario will talk about the issues behind the school boycott. Diana will talk about the arrest of Cleo. Cleo will tell his story and read his affidavit. The other two students don't want to speak but promised to be in the audience and verify the incidents. Severita will close the rally with a call for a consumer boycott with pickets of Speer's.

The crowd went along with the suggestion of a boycott. Severita was to bring up the message contained in the School Board statement she had gotten a copy of. If the crowd didn't react to the Speer's boycott, she was to forget the paper until the next day. We had to have an economic boycott against Speer's. We have to retaliate immediately and show them who is in charge here.

The crowd that night got angrier and angrier as the details poured out of Diana and Cleo's mouth. We had the fired boys stand next to the speaker's stand as the Speer's incident was related. All eyes were on these two boys who had lost their job for the walkout. The parents knew what that meant. They could be next. Mexicans have been held economic hostages for a long time. We needed the jobs, so we'll ignore the fight for our rights. Most of us will think of our personal families first before we think of our raza family. But, their anger and hate seems stronger this time than their reflection on the clear threat of job reprisals. Severita outlined our plans for defense and offense. Against these gringo tactics, we must boycott Speer's.

The people gave her a long, long and loud ovation tonight. Severita is real good. People know that we were the majority of the population AND majority of the consumers. We have Chicano Power and Money Power.

Carefully, Severita got into the School Board statement. She first reviewed the two incidents involving Cleo and the fired students, then, placed the demands in the perspective of events dating back to the Spring of '69. The obvious conclusion she wanted the audience to reach was that, first, gringos didn't keep their word, and second, the gringo contempt for the parents was the same as for them. The gringos would fight us before they would give in to us. Finally, she wanted it understood that fear was our biggest weakness. That we had to stand together and be powerful was her answer for all problems. The crowd agreed.

She read the school board statement quickly in English, then translated the consequences in Spanish. She lectured the crowd on not going back to school first, to then negotiate. She refused to even consider an unofficial meeting with the Board. She spat out the word "unofficial" over and over until the audience got the message. Acting officially, the Board had refused to listen, now, they believed the Chicano dumb enough to have faith in their "unofficial" actions. The section of the statement calling for a meeting "with parents only" was ignored by Severita, like we asked her to.

She felt she had gotten the maximum from her speech for that night. She was right. The crowd was going to boycott schools and anybody else until we got what we wanted. [Note: what follows is the affidavit of Cleofas Tamez, age 14, presented here as written by him.]

I was going toward the rally when a police car passed by. They returned, stopped and also stopped me, asked me for some identification. To my surprise, I asked why and their answer was "Boy, you don't ask me what for." My answer was I don't. Since they talked to me in a rash form I got frightened and ran. They caught up with me and told me to get in the car. Since I did not want to, they grabbed my arm and pulled me in and locked the door. They said they were going to ask me some questions. They asked my name as well as my mother's, what mine was and told me if I did not sign it I could wait for my Mom to come and get me out of jail in Carrizo. They took me to the sheriff's office and pulled me into it. They kept asking me the same questions over and over. Also who my father was and where he worked. I told them I would not answer because I did not have a Lawyer. I also asked "why was I picked up, is it because I am a Chicano?" "No" was their answer "we don't discriminate, besides all the officers of the High School are Chicanos." They also said that "we the Chicanos were going to School because they were paying most of the taxes." I told the skinny one I wished he would die and his immediate response was wish you were over 21 so I could beat the shit out of you." They criticized me because of my accent and mocked me because of my fears. While in the office I was sitting down and got up and was severely pushed back into it. I asked them if I could go and they said I would go if I would apologize and signed the paper. After a short wile I asked again if I could go and they said go wipe your tears off and start walking home. So I left.

December 13, 1969
There was little action on Saturday. Pickets had set up in front of Speer's Mini-Max early in the morning. We made them cardboard signs last night. The customers were respecting the picket line. Nobody was buying groceries. We directed our attention to improving the delivery of services to the boycotters. We had a meeting with the student leaders and men from Ciudadanos Unidos. The students not on the picket line were given these other tasks:

1. Arrange for the use of bathrooms in people's homes around the school and parks.

2. A youth corps of tutors must be developed. The older ones teaching the younger ones.

3. Find out and inform all students, by grade and classroom, the assignments given inside the school.

4. Nobody will go home for lunch. Bring your lunch or have someone bring us lunch.

5. Rotate the pickets and assign duty all week.

6. Find homes and places to hold classes.

7. Make more posters. The old ones are getting bent and ugly looking.

The group broke up shortly after the arrival of the MAYO leaders from San Antonio. The group promised to work out the details for the giant rally at the park the next day. Mario Compean, the others from MAYO, and I, began discussing the Walkout developments. Juan Patlan quickly informed that the trip to Washington was on for next Wednesday. The appointment with Kennedy had not materialized; however, Ralph Yarborough, George McGovern and John Tower would see them. These Senators are to send me a telegram to that effect.

Luz took it upon herself to begin prepping the parents to let their kids go to Washington. The rest of us began making the final agenda for our National Conference at La Lomita, near Mission, Texas, on the 28th of December. I was told that Narciso Aleman was going to cause an internal fight by forcing MAYO delegates to choose between continued support for the Winter Garden Project and his idea of a Chicano college.

December 14, 1969

By Sunday, Luz had already gotten parental permission for our student leaders to travel to Washington. At our Ciudadanos Unidos meeting we discussed the boycott of classes and Speer's Mini-Max grocery store. People involved with Los Cinco before compared this boycott to that of Lone Star beer. We went over to the park. I greeted our visitors from San Antonio, Commissioner Albert Peña Jr., Rev. Henry Casso, and the TIED [Texas Institute for Educational Development] staff. Local volunteers were putting the newspaper together. This was a first, without our direct supervision. We all are too busy. *La Verdad* is going to be a great issue. It will have plenty of photographs and a detailed account of the issues leading to the walkout, the board meeting confrontations, and the boycott.

Our community is rapidly polarizing into the Chicano side and the gringo side. Some of our people are confused. Others have joined the

enemy camp. I know who they are. The white community is beginning
to retaliate with threats of dismissal for employees. The police was cir-
cling our groups constantly, now. The media, both local and from San
Antonio, have been criticizing our efforts. The gringo taunts and jeers
directed at our demonstrators are wearing thin with me. This week
seems like a month. Too many of our students are tired of the routine—
picket, march, chant, picket, chant, march, meet, go home, and repeat
that again and again, the very next day, from early morning to late
evening. The boycott is a new experience and will break the routine. We
must get our own classes started full time.

Some parents expressed the need to reflect on the week's events.
They tabulated all the "zero[s]" their children were getting at school for
missing and got nervous at the prospect of grade failure. Some key people in Ciudadanos Unidos wanted to volunteer to negotiate with the
Board for the students. I didn't stay in the background here. It was at
these meetings that I could really speak. We took great care to keep me
far in the background, behind the scenes, regarding the walkout. The
early publicity could be very damaging to our cause. But at Ciudadanos
Unidos, I am the Legal Advisor. In that capacity I raise any and all questions before the membership. This parents as negotiators is a gringo
trick. The parents will crumble before the gringos. They will lose their
jobs. I told the people at CU [Ciudadanos Unidos] how that is the oldest trick in the book. No Way! I asked them to let me pick the parents, if
any at all, to let me decide. I got the vote but it was not unanimous. Too
many abstained. [I've] got to work the members more.

The giant rally began at 3 P.M. Severita again was great! She linked
the School Board, TEA, and Washington in a conspiracy to deny Chicanos educational opportunity.

Albert Peña Jr. brought the crowd to a height of emotion. People here
still like him from the Cornejo revolt days. He praised the kids and the
parents for raising these kind of Chicano kids. If all Chicano parents did
that, he said our troubles would disappear in a generation. Good line.
[I'll] use it someday.

I spoke today in public for the first time. The folks had not heard me
since the speeches I gave at La Placita during the 1963 elections. I was
18 and green then. My talk had to do with denouncing the School
Board. Everyone could do that now, since all Chicanos involved with us
heard the litany of demands over and over. Toward the end of my talk
I openly supported Severita and the students in the Walkout. I, too
compliment their parents and all parents for trusting their kids to do
right. To fight when they couldn't. I also used Severita's line on a conspiracy to say "Let's take the fight to Washington. We'll call and de-

mand an audience with Senators. We'll go to them before they send more investigators here." The audience loved that idea and it caught like fire on dry grass. I promised to call Washington and get it done. I also took out $5 and gave it to Severita for the pot of money to raise for the trip to Washington. Many others eagerly gave money. I gave a very good speech. Knowing my raza, they will want me to speak again and again. I have to watch this escalation carefully. No need to make speeches; the kids are doing great without me.

Armando Treviño closed the rally. He talked about the numbers quoted in the various newspapers about our school boycott. He cautioned them about believing all those low estimates. The need for continued support of the student cause was stressed. He called for getting more students out of classes. Pointing out that practically the entire High School student body of 670 was out by Friday, now we needed to pull out the Junior High kids. Dramatically, he asked the parents to vote for pulling out those grades by applauding. The rousing ovation was powerful encouragement for all. Armando has consistently shown great speaking ability and great thinking ability. He should be one of the MAYO organizers. After the rally, we had a cookout and beer at the house with our friends from San Antonio.

December 15, 1969
The applause of the previous days was transferred into warm, smiling, bodies on Monday. The news reporters estimated the student strikers at 1000 that morning. Finally, the news began to break in our favor. Even they could not believe how good our work was in Cristal. This is going to be our greatest victory! The cars bringing water and food were busy all day. The main body of demonstrators was split into three groups. A contingent marched on the Airport Junior High. The second group stayed at the High School because Fly Junior High was next door. Through the downtown area marched the third group on their way to the Grammar School. With so many students out, I have my hands full. We need non-stop activities. I need more help. Mario tells me I'll be able to recruit help at La Lomita. That is still 2 weeks away! I need help now.

La Verdad was brought in from San Antonio by the afternoon. It was consumed by the hungry crowd in minutes. There were so many pictures that everyone involved in the walkout appeared. They were delighted. Chicanos had finally made the front page.

At the student meeting in the afternoon, Severita was in a bad mood. She complained for the first time of the pressure and responsibilities on her. The students started to bicker among themselves over petty items. The strain and tension was taking its toll. What was comforting to them, as well as fearful, was the trip to Washington. They knew I already had that worked out. Today, at the rally Severita and Mario asked the crowd to name the three students to go to D.C. I told them to say that Senator Yarborough had sent a telegram and promised to meet with them. The rally exploded into joy at this news from Mario. The new President of Ciudadanos Unidos is Diana's father, José Serna. He spoke up today at the rally as CU President. He offered money and asked others to give. They all gave. Linda and Luz have counted the money and it is a lot, I forgot the amount. Severita made sure the audience voted on sending the kids and they were the three chosen. I was always told to nominate yourself and then vote for yourself.

December 16, 1969
Activities for this day have been in the hands of the secondary leadership. Severita, Mario and Diana have been in lessons by Richey and Luz on protocol, handling questions, facts and figures about Cristal, our movement goals, and Chicano history. Arrangements have been made for their arrival and pickup and lodging with a staff member of Senator Yarborough. Appointments are going to be had for them with Secretary Robert Finch of HEW and John Mitchell, the Attorney General. Linda Richey is converting the money into money orders and travelers checks. San Antonio MAYO is handling the departure press conference at the airport.

I organized a car caravan to accompany them to the airport. It is a big event in Cristal. To everyone, it appears as if we made Washington listen to us.

Late tonight, I checked with the students left in charge of the activities, Richard Espinoza, Richard Avila, Ester Ynosencio, and Linda Lara, Severita's younger sister. They were upset. Why had I not gone by to see if they were OK? they asked me. How could I tell them I forgot! I lied. I said I knew they were doing just great because nobody called me or looked for me at home. These kids saw through my smile and jeered me for lying. But, they felt good that I said that. Students learn very quickly the dynamics of a crowd, leadership, organizing, and public speaking.

There was no rally tonight. Thank God! I encouraged everyone to go to bed early and get some sleep. Rest? What is that?

December 17, 1969
Before we got on the way to San Antonio, Severita and Diana reported they didn't sleep well last night. Between the nervousness of having a jet ride for the first time in their lives, going to the president's city, meeting face to face with Senators and their parents' emphasis on caution,

care and concern, they had slept little. Their nervous giggles could not
be seen by the people as our car caravan pulled out to San Antonio early
at 6 this morning. Luz and I enjoyed a full two-hour ride, alone. The students' constant presence at our homemade office made privacy a lux-
ury. We hadn't been alone in a long time. I complained of the great effort it was to stay in the background. She complained of having to cook
for an army and wash dishes left in the sink all the time. I told her to assign kitchen duty to those hanging around. She was cooking and washing dishes daily, it seemed, and working with the mothers and many of
the girl leaders. *La Verdad* was also her baby. I just get money to print it
from Nano Serna and lean on businesses for ads. Nano has always put
up $87 dollars once a month from the first edition. Our relationship
needs attention. We promised each other to leave the group beginning
at the airport and go seek the pleasures San Antonio offered the rest of
the day.

The press conference was a calm affair. The reporters were amazed
that these children were hustling to Washington to see Senators, Secretaries, and others of rank. Their poise before the press was outstanding.
It is a credit to the job Richey did. He has done an excellent job, as usual.
These kids have matured immensely. This walkout will change their
lives for the better, regardless of outcome. Armando has also done a
good job. The press asked these kids about the ritual at the school held
every morning. The ritual is the flag raising and prayer that Armando
started that day of the first aborted negotiations. The kids go into the
High School and ask for the U.S. flag, they take it outside and raise it on
the flagpole and recite the Pledge of Allegiance and then say a prayer.

This single act has generated more favorable publicity than meetings
and rallies. The press loves it! The patriotism and reverence they read
into it is amazing. We love the press for loving the ritual. They forget to
write the trash about MAYO's militancy, radicalism, reverse racism,
and our plan of action for Aztlan.

At the airport, the press and parents took enough flash pictures to
light up Cristal for a night. Before we realized it, the bags were checked,
boarding passes issued, and the kids were past the gate and down the
ramp to the huge mouth of the 727 Braniff jet. We crossed our fingers
and their parents made the sign of the cross. They closed their eyes as
the big jet pulled away from the ramp.

December 18, 1969
The Texas Education Agency investigators arrived once again in Cristal
while we were in San Antonio. The School Board is beginning to soften.
The money lost by the school district as a result of the student absence

is causing concern in Austin. The School Board now will meet with parents without the students being back in school. We rejected the offer without consultation with the entire group and our leaders are in D.C.

The local gringo newspaper had tipped us off! I don't think it is a trick, just Freudian. This morning's issue encourages all students to return to classes. His interest and concern is the education of the children of Cristal, he wrote. Nothing is said about conditions for negotiation. In fact, he says the school board is being encouraged by TEA to negotiate directly with the students. Great!

Another major problem and headache has been solved for us this day. Josue Gonzalez, the President of TEAM (Texans for the Educational Advancement of Mexican Americans) called to inform us that his organization had voted to come and set up classes for our students during the Christmas holidays. This morning a San Antonio paper carried the story of our leaders' trip to Washington. The press was more favorable this time.

This publicity and general good mood of the Chicano community prompted us to call a vote on pulling out the kids at the elementary grades. This is like the Kingsville walkout! We were going all out to close the schools ahead of the holiday schedule. At the rally, the voice vote taken on that gamble assured us of continued and growing community support. The people are 1000% behind their kids and our cause. Buttressed by this knowledge that teachers are coming from all over the state to help keep our children updated on the instruction they are missing will aid us in obtaining simulated classrooms in homes and buildings. I think I will also try the bars. These have plenty of chairs and tables.

December 19, 1969
Severita, Diana and Mario made the headlines of the area newspapers. A photograph, next to the story, had them meeting with Senator Ralph Yarborough. The story reported they had a full day Wednesday at the Office of the Deputy Director in charge of the Office of Civil Rights for H.E.W., Chris Roggerson. The students had made contact and gotten a promise by Gilbert Pompa, Deputy Director of the Community Relations Service at the Department of Justice to send investigators to Cristal. Mario called early this morning. He told Luz their arrival time into San Antonio this afternoon! A car was quickly found to go greet them and drive them to Cristal. Our sound truck was sent all over town informing the public of a welcome reception for our champions that evening. That the schools were practically empty was good news to them.

Josue Gonzalez arrived today, this afternoon, with a car load of teachers. They were sent over to the various addresses where people had offered their homes to them. Josue placed his people in charge of organizing the classes and schedule. He and I discussed the content of the classes. I stressed to them that reinforcement of the Chicano Movement toward liberation should be the priority. Secondly, I suggested they utilize their best teaching techniques on our children. Spoil them. So they will demand excellence when we go back to school. I think I said that.

That evening we waited for our heroes to arrive. The Chicano teachers, superintendents, we have 2 Chicano ones here! and college professors, white liberals, who had arrived were introduced to our community at the rally. Each one was received with great enthusiastic applause. They had never seen anything like this! Josue kept telling me, "This is fabulous! This is fabulous! ¡Que padre! How wonderful!"

The best outburst of emotion was saved for the student leaders. Cars honked, kids yelled and whistled, others screamed with joy. The applause was deafening as Mario, Diana, and Severita, beaming proudly, emerged from the car and made their way up to the speaker's platform. Once up there, where everyone could see them, all hell broke loose. The crowd went wild and surged toward them wanting to hug and kiss them.

The noise stopped finally to let them talk. Severita grabbed the microphone. Her opening remark was "¡Nos aventamos Raza!" We outdid ourselves, People! That comment again made applause drown her out. When the cheers subsided, she outlined the commitments they had obtained. Mario showed the photograph they brought back and Diana unfolded a copy of the *New York Times* to show us the article that had been printed in New York about us. Feelings are real high tonight. It is going really good.

December 20, 1969
This Saturday was spent in de-briefing the students about their mission to D.C. A class schedule was agreed upon. Luz has ordered it printed in leaflet form. More TEAM volunteers have arrived. Luz got students and mothers to help in our kitchen. She tells me she will supervise the teaching. That is the teacher in her. She also tells me the bars for classrooms is out because the TEAM people scouting reported posters of naked women on the walls. I asked her if it occurred to them to take them down. Not funny.

Much to my surprise, the HEW investigating team promised to the students in D.C. also arrived. They must have been in the airplane before the students left from D.C.! They were already conducting interviews in the community and with the administrators at the school. That was a fast response from Washington. We must present our side of the story. We will fill their ears.

December 21, 1969
The TEAM people and HEW investigators were taken to the Ciudadanos Unidos meeting. Mario Compean drove into Cristal again this Sunday for additional planning for our National MAYO Conference coming up next weekend. He observed the CU meeting and was most impressed. He suggested I write something up for all of MAYO to follow in organizing. As if I have time to write.

We missed the rally this evening. Luz and I are tired of meetings and rallies. The people aren't. They are beginning to plan a huge Christmas Party for everyone. Again, the new TEAM arrivals and the investigators from HEW were introduced to our citizens at the rally. I hear it was wonderful and the outside guests love it.

I heard that it was difficult to gauge who was more shocked at witnessing the rally—the Feds or our people. Our people, some 3000 strong, gaped at the "Federal Officials" as if [they] personally had come from Nixon's office. The Feds, according to Bill and Linda Richey, think they are in another world. They are! A new brown, Chicano world!

December 22, 1969
Our liberation classes got off to a great start. There was activity all over town. The leaflets announcing the class schedule and locations that were passed out at the rally paid off. People got their kids to our classes. The newspapers were busy taking pictures of the classes being conducted. Of particular interest to them is Dr. Hubert Miller of St. Mary's University in San Antonio and Superintendent Homer Sigala from San Felipe Independent School District in Del Rio. This is the segregated school district in Del Rio so that the white kids from the army people can go to their own school without Mexicans. It is on the border! How can we permit this shit to go on? TEAM is doing just great; they have done a tremendous recruitment drive among their members and supporters to pull this off. I am so grateful. If we would have had this cooperation in other walkouts, we would have won them all!

The HEW team headed by Dan Morales and Carlos Vela was shaking up the white community. Their probe into the skeleton-filled closets of the Crystal City Independent School District is getting out of hand. Since the schools were closed, all personnel are available for them to question and investigate in the privacy of their homes, not in front of the Principals and Superintendent; I can imagine what their people are saying without coaching or monitoring. Rumor has it that the whites are alarmed by the speed with which these Washington officials had turned up in Cristal. People don't know they just came from Dallas. They began suspecting a conspiracy of sorts. The entire walkout was proceeding too smoothly and growing every day. Now with school out for Christmas, the students are everywhere. We hold classes, double up in the picket lines at Speer's and are now registering voters.

Last Tuesday, carloads of our students [were] being sent to Cotulla, Carrizo Springs, Uvalde, Asherton, Eagle Pass for meetings and voter registration. The gringos in these communities wasted no time in calling their cohorts in Cristal. They are complaining and want our locals to contain us here with any means necessary. After the meetings, our students recruit from the ranks of the local group those interested in registering voters. In Cristal, the students did a fantastic job. I don't think there is anybody left to register. The have gone house to house, block by block, precinct by precinct, registering everybody who was warm and breathing, but only with a Spanish surname. Bill Richey had flown to Denver to sub for me on a talk I was supposed to give at the League of Women Voters conference and talk with Vernon Jordan from Atlanta and head of the Voter Education Project. He also attended this conference. About Chicano voter registration money, Jordan has sent us $3,500 to get started.

Voter registration among Chicanos alarms the white community. Next to Feds showing up and the TEAM people supporting us openly, voter registration scares white people the most.

Our sources within the enemy ranks told us that the area ranchers and businessmen were demanding the School Board accept our demands. The merchants are afraid that the boycott against Speer's will spread. We have virtually cut his clientele in half. Some of the gringo stores are purposely hiring the boycotting students part-time. To them this is a form of boycott insurance. The white community is coming apart from within and from without. Going to the area cities is a great move.

We got copies of the letters the right wing is mailing in an effort to stop the investigation by HEW. Little do they or anyone know that the investigation is over. Their letters are too late to reach Washington. Yarborough wrote to Roggerson today. I am going to get a copy. The HEW team is due back in Washington with report in hand tomorrow.

HEW and TEAM are pressuring the School Board to negotiate with us. We figure our position is as strong as it will ever be and we may have reached our peak. There are no more students to take out. We must now go into negotiations. Nobody knows what the New Year will bring.

Nothing will be the same, however. The students and parents met at the Salon Campestre tonight to set down the conditions and terms of our negotiation. We are getting ready. I don't think they are ready for us. I don't have time to be tired.

December 23, 1969
The letter offering to meet the school board and outlining our conditions for negotiation was typed and hand carried to Eddie Treviño, the only Chicano on the school board we trusted to be right with us. He has been very cooperative and supportive at Board meetings. Eddie is usually the dissenting vote. Forget the other Mexican, Esquivel, what a sell-out, *un buen vendido y Tio Taco*. Too many times Eddie's motions died for lack of a second.

Classes continued remarkably well attended and organized up to now. Parents in large numbers were coming to hear the professor and teachers, from time to time. Word spread that Dr. Miller gave a great class on Chicano History. Our parents have gone to hear him and to see a Chicano Superintendent, Homer Sigala. He is teaching also. A Chicano Superintendent is a rarity. I hope we get one soon. I talked with Sigala about this possibility. He recommended the TEA guy, Ibarra. Sigala is impressed with our students and parents in our community. His corps of teachers from San Felipe expressed the same opinion to me. We are impressed with them. No one has seen so many Chicano teachers in one place. And, yet they say they can't find any, that we are not qualified.

The pickets at Speer's continued and so did the voter registration drives in the area. I've almost gotten arrested at Speer's but young Allee, the Ranger, is no match for me. He is not his father! Younger Allee doesn't know what to do with me. They have arrested Linda Lara and Ester Ynosencio at the picket line. I'll get the students out myself. They are juveniles. Better get MALDEF help if this keeps up.

December 24, 1969
Most of the classes were canceled or closed up early. Volunteers want to go home for their Christmas. Our students did not attend like they did before. Christmas is in the air. A few of us worked on the preparations for the negotiations and for the Christmas party tomorrow. All of us are wondering what the HEW people are going to do with that report. Are they going to be on our side? I know what our people told them and who they talked to about what but what did they write? Is TEAM going to come back, will the kids stay out of school when the holidays are over? It is a bad day. Too much time and too many questions. Too much

time to think and not do! I can't believe I'm writing this as tired as I am and have a chance to rest for a couple of days and I want more work! Crazy?

Luz and I went to midnight Mass at church, la misa de gallo.

December 25, 1969
Today everything stopped. The Christmas Party was great. There were no pickets, no meetings, no marches, no registration, no classes and no rally. Even our office was closed for the first day in two months. Nobody came to the house. Everyone rested and enjoyed the calm.

PS Some people did come to the house but only to bring *tamales.*

December 26, 1969
It took a while to get the day started. Some TEAM personnel showed up for classes. I can't believe it! They are committed! Our pickets and registration finally got going toward noon. I almost got arrested again.

Several key students leaders made plans for the weekend. They were going with us and the Richeys to La Lomita, outside of Mission. Linda Richey wants to look at birds and take pictures, of birds not the MAYO members!

MAYO's National Convention began today. We must pack and get over there.

December 27, 1969
Mario Treviño issued a press statement calling for a statewide boycott of schools. He told the media we were going to spread the walkout all over Texas but especially the Winter Garden area. We left for the Valley, for the MAYO conference.

Our workshop on Cristal, el walkout and the Winter Garden Project at La Lomita was scheduled.

Word from Cristal was that area voter registration, classes and pickets had gone on as scheduled this morning. It is a good feeling to know they carry on without us.

December 28, 1969
Reports from Cristal were that at the Ciudadanos Unidos meeting they voted to boycott the Winter Garden Cleaners, a business operated by Urbano Esquivel. He was on the School Board but very much against our movement. Ciudadanos Unidos was going to make such a presentation at the next rally. There has not been a rally for several days now.

A favorable article appeared in the *Houston Post*.

The MAYO convention was heading for a showdown between support for the Winter Garden Project and the establishment of a Chicano college, Jacinto Treviño. Mario Compean is right. This Narciso Aleman is a real handful of trouble and very calculating. I got to check on him and watch him in MAYO. His idea is good but why the unnecessary fight? He can become a leader without a fight. Why is he trying to divide us?

December 29, 1969
The Richeys, students, and Luz drove back to Cristal to begin work on *La Verdad*. Luz mailed some letters to the U.S. Commission on Civil Rights requesting a conference to be held in Cristal. When she went into San Antonio with the paper she talked to Richard Avena, the head civil rights guy in the office, who gave a final commitment for January 24th and 25th.

The Department of Justice, Office of the Community Relations Service called and left word at the office. They will arrive in Cristal on the 30th, *MAÑANA!*, tomorrow! for a two day visit. I got tangled with some MAYO chapters on program priorities and it was messy. It's that pinche Narciso.

The compromise effected was to support both the Winter Garden Project and the Colegio Jacinto Treviño. I beat Narciso without a fight. I made sure we'll not get any less money resources from MAYO than before and he has to raise his money without MAYO support. Show us what you can do, *cabron*.

The new recruits Alberto Luera, Viviana Santiago, and Ruben Barrera signed up to return with me to Cristal. We met that evening and discussed the Cristal situation in depth and the larger Winter Garden plan.

December 30, 1969
The national meeting finally came to a close. The new recruits, Alberto "Beto" Luera and Viviana Santiago said they would be in Cristal by the next day. Ruben rode back with me. Luera was going to be late in arriving. Something had gone wrong in Corpus and Laredo, where he was from.

At home, I made the rounds of the various areas of activity. It is revealing that I could have stayed a week in the Valley and not be needed. Some people didn't even know I was gone. That was great!

Jesse Gamez called regarding the incorporation papers of Industrias Mexicanas. Since the Speer's boycott, we had proceeded to contact the Fleming Corporation who supplied him his products for a line of credit. We looked everywhere for money with which to start our own store. José Serna, a butcher by trade, and Ramon de la Fuente Jr. were both interested in running the business. We wanted to break Speer's and set up our own Chicano owned and operated food store. Luz was to pick up the papers.

By late afternoon, Eddie Treviño called some parents. It seemed the Board wanted to meet with some parents and students. The parents called me to tell me of this development and also to tell me that some FBI agents were in town. The agents turned out to be Tom Matta and Robert Greenwald, the representatives from the Department of Justice Office of Community Relations. What a long name.

The students and I met with them. The Board offer, it turned out, had been made at the insistence of the Justice men.

The School Board was now letting outside influence dictate their actions! Victory! They simply may be using this ploy to back out, if things took a bad turn. We agreed to present an offer to settle through them and see if we get an acceptance. We want a negotiation session. If we get what we want, it will be great. If we didn't get any major concessions, the group will get a shot in the arm anyway because we have made them come to their knees. We are in charge. We need this in order to carry the boycott on after the holidays. These holidays have made everybody lazy and sluggish. We are out of the routine and getting comfortable. NO! More time has to be spent checking and on organizing new activities than before. Everything must again proceed on schedule. The old spark of anger and solidarity seems to be fading. *La Verdad* came in late, late tonight.

December 31, 1969

All activity was canceled by mid-day. Word of the offer had gotten around and rumor has it that meetings had already taken place. Some rumors have it that the students had sold out. Other rumors have it that the parents had voted to forget the boycott and send their kids back to school. There are all kinds of rumors. We must start our own. We need rallies to get the word out again. That is the official version our people depend on.

Our sound truck was dispatched into the barrios, calling for a rally at the teatro Luna early this morning. We had to get our business over with quickly before the party mood of the New Year's Eve hit our audience.

This rally didn't turn out our usual 1000 or more people. It was a small group. They were the hard core students and parents. The offer was discussed. Word from the Justice men was that our conditions for negotiations were finally accepted. Severita was to inform Eddie Treviño that five parents and five students would represent us. We insisted on the Community Relations Service investigators serve as the moderators for the get together. We would not meet at the school and we reserved the right to withhold final approval of any item until a mass meeting would be called and approved there.

As a final touch, the student demands were amended now to read:

18. No reprisals against students participating in the walkout

19. That an advisory board of Mexican American citizens, chosen by the Chicano citizens be established by the school board in order to advise them on needs and problems of Mexican Americans.

La Verdad was sold at the rally. The bulk of the newspapers had already been placed at stores and businesses.

The Richeys, Luz and I, with the kids, hid at Richey's house. We left our cars parked at our house to make people think we were there. We played "Risk" and drank beer most of the night. We toasted for it to be a good New Year.

January 1, 1970

Matta and Greenwald came into town late this afternoon. They were presented with a list of our representatives and conditions for negotiations. We stressed that the final demand on reprisals must be the first item on the agenda. No amnesty, no negotiations. The parents and students felt that amnesty must be a precondition to the real stuff in the petition.

The incorporates of Industrias Mexicanas were sought out for their signatures. The legal document was mailed to Austin this afternoon.

January 2, 1970

The first round of negotiations was scheduled for 3:30 P.M. The sound truck was dispatched with that information. People were told to congregate and meet at the Salon Campestre for the purpose of voting on the negotiated agreements as they came out. Response to our call was tremendous. People filled the hall to capacity. Armando Treviño was made the chairman of the meeting. Around 5 that afternoon, news reached the audience that amnesty had been given all boycotters. Victory! A sigh of relief gave way to wild cheering and clapping. The students had scored a major breakthrough.

I was stationed not far from the First Baptist Church by the grammar school in order to caucus with our delegation. They frequently called for breaks in the negotiation. We would meet down the street in order to iron out differences within our group. I had real trouble with the parents. The parents are too anxious to concede major points. I always knew that! The students were too adamant about their desire for total victory, with no concessions. It was a difficult situation. Complicating matters was the new role the CRS [Community Relations Service] moderators were taking. Our group frequently found themselves, as well as the School Board, negotiating with the Federal Officials. Their main goal it seemed was settlement of the walkout, at any price, to whichever side.

The only other issue settled that night, with community approval, was the establishment of a parent's advisory committee. While we wanted only Mexican-Americans on the committee, our negotiating team settled for 8 Chicanos and 2 Anglos.

Negotiations for the following day were set for 7 P.M.

January 3, 1970
Saturday's negotiations were tougher that ever. The board got tough. This session lasted until well past midnight. The student elections were compromised. The twirlers and drum major would be selected jointly by four out-of-town judges and four band members (chosen by the band). The cheerleaders would be elected by the student body. The Most Representative student would be changed in designation to "Faculty Student Representative," and the teachers would continue to select this one. The baseball sweetheart would be chosen by the team. The prom servers would be chosen by the Junior class. The Student Council was agreed upon as the body to write up a dress code for approval by the Board. The 16th of September [holiday] was accepted as a day of observance. An assembly program was guaranteed, but no holiday. Custodial duties would be made optional, not required, to Physical Education students.

At this point, the Board had enough for one night. Negotiations were rescheduled for 12:30 P.M. the following day. While our representatives were in negotiation, we held a farewell party and rally for the TEAM people. They had to go get ready to teach their regular classes where they came from. Our people were deeply moved by these fine teachers and the Superintendent who had come to our rescue. Many of ours were confused about several Anglos in TEAM. These Anglos were as Chicano as us, almost. Cristal had not seen such a thing.

In order to apply more pressure to the Board, a petition was circulated that demanded of the School Board that all student demands remaining be accepted on our terms or the boycott would continue. Some 350 voting people had signed the petition. It was given to Tom Matta.

January 4, 1970
Albert Peña Jr. came to Cristal again today. At our afternoon rally, he told the group that Cristal was the showplace of the Chicano Movement. It was here in Cristal that the Chicano had begun a new era in 1963, he reminded the crowd. Because of this second effort, Cristal stood out

again in 1970 to welcome this new year, *"el Año del Chicano,"* he said. The people loved it. That phrase became a slogan all over the state.

The session today got even tougher. Our leaders were having a hard time staying together. The pressure and intensity of negotiations was taking its toll. I had hell with them. I had to yell at two parents on the team, in front of the students. I can't do that! However, the group stuck it out, partly because he had not chosen alternates and they HAD to do stick it out and do a good job. The timing of the impasse in negotiations couldn't have been better.

After Peña spoke at the rally, the crowd got the word of what was being asked to be approved in the agreement on bilingual and bicultural programs and implementing them in accordance with recommendations by TEA. It was accepted. Our negotiators hit a stone wall on the issues of terminating racist Personnel. The School Board offered to hire a qualified bilingual candidate as a counselor, "if funds are available." This last phrase is the catch-all. They now agreed to do everything, "if funds are available." This session broke up at 6 P.M. We caucused intensely. I told them it was a game now. Everything was "if funds are available." I told them to put up a good fight on each item but to accept the language. I told them we had already won.

They returned at 7:30 P.M. for a second session. We praised the negotiating group during their break at the rally. Many people warned them of conceding too much ground. They were caught in a dilemma; it seemed the boycott could be settled, if they kept pushing. The more they pressed the issues, however, the less willing the Board became. Our public gathering approved a few more items, as they were cranked out by the negotiators. The school facilities would be open three days a week at night. The shower facilities would be installed, as money became available. The Board accepted to make this a high priority item for them as well. The student number, the size, of each class was going to be "looked into" by Superintendent Billings. He would take corrective steps next September. The Board conceded the training of parents for teacher aide positions. In fact, they acknowledged that such a resolution already existed. Again, they told our people they couldn't find qualified Mexican Americans to fill them and hardly anybody ever applied.

People at the park were getting weary with the slowness of the negotiation. They wanted to know if the walkout was on or not. School is to start tomorrow.

Several new speakers got the microphone and began urging all people to keep the kids out, especially now that we were negotiating. They pointed out that if we went back the negotiation would stop. We had to continue demonstrating our determination, they argued. After the speeches, most people left. It was late. The group was still in session but nothing seemed to be coming out. I sat alone in the car waiting.

January 5, 1970
The session from last night went on until 2:30 this morning. At that time, our representatives felt they had gotten all they could. The major concessions were the posting of grades for the National Honor Society; the most Handsome and Beautiful procedure would remain the same; they would not purchase any new books until consultants came with recommendations on books with good Chicano information; there would be no "free speech" area; no outside speaker would be allowed into the schools without approval of the Superintendent; the student paper, *The Javelin,* would remain the only newspaper allowed in the school; the Principal Harbin and teachers Rutledge, Harper and Lopez would not be fired; and teachers would not get special treatment because of their political or philosophical beliefs. The Board insisted that no teacher is pressured into [toeing] the administration's line. Our people were concerned about several Chicano teachers who had openly supported the student walkout.

Hardly anybody was around at that hour to approve the final agreements which concerned many areas. The concessions were worded vaguely and stated many conditional terms. The negotiating team and I decided to accept the concessions and call a meeting for final approval.

This morning some 1700 students still stayed out of classes. We can declare it a victory right now or keep on with the fight. The boycott is still on. By noon, when word of the agreement got around, our student ranks on the picket line had been cut by about 400 students, mainly elementary kids who went back to school. Parents said it was too cold for them to be out in the street and better in class because we were now going to win anyway. Rumors are bad news and good news rumors are worse! We could lose our picket line to a rumor that the boycott is over.

At the evening rally, thousands of people attended. Too many wanted to voice their opinion on the final points of the agreements. The overwhelming numbers of student participants felt we had won a tremendous victory. Just the thought of having had the walkout and the marches of defiance, to them was victory. Nobody believed we had gotten this far. Everybody was hugging and kissing and feeling really great. La Raza had beaten the gringos again.

The agreement was accepted and signed by our representatives. I felt bad about the agreement. The school board got too much. They pulled it out at the last minute by hardball negotiations.

The document signed by our negotiators was delivered to Superintendent Billings for his signature and that of Ed Mayer, the school board President.

The walkout was almost over.

January 6, 1970

The schools shook with activity this morning. All day we monitored the reaction of teachers to our students. With the exception of a few incidents reported, amnesty was going to be honored. The students and our staff met after school to evaluate the day's happenings and to set up our new schedule for picketing at Speer's and Esquivel's. The walkout was over but not for those businesses.

9

The MAYO Plan for Aztlan

We wanted, all along, to build Aztlan, the Chicano nation. Those of us in Cristal thought we were on the right track toward that goal, beginning with the walkout. Now that that struggle was nearly over, victory over the school board was virtually assured. We needed to continue the momentum. MAYO needed to implement the remaining part of the Winter Garden Project plan toward electoral victory in the upcoming April 1970 elections.

The next step in the Winter Garden area was to start organizing for an electoral strategy and economic development to take power for la raza from the gringos in the three-county area. How were we going to do that? I had to interrupt my participation in the walkout for a few days and travel to Mission, Texas, the site of the first and only national MAYO conference, held between Christmas and New Year's Day.

MAYO members from across the state and other parts of the United States attended the first national MAYO conference. We gathered near Mission, Texas, some two miles from the border with Mexico at a place known as *La Lomita*—the little hill—owned by the Catholic Order of Oblate priests. Luis Diaz de Leon, director of the Texas affiliate of the Michigan-based Migrant Head Start Program operated an early childhood program there and used only a very small section of the building. He had leased the huge building that sat atop *La Lomita* from the Oblates. I had asked him to lend us the building for the Christmas to New Year period when his program was closed. Mario Compean, our

MAYO leader at that the time, designated Alberto "Beto" Luera and his companion, Juanita Bustamante, to care for food and shelter. "Tiger" Perez, was head of security. During the first days of the conference a Mass was held for us by Rev. Roberto Peña. Tiger Perez draped him with a *zarape,* a colorful Mexican wrap, and handed him tortillas to pass out as hosts for communion. Meanwhile, the other MAYO activists led by Pancho Ruiz from Houston began painting over an alabaster statute of a madonna with brown paint. This ceremony was caught by photographers covering the conference and made the area newspapers. The local Catholics were enraged and protested to Bishop Madieros, who later became a cardinal from the Boston area, now deceased. I thought it was only bigoted Anglo Catholics that protested. I was wrong. The overwhelming callers to the archdiocese were Mexican Americans who felt we were being blasphemous and sacrilegious in making over the madonna to look brown like us. Both Luis Diaz de Leon and Father Peña received many criticisms for supporting MAYO. I learned not to be perceived as attacking a religious icon or church ritual. A special guest at the conference was the brother of Reies Lopez Tijerina, Ramon Tijerina, who attended as the representative of the *Alianza* in New Mexico.

MAYO was going to attempt a national expansion. Groups in Southern California; Kalamazoo, Michigan; Milwaukee, Wisconsin; and Minnesota had already formed calling themselves MAYO chapters. In East Lansing, Michigan, a group calling itself and claiming affiliation with us as MAYO had negotiated a school walkout. We had no formal method of recognition or credentials for such groups; we were an organizers' organization without membership as such. I recall Minnesota, Wisconsin, and California delegations being present at La Lomita. I arrived late in the day on the 26th and brought some students from Cristal, Bill Richey and his wife, Linda, and my wife, Luz, with me. At this MAYO meeting, we had a knock-down, drag-out battle between those who were following the lead of Narciso Aleman and those supporting my work in the Winter Garden area. Aleman was trying to establish the alternative institution of higher learning, Colegio Jacinto Trevino, in the Valley. Most assuredly Chicanos needed, and still need, a university of our own to learn about ourselves and train ourselves. The goal of building a Chicano college was worthwhile, but the MAYO policy called for one project per year, and mine was it for 1969–1970; Aleman would have to wait until May or June, 1970 to present his ideas and plan. At the national MAYO convention, my immediate job was twofold: to explain the MAYO plan of the walkout, and to present the national MAYO plan for the building of Aztlan. Personally, I was also recruiting at La Lomita for volunteers to help us with finishing the Cristal walkout and with the expansion the Winter Garden project.

MAYO, as had been our policy, met twice a year. Each MAYO chapter sent two representatives, and collectively the representatives would sit and deliberate as a body. During May or June of each year, we would meet to discuss program objectives to set goals, and to choose leadership. In the winter months, usually December, the chapter representatives would again meet to evaluate the program development, discuss personnel, and target resources to be sought. Since this was winter, it was out of order to adopt new program activity such as Aleman's. The Winter Garden Project had been previously voted as the ongoing project for the year. MAYO's other focus at this meeting was national expansion—an additional staff burden, but not a new program. I was at this meeting to report on the progress, ask for help, and accept suggestions toward improvement of the plan for the Winter Garden Project; it was the main agenda item at La Lomita.

The discussion centered around organizational goals and the evaluation of our current strategy to include the prospect for national expansion, but Aleman made it a personality conflict by attacking my organizing ability and views. He accused me of simply wanting to make headlines. I made sure that Aleman's attack on me was perceived as an attack on MAYO because the organization had for years been attempting to take over existing local educational institutions, namely school districts, and I was following that directive. My strategy in Cristal was working better than in any of the previous thirty-eight walkouts MAYO leaders had organized around the state. I personally sought out individuals that had participated in those walkouts and impressed upon them the need to stay the course with the Cristal walkout because we were sure to win any day now. I thanked each one of the other organizers for laying the foundation that allowed me to currently enjoy success. That was a good approach, because they then took personal offense at Aleman's cheap shots at me and MAYO's walkout projects.

The convention, ultimately to avoid a raucous split between factions, chose to support both activities. MAYO members were encouraged to gravitate toward either of the two proposals. I made sure that no official vote was taken on this new proposal so that money commitments made previously by the state MAYO office to us in Cristal was not diminished or redirected. I also made sure no new MAYO money flowed into Aleman's project: he was going to have to raise his own money.

Continuing with the Cristal walkout and the Winter Garden Project was ultimately favored by most MAYO chapter delegates and individual members. Recruiting help for either project began in earnest during the meeting at *La Lomita*. I had a session on the program agenda, and there I discussed at length the concept of organizing the Winter Garden Project. I lectured on how to enact a school walkout and used the Cristal example as a model. Alberto "Beto" Luera, Viviana Santiago, and Ruben Barrera had all volunteered for duty in Cristal. They were most interested in the walkout strategy and the development of an ultimate plan for building Aztlan. Many of us who had attended the Crusade for Justice's National Youth Liberation Conferences in Denver were extremely attracted to the ideology of cultural nationalism.

Ruben Barrera drove back from La Lomita with me, as is mentioned in my diary, while Viviana Santiago and Beto Luera drove themselves to Cristal within days. On the road back Barrera and I went over the plan for the Winter Garden. I told him that power is found locally; therefore the birth of Aztlan should be local, built from the bottom up. We were going to do it. I promised him that when the Cristal Walkout culminated in victory he would see the beginning implementation of the greater plan. Unfortunately, it has not happened to this day because the plan was not replicated in other school districts and therefore made no regional impact.

Our vision was to penetrate the power structure. The situation of la raza has always been one of exclusion from government, not lack of willingness to participate. But participation only serves to legitimize the current public policy of that institution. One changes nothing fundamentally—one only makes minor reforms. The status quo serves those already in power. Being neutral or uncommitted to *la causa* as a Chicano only serves the interests of those in power.

In order to make fundamental changes, we need to take complete power over schools, cities, and counties in order to reach the state and national levels. To make changes for la raza we need to make personnel changes, followed by programmatic changes within each governmental level that will better the quality of life for people.

The MAYO Plan for Building a Homeland

The ultimate plan for building a Chicano Nation that I laid out to the MAYO delegates and others in attendance at La Lomita was relatively simple. It was as attractive to many then as it still is to some today. The plan was that we would use a walkout situation or any education issue that galvanizes la raza to build an organization to take over school districts. The school is used to establish a political powerbase. The school districts were the target because these institutions have money, jobs, talented people—both students and teachers—and power over curricu-

lum. The financial aspects of a school district, its business side, are seldom perceived by the general public. People simply do not think of
school systems, school districts, as businesses. Yet they are. Schools are
massive business endeavors, usually the largest enterprises in small
communities. School districts consume hundreds of thousands of dollars, if not millions, in products and services in order to carry out their
mission. As a source of jobs, the school districts are usually the largest
employer in any given small community. Jobs mean money for people
and stability for a community; they mean extra income to donate for political causes and related projects. At this particular time in 1969, most
of the jobs in South Texas of a professional and semiprofessional nature
were exclusively in the hands of Anglos.

School districts also have, in one place, the largest collection of talented individuals. Under the schoolhouse roof are found students with
ideas and teachers with skills and knowledge. We thought that if we
could recruit teachers who shared our philosophical and ideological
goals for the building of Aztlan we could then influence the curriculum
directly and make militants out of all Chicano students and teachers.
As a group, Chicanos now had large numbers of college graduates with
teaching certificates. And the majority of students in the South Texas
public schools were Mexican Americans. Today, Chicano students are
the overwhelming majority in all of the schools in Texas, at about 55
percent of the entire student population. We thought that if we could
graduate militant Chicanos among the senior class each year, transfer
them to area community colleges and universities for graduation with
Bachelor's degrees, within one generation we could transform the professional personnel in South Texas. To put it another way, we thought it
was easier to make professionals out of militants than militants out of
professionals. I still think that is true today.

In addition to taking control of a school district, Chicanos must look
to city hall, which has great power because it has ultimate police power.
It has the power to provide social services, utilities, eminent domain,
taxation, justice, police, jail, fines, and zoning for development. Zoning
lets business in and keeps business out, and—like licensing by a city, ar-
tificially can create need and exclusivity. City hall regulates the number
of taxi cab permits, beer halls, waste management companies, and dancing establishments. It can also be in charge of delegate agencies such as
libraries, public housing, mental health, legal aid, airports, toll roads
and bridges, and cable television. These entities also have powers and
are mini-businesses, protected businesses. City hall, like the school system, is a business and a source of employment.

The next level of government is the courthouse, the seat of the county's political power. Unlike a city, the county has constitutional power that only the people can take away, by amending the constitution of the state in an election. In a city, the legislature can take away power without an election. County government is unique: it is fragmented and each public office has its own power domain. Unlike a city or school district in which power comes only when you obtain a majority of the seats, in county government each position is paid a salary and has unique powers. County government, for example, has the county clerk, sheriff, tax assessor and collector, justice of the peace, constable and the like. Each one of them is independent of other officers and has its own source of power. Ultimately, each of them depends on budget allocation from the county commissioners.

There are also other local units of government, such as water districts, hospital districts, community college districts, and the like. All have the power to tax, to finance capital projects, to provide services, to go into debt, to make purchases, to hire personnel, to hold elections, to engage in planning, or to contract for consultant services. More importantly, they have offices with equipment. If you take over local government, you no longer need to form nonprofit organizations that forever are seeking grants. Local government is the best nonprofit organization around.

At MAYO, we thought that if we took over the various local governments within a county, we could hire and pay our militants to do more community organizing while also providing social services. We could use the police power to make fundamental changes as needed. We could provide jobs and promote businesses. We could even buy back the stolen land of Aztlan, lot by lot, acre by acre!

A collection of counties under our control would give us the leverage in state politics necessary to negotiate our destiny. Planned carefully, these raza-controlled counties could become a state representative district, a senatorial district, or even a U.S. congressional district. We could build a strong base and have leverage in other areas. The powers that be needed our votes in order to reach higher levels of power, and *we* needed our votes to make changes at the local level. We needed not forfeit power at the state and national levels; we just needed to organize, and bide our time. As we grew in power, maturity, resources, and numbers, we would take power at higher levels; it seemed inevitable that this would happen.

The plan for Aztlan remains unfinished. The local government is the source of all power for Chicanos, where we are the majority and can take power immediately. Aztlan begins at the local level. The only decision we have to make is whether it will be our *Chicanos de Aztlan* tak-

ing power or some other Hispanic group using Chicano votes and population figures to take power for themselves. To be Chicano is to be a
militant nationalist and have a plan to build Aztlan. To be Hispanic is
to want to be assimilated, to become an Anglo-American and participate in the system as it is. But "as it is" is hurting la raza big time!

Back to Cristal

Once I returned from *La Lomita*, it was clear to those of us involved in
the walkout that we had to bring this matter to a close. The organizers
knew that the April elections were just around the corner. The filing
deadlines were soon. We also knew that these elections for the school
board were nonpartisan. Nonpartisan elections for both the city council and the school board were going to coincide in the year 1970. We also
knew that we had achieved the maximum public and government pressure from Washington and Austin on local officials. Our assessment at
that time was that we could not hold out much longer for a walkout as
a form of protest due to what we were sure would be waning interest in
the new school semester.

On the other hand, the school board officials and their cohorts had
begun a campaign of terror and threat against the Chicano population of Cristal. The Texas Rangers maintained their daily vigilance over
us. In some cases, arrests were made by the local police, via the sheriff's
department under Sheriff C. L. Sweeten. We were fortunate in that
MALDEF, and attorney Jesse Gamez out of San Antonio, were always
available to us. No permanent conviction ever hurt any student involved
in the walkout, but two important incidents, do come to mind.

The first was the boycott of J. L. Speer's Mini-Max store, where the
grocer fired two part-time student employees because they were involved in the walkout. We immediately retaliated by picketing his store.
We were so successful with this picket, with the help of the parents of
the protesting students, that hardly a product moved out of his store.
Speer was brought to his knees almost immediately. It was the only retaliation we had against the gringo business establishment. After that,
Anglos stopped firing students involved in the walkout, since it was
not good for their businesses.

Communities like Cristal in South Texas are found throughout the
country, even in the inner cities of urban areas. The majority of consumers and laborers in cities are ethnic minorities. Our people have unorganized and misdirected labor power and consumer power. The
owners of inner city businesses are not Chicano. With the lessening of
segregation and the introduction of shopping malls and franchise busi-

nesses, most of our Chicano entrepreneurs were put out of business in the barrio. A few remain, such as a bar, a funeral home, a restaurant, a beauty and barber shop, and a mechanic's shop. But the small grocery, the dress shop, the fruit stand, the meat market, the hardware store, the dance hall, and the gasoline station are gone. The businesses found at the edge of the barrio today are predominantly owned by Anglos, Jews, Koreans, Pakistanis, and East Indians. The hard-earned money from our labor leaves our hands as quickly as water through a sieve, flowing directly to these other businesses—we don't keep our money in the barrio. The exception to this erosion is the rise of Mexican-owned business development. Some Mexican migrants, recently arrived, are opening up small businesses of every type in the large metropolitan areas of Texas and around the country. Perhaps change is in the making.

In the aftermath of the walkout, scores of Chicano parents were fired or laid off from the Del Monte plant on two occasions: the city elections and the forming of a new labor union, *Obreros Unidos Independientes* (United Independent Workers). The Teamsters Union had been the official bargaining unit at the plant for years. During 1963, the Teamsters had been partners with Chicano union members and helped Los Cinco Candidatos take power at city hall. But by 1970, the Teamsters were opposed to the New Chicano electoral effort and worse, ignored the grievances of Chicano workers at the plant. The dismissals of Chicanos from Del Monte prompted us to expand our organizing efforts to include forming an independent union. First, we decertified the Teamsters union as the official bargaining unit. Paul Rich, the attorney from *La Oficina de la Gente* (The Office of the People), our own city-funded, legal aid program, filed the necessary papers with the National Labor Relations Board to call the election at which the Teamsters were decertified and our own Chicano union elected by the workers to be their bargaining unit.

The negotiations for a contract between Del Monte Corporation and Obreros Unidos Independientes were a challenge. Del Monte hired lawyers from the Houston-based lawfirm of Fulbright and Jaworski. A team of tough Anglo lawyers for Del Monte met daily at the courthouse to hammer out an agreement. Our negotiating team consisted of Elena Diaz, Gregoria Delgado, Paul Rich, and I. Occasionally, the local Catholic priest, Sherrill Smith, would join the team. When the negotiations reached an impasse over the solid economic package we demanded, the Del Monte plant experienced a major water leak that required service to the plant to be interrupted. After that was fixed a couple of days later, the plant developed a gas leak which took time to fix. When the second crisis with utilities developed, lawyer Robert Bombace for Del

Monte, invited me for a beer to discuss the status of the negotiations. We met away from Cristal City, in an Anglo bar in La Pryor. Before the beer had even arrived, he accused me of plotting these interruptions in service at the plant because he was sure that I controlled city hall and the city employees. I told him that these accusations would not fix water or gas leaks at the plant, that these things happen to customers daily. I asked him point blank what Del Monte would rather have—satisfied and loyal employees with a good economic package or more disruption of services? He got the message and said, "You'll get a good offer tomorrow. Take it or I'll see you in federal criminal court." I responded, "If it is as good as we want it to be, you'll have a safe trip back to San Antonio tomorrow." Neither one of us drank our beer.

Pickets and the Pinches Rinches

During the time that we had the picket lines at schools and businesses, the pickets were kept apart from the supporters across the street by lines of law enforcement officials: Texas Rangers, sheriff's departments, and local police. I remember vividly one particular incident when I was monitoring the picket line. I regularly had to walk across the street from the picket line supporters to the sidewalk in front of the store, to assure the student picketers that everything was all right and to encourage them stay on the picket line.

I was on my third or fourth trip across when I was stopped by the son of Ranger Captain A. Y. Allee. This young Ranger, even though he was the son of one of the most brutal and murderous Texas Rangers, did not have his father's temperament or guts. He stopped me in the middle of the street and told me that I was going to be charged with inciting a riot if I crossed the street one more time. I stared blankly at him, said nothing, and finished the walk across the street to talk with the picketing students. Then I came back across the street to where the community residents were. When it was necessary again to walk across, I took a deep breath and started over. He stopped me again in the street, saying that he had warned me previously, and that now he was going to arrest me for inciting a riot if I were to cross again. But, before he could finish the rest of the sentence, I decided to play the macho role. At that time, I used to smoke cigarettes and carried matches. Both Allees, the Captain and his young son, had the habit of having unlit cigars in their mouths. I nonchalantly reached into my pocket, pulled out a matchbook, and held a lit match, with untrembling hand, to his cigar. He nervously puffed on the cigar as it lit. With those puffs I knew, psychologically that the victory was mine; all that was necessary was to wrap it up with words. I said to young Ranger Allee in front of all his police backup, "You are not going to arrest me. If you so much as *dream* about me tonight, you better wake the fuck up and come apologize to me!" I proceeded to walk on across the street without waiting for a comment or reaction.

We had learned over time to have cameras and recorders always present and trained on the police. I felt safe that no violence would occur because of the cameras. God knows what would have happened to me in jail, had young Allee arrested me. But he backed down—he didn't know what to do. Cautiously, I did not risk crossing the street again. I had already won. This incident elevated me to folk hero stature among the local raza. I had unnerved Allee Jr. and his armed Rangers from Company D.

Severita's sister, Linda, and Ester Ynosencio, secondary leaders in the walkout, were both arrested at the Speer's picket line on another day. They were charged with parading without a permit and disturbing the peace. We subsequently went to court on both those charges and got them dismissed on technicalities. Another young man, Cleofas Tamez, was also charged with parading without a permit and walking in the street. He was convicted in Municipal Court. We subsequently were able to overturn his conviction at the County Court because we had good lawyers. These are examples of some of the terrorism that was used against the protesters.

The threats that were made to parents were very real. That is to say, parents of the striking students were called by their employers or members of the school board and told that the walkout was not good for their children, that the children were going to be flunked, that this protest was destroying the relationship between Anglos and Mexicans. They accused MAYO members of being outside agitators, Communists. Fortunately, the parents did not succumb to those threats, although many individuals were subsequently fired in the spring of 1970, when we won the election to the school board.

One of our greatest errors in those earlier boycotts was not knowing when to quit. We agreed to end the walkout in Cristal even though many of the demands were not fully met. Leaving some issues to be resolved in the future would help keep us organized and alert. We were keeping alive the collective protest until the next school board election, where we could institutionalize the gains of the walkout. More importantly, la raza had tasted victory, and wanted more.

Targeting the school board as the next needed victory was critical to our organizing concept. First, we had to learn how to define victory. We determined what victory was, when we had achieved it, and how to celebrate it. We did not let the media, the enemy, the critics, or anyone else define victory in our struggles; we claimed it ourselves! Second, we set ourselves goals; not group goals, but goals that could be reached only by our acting as a group. In other words, we made the organization stick, and made it mobilize collectively, in order to reach our goals. This lesson in mobilized group effort was practiced at the Ciudadanos Unidos meetings with raffles, with voter registration, with marches and boycotts. Third, we kept the focus clear. The struggle was *us* against *them*, the gringos. We had to continue to struggle until we eliminated them completely from power. As Chicanos we cannot have control of our destiny unless we have the power of control over the institutions that affect that destiny. We also realized in early January, 1970, that we already had enough people registered and would be able to register more to vote before the month was out. At this time, voter registration could only occur between October 1 and January 31 preceding the election season. We had also been registering voters during our off time, not only in Crystal City, but in Cotulla, Uvalde, Carrizo Springs, Asherton, Eagle Pass, and other areas in the Winter Garden district. This was an example of an activity used to keep the students busy and politicized during the walkout.

We knew after the holidays that we were in good shape to carry on the next step of the plan, which was the formation of La Raza Unida Party. I had brought up that idea back in 1968, to no avail. Even the MAYO leadership of the time, Mario Compean, Juan Patlan, Ignacio Perez, and Willie Velasquez, all rejected the idea. They all, particularly Willie ridiculed my even thinking along those lines. They felt that our people were too solidly entrenched within the Democratic Party. Willie actually believed that loyalty to the Democratic Party was a must for us, but I vehemently disagreed with him. This ideological and philosophical disagreement between us was never resolved. Texas was and had been since Reconstruction a one-party state, controlled in every way by white Democrats.

I was not to be daunted; I brought up the idea again during the meeting at La Lomita. MAYO decided to let me try implementing such an idea as part of the conclusion of the walkout. So on January 10, 1970, just days after the walkout had officially ended, we called an organizational meeting of La Raza Unida Party for Zavala County at the Campestre Hall, on the outskirts of Cristal. We filed the preliminary papers and documents to establish such a political party in the other counties of the Winter Garden region, plus Hidalgo County, which is where La Lomita is located, near Mission, Texas.

We were ultimately thrown off the ballot by the local county judges and subsequently, the Federal Court. We argued for equal protection under the law to permit us ballot status, but to no avail. The federal judge decided that we were not being denied opportunity. He reasoned that the voters, even without having us on the ballot, still had a choice. They could vote for or against the nominees of the Democratic party. No such problems existed in the city and school elections, as those were nonpartisan. We filed candidates for every available office in the three cities in the area, Cotulla, Carrizo Springs, and Crystal City, sixteen candidates in all. On election day, we won fifteen of the sixteen races. In two of those cities that gave us majority control because there were already Mexican Americans on the board who subsequently changed allegiance and voted with our group. This was the case in Crystal City: three of us ran—Miguel Perez, Arturo Gonzales, and myself—and we won. We were joined by Eddie Treviño, who already was on the board and an employee at Del Monte. He began voting with us to make a majority for the three against the remaining incumbents. The same thing happened in Carrizo Springs, although the newly elected mayor, Rufino Cabello, a local attorney, did not live up to the militancy and the leadership that we had expected. Carrizo Springs never developed into a Crystal City. On the contrary, it developed into the antithesis of Crystal City, as Mexican Americans continued to be docile and led by Anglo interests in the area. In fact, Carrizo Springs became the location site for many businesses and enterprises leaving Crystal City, only twelve miles away. The only other Crystal City-like community was Cotulla. There, the candidates emulated our activity. Every mayor elected in Cotulla from our movement during that decade was subsequently fired. There developed a relationship, a new level of migrant travel for mayors, Chicano mayors of Cotulla. They had to go to Milwaukee, Wisconsin, to work part of the time in order to sustain their living. It became a pattern: you got involved politically with La Raza Unida, you got elected, and then you lost your job.

The winning of elections in Crystal City got to be an art form. No one in another community had ever paid as much attention to the methodology of winning an election as the people in Cristal did. The antecedent victory in 1963 had been pulled off, but the subsequent election was lost by 1965. People stopped trying during that period, until 1970 when we introduced a new concept of organizing and getting out the vote. We organized around the family unit—the extended family unit to be more exact. Among Chicanos, and I suspect other Latinos regardless of nationality, there exists an extended family, a complete network of kin stretching beyond the nuclear family into several other nuclear families. The Chicano families are large, very large. If you add to these extended families the additional semiextended family of *compadres* (cronies), *cuña-dos* (in-laws), *camaradas* (comrades), *padrinos* and *madrinas* (godfathers, godmothers), *paisanos* (fellow countrymen), *vecinos* (neighbors), and all those related by affinity, you have very large numbers of people related to each other by blood or by the social politics of the family.

The family became our basic unit of organizing. Our goal, when working with extended families, was to recruit every eligible member to vote for our candidates or to be in favor of our issues. If we couldn't obtain their affirmative vote or support, we then sought them to pledge to be neutral and not provide any opposition in terms of a negative vote or negative campaigning on an issue. The least desirable was to have someone voting against our nominees and being in opposition to our ideas. We were most successful in using individual family members with their social political ties to not only get us votes, but to neutralize those who possibly would be in opposition. In politics, the neutral vote is far better than the negative vote because it doesn't factor into the equation. Political math is different from regular math: if you have five votes on one side and five votes on the other side, that is dead even. If, however, there are fifteen votes available and from the remaining five, three join your side and only two go to the other side, you have won by one vote. If you neutralize their two in opposition, then you win by three votes and if you can take a vote away from the opposition, they need one vote to make it up, a second vote to even out the numbers, and a third vote to defeat you. So, in politics, one plus one does not equal two; one plus one may equal two or three, as my example suggests.

We also organized the families, block by block, street by street, neighborhood by neighborhood, precinct by precinct, community by community. We had people in every block of every street in every barrio. From each street, one was our representative, our "team captain" if you will. We taught people how to walk the streets, door to door, canvassing, doing solicitation, getting out the vote. At that time the absentee voting was our main strength. People not keenly aware of how politics work or how to make maximum use of resources will try to get all their votes in on election day. What a mistake! The key is to use every single day of the open voting period of early voting to get as many votes as you can, every day prior to the election. You should win the election in advance. We did this repeatedly.

We had index cards on every registered voter; this Chicano-style database—index cards in a shoe box—was most useful. If we wanted to know who voted, in what previous elections they voted, what families they were connected to, how many family members there were, and where they worked, we looked at the index card. We knew voter his-

tory, family history, and political history, and could find the appropriate familial nerve endings to touch to get the response we wanted. It is
true that blood is thicker than water. Needless to say, we won election
after election for a number of years. We only began losing as split factions developed within us.

The entire complexion of politics in Texas and across the country was
changed by La Raza Unida Party: Anglos could not win, but Mexicans
could lose elections in South Texas. When factions developed among
Mexican Americans, then Anglos could pick between rival Mexican factions, as to which faction would win.

Election day was a marvel of organization. Literally hundreds of
people volunteered to help us get out the vote. We would canvas every
street and knock on every household with voters several times a day.
We would hound people into voting simply to stop the door knocking
and the calling on them to go out and vote. And they were festive times:
our volunteers got fed; our poll watchers got treated royally, when we
remembered them. On many occasions, though, we forgot about the
poll watchers and they went hungry and drinkless because the enemy,
especially in the early years, would not treat them to a glass of water or
let them leave the polling place to get refreshments or food. You dare
not leave the polling place after admission as a poll watcher unless you
dare risk losing the right to return. I don't know which would have
been worse: to have lost your place as a poll watcher, or to face us, the
organizers, had we lost the election because you left your watch.

There were many incidents involving the admission of poll watchers.
I recall a particular incident involving Joaquin Jackson, another Texas
Ranger, who to my recollection was the only decent Ranger in an old-
fashioned kind of way. One could cut a deal with Jackson and he would
honor it. Not that it was legal or that he was doing us a favor; he was
simply being practical and doing the best he could under the circumstances. The election that I recall and the incident took place at the
county road administrator's office on Highway 83, on the west side of
Crystal City. The election judge there wanted our poll watchers evicted.
Upon learning of this incident, we gathered across the street by our
table. We stormed the polling place and were at the door screaming ob-
scenities at the election judge. Ranger Jackson showed up and proceeded to tell me that the election judge had the power to evict poll
watchers. Luz was among those being evicted, as were Richard Diaz,
and Rebecca Perez, the wife of Rey Perez, our candidate for county attorney. The county police were there, sheriff's deputies José Rodriguez
and C. L. Sweeten, and some others. The police were literally, physically
pulling the poll watchers out the door as we were pushing them back

in. Joaquin Jackson came in to mediate. Jackson knew that our paperwork was in order, that is to say, the applications for designating a poll
watcher were properly filled out and presented before 7:00 A.M. There
was nothing wrong with the appointment. The election judge simply—
arbitrarily—didn't want our watchers in the polling place and he argued that the polling place was too small to have all these people standing around. He wanted them evicted and had called the Sheriff. Jackson
was able to put a hold on the escalating potential for violence while he
would confer with the district judge in far away Sabinal via telephone.
Ranger Jackson wanted me to go with him to the courthouse to call the
district judge and see what could be worked out. I refused to go with
him. On the contrary, I told him that he should go with me in my car,
with my bodyguards. I proceeded to pin a Raza Unida Party button on
his jacket, which he left there. He accepted a ride in my car, and we drove
to the courthouse. The crowd loved it; word got around quickly that I
had arrested Jackson and had taken him to the courthouse. To this day
some people still believe that, which certainly was not the case.

We went to the sheriff's office, and Jackson made the call to the district judge. Jackson proceeded to tell the judge that our paperwork was
in order and that we were entitled to that many people. He knew that we
were right, and he also knew that the election judge was in the wrong.
All the election judge had was the absolute power on election day to
conduct the election as he saw fit, and he was abusing that power. Jackson said that to the district judge in front of my ears. Judge Woodley
talked to Jackson awhile then asked to put me on the line, where he
asked me point blank if I would accept a compromise, half of the poll
watchers or none. He explained to me that he had no authority to order
the election judge to accept any poll watchers. That the election judge
would ultimately prevail during election day because he had the authority even if he was exercising it wrongly was something I already
knew. Our choice was to sue and bring court action after the election.
We might lose the election, if we were not there as poll watchers to
watch the conduct of the election. I had always been a practical man,
even under the heat of adversity, and reluctantly accepted the compromise. Sometimes, anger and rage will make me lose my composure, but
not this time. I did tell the district judge I thought it was most peculiar
that he could not order the election judge to take our poll watchers but
could order him to let us have half of them.

I went back with Ranger Jackson in tow, and put in our best watchers, Luz and Diaz, with instructions to give the election judge hell. Jackson would not come back to evict them, he had told me that indirectly.
So, we both won on that particular day, and Jackson and I developed a

working relationship. I suspect that he would say mutual respect, rather than a working relationship. We both had jobs to do and we were both going to do them, even at the expense of each other. We just simply sought to avoid that type of confrontation.

I never had any problems with Jackson after that. Later, when I became county judge, we worked well together even when I was under his investigation and his surveillance. He knew I wasn't crooked or a dope dealer. It is solely my politics that gringo people don't like about me. He was always straight and honest in his dealings with me, and I with him. Later still, in 1996, Ranger Jackson and I took part in an interview with Dean Lawrence Clayton and Dr. Susan Allen of Hardin Simmons College in Abilene. Jackson and I recounted numerous stories of Chicano confrontations with the Texas Rangers, stories that appeared in the January 1998 issue of *Texas Journal*, a local magazine.

10

Ciudadanos Unidos

The Base

The basic party organization was our community based group, Ciudadanos Unidos or CU. We had started this group early on, my wife and I, each of us organizing the men and the women separately. Usually, in social, cultural, or political settings, the sexes arrive together but will gravitate away from one another as time progresses, ending up in segregated enclaves by the end of the activity. We knew that promoting an egalitarian agenda for the sexes was not timely; to initiate cultural reform and fight the gringos simultaneously would be suicidal. And in fact the few skirmishes we had with older Chicanos over equality of Chicanas as members and voters within the organization were counterproductive to the immediate task at hand, the walkout. We chose to delay the integration of the women into the men's organization for several months. At that time we lowered the membership and voting age for Ciudadanos Unidos to eighteen, and had the women march into a men's meeting at el salon Miguel Hidalgo, where they demanded the right to join as equals and proceeded to vote. (At a later date, we also persuaded the group to lower the admission for voting members to the age of fourteen.) It aided the women's efforts immensely that the president of the men's organization was José Serna; that his wife, Olivia, was one of the leaders of the delegation, and that his daughter, Diana, was a leader of the walkout. Mrs. Serna was one of the speakers in favor of integration. We integrated Ciudadanos Unidos in that fashion.

Ciudadanos Unidos met every Sunday at one o'clock. That is, after church and after lunch, we would gather at one of the available auditoriums in the city large enough to handle the group. We had started at the Teatro Luna and Salon Campestre during the walkout, but now regular meetings were held at the Salon Miguel Hidalgo. Soon after the initial electoral victories, we moved to larger accommodations such as the city library, swimming pool building annex, and, most frequently, the new junior and high school cafeteria. These locations were a far cry from the all-male meetings held in the cactus patch at the Ynosencio or Galvan ranches, after-hours behind the Oasis Drive-in, or the un-air-conditioned Salon Miguel Hidalgo. The CU meetings were social and political events; social in that families and individuals mixed with each other, had a chance to visit, talk, and network with one another on the various things they were working on now, such as their jobs, their programs, their responsibilities, and their lobbying. This was a new experience for every one in Crystal City. Usually, husbands and wives would be the regular attendees, occasionally with children in tow. The participation by children wasn't because parents didn't have baby-sitters; rather, it was because they wanted their kids to continue sharing in political experiences, as they had during the walkout. The activist students came on their own, and most often sat apart from the parents, but if they were fourteen or older they were admitted as voters.

The CU meetings were also good for political socialization and accountability. A meeting would begin with a call to order and the reading of minutes from the previous meeting, followed by a treasurer's report. Afterwards individual office holders and program administrators were asked to give a five to ten minute presentation on what they were doing with their program or position that week. It was expected that major decisions would be made in consultation with the CU membership therefore the group had to be told in advance of what was going to happen. It was also assumed that the presenter would bring up not only the successes but also the controversies, dissension, and problems facing them in the discharge of their job and program mission. CU, in consultation, would offer its suggestions and advice on how to remedy those problems. Individually, members would take note and see if any extended family member was involved in creating the problem so as to take internal familial corrective measures. The agenda was designed to make people accountable. Votes on issues and on the overall reports would be taken, from time to time, with instructions to program heads, office holders, and other party functionaries. This did not sit well with many of the administrators at the school and with some office holders. Given, however, that CU was the base of support and the main organ for the political party, everyone soon learned to become accountable and responsible to its membership.

I recall that early the career of Angel Noe Gonzalez, the first Chicano school superintendent, he presented his budget proposal for the schools to CU for support and leverage with the members of the school board. In his budget, Gonzalez had not given a pay raise to the janitors. One of them in attendance at the CU meeting noted the discrepancy and pointed out that others had gotten salary increases, but not them. He made a motion flat out for CU to instruct the school board members to add such an increase. The superintendent protested that he was in charge of this responsibility for salaries and increases and it was his budget proposal. He was simply providing information to CU, not subjecting it for amendment. The janitor in rebuttal stated that in CU he was in charge as member and Gonzalez worked for him in his capacity as superintendent. The motion passed. Those of us on the school board advised the superintendent to revise the budget on that issue, and he did.

Selecting Heroes and Candidates

One of the more salient activities of CU, in addition to political party work, was the Chicano Del Año (Chicano of the Year) banquet. The event was a fund-raising tool: donations and sponsors would be sought out to pay for the cost associated with the dinner dance and the plaques given as awards. The annual event was in celebration of two CU members, a man and a woman, for outstanding work done on behalf of la raza, and it was a very festive banquet and dance. At the midpoint of the evening, the honorees were announced and presented with the engraved plaques. It was quite an honor to be so recognized by one's peers, and it was our way of creating our own heroes. The sponsors were also recognized and given a small plaque of appreciation. These were publicly displayed in Chicano businesses as symbols of distinction.

Another important event held by CU was the candidate selection process. Basically, the CU board would look for potential candidates from among five sectors: the Mexican American business class, the youth, the women, the labor union people—both farmworkers and at the Del Monte plant—and finally, party officials and workers. We also had term limits: officeholders could not run for reelection. From among these five groups, the Ciudadanos Unidos board would ask for names of candidates. Very early in the process each person nominated was asked whether they would support whomever became the final nominee. A response in the affirmative permitted you to go forward; a response in the negative disqualified you from the beginning. Since this was asked in public at the nomination of every potential candidate at a CU meeting, everyone had to answer affirmatively. The ritual was a commitment by the individual to the group, to be disciplined and adhere to party loyalty regardless of the final outcome. For two Sundays prior to the actual vote, all the candidates would be interviewed in front of the membership. The candidates would make presentations at the meeting, and there would be two pre-primary votes taken. These preliminary elections reduced the number of potential candidates to just twice as many as were necessary for the offices to be contested. For example, if three seats were coming up on the school board, the last cut contained six nominees who would be presented at the last Ciudadanos Unidos meeting prior to filing. The membership would vote for only three candidates by secret ballot, and we ran complete slates of candidates for each election. The Ciudadanos Unidos membership would take care of getting out the vote, raising the money, doing all things necessary for them to win. It was fairly understood by all that being selected by Ciudadanos Unidos as the candidate meant that you would be the officeholder, simply waiting to be confirmed by the votes on election day. On at least two or three Sundays prior to the beginning of the absentee voting period, the CU meeting would end early and each member was given a street to canvass. The entire election district would be canvassed two or three times by the membership.

The candidates would follow up with personal calls to undecided voters, and some "no" voters if it was deemed appropriate, though most negative households were ignored so as to encourage their active opposition. On election day, the entire CU organization and the extended families of the candidates were expected to work during the election, *a correr las calles* (to walk—canvass—the streets). Organizations always had to be recruiting new members because existing members would lose interest, move, die, move on to other interests, or become disaffected. This lesson was ignored by MAYO and is largely the reason why MAYO disintegrated. Most of the MAYO leaders and members of my political generation went on to do political party organizing and forgot to replace themselves with new recruits. Some loss of members occurred in CU from the very beginning of the movement. At first, when the first walkout began, every Chicano was for the walkout and against the repression that had gone on for decades. As programs were implemented people began asserting philosophical differences, ideological differences, personality conflicts with those in power, competition for jobs, and petty jealousies. Particular criticism was leveled against the "out-

siders" that were coming into Cristal to support the movement. These
Chicanos had the credentials required for jobs such as superintendent,
principal, or director of federal programs, and were made the targets of
locals. This in-house, intragroup nativist movement grew to great proportions in later years. Eventually, Ciudadanos Unidos split into two
factions over this issue and that of accountability to the organization.
CU had voted to instruct the city council to hire someone other than the
leading candidate as police chief. The city council members ignored
CU's recommendation and hired their school board member favorite,
also making him the police chief. This was their Chicano version of interlocking directors. The group that broke from the main Ciudadanos
Unidos was the faction comprised of recently trained school administrators from the area, some of the younger members of Ciudadanos
Unidos who had risen to leadership within the organization, some public officeholders who did not want to continue with the new politics of
accountability, and members of the Barrio Club, an all-male Chicano
club of drinking buddies that early on was the backbone of security for
the student boycotts. They wanted Cristal for the Cristaleños. It was a
very nativist appeal, a very selfish appeal, because many of the relatives of these individuals who opposed the "outsiders" were the first to
get jobs. These families had strengthened their hand politically through
patronage as they had learned by experience over the years. The extended family network proved to be useful in both a proactive and reac-
tive mode. The breakaway faction utilized the extended family network
effectively to create and breed political nepotism in which only their
family members from Cristal got jobs. This phenomenon is found extensively in South Texas today, as it was when the white power structure had control. The Anglo families were the first to get jobs and only
those Mexicans willing to do their bidding got the few jobs dispensed
outside the white group. Anglo political culture, when intertwined with
Mexicano culture (where a person is expected to look after the welfare
of the family members in order to be a good person) creates a new and
difficult paradigm.

The Ciudadanos Unidos meetings became very large over time, with
some three to four hundred people attending for three to four hours
every Sunday afternoon, so we had to create a second meeting on Wednesday mornings. Having it on a weekday morning meant that it was
available only to people who controlled their own employment or who
held public office and could come and go at will. At these Wednesday
meetings were the heads of programs and the officeholders of the party,
and whatever members of the leadership of Ciudadanos Unidos was
able to attend. At these Wednesday meetings we tried to work on bu-

reaucratic and programmatic problems that developed, not realizing that *we* were now the bureaucracy.

Invariably, jobs were everyone's main concern, followed closely by some of the politics of Ciudadanos Unidos: where we were headed, what we were doing, who had turned against the organization, who had defected, who was going to answer which criticism, and so on. We recognized that the elimination of poverty was an intractable problem. And poverty was endemic to South Texas and rural areas where Chicanos were located; there were never enough jobs for every person in need of employment. South Texas, like most rural areas, has a colonial system: the few control the many through unemployment and coercion. We beat the coercion and fear but were in turn beaten by the large reserve labor pool of unemployed migrants. Our people actually went to work in the summer months in the northern states and returned to sign up for unemployment the remainder of the year. When Chicanos were asked if they were working, or what they were doing for money, they would often reply, *"Estoy firmando"* (I am signing [for unemployment compensation]).

We tried, as a political machine, not to hire more than one family member in a job. Unfortunately, the school administrators were the visible exception. Both spouses were employed and paid great salaries. My wife and I were both employed and paid good salaries—not as great as the school administrators, but good wages compared to migrants. Whenever a job was filled, we created potential enemies as well as reinforced support from the family of the person hired. It was a two-way street, but a narrow one.

The Rise of Factions

It was about this time that the Ciudadanos Unidos group split into two factions. From then on, there were two CU meetings, two newspapers, two political campaigns for the party, and two sources of jobs. The faction that split off, Ciudadanos Unidos II, were joined by an earlier faction, La Raza Libre, the free people. Together, they had control of the city and soon took control of the school board. They fired the school superintendent, Amancio Cantu. Soon, they began to hire their own faction supporters.

We had three challenges to our power position now. There were the gringos. There were the former Mexican American favorites of the white power structure. And, now there were former Raza Unida party members. One faction of La Raza Unida contended against another, with the gringos and the Mexican American Democrats as the balance of power, the gringos choosing which group to favor. Obviously, they were not going to ally themselves with the more radical and militant Raza Unida faction to which I belonged. Invariably, these factions all voted for their side and we, the original founders, began losing elections to the more moderate, reformist faction that enjoyed gringo support.

It took me awhile to figure out why this family fight had happened. We didn't disagree over the goals; we didn't disagree over the program. The Barrio Club did disagree with my leadership, particularly their leader, Guadalupe "Lupe" Cortinas. He simply wanted to replace me with himself. The old intraethnic challenge-to-the-leader trick was rearing its head. I had brought him and his wife back from Chicago to help operate the computer system we were installing at a local school. We gave them both good jobs. She became a school cafeteria manager, and he was the computer technician, allowed released time to begin classes at St. Mary's University Law School in San Antonio.

Back in our childhood and high school days when I first recall knowing him, Lupe was a puny kid, sickly, with thick glasses like Mister Magoo in the cartoon, and forever had a racking, phlegmy cough and seemed out of breath. After high school he joined the military and I never saw him again until my colleague on the school board, Arturo Gonzalez, suggested we bring him back to help with computers. Arturo billed him as an expert, and he was: he made those computers work. Once back in town, Lupe joined the Barrio Club and became the intellectual leader. The Barrio Club members as a group were not involved in illegal activities but it was said that the Cortinas brothers and some of their allies were. The Barrio Club acted as if they were a group of delinquents, a childhood gang. They opened a bar and had topless dancers; they congregated together at meetings and rallies and at parks as a separate group. Lupe soon opened a liquor store and other businesses. His frequent absences from work, law school, and the city were curious; on several occasions, I had to intervene and persuade local police and county deputies not to press charges against him for assault, as he was prone to drinking and fighting. Each of these offenses was a felony and could have cost him his law career upon conviction. In retrospect, I should not have stepped in on his behalf. I regret not letting things run their course in these criminal matters, because Lupe would then not have become a lawyer. Soon, he got his law degree and license and filed lawsuit after lawsuit against the *Partido* and me. Together with Louis Segura he regularly received money from Mary Nan West—a rich rancher who resided in Batesville and would later serve on the board of regents of the Texas A & M University System—to finance their legal war against the partido and our programs.

Lupe was able to merge the interests of the Barrio Club with those of the other partido faction, which was mostly made up of local second-level leaders. Some were trained in the school administrators program, others were already in the public schools. The Barrio Club sought the nomination of its members as candidates at every election. A couple of them got in but only because we had picked them before their club had organized, such as Arturo Gonzalez, Rudy Palomo, Issac Juarez, and Rey Perez. Lupe got nominated and elected to the city council of Cristal. In the next election, the Barrio Club discovered the fraud committed by one of our own, José Herrera, a CU candidate for the city council. Herrera claimed teaching credentials that actually belonged to his brother Saul. CU immediately sought his removal and because time was of the essence, we did not go through the selection process. Instead, we negotiated with those not previously chosen in order to pick a replacement. We settled on Eugenio "Gene" Ruiz. He was a school administrator and his sister, "Cha Chi," was on the school board already. This was the only negative aspect, a brother and sister team on two of our major governmental entities. Shortly after we won the election, it was necessary to hire a police chief. The Barrio Club wanted as police chief Ramon Garza, the former county deputy and now a member of the school board. We saw the danger of that close knit group becoming interlocking directors. CU wanted Antonio Yanas, a former patrolman from the days of Los Cinco. CU voted to instruct the city officials to hire Yanas, but a the split occurred over that issue with the fear of the interlocking directors. On the city council, Lupe Cortinas, Issac Juarez—both Barrio Club members—and Gene Ruiz made a majority. At the school board, "Cha Chi" Ruiz, Ramon Garza, and Raul Flores, the head of CU II, made the majority. The CU II faction instructed its public officials to hire Garza and fire the school superintendent, Amancio Cantu; they took control of the school district. Local Cristaleños were promoted into positions of educational leadership. Those from other parts of Texas and the nation that had come to help were no longer welcome or needed. They soon left either by resignation, termination, or voluntary departure.

La Causa was now a personal one. The professional careerists had won over the militant Chicanos. The new leaders did not seek to make further changes, other than personnel changes, in any area. They often stated that the goal of the *movimiento* (movement) had been to rid ourselves of the gringos. We had done that. Now, according to them, there was no need to make further changes. They saw themselves as both the cause and the result of the movement: the job was done, according to their perspective.

Local organization was still vital to the success of governance at the local level and to the development of a political party. Prior to the split in Ciudadanos Unidos, we did enjoy solidarity of purpose and goals which allowed us to take control of the schools and city government, even the county.

11

Chicano School and City Governance

An organizer has the ability to put a human puzzle together, and is then the one who has an idea of how to solve the problem or puzzle and has the necessary creative and leadership skills to make others willing to listen, to trust the organizer to recognize an opportunity or provide an avenue toward seeking a solution. Organizers do not ask for a vote of confidence from the group they are working with. They simply begin to act and work at attracting supporters. In this process an organizer will identify and gather available resources for the group's needs and advise them on strategy. Ultimately—win or lose—the organizer walks away, to repeat the scenario another day with another group. Regrettably, we insist that community work done by organizers be mostly voluntary and without remuneration. There are no fringe benefits. It is as if organizers have taken vows of poverty in order to serve the community. Personal power for an organizer is not an end in itself; this is one of the fundamental differences between organizers and politicians, as the latter only seeks personal power. They pretend, and we let them, that their election empowers us as a group. The most empowered by the election of a person to public office, besides the elected official, are their big-money contributors, who will have unlimited and unqualified access to the so-called public servant.

The Transition From Organizer to Elected Official

In my case, I could not give up the persuasive power and influence I had earned over the membership of Ciudadanos Unidos or among the students. If I stopped organizing, the entire agenda would be jeopardized. If I continued organizing toward an electoral takeover of local government, I would not have the complete loyalty from those elected once they realized they had acquired personal power as politicians. I had to become a central part of the first cadre of elected officials in order to direct the development of our political party as it was built, and create a culture of Chicano governance at the school board and city council.

The challenge after the walkout victory was to capture political control of the municipalities and school boards in the three counties of the Winter Garden district. Organizers by nature spend 99 percent of their energies on organizing the group effort to take power, and one percent on teaching them how to wield that power to govern after a victory. I decided that I would not make that mistake. MAYO had not had a single electoral victory in conjunction with a school walkout. Cristal was the most effective and efficient walkout organizational effort I had been involved with, after thirty-eight previous tries. I only had one choice: I had to accept a leadership role as a political candidate.

Mike Perez and Arturo Gonzalez and I became the first Raza Unida slate of candidates for the school board elections of April 3, 1970; Pablo Puente and Ventura Gonzales became the candidates of our newly formed political party for the city council. In other communities in the Winter Garden area, similar Raza Unida party slates were organized, and on election day in April, winning fifteen of our sixteen races was exhilarating.

At the first meeting held after the school election, the school superintendent usually presides for the purpose of electing board officers, the president and a secretary. Up to that point, not one Chicano had ever been elected president or secretary of the school board in Crystal City. The other three Chicanos on the Board and I had agreed to elect me as president at this first meeting, but the three gringos on the Board had their own plan. Arturo Gonzalez sought to get recognized by Superintendent John Billings in order to nominate me for president. Billings ignored him, and also ignored Mike Perez when he tried to get the floor. Instead, Billings first recognized Wayne Hamilton, who in turn nominated Eddie Treviño for president, but Eddie quickly declined. Hamilton then nominated Mike Perez, one of my slate members, because he had received the highest number of votes in the recent election with 54.9% of the vote. He declined the nomination and used the opportunity to nominate me for president. I was elected by a vote of four to three. The crowd in attendance, mostly Chicanos, exploded into sustained applause.

As the presiding officer, I quickly sought nominations for secretary. Perez nominated Eddie Treviño and he won by the same margin. The gringo board members objected to my voting on Eddie Treviño's nomination because "the president votes only in case of a tie. Board policy." I recalled that my prior research of the board minutes had not indicated such a voting policy for the election of officers, and that it pertained only to voting on issues. And even then, the policy had been invoked only haphazardly. I looked individually and slowly at gringo board members Wayne Hamilton, "Buddy" Maedgen, and Ed Mayer, the now ex-president, and said, "This president will vote on every matter before this board. Every matter. The old policy is just that, old. Anybody have a problem with that?" Then I announced that since there were no objections, this would be the new policy.

I learned three lessons from this first encounter with the powers that had been. First, the opposition will always try to divide and conquer; be organized and expect the worse. Second, if you have the votes, you don't have to explain, convince, argue, or present evidence in support of your position—just vote. When you have power, use it! Lastly, the tactic of looking at gringos in the eye is the use of a reverse stereotype. Anglos believe that if a person does not look you in the eye when talking or being addressed, they are "hiding something," "lying," "being devious," and/or are "afraid." I think they got this from the old westerns, where the burly cowboy always demands, "look me in the eye when I'm talking to you." I called it "the John Wayne Syndrome." Parents use this rhetoric with their children all the time, "Look at me when I'm talking to you," to assess honesty and truthfulness. By facing down the gringo board members at the first meeting, they knew who was in charge and that I intended to use my power fully. They also had to defer to the power of my position. And, worse yet, they had to defer to me and the other Chicano board members in public. La raza present at this first meeting, and there were hundreds, loved the display of legitimate machismo. Being macho often carries negative connotations because male prerogative and power regularly abuses the female gender and domain. But in this case the people loved my machismo because here was a young Chicano male not only facing down the older gringo board members in public but also putting them in their place, at his will.

During subsequent meetings we busily began voting for changes that would allow us to hire Chicanos, begin programs, and create a new educational environment. The Chicano members voted in a solid bloc for our agenda items. The votes during this first year on the school board were typically four to three, Chicanos to whites. The first item we needed to take care of in order to pave the way for others was the making of personnel changes. I learned that there are only two kinds of executives, ones who by their skill, finesse, and political acumen direct and control the board members who hire them, and those who are directed and supervised totally by the board members who hire them. We were not going to be directed and controlled by *any* of the gringo superintendents—John Billings, John Briggs, R.C. Tate, or Darrel Ray.

At that time, we had two active superintendents, John Billings—who had put in his resignation in January, 1970, over the walkout of '69—and the newly hired John Briggs. Billings was hanging around in order to serve out his contract because Briggs was now the executive in charge. The two other ex-superintendents, Tate and Ray, were also employed by the district. Tate was the director of the federal migrant program and Ray was a school principal. The entire district had old, worn-out Anglo administrators, teachers, teacher's aides, and support staff. No Anglo was ever fired, demoted, or removed; Anglos never faded in Cristal, they died in office. The district had no mandatory retirement age for employees, professional or otherwise. We immediately implemented a policy to force retirement at the age of sixty-five and that netted us the removal of thirteen Anglo teachers and administrators. There were very few Chicanos employed in any capacity, particularly in positions of power over money, policy, curriculum or instruction. We also voted to require the learning and speaking of Spanish by teachers within three years because we were going to start a comprehensive, district-wide bilingual education program. We began a concerted campaign to hire Chicanos and replace Anglos at every available opportunity. We also fired many whites, beginning with the new superintendent, and twenty more teachers during the next year.

Often, to mitigate the charges that we were only hiring Chicano militants, we hired the very persons John Briggs had interviewed, already hired, or recommended for other positions. This is how we found our first Chicano superintendent, Angel Noe Gonzalez, and Erasmo Andrade, the federal programs director, for example.

The Removal of Superintendent Briggs and
the Beginning of Bilingual Education

Among the many charges we brought against Briggs, one was of particular interest to me. He had instructed all staff, support and professional,
to inform him of our presence on any campus, building, or activity. He
had persons assigned to monitor us as we went about the business of
supervising the implementation of school board policy and state law. I
could not set foot on a campus or in a building or attend an activity
without being summoned by some Anglo to the nearest telephone.
Briggs invariably was on the line telling me that he didn't appreciate
my uninvited interference with his educational program. I always
laughed into his ear as loud as I could and would tell him, "You work
for me, Briggs, I don't work for you! If you want to watch me, get your
ass over here and see what I have just found out." Any one of us that
made a visit to a school or activity would find de facto segregation of
students within buildings or programs and that our recent policy direc-
tives were not being carried out. Because of his surveillance of us, we decided to replace Briggs at the first opportunity. The summer of 1970 we
hired Angel Noe Gonzalez as superintendent. He turned out to be an excellent choice: tireless, energetic, tough, and eager to gain a reputation
as an educator. He had previously been denied an opportunity to become superintendent and now turned with enthusiasm to the task. He
built a great team and made miracles happen regularly with the finances available. His wife, Diola, became a bilingual education supervisor and was a quiet supporter of our efforts.

From day one, we did not accept any of Briggs' recommendations
and made our own official policy, by voting on the board. We not only
instituted personnel changes but also began innovative programs, the
most controversial of which was that of bilingual education. Most people find fault with the program on two grounds. The critics of bilingual
education either disagree with the philosophy or the approach, blaming
the content or the method. Critics argued that teaching in any language
other than English is divisive and would lead to the ethnic balkaniza-
tion of our culture. This would be so because language transmits culture. "English only," then, both transmits Anglo culture and also exter-
minates any other culture via displacement. Other critics fault bilingual
education because students often experience confusion, and lag behind
in both languages as they struggle to gain proficiency in both. The problem here is with the approach to teaching: the teachers mix different
methods of instruction and do not focus on one approach in either English or Spanish long enough for the children to demonstrate any com-

petence. The bilingual program we proposed was going to be from the
first through the third grades. We ordered that instruction take place in
either Spanish or English, not just English. Our Chicano kids came to
school from homes that spoke only Spanish; very few spoke English.
We insisted that English proficiency be made an exit criterion from elementary school, not an entrance criterion for the first grade or kindergarten. Later, we expanded our ideas for bilingual education to include
the high school. We thought that learning in two languages was a
worthwhile goal, and we decided that a high school diploma with both
language proficiencies was the ultimate goal. We disagreed with those
who wanted Spanish utilized only as a means, a transition, to English.
We disagreed vehemently with those who wanted our kids immersed
only in English from day one. We called immersion the sink or swim
method. Yet most schools in Texas and the U.S. still use that approach
today. When kids in this type of program fail, the educators blame the
program, or the kids, when they should be questioning the educational
method.

Since we had the power to implement school policy, including curriculum, we voted for a bilingual program that would maintain Spanish, build proficiency in that language, and also teach English proficiency by the twelfth grade, if not sooner. Because we added a strong
cultural component to the language instruction, the critics—internal
staff, community residents, outside influentials, and some students—
opposed our initiatives.

White Backlash by Teachers

Anglo teachers and staff retaliated in 1971, the year following our inauguration, with a strike of their own. The Texas Classroom Teachers' Association (TCTA) declared a boycott of our school district, urging teachers not to seek employment in our district. They published a notice in
many professional journals and posted leaflets at area universities and
teacher colleges. We promptly sued TCTA for $350,000 in damages (the
disruption of instructional programs, the hiring of temporary teachers,
defamation and breach of contract), but the court only granted us $500,
plus attorney fees.

On the other hand, and because of the Anglo teachers' boycott, we
got rid of more than a hundred teachers and most administrators, all
white. The local Anglos honored the call for a boycott and did not seek
work in the Chicano administration.

I spoke directly with new employees hired by Briggs, such as Elpidio
Lizcano, the band director, and his wife, Janette. We charged Mr. Lizcano

with the responsibility of teaching the band Chicano music and marching routines that would reflect our Chicano culture, and he was overjoyed at the prospect. The marching band learned to play the favorite Mexican tune "Jalisco" and added it as its fight song. It was played at every football game, particularly when we scored or made a significant play. When the band marched defiantly onto the field at half time, it was to the tune of "Jalisco," with many of the marchers thrusting a clenched, left-hand, power fist into the air. Our critics fumed every Friday night during the football season at this spectacle, especially at out-of-town trips. Our football team never won many games, but our band became and remains the premier musical and marching band of the region, regularly winning awards for its performances and marching routines.

Unequal Educational Opportunity

State funding of schools has always been skewed in favor of rich districts, while the poor districts remain poor. Because we had boycotted the schools for many days during the fall of 1969 and early 1970, slightly over 10 percent of all school days in the year, operating revenue was scarce when we took over, since per-pupil allocation of state money is based on school attendance.

The schools in Texas get money from three sources: taxes, federal grants, and state grants. This fight to equalize funding was an issue we attacked, joining with another Chicano urban district in San Antonio, Edgewood Independent School District, to sue the state. The fight continues today. Texas does not provide money for all students to receive the same quality education across the state and probably never will, as more students in the public schools are Mexican and African Americans. Many Anglo taxpayers and voters question why they should continue to bear the burden of educating some "other" group's children. As members of the school, we went after the two sources we could affect, taxes and grants. During my three-year term we nearly doubled the property valuations for tax purposes and therefore increased the operating budget. Across Texas, as in the country, a major task of officeholders is to keep property taxes low. This unofficial policy hurts governmental entities that seek to provide services to constituents previously underserved or ignored, as in the case of Chicanos, while helping the rich landowners and those with extensive real estate holdings and taxable assets. I had studied the land-ownership patterns in the Winter Garden area of Texas, which includes Frio, La Salle, Dimmit, Zavala, Uvalde, and Maverick counties. In Zavala County, I found that twenty-six people owned 85 percent of the land and of these nineteen did not live in Zavala County. In Maverick County, to provide a contrast, ten people owned 91 percent of the land. Land in general was evaluated lower than in other comparable areas of the state. Moreover, the rate of taxation was also lower than in almost all other areas of the state, except for far West Texas.

The Anglo taxpayers fought back. They refused to pay their taxes, they sued, and they hid assets. The rich ranchers moved their cattle, horses, airplanes, tractors, implements, and vehicles from one county to another to avoid the tax appraiser. They underreported the value of the minerals in their land. They challenged the categorization of irrigated land on their holdings, insisting that their land was underdeveloped and all in brush. We took them on and ultimately won all legal battles, but they were costly.

Our needs as Chicanos, long ignored, were dramatic. Not only did our new staff have to get busy and take over the reins of power, but it also had to begin to address the decades of neglect in a hurry. We instructed the staff to draft proposals seeking funds at all government levels and from private sources. Virtually every proposal our staff wrote requesting funds was accepted. In the past, the Anglo administration had rarely sought grants of any type. Philosophically, they were opposed to such handouts and welfare. The farm subsidies, oil depletion allowance, tax credits, old age assistance, and social security they had long enjoyed, however, were the same as handouts and welfare. But when federal money flows to the rich, it is not called welfare.

Grants from Washington, D.C., began to pour in. Our critics began to accuse us of being in bed with the Republican White House, then occupied by Richard Nixon. We thought it curious that only when Chicanos get federal money is it considered a "buy out." When other groups get money from Washington it is assumed they deserve it, because they wrote a good proposal, because they are fiscally responsible or because they are eligible. We nearly tripled the size of the Cristal school operating budget, from $1.3 million in 1969 to $3 million in 1973, when I turned over the reins of power to the next group of Raza Unida party militants elected as trustees of the Cristal school board. We also succeeded in persuading the voters to pass an additional $2.8 million in construction bonds with which to build new schools to replace the old Japanese American internment camp barracks used as schools for Chicanos.

When MAYO first began to target the schools for protest, particularly in Cristal, we knew that there were only five Chicano superintendents in all of Texas. The idea for training Chicano superintendents came during a most unlikely moment: Angel Noe Gonzalez and I were

Gutiérrez speaking at the dedication of the Maria Hernandez Resource Center, 1972.

returning from a trip and stopped to gas up his Cadillac. The attendant took his money and gave him a set of drinking glasses and some Gold Bond stamps redeemable for additional prizes. We discussed the transaction and how we both thought and felt we were getting something more than the gasoline with the prizes and stamps when in reality it

was all included in the price of gasoline. I began to list ideas and figures on a piece of grocery bag, as we had no writing paper handy. We
had been trying to figure out how to get money to pay teachers to study
and become certified as superintendents. The glitch was that we did
not have access to a university, much less control of such an institution,
that would accept our training program or professors and extend certification to the participants when we deemed them ready to assume positions as superintendents elsewhere. The drinking glasses and Gold
Bond stamps provided us with the answer. Colleges and universities
are driven by tuition payments from students and state funds based on
those enrollments. If we guaranteed a university the money for graduate level courses and paid their fees, they probably would accept the
idea of an off-campus program taught by professors that we hired.
Then, certification of the teachers as superintendents was only one
more step, a formality. Everything the university wanted was paid for,
we just gave out the Gold Stamps in form of administrative competence
certificates.

The Dynamic Duo Goes to New York

At first opportunity, Viviana Santiago—my right-hand person since
her recruitment at the MAYO conference at La Lomita—and I sought
funding from the Carnegie Corporation for a training and certification
program of school superintendents. Viviana was my most trusted companion, a smart and tough negotiator. Her managerial skills kept the
various political offices and funded programs running smoothly. She
and I traveled to New York to negotiate funding for the proposal. I tried
to add the city managers to the list of training needs but was not successful. Before the Carnegie funders I played the heavy by berating
these administrators on their historic insensitivity to Chicano needs
and Viviana, the smoothie, explained most rationally how the need for
superintendents was the very answer to high Chicano dropout rates
and the innovative curriculum changes that needed to be made. It
worked: the Carnegie Corporation funded the first training cycle of
Chicano superintendents, and even a second cycle. We began "buying"
certification with tuition payments from various universities in Texas
and California. We graduated and had certified nearly thirty new Chicano superintendents in four years.

   We also began a "grow-your-own" training program for teachers'
aides to become teachers, for teachers to obtain Master's degrees, and
for community residents and school support staff to obtain Graduate
Equivalency Diplomas (GEDs). On one occasion during a graduation

ceremony we had four graduating classes: the high school kids, parents receiving GEDs, "home-grown" and educated teachers through the Urban/Rural Federal Program, and the superintendents from the Carnegie Corporation program. Witnessing that graduation program made me cry. Education for Chicanos by Chicanos had finally come to la raza of Cristal.

The accomplishments at the city council were similar in quantity and scope. Bill Richey, my co-organizer in La Salle County and assistant of economic development in the Winter Garden, became the first city manager in Cristal under our direction. With the city's support we were able to begin a model mental health program and a community health center, to pave streets in the barrios, construct hundreds of homes with urban renewal monies, and establish La Oficina de la Gente (The Office of the People) a legal aid clinic staffed at first by Sylvia Demarest, and then Paul Rich.

The Richeys decided to relocate to the Northeast in 1972 so that Bill could enroll in law school at Harvard. The next city manager was Francisco Rodriguez, a former high school classmate of mine. Rodriguez moved the foreign policy relations with Mexico into high gear and modernized the office and operations of the city.

The Legacy

My three years on the school board passed quickly. Ciudadanos Unidos selected new faces from among its membership to succeed us, and won. Among those that also served on the school board during the years 1973–1976 were Ernesto Olguin, José O. Mata, and Viviana Santiago. The Raza Unida party continued its string of electoral victories at the city council and school board levels in the three counties. The partido had already won important seats among those available in the county government, but not the control of the county judge and the commissioner's court, which is the county executive department. In our position in the Winter Garden area, this seemed to be the inevitable direction to head in expanding our power base.

We had an idea of a plan to take control of county government. Once in power, few of us thought of training successors. It was the notion of rotating leadership in our organizations that forced us to face the need for replacements. In political positions, the incumbents seldom voluntarily relinquish the power of the office. Voters either vote them out or officials retire or die in office; a few politicians move to higher office because they seek greater power. Most people want to follow their political leaders, not lead them. The three of us that had first been elected to

the school board, Arturo, Miguel, and I, did not seek reelection. Our political party did not permit it, as we had term limits. Besides, there were
other positions, in higher levels of government, to seek.

Challengers rise from among our own ranks when there is no shared
power with Anglos. The views of challengers often pose a counterview
to the existing programs, personnel, issues, ideas, policies, and allocation of resources. They rise as opposition leaders when only other Mexicans hold power and there is no additional room for them. In Zavala
County, Chicanos had been virtually excluded from holding public office since Texas was a republic and the county had been created. It was
time now to make room for ourselves: We had control of the City Hall
and the schools and now needed the courthouse. We abided by term
limits as a way to increase the number of elected officials with experience and to minimize the chances a political machine might be developed by a few Chicano militants turned politicians.

When I left the school board we had a district with a comprehensive
bilingual program and Chicano Studies incorporated in all subject matter. Our dropout problem had been cut in half, the placement rate of
Chicano graduates into colleges and universities was very impressive,
and we sent kids off to college with money obtained from scholarships
and grants. The personnel in the school district was almost completely
Chicano; the few Anglos working with us were new, and in total support of what we were trying to do. The money generated by the school
district in terms of payroll and consumption of supplies, goods, and
services began to create many jobs and because of that, a Chicano middle class in Cristal. The voter turnout among la raza was the highest in
the state. People had a reason to vote for something—the control of their
schools and city. The federal programs being brought in were making a
difference not only with kids but also the parents who availed themselves of the opportunities. By 1973, we were already planning on training school superintendents for other communities with the Carnegie
Corporation's funding, and were graduating teachers and teachers'
aides with Master's and Bachelor's degrees, respectively, through federally funded programs.

The city officials had turned the focus of the urban renewal program
toward building homes for Chicanos. Construction was constant.
Cristal had the most beautiful barrios now, with paved streets, sidewalks, and parks. Many programs were initiated in the area of mental
and public health. *El Centro de Salud* (The Health Center) became a very
extensive and comprehensive health program that today serves the entire county. The locally funded legal aid program eventually merged
with the program served by Texas Rural Legal Aid Foundation, and the

workers at the Del Monte plant had decertified the Teamsters Union and now had an independent union, Obreros Unidos. With the election of Sheriff José Serna in 1972 we invited the farm workers union to organize in Zavala County without fear of legal reprisal from law enforcement officers. We were on a roll toward building a Chicano-controlled school and city, serving the first real Chicano community in Aztlan.

12

El Partido Nacional de la Raza Unida

Immediately after the April, 1970, elections in Cristal, I traveled to as many places as I could, spreading the word of the political organizing going on in the Winter Garden area. The zeal among Texas activists for the creation of a statewide political party and the subsequent building of Aztlan was tremendous. Groups and individuals in other states were bit by the same bug. Chicanos who had heard of the victories in Cristal and the Winter Garden area by our Chicano political party wanted to replicate the successes in their area. Chicanos in Texas wanted the political party to go statewide. Together, local and regional political groups wanted to expand the concept of an alternative political party to include them. These groups wanted a national Partido de la Raza Unida. Invitations to speak, after our inauguration and swearing-in ceremony on April 17th, poured in from all regions of the country. Chicanos everywhere wanted to hear the story of the takeover of Cristal and the birth of La Raza Unida party.

People interested in the concept of the *Partido de la Raza Unida* fell into two camps: those who longed for the creation of Aztlan, the Chicano homeland, and those who wanted to use the electoral strategy as a political arm of the Chicano movement. The difficulty I initially had in organizing was in being able to tell the difference between these two goals and potentially contradictory ideologies. A person wanting to be part of the partido did not necessarily want to become a Chicano nationalist. A person wanting to be part of the political strategy could also

La Raza Unida Party poster from the 1970 campaign. The poster reads "One Hand Doesn't Wash Itself."

be interested in remaining a national Democrat and only interested in taking power locally, under the umbrella of our political party.

The interest in forming the partido seem concentrated in certain regions of the country. California was a hot bed of organizing activity. Armando Navarro was the prime organizer for the party in the area around San Bernardino, California, called the Upland Empire. Herman Baca, a printer and a party delegate from National City was organizing a group of La Raza Unida party supporters in the San Diego, California, area. Bert Corona, a labor organizer forever looking for a new political opportunity, invited me to attend a MAPA convention, comprised mostly of Democrats. In Denver, Colorado, the Crusade for Justice was the local partido. This group saw itself as a revolutionary, vanguard cadre of cultural nationalists. The Crusade was formed around a charismatic leader, Rodolfo "Corky" Gonzales, who sought to organize urban youth. The nickname "Corky" was a holdover from his amateur and professional boxing days. Reies Lopez Tijerina from New Mexico kept telling me via occasional telephone calls that he wanted to meet and discuss my organizing plans for the political party, particularly in that state. The cities of Albuquerque and Las Vegas in New Mexico had a mixture of Black Berets, Brown Berets, and Alianzistas (members of the Alianza [Alliance], another activist group) looking toward the formation of a party apparatus, and Juan José Peña and Fred Hill were attempting to forge them all into one organization. In South Tucson, Arizona, Salomon Baldenegro was finding support for the partido among the *indios "Papago,"* now called Tohono O'Odham. The various Berets groups, the Black, Red, and Brown, were organizations that viewed themselves as the defenders of la raza and their barrios. They patrolled the Chicano neighborhoods and provided protest activities with security. They dressed in paramilitary garb, hence the colored berets. The Alianza was another matter altogether: this movement was established to recover the lost lands—land grants from Spain and Mexico made to our ancestors in the Southwest. The principal leader of the Alianza, the short name for Alliance of Free City States, was Tijerina.

The area around Lake Michigan—from Milwaukee, Chicago, and Gary, Indiana, over to Michigan state—was another important center. La Raza Unida organizations were in some cases, as in Indiana's, nonprofit, tax-exempt organizations. There were isolated spots in Kansas, Nebraska, Washington, Oregon, Arizona, and Washington, D.C., that when joined together ultimately formed a Raza Unida organizing committee.

Local leaders began to emerge in the other regions, such as Ernesto Chacon in Milwaukee, Angel Moreno in Chicago, Betty Cuevas and Fred Aguilar in the San Fernando Valley of California, Lupe de Leon in

Indiana, Manuel Fierro in Kansas, Raul Ruiz and Charon D'Aiello in East Los Angeles, Elena Minor in San Jose, Calfornia, Frank Shafer-Corona in Washington, D.C., and Lupe Angiano in Maryland. While Reies Lopez Tijerina was in dialogue with me about the purpose and direction of the party, he did not seek help to build another political party. He had already formed a party previously, the People's Constitutional Party of New Mexico. He simply sought our support for the land claims being made as part of the land recovery movement, as a seasoned veteran of the Chicano land wars in New Mexico. He had physically taken several portions of national parks and held them against the U.S. Forest Service. He had been tried and jailed for these attempts at getting the land back.

Locally, in Cristal, Cotulla, Pearsall, and Asherton in the Winter Garden area, we won more elections in 1971. Pressures mounted for me and the MAYO leadership to expand the base of the electoral organizing across the state. At a special MAYO meeting called for this very purpose, the members voted to go statewide with the partido. I voted against the proposal but lost. I had no choice but to lead the charge to what I thought ultimately would be electoral disaster. To me, the reasons for the ultimate failure were obvious. First, our ethnic group had majority populations in many rural areas but not in any urban area. Second, the resources necessary for such a statewide effort were not available to us at the time. Third, I argued that we need to consolidate our electoral strength first in the rural areas to have resources and political power at the local level; we needed a regional party which was permissible under the election code. (Basically, that is what we already had begun in the Winter Garden area. I felt we should build on solid ground, not engage in symbolic statewide exercises. This point offended many supporters in the urban areas because they felt I was leaving them out of the future of the political party.) Fourth, the majority in many other communities or sections of urban areas like El Paso, Corpus Christi, San Antonio, and Del Rio did not mean a majority voting population in which all Chicanos could register to vote.

Older Chicanos came into the United States during the Mexican Revolution of 1910 to escape the violence. The stream of immigrants continued during the aftermath of the Revolution until about 1930 when the situation began to normalize. These older members of our group are not citizens; they merely have lawful status as resident aliens. As such, they are ineligible to register to vote. I call this "the Rule of 1, 2, 3." Because Anglos are older—mostly over the age of twenty-one—and have money and education, they vote in higher numbers than any other group. If you pick out one hundred Anglos in the street, almost all of them are eligible and have reasons to go vote. If you pick out two hundred Blacks, about half of them will be old enough to vote and have good reasons to actually go vote. Blacks have a younger median age than whites but are older than browns, la raza. Chicanos need three hundred of our own to have equal power with one hundred whites. Blacks need two hundred of theirs to have equal power with one hundred whites. Hence—1, 2, 3.

At the organizing convention of La Raza Unida, the delegates voted against my proposal to form the political party county by county, a regional plan. They didn't listen, and voted with their hearts. They voted to go statewide with me knowing we would surely lose. The rules governing elections and political parties are strictly a state matter: the applicable law over La Raza Unida was Texas election law. The election code contained two major requirements for the formation of a statewide political party: that a petition of voters requesting the nominees of that political party be placed on the November ballot; and that an organizing convention be held, comprised of delegates from across the state. The organizing convention of a political party has apportioned delegate strength based on the votes cast for governor in the previous election in each county. To meet the first requirement we were going to have to obtain some 23,000 notarized signatures from voters who would not vote or had not voted in the primary elections of any existing political party, and that was not going to be an easy task. We allocated quotas for signatures across the state. I insisted that those who voted for the statewide option bear the burden of getting the signatures, which was a nightmare and an ordeal. Toward the deadline, we encouraged the organizers across the state to gather their supporters and promote petition-signing parties, in the same way they held social parties and fund-raising parties, and finally we did get the required number of signatures.

Mario Compean, the state chairman of MAYO, and I drove to Austin to present the box of petitions to Secretary of State Bob Bullock. The election code stated that the secretary of state had to receive the petitions and certify that the signatures were both sufficient in number and legitimate. Our first hassle with presenting the petitions came from his receptionist and assistants, who wanted us to leave the box with them because the secretary was "busy." We had called for an appointment and told them we were coming at the designated date and time. We reminded them that the law clearly stated that we were to tender the petitions to the secretary of state, not his representatives. We were made to wait for hours. Finally, in the face of our determination and stamina, we were ushered into the spacious back room of his office. His door had a large nameplate above the seal of the state of Texas; the chairs in the room all had the same seal embossed in gold on their leather backs and his desk was enormous. As we were announced upon entry, he barked questions at us with low, raspy voice made that way from too many cigarettes and Jack Daniels, "What do you people want with me. Can't you give that shit to my staff? It's papers, no?" Moving closer to his desk I repeated the election law section about tendering to him, not his representatives. He popped off immediately, "Oh, you're a goddam lawyer, eh?" He made a comment about everything I said from then on.

Bullock took the box and our letter, then lifted the first set of petitions, read a little, and looked up at me, then Mario. He said, "This shit is all wrong. These are no good at all. Look here, you claim to know the election law! Look here, this name has to be in American, *comprende?* This *Ratt-zah You-Nig-Dah* [Raza Unida] name is no good! It must be in regular English, not Tex Mex." We got into it, he and I, over what the election code said and meant and what the U.S. Constitution said in the First Amendment on free speech. I argued that the requirement for the name of a political party was three words and one of them had to be "party." I said, "Raza Unida" is two words and "party" is the third. He argued language: "Goddam it! Cut the crap! You know goddam well this name has to be in English. This is America, goddam it! Texas is still in it, so I hear, goddam it! The three words must be in English and that is all there is to it!"

Mario Compean by nature is a most nervous individual, his face twitching as he speaks, and soft spoken. He tried to get a word in edgewise during the harangue, but to no avail. I thought we were lost. We had gone through all of that Herculean effort for nothing. I didn't have a clue as to what to say now to lift this dark cloud from over us. Nervously, I looked around the room, my mind blank. "Raza Unida is the same in English," I finally said. "What is your name, sir?" I asked him. He began shouting: "Goddam it! What nonsense question is that? What are you talking about? You know exactly what my name is, goddam it! It's on the fucking door! Didn't you see my name, bigger than shit, on the fucking door? Huh? Didn't you?" All the while he was gesturing wildly, throwing the petition and letter back into the box, and pointing to the door. With as much composure as I could muster, I asked him one more time, "Sir, what is your name? Please?" He stood with his nose almost touching mine and bellowed, "Bob Bullock, goddam it! Can't you fucking read? Bob Bullock! Who do you think you're talking to?" Again I said, "Fine. What is your name in Spanish, sir?" Without a moments hesitation he barked at me, "Goddam it! It's Bob Bullock! Bob Bullock in English! Bob Bullock in Spanish. It's still Bob fucking Bullock!" Grinning as best I could, I said, "Then sir, Raza Unida in Spanish is still Raza

Unida in English, no?" To his credit, his eyes opened wide, then shut tight as he roared with laughter. We could hear between the breaths for air and his unrestrained laughing, "Goddam that's good, that's real fucking good. *Ratt-zah You-need-dah* in Spanish, *Ratt-zah You-need-dah* in English. Okay, I'll sign off. You boys gave me a good laugh. Hot damn!" Bob Bullock kept his word: He signed off on the name and certified the signatures on the petitions.

The party obtained ballot status in 1972 and was running a statewide slate, headed by Ramsey Muñiz for governor and his running mate Alma Canales for lieutenant governor.

By late spring of 1972, in consultation with Reies Lopez Tijerina and Corky Gonzales, we decided to call a national meeting, a Raza Unida party national convention. I had traveled to Albuquerque to speak with Reies several times and had convinced him that this political party would help him because of its national appeal to Chicanos and that this base of voters could pressure for his demands as could his supporters, most of whom were actual land-grant heirs. I also went to Denver several times to speak with Corky about the national organizing effort and direction of the partido. In talking to each one about the other, I noticed that Corky and Reies did not get along well, did not speak well about each other. Their rift began when Corky came to Albuquerque to help keep the Alianza going when Reies was jailed for the 1965 Rio Arriba courthouse raid when Tijerina and others tried to execute a citizens' arrest of District Attorney Alfonso Sanchez and engaged in a shootout with police officers. Members of the Alianza did not accept Corky's surrogate leadership. He couldn't speak Spanish; he spoke in English to his rural New Mexican audience about imperialism and the need for revolution without tying it to the land grants. These Alianza members wanted their old nation, Spanish *Nuevo Mexico*, back, not Aztlan. They were not interested in creating a new nation. And, he was out of his league with the rural, *manito* ("little brother," a term of endearment) culture of the membership. Corky was not one of them. Even though Reies, a transplanted *Tejano*, was not a native *manito* either, he had endeared himself to them after decades of struggle on their behalf.

Later, during the preparations for the Poor Peoples' Campaign on Washington D.C., Martin Luther King Jr. accepted Reies over Corky as the spokesman for La Raza, and tensions between the two Chicano leaders grew to impossible proportions. Corky's members involved with the march were reduced to handling group logistics for all raza showing up—kitchen patrol, camp security, defense of the women from sexual attacks, and general clean-up—while Reies went to strategy meetings and press conferences with the Southern Christian Leadership Conference (SCLC) leaders. Crusade members nicknamed Reies Lopez Tijerina "TV-rina" for his dogged pursuit of the media and his staged media events.

As our Texas-based organizing plans were being carried out in the Southwest and Midwest, I made time to keep both of the men informed. Corky, however, remained upset at Reies for upstaging him in Washington, D.C. I had underestimated the degree and intensity of the rift between them.

Recruiting Cesar Chavez

Through the years I had had several conversations with Cesar Chavez regarding his cooperation with the partido. Like the visits to Tijerina's home and that of Gonzales's, I also traveled to La Paz, the farm worker's headquarters near Keene, California, to visit personally with Chavez, who declined involvement from the beginning. He said something to me that I never forgot: he told me that he was a labor leader and not a Chicano leader. He explained that he was a "[Robert] Kennedy Democrat," a national Democrat, and would not change that affiliation. With every conversation on this subject, Chavez sounded more and more like my old mentor, Albert Peña Jr. Both Peña and Chavez used the phrases "national Democrat" or "Kennedy Democrat" to indicate their separate identity, an apartness from the local, racist Democratic power structure and officeholders, the very people who sought our votes and gave us nothing in return. When they used these phrases they meant that they were liberals, not conservative Democrats. Chavez, like Peña, counseled me on how difficult a road I was traveling. They both expressed grave reservations that our people would abandon the Democratic party of Franklin Delano Roosevelt for a new and all-Mexican party.

Chavez did offer to help me directly when he could, told me he would not criticize my efforts in public, and would help me with nonpartisan election campaigns, and he delivered on that pledge several times. First, he came to campaign in Cristal for our Raza Unida party slate running in a nonpartisan election for school board and city council seats. He also accepted my invitation to attend the national convention and speak on the need for political unity, and support for his own efforts. During his speeches Chavez again sounded just like Albert Peña Jr.; he spoke out against the local officials of the Democratic Party but praised the Kennedy Democrats and organized labor. Peña had always distanced himself from the Texas Democrats by invoking an allegiance to something he called the "National Democratic Party."

Both Corky and Reies, by the summer of 1972, wanted to form La Raza Unida as a political party. But, each had different motivations and goals. Reies wanted an electoral instrument to take power in New Mexico. Because he had mass support, he wanted to elect his own people to positions of public power at all levels. Unfortunately his earlier foray into electoral politics with the People's Constitutional Party had not gone well for him: he had lost every position contested to the Democrats. He was not sure that the Raza Unida party was any better, but he was willing to try again. Corky wanted the political party to be a revolutionary, vanguard, cadre-based arm of the Chicano Movement. He was seeking to build a revolutionary nationalist agenda leading toward a Chicano nation. I was caught in the middle. Already with the limited experience of taking power in South Texas cities and schools, I knew how important it was to use the power of government to effect change. I also shared with Corky the notion of a Chicano Nation. But Reies and I did not share Corky's organizing strategy of a revolutionary cell-like organization. Corky's urban experience, without the mass support Reies and I enjoyed in our rural areas of northern New Mexico and South Texas, made him blind to our strategy of organizing to take power electorally. I was less than enthusiastic at the prospect of all three of us working together.

There were two additional problems. First, Reies and Corky both saw me as an apprentice to each of them, and each individually had alluded to my being his successor after I grew in political maturity. In my own mind and public comportment, I accepted their ascribed role of student and heir apparent. I knew that as a matter of age, though, I would outlast them, and regional leadership would fall to me regardless of their wishes. Secondly, I had already seen first-hand the dilution of power with the statewide strategy of the partido in Texas. We had to build a local to regional base of power before we could attempt any statewide activity or we would lose the election and dissipate our resources for no meaningful gain. I had also seen the very effective means by which the Socialist Workers Party (SWP) had used running for public office to organize, to proselytize, and to educate the public on issues.

After several trips to Denver and Albuquerque, I agreed with Reies and Corky that I would be their understudy within the party. The leadership mantle of the partido was going to fall on either of them, initially; the question was, which one?

By early summer, we agreed to have a national convention in El Paso, the more central location. We agreed on an agenda that would call for the creation of not only the top leadership of the party on a national level, but also a governing body called "El Congreso de Aztlan." Without saying so, each one of us could see in this bifurcated structure that there would be a role for both Reies and Corky, one as head of the party, and one as head of the Congreso. Corky wanted to be the head of the political party, and understood that Reies would take the Congreso position. The problem was that we had not cut any specific deal among the three of us. Their ambitions for these positions had not even been articulated to me or to each other.

Organizing the El Paso National Convention

I quickly began to make logistical arrangements for the meeting in El Paso and Juarez, Mexico, just across the border. Symbolically, we wanted to hold our meeting in both cities to indicate it was in reality only one metropolis, one nation, *un pueblo sin fronteras*—one people without a border. By dealing with Mexican President Luis Echeverria Alvarez, I had infuriated both Tijerina and Corky. Tijerina had been deported from Mexico by Echeverria when Echeverria was attorney general under President Gustavo Diaz Ordaz, and Corky pinned the label of assassin on Echeverria for the massacre of Mexican student protesters at *Tlatelolco* in Mexico City during a protest over the Olympics in 1968. I didn't see my dialogue with the Mexican president in that limited sense. We needed resources from wherever we could get them and we needed to be legitimized by the leaders at the highest levels of our other mother country.

I printed the preliminary advertising poster, and we scheduled the meeting for Labor Day weekend. Up until the last few weeks prior to the actual convention, I had no inkling that the folks from the Crusade for Justice were undermining my organizing efforts for a successful conference. I had invited not only Cesar Chavez, Bishop Patricio Flores, and Reverend Ralph Abernathy of the SCLC, but also leaders from various Indian nations and both presidential contenders, George McGovern and the incumbent Richard Nixon, to the conference. Tactically, the invitations were designed to put each of them on notice and their party platform on the spot because our convention could either field a presidential candidate of our own, endorse one of them, or ignore them altogether and concentrate on our own statewide and local election campaigns.

I had prepared a position paper on the Chicano voter as the balance of power in the upcoming presidential election and made suggestions for the type of political demands Chicanos should make in voting for either presidential candidate. That letter circulated around the country and was read at a regional political meeting of Chicanos in San Jose,

California. No Raza Unida party leader or group had publicly declared an interest in running our own candidate for president and neither Corky nor Reies had ever stated an interest in running for the presidency. I had broached that possibility with Reies once and he neither rejected it nor brought it up again. It seemed to me that everyone seemed focused on serving as the balance of power, whether we voted for President, abstained, or boycotted the election. I personally had made some demands of the declared presidential candidates in response to questions from reporters as to which of the two contenders was the lesser evil. Corky and I shared the similar opinion: both Nixon and McGovern were fingers of the same hand. They were both evil for la raza.

Behind my back, Crusade members directed by Corky let it be known that Cesar Chavez was not welcome at the convention and would be booed if he appeared. I did not know that plans by Crusade members were also afoot to withdraw the invitation to the top leadership of the American Indian Movement (AIM), the Spanish-speaking Catholic activist priests, and Ralph Abernathy. These tactics embarrassed me and the Texas delegation of the partido tremendously. Reverend Abernathy had recently made a trip to Dallas and publicly endorsed our candidate for governor, Ramsey Muñiz. Cesar Chavez had been campaigning in nonpartisan elections for our candidates, as he had promised, since 1970. Dissidents from other states and in support of the Corky camp were going to propose that only delegates be permitted on the floor and guests were to be precleared by delegate vote or be denied access to the floor and the speaker's platform.

I arrived in El Paso in the last days of August to make final preparations for the conference and to set up my headquarters at the convention hotel, El Paso del Norte. At several meetings with arriving delegations and volunteers, there was an expectation of having a tremendous conference and the beginning of a truly organized national Chicano movement. Reies Lopez Tijerina and Corky Gonzales arrived a day prior to the first plenary session of the convention. They both checked with me on last minute details, arrangements and the agenda.

Corky and some of his people told me on the eve of the convention of the killing in Oro Grande, New Mexico, of Ricardo Falcon, a Colorado delegate. Falcon apparently was shot in cold blood by a gas station attendant who refused to give him water for his overheating car. Corky was very upset; he wanted an immediate press conference demanding an investigation by the Department of Justice on the failure of local police to arrest the killer. He wanted a public commitment to the investigation by both Nixon and McGovern. I arranged a press conference for this purpose the next morning but was excluded from participation by

Corky and Falcon's widow. I told Corky to mention the killing of someone named Anaya in Juarez, across the border, and to demand the same
of the Mexican president. He ignored my request. Reportedly, Anaya
was a potential delegate but I did not have all the details. He turned out
to be related to Rodolfo Anaya, the writer.

I arranged for the three of us to meet as soon as possible in Corky's
suite. The incidents involving Anaya and Falcon were but two pressing
concerns. Corky, Reies, and I met alone in his bedroom, with Corky's
bodyguards right outside the door, on the evening prior to the convention opening. After a brief and stiff welcome to the suite, and once inside his bedroom, Corky began the conversation between us by asking
me what I was going to do personally about the killing of Ricardo Falcon. I told him the press conference was arranged for the following
morning and gave them both the sketchy details of the killing of the
other person in Juarez. I also told him I would make a comment about
these deaths to the press at that time but that I was worried about some
people who were encouraging a protest march to leave from the convention to Oro Grande, New Mexico. I asked them to stand with me in
stopping that effort. Corky brushed aside my remarks and without asking us to be seated, asked me for our support to elect him as the national
chairman of La Raza Unida Party. Tijerina immediately expressed dis-
pleasure at this notion. He asked Corky, *en español,* if this was a plan to
run for President of the United States, as some people said. The question
in Spanish was a double insult to Corky because he barely understood
it, and the question itself was insulting enough. Corky wanted to lead
la raza, not lead white people. Tijerina also wanted to know, turning to
me and without waiting for an answer to his first question from Corky,
if I had invited Nixon and McGovern to speak at the convention. He
pointedly asked me *en español,* again excluding Corky, if we were going
to vote on endorsing either of them or support Corky's run for the presidency. The questions came very fast and were stated in hostile tones.

Corky got very angry. I guess he was angered at the tone of Tijerina's
questions because he barely spoke Spanish. Corky may not have even
understood what Reies was proposing. Reies was moving on to a higher
level of strategy and issues without resolution of support for Corky's
candidacy. Corky vocalized his anger in English, launched into a tirade.
He told Tijerina that he had followed Reies's leadership in the past, had
led his organization in his absence, and found them to be lacking in ideology and a real commitment to revolution of the kind that he was prepared to undertake. He accused Tijerina of not being a nationalist but a
reactionary because of his fascination with things Spanish and royal.
He used the example of Jerry Noll, a rotund blue-eyed fellow that Reies

had introduced at some Alianza gatherings as the King of the Indies, the New World, our Aztlan included.

Tijerina became incensed, and I was caught in the middle. Fluent in both English and Spanish, he prefers his primary language of Spanish among la raza. He lectured Corky in Spanish, beginning with a caustic attack on his inability to even speak Spanish while seeking to lead Spanish-speakers, and proceeded to detail how he had already built an alternative political movement and political party, the People's Constitutional Party in New Mexico years ago. The Raza Unida Party was nothing new. He charged that Corky only paid lip service to his revolution, that the call was empty. Tijerina had yet to see any real activity on Corky's part. He accused the Crusade leadership, beginning with Corky, of being cowardly, *no tiene huevos* (of not having any balls). The Crusaders were nothing but thugs acting as bodyguards for Corky, Reies charged. Before long, they were shouting at each other. I couldn't follow all the allegations, they were coming so quickly.

Needless to say, the meeting broke up immediately after a disgusted and very angry Reies left the room. Corky asked me what I was going to do about withdrawing the invitations to Nixon and McGovern. He insisted on my pledge to select him as national chair. I asked him who he was going to have as his second, or vice chair, of the party, if not Reies. First, he said there were not two offices, only one—the head of the Partido was the only head. The Congreso was a legislative body and he as president would preside over that as well. I was shocked at this, and the specter of Corky holding both positions without a Tijerina-like leader also at the top for balance. Secondly, he told me that he didn't need a vice chair at all, much less Tijerina. He would rely on all his lieutenants when necessary, as he had in the Crusade, to help lead the party. I was in disbelief at this open display of arrogance and ruthless grab for power. In all the previous discussions, we never had entertained the idea of one person holding both positions in the national party structure.

He asked me again what I intended to do. He asked pointedly, "Are you going to back me or run against me?" I was floored at the train of events and the content of his remarks. I had never thought that I would run for national chair or Congreso chair. I had always assumed I was the apprentice to both him and Tijerina, that my job was to be the field organizer for the Partido. To buy time while I figured out what to do, I told him that I would let him know very soon.

I conferred with the Texas group over what had happened. I asked them if they thought we should offer an alternative candidate to challenge Corky for the chairmanship. Most everyone agreed that I should be that person. I tried to locate Tijerina and ask if he was going to run and what his opinion was if I were to run. When I found him, he said that I was the only one who could keep things going as successfully as they had been because Corky simply was power hungry and an ego-maniac. Other delegates that I called to inform of this dangerous split also encouraged me to run against Corky. With this quick but emerging show of support, I was willing to fight Corky for the leadership man-tle. I had done all the work for the convention and knew who was com-ing from where. I knew I could win if I worked quickly.

Rumors, events, and meetings began to happen fast after I decided to run. My closest friends from Crystal City, members of the Barrio Club, and delegation leaders from other states—like Baca, Navarro, Angiano, Shafer-Corona, and Fierro—and I personally set out immediately to contact delegates for support. My impromptu campaign staff began to organize the convention delegates into voting blocks and count the votes we had committed to me. Small groups were invited over to my suite to talk about my plans for the partido. I worked many undecided delegates one-on-one in the halls of the hotel, at the convention site, and by telephone into the night. It became perfectly clear, very quickly, that my organizational training and the work I had done in developing the convention had paid off.

I went back to Corky's suite and was met at the door by Ernesto "Ernie" Vigil, a young Crusade insider and second-level lieutenant. According to Ernie, Corky was not available. I told Ernie that I was run-ning for the chairmanship of the party, that I would welcome him as my running mate to head the Congreso, and that I was sure that I would win. He was incredulous and astonished that I would so obviously at-tempt to co-opt him from Corky's side. He told me, while smirking, that he would tell *el jefe* (the boss, Corky), about my statement, as if to signal that I would have hell to pay for my challenge. I never heard from Corky. As Corky and I made the rounds of the different delegations, the con-vention divided into those who were for a practical approach using elec-toral tactics to take power and those who sided with the need for a rev-olutionary nationalist agenda and little electoral activity.

The Winning Strategy

The convention was quite a showdown between the two poles begin-ning with the credential process: who was and who was not a bona fide partido member entitled to vote. Delegates were being pressured indi-vidually and collectively to chose between Corky or me. Several ma-neuvers were employed by the Crusade to try and capture blocs of votes by invoking the Southern racist "unit rule," a tactic used by Southern

Democrats at the national convention of the Democratic Party to hold all their state delegates bound to the will of the majority within the delegation. Candidates A and B would run against each other for delegation votes. Candidate A would get 51 percent of the vote and Candidate B would get 49 percent of the vote but under the unit rule 100 percent of the vote could only be cast for A. The minority of delegates would have to vote for the majority decision, as a unit. This device was tantamount to a dictatorship of the majority over the minority. With this procedural voting device, the Southern states had a stranglehold on the presidential nominee of the Democratic Party and snuffed out any dissent within their individual ranks of state delegations, particularly from liberal factions or blacks.

I lectured my floor leaders on the dictatorial effects of the unit rule and argued persuasively for an open, democratic, and participatory convention as opposed to a tyrannical, hierarchical anointment of Corky as national *jefe*, or boss. That pitch worked and we blocked that move most successfully, making Corky look dictatorial and heavy-handed. It also gave me an early signal of my voting delegate strength.

I took advantage of the large California delegation. We had observed that it had various factions, some committed to our practical electoral strategy of winning elections at the local level and others for Corky's revolutionary vanguard party. I began to recruit Raul Ruiz from Los Angeles, a most effective and articulate regional leader. I talked him into accepting the nomination as temporary chair of the convention. Ruiz naively accepted the responsibility and took many of the lumps meant for me during the fights over credentials of individual delegates, the credentials for seating delegations, and many procedural matters, including the vital defeat of the unit rule. Free from the details of convention management and parliamentary process and the personal acrimony that is directed at the individual presiding over such raucous skirmishes, I then had time to organize and obtain key delegate support from across the country.

My people had also been in charge of registration. I knew exactly who all the delegates were, where they were staying, and the background information on them from their registration forms. Corky never asked for access to these records. When I approached a delegate I knew in advance who she or he was. I had copies of registration forms with me to refresh my memory or someone with me usually would whisper in my ear other tidbits of information I needed when someone approached me. People were very impressed with the knowledge and time I took to familiarize myself with each of them.

I caused to be appointed many of my supporters within other state delegations and workers of the registration table to the important Credential Committee. The unit rule was defeated on the convention floor by a narrow margin. Individual delegates could now vote their conscience and not be bound to their local jefe. We split California in two, kept Texas solidly for me, except for one vote, and broke off enough individual delegates from Arizona, Illinois, Utah, and New Mexico to put together a winning coalition of delegates.

The Crusade people accused many delegates of being migrants sent by me to northern states, now claiming to be Raza Unida party groups in those states. People in that category got very angry with him over that accusation. Historically, most migrants have come from Texas and did settle out of the migrant stream in northern states; but to say that I had sent them there years prior and now was calling them back into service for a political party was ludicrous. Being ignorant of the migrant stream phenomenon, Corky could not appreciate my prior work in traveling to migrant communities in the Northwest and Midwest regions of the country. Our people are found in every state of the union and, within each state, in nearly every county. I had learned to organize in the migrant stream from Los Cinco Candidatos and Virginia Muzquiz. She had handled the absentee voting for migrants since the days of Juan Cornejo in 1963, and had served me in 1970 in the same role. In 1972, she was elected with me to the county government as county clerk, officially in charge of the absentee balloting process. She was my resident expert. Corky had no such person. Every community in South Texas, including Cristal, has a direct connection to migrant communities in the other states. Migrants from Cristal, for example, have twin communities of relatives in other places such as Moses Lake, Washington; Milwaukee, Wisconsin; East Lansing, Michigan; Gilroy, California; Findlay, Ohio; and Fargo, North Dakota. In other words, there are other Cristals in other states. One finds the people in the other states by asking the relatives still in the original Cristal where they are. The same is true of all Chicano communities in South Texas, like Weslaco, Donna, San Juan, Eagle Pass, Carrizo Springs, and San Benito, to name a few.

Today, the migration from Mexico follows the same pattern. Relatives of people from certain *pueblos, villas, ranchos, ejidos, ciudades* and *estados* bring others to the United States. In every large metropolitan area of the U.S., there are congregations of people from the various states and cities in Mexico. The largest number of Mexicans in the United States come from one state, Jalisco. These Jalisenses are found predominantly in California. Pacoima, California, has thousands of Mexicans from Arandas, Jalisco. New York City has thousands of Mexicans from the corner region where the states of Mexico, Oaxaca, and Hidalgo meet.

The grocery chain Randall's, in Houston, employs only workers from a certain region in El Salvador, and Washington, D.C., has the second largest concentration of Central Americans after Los Angeles. In Dallas, today, the largest concentration of people among our population of 840,000 Mexicans and Mexican Americans are from the state of Guanajuato. These *paisanos* still live together, drink in bars and dance in halls together, and even socialize together where they now reside as if they were back home. These are the informal, yet real, sister cities of the continent. All this information was unknown to Corky. He had never been a migrant, and I had.

Politics after the Convention

I was able to out-organize and out-maneuver Corky at every step of the campaign. After we were both nominated and made the traditional campaign speeches to the delegates, voting by state delegations began. The election results showed how well we had organized the campaign. I defeated him rather substantially for national chairman of the Raza Unida party. Everyone forgot the Congreso chair or vice chairman position, for which no election was thus held. Every state designated their three members to the Congreso de Aztlan.

For a brief moment, there were many delegates who felt euphoria at the display of unity immediately after the convention. The classic photograph that emerged from the convention was of Tijerina, Gonzales, and myself, joined hands held high with raised clenched fists, in apparent solidarity. This photo graces the cover of the book on the Raza Unida party written by Ignacio Garcia, *United We Win.*

The unity was superficial however, and short lived. The pose had been a symbolic gesture, a photo opportunity at best. The next order of business was to constitute the Congreso de Aztlan, the governing body. Corky did a tremendous disservice to the growth of the Raza Unida party after the election. At the convention he had argued that the National Chair was also the head of the Congreso. After the convention had not elected a vice chair, he now argued that the members of the Congreso should elect from among their own the vice chair of the party. Corky never attended any meeting of the Congreso; had he shown up to these meetings and faced me, perhaps we could have worked out an acceptable relationship of shared power, but his ego kept him away. I, he felt, was not his equal. He had illusions of being *el jefe* of all Chicanos. He sent his underlings, youthful and inexperienced militants, with instructions to vote no on every proposal I made. They had no inkling of how to run candidates in elections, how to govern, or how to

keep and exercise power, much less how to negotiate and build a working political party. I was as young as they were but had years of experience in electoral campaigns and with governance structures. Corky, as
a leader in the Democratic Party in Denver and Colorado state politics
just before he joined in building La Raza Unida, had ample experience
but he did not participate in any subsequent meeting of the Congreso
or La Raza Unida. He quit.

The proposal for the governing structure for the Congreso reveals
the inexperience, impracticality, and narrow vision of the dissident faction within the national committee. It was outrageous. The Colorado
proposal was to place the vice chair of the party, chosen by the national
committee members, in a different geographic location than me, the
chairman, and put the treasurer in yet another location different from
the chair and vice chair. Their rationale was to avoid a concentration of
power in the hands of one person. The national headquarters of the
party was not to be in Cristal or in Texas, because I lived in a small,
rural, inaccessible town and Texas was too far out at the eastern edge
of the Southwest. It was to be centrally located in another state, and
with a paid staff. These committee members, like Corky, had assumed
no responsibility for debt incurred under the name of the party for the
national convention. They argued that the El Paso debt was my sole responsibility because they had neither been consulted nor committed
previously to assuming the debt. The fact that no one knew previously
what the outcome would be, other than the ultimate goal of building a
national structure, was ignored. I asked the maker of the motion for
this ridiculous structural and organizational set up how they were
going to pay for staff and travel for officers. I was told that was my job,
to raise the money for them.

We made several attempts then at building the Congreso. Meetings
were held in Las Vegas, New Mexico, in South Chicago, Indiana, in El
Paso, and in Denver over the next two years. By 1974, it was obvious to
me that there was not going to be any national Raza Unida Party structure or program. We simply did not work out our differences. Rudy
Acuña and Raul Ruiz, on one occasion, tried to get Corky and me to
meet face to face, to iron things out. One such meeting took place in El
Paso, without success. Corky arrived with a retinue of bodyguards and
I, alone. For the meeting, I called Gloria Garza, a former teacher from
Cristal now living in El Paso, and asked her to pick me up at the airport
and transport me to the hotel. I explained the purpose of the meeting and
asked her to come out to the pool area every fifteen minutes or so, and
without making eye contact with anyone else, simply walk directly
and slowly toward me and whisper in my ear any nonsense she could

Mario Compean, the Raza Unida Party state chairman, and Maria Jimenez, RUP candidate for state representative, Houston, Texas, 1974.

think of. She wanted to know why that was necessary and how it would help the discussion. I told her that I honestly didn't know but that it would probably help keep violence out of the situation and maintain a low-risk environment because Corky operated from a premise that the threat of violence from his thugs was necessary and I was attending alone. Corky would never imagine that I was there alone: her coming and going would give the appearance of carrying messages and relaying information to and from others. Corky's own imagination would work against him. It did. Corky's bodyguards searched the hotel, floor by floor, looking for my nonexistent bodyguards.

We sat by the hotel swimming pool near the El Paso airport, but at separate tables. Corky and I never faced each other across the same table. The preliminaries to the meeting went on with Rudy Acuña or Raul Ruiz attempting to mediate our differences. We talked to one another, Corky and I, through them but never progressed beyond the preliminaries of deciding what exactly to talk about. Corky wanted retraction of some statements made to the press while at the convention and attributed to me admissions of voting fraud by some members the Texas delegation at the convention and receipt of financial kickbacks from the Republican Party as prerequisites to a dialogue. I wanted to know if he would put up some money for the debts of the convention, show up at the Congreso meetings without an entourage, and participate as a delegate. And, of course, I refused to even consider his allegations. The mediation failed and we never met again face to face until the summer of 1994 when my younger daughters and I visited him at his home. After the death of Cesar Chavez, I wanted to bury the hatchet between us before Corky died. He had been very sick since a terrible automobile accident.

Going It Alone

As best we could and with the meager resources we could muster, those of us committed to the idea of a national Partido continued to organize across the country and encourage people to seek ballot status in their respective states, or to sue to obtain ballot status, as was successfully done in Chicago by Angel Moreno while running for the U.S. Congress. Another individual that succeeded in putting together a winning coalition and campaign was Frank Shafer-Corona, in Washington, D.C., who was elected to the school board there.

By 1974, we had already had a second gubernatorial swing in Texas. At that time the term of office for governor was two years. Ramsey Muñiz was again our candidate. He obtained the same percentage of the vote as before, although lower in numbers. It was not a presidential year and again the Republican challenger benefited from the presence of La Raza Unida party on the ballot. The party began receiving invitations from foreign countries to visit and dialogue with representatives of other political parties around the world, and heads of state. I was amazed at the interest that others had in our politics.

Since 1971, we had begun to establish links with the government of Mexico. We had our first meeting with Luis Echeverria Alvarez, president of Mexico in 1972, in San Antonio, Texas, shortly after the Raza Unida convention in El Paso. President Echeverria had come to the Sixteenth of September festivities in San Antonio to inaugurate the Mexican Trade Fair that was going to be held in that city. The meeting was arranged between us by several advisors and staffers of the Mexican president. These Mexicans had long been interested in keeping abreast of developments in the Chicano movement. Some of them, Jorge Bustamante, for example, had been in attendance at early organizing meetings of the issues conferences. The U.S. State Department was very upset at these developments. They wanted Echeverria to meet with Chicano celebrities like Trini Lopez, Lee Trevino, and Vicki Carr, not with the militants.

Reies Lopez Tijerina and Gutiérrez at the breakfast honoring the 1973 visit of Mexican President Luis Echevarria Alvarez to San Antonio.

Echeverria and I hit it off very well. I was able to obtain many concessions from him over the balance of his term. Echeverria made Chicanos respectable in Mexico and made it part of the international posture of Mexico to include us as part of the third world peoples, and it was he who institutionalized the dialogue between Chicanos and the Mexican presidency. Many others in the party castigated me, as Corky Gonzales had, still for the relationship with Echeverria. They could not see beyond the massacre of students at Plaza Tlatelolco, nor could they understand why it was important for us to have contact with other governments such as Mexico. They could not see what there was to be gained. I saw that it was necessary for Chicanos to have an independent position in foreign affairs and, more importantly, our own voice and contacts abroad.

Cesar Chavez, SCLC, and AIM leaders were very upset with me as a result of the goings-on at the El Paso convention. Though their invitations to speak at the gathering had been withdrawn by the convention delegates in the preliminaries, I had chosen not to fight that fight during the convention. Most of these guests or their representatives had sat for hours in the gallery waiting for a decision on whether they would be allowed onto the speaker's platform. When the vote came back negative, I couldn't get to them in order to personally apologize for the vote.

Chavez would have attended. He had given me assurances that he would, but news of the fight on the convention floor over speakers kept him away. It took a while to work things out with him again.

Chavez was opposed to contact with Mexico. At that time, he viewed Mexican labor as potential scab labor. He did not want to deal with the government of Mexico unless they could guarantee no scab labor would come across the border to break his strikes. Reies Lopez Tijerina was the only one willing to try again to renew contact with Mexico. On a prior occasion, in 1964, he had attempted to discuss land titles and grants with the president of Mexico, only to be deported by Attorney General Echeverria on orders from then President Diaz Ordaz. I labored with Tijerina to convince him that it was Diaz Ordaz, not Echeverria, who was to blame. Tijerina believed Diaz Ordaz to be in the pocket of the Central Intelligence Agency (CIA). I urged him to try Echeverria now as president. Later, as a result of our contact with Mexico, we were able to obtain funding from President Echeverria to make a movie about the exploits of Tijerina. The movie was called *Chicano,* a hastily put together film that depicted some of the travails that Tijerina had encountered in the pursuit of the land grants. Echeverria liked Tijerina also, but the problem with Tijerina was that he wanted reparations for the lost land grants from Mexico. The land grant issue to this day is not so much a legal battle against the title holders as it is against the government of Mexico for not compensating the heirs of these land grants for their land or the mineral rights. The question of mineral and land rights is still open in Las Vegas, New Mexico, and Catalina Island, off the coast of California. These two parcels of land have never been adjudicated or entered into the documents that conveyed land.

Much of the land taken from Mexicans during the Texas Revolt and the subsequent invasion of Mexico by President James K. Polk remains in the hands of private land grabbers today, with the help of the courts, the pinches rinches, unscrupulous lawyers, and the gringo courts of law. For the most part however, the land remains in the possession of the United States government, and has not been paid for. As well, the mineral rights to all the southwest have never been paid for. Approximately two-thirds of the land mass west of the Mississippi is held in trust by the United States government in the form of parks, sanctuaries, reservoirs, and leased land. In Arizona, the federal government owns about four-fifths of the state. Western ranchers, farmers, miners, and energy companies obtain leases to this land, *our* land, at bargain basement prices. Tijerina learned to ask for programs from Mexico; previously, he had always asked for monetary reparations.

Meeting regularly with the president of Mexico was a most educational experience for me. I learned a great deal by observing the Mexican politicians, operating at their best at these higher levels of government and foreign affairs. I also saw how poorly we acted in their presence. Many of our leaders from LULAC, the American G.I. Forum, MALDEF, The National Council of La Raza (NCLR), IMAGE, Project SER, and national-level politicians cannot speak Spanish well enough to make a coherent sentence, much less have a conversation. Too many of our leaders do not have any knowledge of Mexican history or politics.

I sat with a Chicano delegation comprised of national presidents of organizations while in the office of the Mexican president and heard one of us, a national LULAC president, state, while pointing to a portrait hanging on the wall of a presidential office, "That is a great picture of Santa Ana." In Mexico, the conventional view of General Antonio Lopez de Santa Ana is that of traitor—his picture would never be in the Mexican presidential palace! This ignorant Chicano leader was pointing to the great General Ignacio Zaragoza, a Tejano from Goliad, Texas, the hero of the battle of Puebla who fought against the French. This person not only did not know which man was which, but also did not know that Zaragoza was a Chicano from Texas, like us.

Our national leaders, by and large, don't know how the Mexican system works. For that matter, they don't know how our own U.S. system works, or how the world works. They are ignorant of many of the international relations and foreign affairs of Mexico and other countries that deal with the United States. It is imperative that our leadership learn the skills necessary for this high level kind of communication. It is in our best interests for the future.

Internationalizing the Chicano Movement

For Chicanos, contact with the world began with Echeverria. This president also raised the reputation of Chicanos in Mexico. The rich and upper-middle-class Mexican doesn't think about us at all. To members of these social classes, Chicanos are an embarrassment because we don't speak Spanish, don't know Mexican history, and often, are poor imitations of gringos. Many Chicanos don't like Mexicans because they remind them of how assimilated we really are as Mexican Americans. And we have more in common with Anglos than Mexicans—food,

The dedication of the Chicano movement mural at the University of Houston, 1975. *Left to right,* Tatcho Mindiola, acting director of the Mexican American Studies Program, Gutiérrez, and Lorenzo Cano, a graduate student.

music, work, business, socializing, school, language, holidays, politics, and our future. Most of us believe our destiny is governmentally tied to Washington, D.C., and not Mexico City. But some of us wish it was not that way.

I recall a meeting with President Echeverria on the eve of his designation of the candidate to succeed him as president. He had summoned all his cabinet members, as the successor would come from this group. Upon arrival they gathered in the portico of the presidential residence at Los Pinos. Echeverria introduced us to each one of them and told them, bald-faced, that Chicanos were the single most important people outside Mexico. He said the future of Mexico rested with the Chicano people and that his successor would be well served to pay attention to relations with Chicanos. From that moment on, contact with Chicano groups became part and parcel of the Mexican presidential sweepstakes. Every official candidate for the Mexican presidency not only meets with Chicano groups during the campaign but also initiates programs to maintain the contact with these groups as president. Chicano relations with the Mexican president have evolved from the days of a scholarship program administered by the Mexican equivalent of the

U.S. Housing and Urban Development cabinet department—*Obras Publicas*—to the current Department of State—*Secretaria de Relaciones Exteriores*—and support for a nonprofit binational organization, *Fundacion de Solidaridad Mexicano Americano* (the Foundation of Solidarity between Mexicans and Americans). This latter project is a joint venture between the National Council of La Raza and the Mexican government via the foundation.

In 1975 Raza Unida party leaders and I were invited to spend a month in Cuba by the Casa de las Americas and the Cuban government. This was another occasion where the "Corky loyalists" refused to participate, mostly because I was organizing the trip, and Tijerina expressed no interest in meeting with any member of the Cuban government, being leery of the "communist" tag. Cesar Chavez similarly had no interest in going to Cuba. We organized a nineteen-person delegation from the various chapters across the country. People from Indiana, Wisconsin, Illinois, New Mexico, Texas, California, and Washington, D.C., comprised the delegation. I also recruited a news team from CBS, headed by Ed Rabel and Mexican Congresswoman Maria de la Paz Becerril de Brun, to accompany us. We went in the latter part of April through mid-May for an incredible journey in Cuba. We did not get a chance to meet Fidel Castro, but we did meet with many other high level government leaders including Castro's brother, Ramon, and many regional leaders as we toured the island. At the May First Workers' Parade in Havana, our Chicano delegation sat just below the reviewing stand where Fidel Castro and the Cuban Politburo sat. Raul Castro, another brother, stood just behind and above me. We exchanged a handshake and a brief introduction.

While we were there the Cuban experiment with socialism was most attractive to many of us, particularly in the area of health, education, housing, and agriculture. It was not difficult to figure out why the rich left Cuba and why the poor were in total support for the Communist government. Poor people had access to all the essentials that make for a quality life. Everyone had a house, a job, health care, and paid annual vacations. The Cuban models of development in these areas were fascinating. I, for one, thought then that we had a lot to learn from Cuba, particularly in these fields. My diary of that trip is replete with entries that address the various insights and experiences that made the Cuban model attractive to me.

The Cuban trip caused quite a controversy in Texas. We were severely criticized for that journey and "red-baited," being called communists. In Cristal indictments soon were handed down against Amancio Cantu, our school superintendent, for taking a video camera on the trip that was school property. He was later acquitted at a jury trial. I was attacked

A meeting at the Casa de Americas during the 1975 trip to Cuba *(clockwise from lower left)*, Gutiérrez, Robert Maggiani, Charon D'Aiello, Esequiel Guzman, Lupe de Leon, Raul Ruiz, Abel Cavada, Angel Moreno, Elpidio Lizcano, Ernesto Chacon, John Ramirez, unknown.

by Governor Dolph Briscoe for stating that we needed to replicate successful Cuban programs here in the U.S. What I meant was that the Cuban models for health, housing, agriculture, education, and sports were wonderful examples to emulate. I espoused the notion that we could benefit from these models and should try them here in the United States. I was branded a communist by the gringo politicians, from the governor on down to the local Barrio Club. The media had a field day.

During these years, there were many other MAYO members and Raza Unida party members, such as Jesus "Chuy" Ramirez from Pharr, Texas, Edgar Lozano from San Antonio, Carlos Guerra from Robstown, Texas; Raul Ruiz from Los Angeles; Frank Shafer-Corona from Washington, D.C., and Juan José Peña from Las Vegas, New Mexico, who traveled to other countries. Our MAYO and Raza Unida leaders visited such places as Quebec in Canada (to meet with the French separatists); China; Mexico; Lebanon (to meet with the PLO); Spain (to meet with socialist party members); Colombia; Puerto Rico; Nicaragua; and some Scandinavian countries. There is no doubt in my mind that this international travel had good results. Not only did those traveling learn firsthand of other people's movements and governments, but the people in those countries learned about us, the Chicanos. We learned how problem-solving and decision-making are implemented in other cultures; thoughts of how to govern effectively at home never left me while traveling abroad. It was so gratifying to learn how important these people in other lands thought we were. Even we don't think as highly of ourselves as they did. Perhaps the self-hate we learned in school because of the pervasive emphasis of the curriculum solely in English and solely on Anglo accomplishment and victory over Mexicans is what prevents within us a wholesome attitude about ourselves. The most astounding revelation was how curious they were about our specific plans for recovery of the Chicano homeland. I believe that most Chicanos are, ironically, the only ones oblivious to this issue.

13

Chicano County Governance

I sought the office of county judge in the spring of 1974 and won. Though I was not a lawyer—the qualifications for this office required only that the candidate be twenty-one years of age and a registered voter, a county resident for at least six months, and have no felony convictions—my past political experience and education undoubtedly helped me win election. The election victories of La Raza Unida Party in Zavala County, however, had begun in 1972. In that election, the party candidates that won over Democratic Party incumbents were José Serna for county sheriff, Elena Diaz for county commissioner of Precinct 3, Gregoria Delgado as justice of the peace for Precinct 3, and a few others as constables. These individuals were the first to begin opening the door for raza power in Zavala County. Then, in 1974, we made a complete sweep of nearly all offices remaining in the county. Ramsey Muñiz, as candidate for governor, headed the statewide slate, and I the Zavala County ticket.

In Texas, the office of the county judge is the most powerful position in county government; I knew this since taking my first college course on state and local government. It is an office that exists only in the states south of the Mason-Dixon line, and combines the three branches of power—the executive, legislative and judicial—into one. Additionally, as if these powers were not enough, the county judge is the chief budget officer, chief election officer, and even shares concurrent jurisdiction over family law matters with the district court judge. This position also directly supervises and manages the affairs of the Road and Bridge Department, which is the largest department, in terms of employees, in rural county government. The county judge, by virtue of the duties associated with these powers, is the single most important individual in county government. Additionally, county positions are salaried. The pay is sufficient to support a family, unlike the nonpartisan positions that are unpaid at the school board and city council.

I was temporarily challenged in the primary election by another Raza Unida Party candidate, Manuel Espinoza Jr., but he did not file the proper papers with our party chair and was disqualified as a candidate. I then faced the incumbent Democrat, Irl Taylor, in the general election. He was only the fifth county judge in the history of Zavala County since it had been a part of the Republic of Texas.

The November election of 1974 was not a difficult a contest. I beat Irl Taylor two to one. It wasn't that I was qualified, well-financed, and the *Partido's* number one candidate in the county; rather, it was that La Raza Unida Party, since 1970, had perfected the process of winning elections.

The Raza Unida Party Electoral Strategy

An early lesson learned in politics is that you begin the next electoral campaign on the day after the victory in the present election. We campaigned year round, raising funds, registering voters, making home visits, holding rallies for issues or other candidates, and holding celebrations, like the Chicano del Año awards celebration.

Early in a campaign, six to eight weeks prior to an election, Virginia Muzquiz would hold a school for poll watchers and poll volunteers. This course consisted of several nights of in-depth study of the election code laws, on which Mrs. Muzquiz was an expert. Armed with years of election experience and technical knowledge of the code, down to the page, section, and subsection, our poll watchers and campaign volunteers were formidable opponents for any election judge who sought to violate the law or bend it with interpretation unfavorable to us. Another strategy was to take advantage of absentee or "early" voting, as described earlier in this book.

We used to classify our potential voters into four categories. The most prized voters were the strong partisans of La Raza Unida Party. These were the first voters we took to the polls during the absentee voting period. Then we concentrated on those voters who were in favor of our candidates, accessible but lukewarm. These voters were individuals that we could get to vote for our candidates by getting a relative, a coworker, a friend, or even a *compadre* to talk them into committing to a party candidate or even the entire slate. Those Mexican American voters who were against us we tried to neutralize by using a relative, compadre, coworker, or friend to at least get them not to vote *against* our candidates, or to get them not to vote at all. Lastly, our precinct workers were instructed to avoid contact and any exchange with the European American, the white rednecks, the gringos who were against the Raza Unida Party. The logic behind this tactic of becoming "invisible" was to delude the opposition into thinking we were not working the precincts; thus, the opposition voters would not be motivated to go out and vote for a candidate of their choice. They would think, as voters often do, that their vote is not crucial, necessary or needed, or that there was little or no threatening opposition to vote against.

The Transition to Chicano Governance

Our margin of victory in the county elections was a landslide for most candidates of the partido. We were a most formidable slate, the best organized and resourceful group to challenge the white power structure in the entire history of the county. I went to see Judge Taylor about two weeks after the election and he refused to dialogue with me. In fact, he came out to the lobby, after making me wait for nearly thirty minutes, and told me that he was county judge until midnight, December 31, 1974. "You go get the keys from Sheriff Serna at that time," he said, "There is no point in coming to bother me. We have nothing to talk about." I expressed to him my regret for his attitude. I asked him for basic information such as the county budget, pending contracts, and a few other items. In a scolding tone he said, "Go see the county clerk. What you need is on file there. That is where the records are kept." I left. My parting words were something to the effect that I simply had gone to see him so that we could smooth the transition of county affairs from his administration to mine. I told him that I would remain available, if he changed his mind. He didn't.

I also had an ulterior motive in going to see Judge Taylor. I wanted to inquire about any legal challenge he or anyone would make to the election. I do not recall an election held in Zavala County, since Los Cinco Candidatos of 1963, that did not bring into play one of three legal maneuvers used by losing candidates to challenge election results. Invariably, as a beginning legal challenge, one side or another would seek to impound the ballots alleging the potential of fraud. This maneuver usually brought in the Texas Rangers to physically collect the ballot boxes daily from the polling places and store them in bank vaults or some similar "secure" place. Crystal City had only one bank in 1974, the Zavala

County Bank, and there is another bank in La Pryor, the La Pryor State Bank. These two banks are part of the testamentary gift of the John Nance Garner estate given to the Southwest Texas Junior College. The Trustees of the college appoint the board members of these two banks; the boards of directors are interlocked; relatives, co-workers, friends, and business associates, all gringos, serve on these boards. I never was able to get the Texas Rangers to deposit the impounded ballot boxes in our city or school government facilities. They always took them to private facilities controlled by the powerful white business leaders of the area. In private hands, the ballot boxes can be tampered with readily. And if you can have access to ballots after an election is concluded and before the vote results are announced, you can win any election. White political bosses in South Texas had done illegal ballot stuffing and counting for decades.

Shortly after the votes were counted, another legal maneuver that was used is the recount. The election law provides that a losing candidate may ask for a recount of the votes cast, if the defeat is within a ten percent margin of the victory. In this maneuver a new election judge is appointed, poll watchers designated by the candidates are assembled, ballot boxes are reopened, and the ballots are counted once again. Mistakes in counting, if any, that would alter the results are noted, and the results are again announced. A fee is charged per precinct ballot box to be recounted to the party making the request. This can become an expensive challenge if many precincts or ballot boxes are involved.

The third and most dangerous alternative was an election contest. This is a lawsuit in which one candidate, usually the loser, alleges fraud and other voting irregularities. If the allegations are proven that would lead to a different result or questionable result, the district judge can order a new election, declare the challenger the winner, or leave the results as they were announced before the election contest. Not only is this type of litigation expensive, but also the bond, a supersedeas bond, that the challenged party must post is awesome—four times the amount of an annual salary for the position contested. In the politics of Zavala County, this supersedeas bond would almost kill the winners financially. Irl Taylor did not go beyond the impounding of the ballots. He couldn't ask for a recount given the landslide victory, and he didn't file an election contest.

Cleaning the Courthouse and the Taking of Power

Taylor's rebuff of me in the lobby of my future office angered me. A couple of weeks later, after Thanksgiving, I visited the Road and Bridge

Department in person. I approached the county road department supervisor, Jackie Hooks, and informed him that I expected his resignation before January first, as I wanted my own man in that position. I told him that I would appreciate it if he would assemble all the county crew right then so that I could tell them that they too were going to be asked to resign and that they would be most welcome to reapply for positions in the new administration. Mr. Hooks was even worse than Judge Taylor: he asked me to leave, at once. He told me that it was not my place, yet, to be there. He said, "You're arrogant, coming to fire me and everybody even before you begin." I did not leave the premises immediately; rather, I walked around the shop area and premises, pretending to visibly inspect the facility and equipment. I wrote down some nonsense words on a piece of paper just to appear to be taking notes. He followed me around, barking at me, "Get out of here. You're not the county judge. I'm going to call the police on you." I ignored his threat and continued my walk around the area. In the emotion of that confrontation he forgot that both the sheriff and city police were no longer his partisan white cohorts, but my Raza Unida partisans. I left the building after promising him that I would return with letters asking for the resignation of each employee in a few days. I did.

I did not have the pleasure of firing Mr. Hooks or anyone else in the County Road and Bridge Department. They all resigned prior to the end of December, as I had asked them. Only a handful of them reapplied, of which I hired three. Otherwise, I brought in an entire new crew and I chose my righthand campaign worker, José O. Mata, as the county road administrator to replace Hooks.

The swearing-in ceremony for the new county administration was a wonderful experience. It was done outdoors on New Year's Day, 1975, on the courthouse steps and walkway facing Uvalde Street. County Attorney Rey Perez administered the oath of office to me as the first officer for the county. I, in turn, administered the oath of office to all the others, mostly women, who had won with me in the last election—Virginia Muzquiz as county clerk, Carmen Flores as county treasurer, Esteban Najera as county commissioner, Irene Ojeda as justice of the peace in Batesville, Rosa Quijano as justice of the peace in La Pryor, and others as constables. It was visibly obvious that the Raza Unida party was the political party for Mexican American women seeking to win elective office. We all made wonderful speeches, and the entire courtyard and lawn of the courthouse was filled with spectators and well-wishers. Some people from as far away as cities in West and South Texas and North Texas activists from Waco, Fort Worth, and Dallas came to be part of the ceremonies. *Mariachi* music played before and after the ceremony.

The sheriff, José Serna, hosted an open house in his part of the court-house and offered coffee, pan dulce, tacos *de chorizo* (sausage), and *carne guisada* (meat stew). A tour of the courthouse was also arranged by Sheriff Serna. Some people had never been inside the courthouse in their lives; others had only been inside the jail or the tax office. Inside the courthouse, on conference tables in various rooms including the commissioners' court room, were arts and crafts on display, the work of local Mexicano artists.

There was one incident that nearly ruined the celebration. It re-minded all of us, me in particular, of how dangerous the political road we had traveled really was. As I was repeating the oath of office while being sworn in, a ruckus and commotion began toward the rear of the crowd that was standing in the middle of the street, directly across from where we were taking our oaths of office. People in that part of the crowd were pointing to a building directly behind them as they pushed each other in an attempt to get out of harm's way, and panic set in. The sheriff's deputies, city policemen and other self-appointed body guards, among them my padrino, David Serna, Felix Velasquez (a local restau-rateur and friend known as "La Llanta,"—the tire—because of the thick ring of fat around his midsection) raced into that area. They ran in the direction the people were pointing, and found a man with a rifle, pointed in the direction of the podium. The man sheepishly explained to the police that he meant no harm, he was merely looking through the scope on the rifle to see the activity up-close. The rifle was unloaded when the men protecting us disarmed him. I was given the details of this incident by the sheriff as soon as I finished swearing in the other office-holders. The man was kept in custody in the city jail across from the courthouse. He was a middle-aged, medium build, balding, white man, unknown to any of us. I've even forgotten his name from the identifi-cation he provided at the time. We chose not to press charges; the chief of police released the man, but impounded the rifle. No one ever came forward to claim the property.

After this dangerous moment passed, I was presented with the keys to the office suite and with a can of Lysol disinfectant by Sheriff Serna. He said, *en español,* "Go spray the county judge's office, the commis-sioners' courtroom, and the district judge courtroom to disinfect any redneck germs that may have remained." I promptly obliged. The crowd following me into the offices loved the symbolism. My wife, Luz, and others began rearranging furniture and decorating the offices promptly, and the entire crowd of spectators participated in some form or fashion in rearranging, removing, or placing things about the offices of all the newly elected officials. The collective attempt was to make the offices suitable for officeholders from the Raza Unida party, the first Mexican Americans since Texas Independence to hold power in this area. It was a great day of festivity. People felt it was their courthouse for the first time in their lives, that it was no longer a bad place to come to visit. Now it would become a second home for them because their friends and relatives were there. There was a Democrat incumbent county commissioner, Felipe Torres from Batesville, and a Republican turned Democrat, Frank Guerrero, who had won election as county commissioner from Precinct 4, which held the majority of white voters in Crystal City. Guerrero had been a staunch Republican as far as I could remember, but by running as a Democrat he was able to defeat the Raza Unida party candidate narrowly in the last election. Esteban Najera, the new county commissioner elected from La Pryor, incumbent county commissioner Elena Diaz, and I made a three-to-two majority for La Raza Unida Party on the Zavala County Commissioners Court.

The First Steps Taken in Zavala County

As county judge, I proposed some of the same things that we had done on the school board. Immediate personnel changes were necessary if we were to govern with the uncompromised support of staff. Word had already gotten out to most of the county employees that I or the other officeholders were going to fire them on January first, as soon as we took office, if they didn't resign. That was the message inherent in my visit to the Road and Bridge Department in November, 1974. We didn't fire everybody right then; we waited until the second day of January. I assembled the employees that worked in the courthouse in the commissioners courtroom and asked them to resign and to reapply so that we would have the benefit of employees loyal to what we were trying to do. I was severely criticized for this by the local newspaper, but I saw nothing wrong with it. Presidents, governors, chief executive officers, and other officials wanting change in policy and program direction have always done this. I saw great need for having my own team carry out what I promised to do during the campaign. The voters had a right to expect what we promised. The other officeholders who won with me did the same thing in their respective offices.

Within a few weeks of taking power in the county, the atmosphere of the courthouse changed radically. The smell of *chorizo*, Mexican sausage, was prevalent in the mornings, as was Mexican music and the Spanish language. Virginia Muzquiz, the county clerk, posted a sign on the window of her private office, facing the street, that said SE HABLA INGLES. English was now seemingly as "important" as the Spanish language.

Gutiérrez in his office as county judge.

Our meetings of the county commissioners court, held every other Monday, were as well attended as the evening school board meetings had been some three years earlier. The meetings were held in either language, Spanish or English, depending on the circumstances. Unlike the composition of the school board when I served, the Zavala County Commissioners Court had no Anglo members. The commissioners court consisted of our three Raza Unida Chicanos and two Mexican American Democrats—Frank Guerrero and Felipe Torres. Elena Diaz had won election to the commissioners court in 1972, and thus was our veteran. She knew what had been going on under Judge Taylor's administration, and Najera and I were new to the court.

When I was elected county judge, the majority of the county judges were women. The issue of male or female leadership never became a controversy within the partido: women led and men followed, or men led and women followed. Leadership, without regard to gender, was the criteria. The greater good was community empowerment and group ascendancy, not gender politics, much less selfish politics. The Raza Unida party had been the first political party in Texas to nominate a woman, Alma Canales, for lieutenant governor in 1972. We also had more women as elected officials in the party hierarchy and in public office than the Republican or Democratic parties had ever had.

The First County Programs

Our first major undertaking was to provide services to people in Batesville and La Pryor, communities heretofore ignored. The budget of the county, as in all counties in rural Texas, had historically been allocated for the repair of roads, bridges, fences, and cutting brush on roadways leading to farms and ranches. We began paving streets and building houses in the unincorporated "cities" of La Pryor and Batesville; we provided ambulance service to the entire county; we started a juvenile probation program; we collected child support payments; we encouraged participation in county government; we revived the historical society and built a new type of delivery system for services for the county.

But all of this cost money. We set upon the first equalization of property appraisals since 1917. Among the first order of business was a proposal to reappraise land values in Zavala County, which were totally out of order and created a shortfall of potential revenue for the county. Landowners, on the other hand, were in heaven, with low tax bills. An appraisal of land values is always a good maneuver, rather than raising taxes or assessments. A friend from the early days of the takeover of the school board and the city council—Juan Ramirez from San Francisco, California—had come to Zavala County once again and assisted me prior to taking office in reviewing the county budget. He gave me a financial picture of the county from the available records in the county clerk's and tax assessor's offices. It was his suggestion that we reappraise the land to current market value as a way to increase revenues from taxes for the county. He was correct. We brought substantial sums of money in new taxes into the county and to the other units of the government simply because we appraised real property, minerals, and utilities to their current market value in 1975.

The vote among the Commissioners Court was unanimous for reappraising land values in Zavala County. For the year 1975, however, we had to operate with existing money from the prior administration, and Judge Taylor had spent a great deal of money in the last two months of his term. Our people, the Mexican American community, were hungry for services and improvements. They had long been neglected throughout the county.

A major crisis occurred during my first term of office. The Lo-Vaca Gas Gathering Company, a gas supplier, reneged on its contract terms with the government of Crystal City. Lo-Vaca wanted to void a contract with the city because the cost of natural gas had gone up and they were losing additional profits. They wanted a new contract at a higher price, with the increased cost of natural gas to be passed on to the residents of Crystal City. The city council refused to allow Lo-Vaca out of the contract and wouldn't consider passing the cost on to consumers. The city officials argued that if the shoe was on the other foot and they could find natural gas cheaper than with Lo-Vaca the company certainly wouldn't have let them out of the contract.

The company threatened to cut off gas service to the city if the new prices were not paid. The matter was litigated, and Crystal City lost in all state, federal district, and federal appellate courts. The case reached the United States Supreme Court and Crystal City lost again. In due time, natural gas service to Crystal City was completely shut off. As county judge, I was also the chief civil defense director and the director of emergency preparedness for the county. I immediately declared a state of emergency and authorized the county employees to gather wood from area ranches, so that the public would have firewood for heating. It was a matter of public health and safety. The county employees were to enter farms and ranches and gather dead wood from the land, with or without owner permission. Not a single farmer or rancher protested our activity. In collaboration with the city officials, the county began firewood delivery to homes in the city.

We prevailed upon the United States Army warehouses and government surplus offices of the Government Services Administration, in nearby San Antonio, to give us the wood stoves used by the troops in the Korean conflict, which we promptly distributed, along with Army-issue wool blankets. The more critical buildings without heat during this period of time were the schools and the medical facilities. School days were shortened, with schools opening later than usual in order to be warmer. The medical clinics and hospitals sought alternative methods of heating, such as electric heaters and stoves. The affluent of Crystal City easily converted from natural gas to electricity, from one day to the next. The poor converted to the use of wood products. To this day, Crystal City is without natural gas and relies on propane, wood, and electricity as its sources of energy, and the city remains adamant that it will not pay the new contract price for natural gas.

Through our relations with Mexico, we tried to get the Mexican government to give Crystal City natural gas in exchange for electricity. We approached the City Public Service Board in San Antonio to see if they would fire up their generators to full capacity and trade the surplus electricity for natural gas from Mexico. In Mexico, most of the natural gas is flared, simply burned into the atmosphere. Mexican homes use bottled propane gas because the country does not have an infrastructure of gas lines in its cities to supply gas from a well to homes or industry.

San Antonio could sell the natural gas and pay for the increased electrical production, as well as make a profit on the amount of gas required for Crystal City. The natural gas from Mexico was free. The United States government had an energy policy in effect at the time that called for a boycott, a prohibition against buying any natural gas from Mexico. But our deal was a trade, not a sale; this was a home run, if you will, for all parties concerned. Still the deal fell through: other politicians in the state got wind of this deal in the making and torpedoed the entire program simply to keep Crystal City without gas, and to hit a foreign policy home run. To this day, it amazes me that such a wonderful idea, one still possible, is not attempted. Mexico is still without sufficient electricity along the border, and southwestern electrical plants in the U.S. are operating at less than capacity. This is a win-win situation for all parties concerned: with Mexican gas, we can fire up the generators to produce electricity for Mexico and make money in the process.

Another issue that became of interest in county government was the building of the Centro de Salud, a health center. The city and county collaborated and were able to obtain funding for the building of a health maintenance organization, an HMO, in Zavala County. Health maintenance was—and is—one of the most critical of the unmet needs in rural America, and Zavala County was no exception. Our health center would be the first to provide a comprehensive and affordable health program for migrant Chicanos in Texas.

We organized the area Mexicano home builders and general contractors into a partnership for this venture: they would build the Centro de Salud. We couldn't find bonding for them because they had had no experience with a construction project of this magnitude. Finally, we obtained sponsors for them from among other contractors, Anglos who had done work with the school district and the city, and construction began. We located the Centro in the heart of barrio Mexico Chico in order to build infrastructure to that area of town—paved streets, sidewalks, sewer, and services—leading to the health center.

Another project, as mentioned earlier, was the implementation of countywide ambulance service, as Batesville and La Pryor had no such service. They had previously transported their sick and injured by private cars to hospitals and doctors in Uvalde, Crystal City, or San Antonio. Second, we began a paving program through the Road and Bridge Department of the dirt streets in Batesville and La Pryor and some of the streets in River Spur, near Crystal City.

The three-vote majority of the commissioners court, Commissioners Diaz and Najera and I, rearranged some of the funding priorities under the Community Development Block Grant (CDBG) in order to open, on a part-time basis, an expansion of services by the Centro de Salud into La Pryor and Batesville. The three of us became very creative in using county emergency nutrition money. We proposed that rather than giving people vouchers with which to buy food, that they raise and grow their own food. Before any electoral victories, Viviana Santiago and Bill Richey had organized a pig farm cooperative; now, with county money, we were going to expand the reach of this cooperative into livestock and poultry. But it never quite succeeded. The fundamental problem was the migrant stream: our people would leave for work in the northern states each year, and those remaining had to work double or triple shifts to make up for those absent. Upon return from the migrant trek, the people couldn't and wouldn't pay the money owed to others who worked for them in their absence. They forfeited their equity share rather than pay the salary in arrears, and fewer and fewer persons remained in the cooperative. We never could solve this problem. While it lasted, this program provide a lot of meat for families, but the cooperatives soon became the sole property of a few families.

We also used CDBG money to expand the Women, Infants, and Children program (WIC) countywide. The WIC program is one of the most effective and beneficial programs from the Nixon era, providing protein in the form of milk, cheese, and eggs at low cost to women with small children and women expecting children. The private sector, particularly grocers and food suppliers of such products, benefits immensely from this program. The business with WIC vouchers is big business in small towns; in my view, these business interests obtain more financial gain from these programs than did the people.

Another county program was mired in controversy from the very beginning, and this was the creation of a county-sponsored community development corporation (CDC). The Zavala County Economic Development Corporation attempted three ambitious projects: the buying of five thousand acres of land on which to start a farming cooperative; the establishment of a musicians cooperative for *conjuntos*, Chicano musical combos that play *onda* music, the Chicano sound; and the aforementioned expansion of the existing pig cooperative. Many of us in the Raza Unida party viewed the farm project as buying back land in occupied Mexico—the beginning of the creation of our Chicano homeland, Aztlan.

The CDC was headed by Jesus Salas, who relocated from Wisconsin to lead our program. The proposal his staff developed was excellent, winning endorsement from various federal agencies and local corporations. The Del Monte plant agreed to buy all the produce provided by the cooperative. Labor was plentiful and the farm land ideal, having an ample supply of water from wells and the Nueces River. All we needed was the start-up money from the federal government. The program was pending final funding approval during the waning days of the Nixon administration; had Salas and his staff worked faster on securing the funding before Jimmy Carter took office, the buying of land for the building of *Aztlan* would have gotten started and our *raza* would own the fruits of their labor.

Luis Ramirez, a Nixon appointee to the Community Services Administration, the agency that funded CDCs nationally, was replaced by Graciela Olivarez. President Carter had cut a deal with Governor Briscoe to ax this project, and instructed Olivarez to kill it, which she did, along with that six or seven other Chicano CDCs in the Southwest. She did more to hurt the progress of economic integration for Chicanos in the country than any previous federal administrator ever had. Rather than stand up for Chicanos, she toed the administration's line. To this day many of us wonder what happens to our Chicanas and Chicanos when they get positions of importance: why do they turn on us when we are the ones who demanded and made possible their getting a position, in order to serve our needs?

Some of the lesser county programs became more important in the long run. Meals for the Elderly provided not only a nutritional component but also a social atmosphere for our raza elderly, *los viejitos*. We worked with the Community Action Program (CAP), and the local Council of Governments, and the Middle Rio Grande Development Council, to develop these type of programs. The law required that no less than one-third of the seats in the CAP be from among the poor and not more than one-third of the seats be held by elected officials. The remaining seats came from community organizations, but since Zavala County now was in total Chicano control, the seats for the poor and for elected officials came from the ranks of the partido membership. In the Council of Governments, similarly, the elected officials from Zavala County and its lesser units of government were all La Raza Unida party officeholders.

The Reaction to Zavala County Programs

Opposition from regional and national politicians against Zavala County—that is, La Raza Unida Party—programs began immediately. Richard Nixon was in the White House and Dolph Briscoe, a Democrat governor, was in the statehouse in Austin. The traditional formula of getting money through funded proposals to operate programs in cities, counties, and schools came under attack in our case. If Raza Unida party-controlled governmental entities wrote successful proposals and received money from the Nixon administration, it was alleged by Democrats that it was a political payoff because we were anti-Democrat. Our critics ignored that we were writing good proposals that met the published guidelines in the *Federal Register* and that the need for such programs and services was amply demonstrated and abundant. They argued that we were not deserving of the funds. Democrats tried at every opportunity to cut off these funds and stop the federal dollars from coming to Zavala County or any other Raza Unida party-controlled government in Texas. They maligned our efforts. When Democrats give money to Democrats, it was perfectly okay; when Republicans give money—through their administrations, to Democrats—it was okay; but when the Republican Administration gave money to the Raza Unida party–controlled cities, schools, and counties it was deemed as evidence of political payoff for taking Mexican American votes away from the Democratic Party.

Chuy Ramirez, an early MAYO member and activist of the Raza Unida party, had organized the electoral victory in San Juan, a city in the Rio Grande Valley. He served as city manager there and informed us of the threats of cut-off of federal money to San Juan by Democrats in the state capital. The message to Raza Unida party leaders in this city was clear: remain Raza Unida and the city will never get a federal or state dollar for programs. If they were to come back into the Democratic Party fold, however, they would be able to obtain more federal and state money, as were all the other cities, counties, and schools in the Valley. Chuy Ramirez and the rest of the partido officeholders in San Juan sold out promptly, becoming the first defectors to the Democratic Party. Chuy was rewarded by being elected as the youngest member of the Democratic National Committee.

In Zavala County, the Democrats were not as successful in stopping our money or buying us off as in San Juan, except in a few memorable instances—the foiling of the CDC and the natural gas cutoff in Crystal City. Our opponents during this time were not only the local newspaper, the *Zavala County Sentinel,* but the congressmen, O. C. Fisher and Abraham Kazen, both representing our area. John Connally, the former governor and now Nixon's treasury secretary, and Dolph Briscoe, the governor in the mid-1970s, were both land owners in Zavala County, and both were solidly against us. The local gringos were against what we were trying to do; we had very little support among philanthropic organizations, the Catholic Church, or any other group. In fact, we received more funds from Methodists, Episcopalians, and Presbyterians than we did from the Catholic Church through its foundation, the Campaign for Human Development. It was not for lack of trying; the support from the Catholic Church simply has not been there for the Mexican American movement across the Southwest. Foundation benefits, including that of the Catholic Church, would seem to go to Anglos first, then African-Americans, to the detriment of all other minority groups. Yet, la raza makes up the largest ethnic group within the faith in North, Central, and South America. Consequently, we had no option but to turn to the state and federal government to try and obtain monies. The only secular foundation that stepped up to help us was the Hogg Foundation from Austin. They helped build the first mental health program in our area. The Winter Garden area of Texas had been underserved for years by any state mental health agency, and was not on their priority list for the provisions of mental health services.

Governor Briscoe, at the State Democratic Party Convention, alleged in a speech that we were building a communist base in Zavala County. He cited as evidence the Community Development Corporation, which was building an economic base with the cooperatives and farm project. Briscoe called these efforts the "making of a little Cuba on Texas soil." In 1975, while I was county judge, a delegation of nineteen persons representing various states and the national Raza Unida Party traveled to Cuba. Upon our return from this trip, I was quoted in the press as wanting to make a Cuban Revolution in the United States, which was not what I had said. In response to a question of what impressed me about Cuba, I responded that the poor in Cuba all had access to higher education, health, housing, food, and jobs, and that these would be good goals for our government to establish here. The national media picked up on this fight and Dan Rather came to interview me for *60 Minutes*, the television program. Rather, a fellow Texan, was impressed with our efforts and project but he opined on national television that we would ultimately be "squashed like a bug" by the governor and president, regardless of the merits of the proposal. He was right. Briscoe red-baited me, La Raza Unida Party, and the CDC with his allegations of communism until he convinced President Carter to kill the project. We sued the federal agency for conspiracy, breach of contract, and discrimination. We had information that Carter was reminded by Briscoe that he had carried Texas for him in the last election, and that the payback demanded was to kill this project. Reportedly, the conversation was documented in memos and notes from the Oval Office. Federal District Judge John Sirica ruled, however, that the president and his records of meetings with Governor Briscoe were not available to us for use as evidence of a conspiracy because the White House counsel had taken the position that these documents were a matter of national security.

We suffered an electoral defeat in a bond election for the creation of a recreational area around a lake to the west of Crystal City. Estero Lake is a swampy area that is a flood menace to the city because it empties into Turkey Creek when it overflows, which in turn floods the southern part of the city. The project sought to capture the potential flood water into a permanent lake at the Estero site and promote its use for recreation. When I was on the school board, we had sought bond money to replace the remnants of a Japanese American internment camp from World War II that was being used as a school for our Chicano children. This earlier bond issue had been approved by the voters to build new schools. The Raza Unida Party county commissioners and I figured the voters would also approve this project, to solve flooding and create a new industry built on recreation and water sports.

George Ozuna, the former city manager now practicing as a civil engineer in San Antonio, was contracted to research the viability of such a project. He found it to be feasible and began looking into the process of condemning some of the land and acquiring other adjacent tracts of the land. He found support for this project among the U.S. Army Corps of Engineers and among regional directors of Housing and Urban Development (HUD) in Dallas. He reported to us that there was money available from these two sources to help create such a lake. It made sense to the Corps of Engineers as a flood prevention program and to HUD as an environmental program. In addition to the actual lake, Ozuna also proposed that we construct greenways, bicycle paths, jogging trails, and nature trails, and keep some of the swamp areas for bird and animal sanctuaries, as the area is host to alligators.

Unfortunately, Commissioners Frank Guerrero and Felipe Torres were able to effectively blunt our campaign by promoting negative publicity. They played on the fear of a second property tax hike. The first tax hike, they argued, had come from the reappraisal of the land. Guerrero claimed that the indebtedness from the bonds for this project would hurt the next three generations of Zavala County residents. Instead, he proposed that we build a local hospital, as the existing hospital had shut down and was only operating as a day clinic. And the *Centro de Salud* had not yet reached its peak capacity for providing full and comprehensive medical services. This negative campaign had a dual attack on county programs—the health center would face stiff competition from a new hospital and probably die in its tracks, and the lake project would be defeated. The public's fear of higher taxes and the greater desire for a hospital, not just a clinic, defeated us at the bond election. And neither the CU or Partido memberships worked the bond election as they had other elections. There was not great interest for the project.

The Ammonia Explosion

An explosion occurred at the Carr Chemical Plant, located four miles south of Crystal City, one early dawn in 1979. Democrat Commissioners Guerrero and Torres, and Raza Unida Commissioner Esteban Najera teamed up for this incident, which gave me a glimpse of events to come on the commissioners court. I was called in the early hours that day by José O. Mata, the county road administrator, informing me that an ammonia tank had exploded out at the Carr facility, and a toxic cloud of ammonia released in the explosion was being driven by southerly winds toward Crystal City. We needed to evacuate residents. I had attended one training session for Emergency Preparedness Civil Directors, and as county judge I was the head of the Civilian Defense Board, the local arm of emergency preparedness. As director, the county judge has the power in an emergency to declare martial law, if the conditions are there for such an extreme step. (These emergency conditions are natural disasters, riots, civil disaster from war, or nuclear attack.) The county judge, as civil defense director, is charged with protecting life and property and maintaining the general welfare.

Immediately upon José's phone call, I called the sheriff's office. I instructed the radio dispatcher to call all volunteer firemen, law enforcement officials, and health clinic personnel to an emergency meeting at city hall at once. I forgot about calling the mayor and members of the city council; I simply took charge of the emergency. José, on his own, had already set part of that in motion by calling the school superintendent and other public health authorities. For some strange reason—habit I guess—I jumped in the shower, only to realize within seconds that this was not a time to be taking a shower. My wife, Luz, awakened by the ringing telephone call, also overheard the news and got more details from me. I told her to wake the kids (of which there were now three: our sons Adrian and Olin, and our daughter Tozi) and to go to my mother's house. We would meet there within thirty minutes and decide what to do then. She began calling her medical clinic staff and alerted them to the potential consequences of this disaster.

I grabbed my shotgun and my 9 millimeter automatic and proceeded to city hall while Luz drove to my mother's house, woke her, and told her what was happening. At city hall, I began trying to assert my control over the situation. The troopers from the Highway Patrol, the sheriff's deputies, city police, and some firemen were also there; taking control wasn't an easy task. Those state troopers believed as did the Texas Rangers, that they were of a higher authority. I just began talking louder and louder, acting more authoritatively and barking out specific orders to each one. I did eventually get control of the situation and of the men. They proceeded to implement my orders on how to evacuate the people. They all did what I ask them to do.

I told José Mata to go wake Ignacio "Nacho" Luna, owner of the teatro Luna, and David Mendoza, from Ciudadanos Unidos. He was to tell these men to go up and down the streets of Mexico Chico, the first neighborhood directly in the path of the ammonia cloud, announcing the peril over the car-mounted loudspeakers. "Write it down for them," I said to José. This alert would begin the evacuation. The city police were told to direct traffic in an evacuation route out of Crystal City going north on Seventh Street to Highway 83 toward La Pryor, nineteen miles away. The Highway Patrol were to station themselves along the route on Highway 83 and keep the traffic flowing, not allowing any car to stop on the shoulder or pull into some farm house. The firemen were asked to volunteer to monitor the progress of the ammonia cloud and report its approximate location by radio to city hall. The police dispatcher also began alerting hospitals in Uvalde, Eagle Pass, Carrizo Springs, and San Antonio of our dilemma. The local pharmacists were roused from bed to their drugstores for possible medications or antidotes for this type of noxious gas. Routes to the south of Crystal City toward Carrizo Springs, Dilley, and Cotulla were blocked; these were the more dangerous evacuation options because that was the general area and possible direction of the disaster if the wind changed. Unbelievably, we evacuated the entire neighborhood of Mexico Chico in an hour and fifteen minutes. We also had to shut down the medical clinic, as it was in the path of the cloud. The doctors and other personnel, including my wife, joined the evacuation caravan heading north and set up a temporary facility at La Pryor.

Commissioner Guerrero from Crystal City also left the city. Commissioner Torres from Batesville was called and joined Commissioner Najera of La Pryor at the school site. This trio created a makeshift reception area in the gymnasium of the local school. They greeted each carload arriving in La Pryor. Guerrero instructed the school cafeteria to double their cooking production for the day in order to feed the people arriving from Crystal City. He promised the school superintendent that the county would pay for these extra meals. The commissioners continued their publicity seeking among the temporary refugees. Upon queries as to where I was, Guerrero reportedly told the people that I was not around. Technically, he was correct, I was at city hall, directing the evacuation and coordinating relief assistance with area cities in the event of disaster. No one had seen me or heard from me, except for the police and area officials at city hall.

The overall evacuation was a complete success, logistically speaking. It was done well, it was done in record time, and it was done before the gas cloud drifted over Mexico Chico, as it had been expected to do. We evacuated almost half of the city's residents. What I learned most from this experience, beyond the powers of the county judge as head of civil defense and as director of emergency preparedness for the county, was how quickly others respond to someone who is decisive and speaks with authority. I was not only authoritarian, but also authoritative. I used the power of my title and office as county judge and gave the appearance of knowing what to do. I also learned that Anglos are reluctant to take orders from a Chicano, even if he is the county judge. I had to bark orders to the Anglo volunteer firemen and the state Department of Public Safety patrolmen, two to three times, to get them to move. Only when I threatened to call their superiors did they react promptly.

I began researching the power of the office of county judge even more. I attended more seminars for elected officials. When, three years earlier, the natural gas was cut off to Crystal City, I had also declared a state of emergency for the county, particularly the city, and proceeded to use that power to confiscate firewood from area ranches. I had ordered the U.S. Army in San Antonio to supply me with gas heaters left over from the Korean War, blankets, and other paraphernalia to sustain a winter without heat from natural gas. I had begun looking for a legal team to assist me in expropriating gas wells in Zavala County with which to supply the city, but couldn't find any lawyers interested in this litigation.

The Defection of Commissioner Najera

The gas cutoff and the ammonia explosion incidents signaled the beginning of the "shaving off" of Commissioner Najera from our three-vote bloc on the county commissioners court. Esteban Najera did not drive a car because of hypertension, diabetes, and sleep apnea, which caused him blackouts from time to time. The Zavala County Road and Bridge Department crew leader in La Pryor, Antonio Perez, was instructed to drive the Commissioner to the courthouse at any time he requested, and to all meetings of the commissioners court, which he did for at least two years. Commissioner Torres, in due time, replaced Perez. He convinced Najera that rerouting his trip in to Crystal City from Batesville via La Pryor was no trouble for him and that he would ap-

preciate the company instead of driving alone. While the latter may
have been true, the former was not. The Batesville to Crystal City drive
is only nineteen miles, about twenty-five minutes. The rerouting to La
Pryor, then Crystal City added approximately thirty-five extra miles to
his journey. The trip each way would now take about an hour. Nevertheless, the ploy worked. Najera accepted rides from Torres and the two
of them drove back and forth to the meetings in Crystal City. And of
course Najera had to accompany Torres everywhere as they came and
went. Najera's movements were then controlled by Torres and I couldn't
even talk with Najera after the meetings or during the lunch break.

     This driving situation gave Commissioner Torres great amounts of
time to bend the ear of Commissioner Najera. Frequently, Commissioner Torres would reinterpret the agenda items for the meeting as
grand strategies on my part to exclude residents of La Pryor from some
imagined service or program. Najera would arrive at the meeting with
many questions and apprehension over items on the agenda. And, Torres would manage to arrive just as the meeting was to be called to order
so that Najera could not ask me his questions or voice his concerns privately; he had to ask or make his comments in public session. The appearance of dissension between the three-vote majority was obvious,
and the consequences of the Torres-Najera driving arrangement revealed itself in votes taken at the commissioner court meetings. Soon,
Commissioner Najera was either voting with the other two commissioners against the recommendations I would make, or against motions
made by Commissioner Elena Diaz. On many occasions her motions
would die for lack of a second on Najera's part: I was faced with sec-
onding a motion that obviously would fail. Supporting Commissioner
Diaz became symbolic politics. Najera himself began to talk about being
independent, being his own person, being more responsible and accountable to the people of La Pryor only, and not those in Election
Precinct 6, located within Crystal City and part of his Commissioner's
Precinct 3. Najera became inaccessible for meetings of the partido and its
various caucuses. He began to miss, along with the other two commissioners, the information sessions I would offer on county business and
projects. When he had attended these sessions previously, I needed not
worry about a three-vote majority in support of these business items if
they became agenda items. Without him, I knew that discussing these
items at meetings of the commissioners and calling for a vote would
have negative results. He seemed to prefer the company of Commissioner Torres, and then, more frequently, also that of Commissioner
Guerrero. The trio would be seen drinking coffee and having lunch. In
due time, Commissioner Najera voted against the recommendations for

election judges and absentee voting judges that I had made. In fact, he voted for a substitute motion that the commissioners pick their own judges, in their own precincts, and that together, the trio of himself, Guerrero, and Torres pick the absentee vote election judge. Najera seconded that motion and voted for it. We suffered our first major defeat in the votes cast of the commissioners court. Effectively, Najera had given control of two election precincts to the Democrats, and most vitally, control of the absentee voting to the Democrats. An election judge can sway an election simply by making it difficult for people to vote and engaging in illegal acts that can only be challenged on election day, but not stopped. An election judge can call out the wrong names as those marked on paper ballots during the counting of votes to produce a result contrary to actual votes cast, and can use his or her discretion in deciding how to count a marked ballot, or not to count it at all. The election judge assigns all the personnel to the various tasks during the election day; job assignment is critical to vigilance for voter fraud. An election judge, for example can offer to assist a voter with marking the ballot and mark it contrary to the wishes of the voter or cause the ballot to be classified as "mutilated," if the voter cannot physically mark the ballot, read, or is unfamiliar with the mechanics of voting. Court action, after the election, is the only remedy to these types of voting irregularities.

After this vote, Najera attempted to explain as insignificant his support for that critical and partisan motion. Later, when it was too late, he came to regret it: he lost his next election. We began losing other elections at the county level. What I did not know about Najera at that time was that Commissioners Torres and Guerrero had been turning a blind eye and head to his alleged frequent use of county labor, county materials, and supplies—such as rock and cement—for the upgrading of his drive-in food stand and bar in La Pryor. In short, he was susceptible to threats of a criminal indictment for stealing county property. We simply had not become aware of that activity, even though we noticed the rapid improvements around his buildings and home at that time. This whole Najera situation reminded me of the same tactics used against Los Cinco Candidatos in the early Crystal City days of 1963. The defection of Esteban Najera cost us the majority vote on the Commissioners Court; now we could not deliver on election promises or the party platform. Election contests were filed on the next wave of elections held in 1976, and again in 1978. These election contests took their toll. Anytime the courts interfere with the election process, the people lose. Chicanos and older Mexicans avoid legal entanglement at all costs, including not voting again, so voter turnout began to decline. Various San Antonio attorneys hired by Anglo ranchers and Democrats—such as Louis Se-

Gutiérrez and Riche Diaz putting up political signs for the 1976 elections in Zavala County.

gura, Lupe Cortinas, Peter Torres, and Jesse Gamez—began filing these lawsuits against us. In the early stages of the litigation, during discovery proceedings, attorneys for the Democrats would allege that all Spanish surnamed voters were illegal residents. They would subpoena every voter suspected of being a Raza Unida supporter to testify in open court about their participation. Not a single Anglo was subpoenaed in spite of the fact that some winter residents in the county are from northern states and could be voting illegally, as well. Voting for the Raza Unida party candidates meant a sure trip to the courthouse for Mexican American voters, to testify not only that they were qualified voters, but also how they had voted. So much for a secret ballot in Zavala County.

Second Term

I was reelected in 1978 as county judge for a second term by a substantial margin, even though I was absent from the campaign trail for most of the time. This in itself is a commentary on the efficiency of the campaign organization, despite the lawsuits surrounding us at the time. My wife Luz, the two older children, Adrian and Tozi, and I, courtesy of a

The tenth anniversary of the Crystal City High School walkout, 1979.

consultant contract from the United States Army in Europe (USAEUR),
were able to tour most of Europe for a month. I was contracted to evaluate race relations among U.S. Army military personnel in Germany.
My county judge campaign consisted, then, of phone calls from various
parts of Europe to my office, where they were taped and later rebroad-
cast as a paid political announcement, or on radio news, and at the Ciudadanos Unidos meetings by the campaign workers.

One of the most important results of the 1978 election was the defeat
of Najera by Alejandro Perez in our own party's primary election. Our
party loyalists refused to vote for Najera and threw their support behind
a younger man with ties to an opposing Raza Unida faction. In the November general election, Perez defeated Matthew McHazlett, a Democrat, by a few votes. A recount of votes did not change the result. An
election contest was filed against Perez and the other Raza Unida candidates that had won election to county office: Diana Garcia as county
clerk, Margarita Gonzales as district clerk, Carmen Flores as treasurer.
The District Court Judge issued an injunction preventing Perez from
taking his position which resulted in McHazlett being seated on the
commissioners court. Matthew McHazlett's seat made three permanent Democrats on the commissioner's court against two Raza Unida
partisans, Elena Diaz and myself. The financial cost of defending our

Gutiérrez and Ernesto Gomez in the parade celebrating the tenth anniversary of the 1969 Crystal City High School walkout.

officials in this election contest was enormous. The bonds they had to post to hold office were very costly and made affordable only because local business people signed as sureties, guaranteeing payment in case of forfeiture by the candidate. The defense of this matter became prohibitive. In the surrounding areas, formerly Raza Unida party candidates ran either as Independents or Democrats. We stood alone in Zavala County.

The Beginning of the End

While voting on the Zavala County Budget for 1979, the three Democratic commissioners cut my salary in half. That prompted me to have to augment my salary by other work outside the courthouse. This became a self-fulfilling prophecy. The more I worked outside of the courthouse, the more they alleged that I was not earning my salary, and would cut it down even further, to the ridiculous point of allocating to me a one dollar annual salary. They also withheld the checks for my payroll and began calling meetings of the commissioners court on their own. Three commissioners can post an agenda, call a meeting, and conduct a meeting without the county judge as long as the notice for the meeting is posted timely and properly, which they made sure of. It was apparent to me that this was the beginning of the end and the only casualty of this political tug-of-war, with Commissioner Diaz and me against the Democrats, was going to be the people of Zavala County, particularly the Mexicano poor that were by now reliant on county services and programs. I began to look for a way out.

14

Exile to Oregon

In 1980 the Democrats on the Zavala County Commissioners Court filed a complaint with the Judicial Qualifications Commission for the state during the middle of my second term as county judge. This body investigates complaints against judges and has the power to disqualify the accused from judicial responsibilities. The complaint against me alleged that I did not hold court or trials often enough and that the backlog of cases within my jurisdiction was immense. The county judge in Texas, as is the case for all states south of the Mason-Dixon line, is both an executive office for the county and a judicial functionary with original jurisdiction over misdemeanor, probate, juvenile, and civil cases.

I hired Warren Burnet, a famed attorney from Odessa, to represent me. Earlier, in 1969, Warren had helped formulate the legal basis for the formation of La Raza Unida Party: Bill Richey, Rick Bela and I had spent a couple of days in his law library with the attorneys of the Burnet firm figuring out how to get the party on the Texas ballot.

The hearing on my qualifications to continue to hold the office of county judge for Zavala County was a kangaroo court. The presiding judge would not permit the introduction of the docket book which indicated that many cases had been disposed during the period of alleged wrongdoing, nor would he permit witnesses with firsthand knowledge of court proceedings, disposition, court costs, and fines collected, or the various court dockets indicating that there was no backlog of cases. (The banned witnesses were County Clerk Virginia Muzquiz and Deputy

County Clerk Diana Palacios Garcia.) The judicial panel wanted to probe my comings and goings from Zavala County, honorariums and consultant fees earned, and the nature of my business outside the county. In the master folder of the investigator for the commission were clippings of articles about me and copies of what appeared to be, at cursory glance, FBI reports, as I had been under government surveillance for years. (See appendix for samples.)

Warren advised me after the first round of hearings that I should contemplate resigning from office. He convinced me that the commission, with the process they were following, would find a way to discredit me as a judge, tag me as incompetent, and probably recommend disqualification from the judicial office. If I ever planned to return to law school, this "white" mark would put that aspiration in serious jeopardy, if not disqualify me altogether. The commission, by their vote, could remove me as judge but not as chief executive officer of the county. But the Democratic county commissioners had already effectively done that. The end of my political efficacy as the county judge and highest ranking Chicano elected official of La Raza Unida Party was approaching quickly. I was powerless to stop the train of events.

Born-again Democrats: The Birth of the
Mexican American Democrats of Texas

In neighboring La Salle County, the Mexicanos Unidos base of the Raza Unida Party voted in 1977 to cease affiliation with the Raza Unida Party, and ran candidates as "Independents." This scenario repeated itself within the partido organization of Pearsall in Frio County. Later, these two groups would join the Mexican American Democrats of Texas (MAD), formed explicitly in 1976 to compete with us for Mexican American voters. The leadership of MAD came from former allies such as Joe Bernal and Albert Peña Jr., former Raza Unida Party activists Jesus "Chuy" Ramirez and Juan Maldonado from San Juan, and former MAYO cofounder Willie Velasquez. I visited with many of these individuals in MAD in an attempt to work out a set of rules for the competition for raza votes. I had wanted these born-again Democrats to agree on a fundamental item: they had significant political leverage within the Democratic Party as long as La Raza Unida Party existed. Without us, the Democratic Party would not need them. White Democrats had seen the success of the Raza Unida Party in attracting raza voters to the polls and needed a Mexican American alternative to us. Only when white Democrats saw the massive defection of Mexican American voters from their ranks did they begin to seek out Mexican Americans for leadership roles. White Democrats were soon to become a minority group within the Democratic Party, yet they wanted to hold all the important positions of power, particularly as statewide officeholders and party leaders. The Mexican American Democrats disagreed. The ultimate goal for these diehard converts was the elimination of the partido, not in working a mutually complementary strategy. They refused to consider that this developing scenario would be much like a return to the days when our collective community vote was largely taken for granted by the Democratic Party and totally ignored by the Republican Party. The Democratic Party has always used our community only as a source of votes for white Democrats running for public office, from the courthouse to the White House. The concepts of political leverage and insider/outsider collaboration eluded them in their zeal to curry favor once again with gringo Democrats. The MAD leaders wanted to be accepted, liked, and led by white, male Democrats rather than their own people.

Our Partido and the Courts

The fact that Ramsey Muñiz, our candidate for governor in both the 1972 and 1974 elections, pleaded guilty to drug charges and bail jumping in February, 1977, added to our problems within and without the partido. The media constantly reported that Ramsey had been under investigation by both the Drug Enforcement Agency (DEA) and the Internal Revenue Service for eighteen months. Beginning in mid-1976, he had been charged with multiple conspiracies to possess and transport marijuana. Ramsey told us he had been framed. The monitoring included wiretaps of his business and home telephones and was probably illegally done—without probable cause, much less a court order. We believed him and not the media. We raised funds and hired David Kennedy, a top-notch criminal lawyer from New York with extensive experience in defending drug cases.

The monitoring of Ramsey's telephone records and his travel expenses on credit cards revealed calls made from alleged drug dealers to his home and law office, calls from him to them, and travel to destinations of alleged drug drops and money exchanges. Ramsey told me he was conducting legal work for these clients. This explanation seemed plausible enough. Lawyers, in preparing a legal defense for persons accused of crimes, investigate, interview, and travel to alleged crime locations routinely. And, of course, lawyers are paid for these services, sometimes large sums of money. To make things worse, Ramsey jumped bail in the middle of the process and fled to Mexico. The media had a second field day with me and with the partido. He later was apprehended on Christmas Eve 1976 in Mexico and shipped across to the U.S. We tried to continue with the massive fund-raising drive for his legal defense, but donors were skeptical. The expensive lawyer from New York hired to defend Ramsey couldn't do his job because Ramsey pleaded guilty. I was in shock! All of us felt betrayed by him. The partido never recovered its credibility or integrity. Two subsequent times, Ramsey was charged and convicted on drug related offenses. His third offense in 1994, resulted in a sentence of life imprisonment as a habitual offender. At each arrest, trial, conviction, sentencing, and appeal of Ramsey's, the entire Raza Unida Party was also "tried" and found guilty by association. The crimes of white politicians, Democrats or Republicans, are never attributed to their political party, of this Richard Nixon is a good example. Only our political party was, and still is, even after it has been legally dead for decades.

In 1979 I faced the possibility of having some civil or criminal charge, or a trumped-up charge of misconduct and incompetence, put against me. Texas Ranger Joaquin Jackson had visited me in my office several times and told me he was investigating me for theft of public property and misuse of government property: I was on notice. On many occasions, in Hondo and Rio Grande City, Texas; in Las Vegas, New Mexico; and elsewhere our partido militants and leaders had often been charged with such crimes just prior to elections, only to be exonerated after an election—and at great expense. In Las Vegas, New Mexico, not only did our party loyalists prove the charges to be false but also proved that the Democratic party leaders and county sheriff had planted the drugs on our people. The sheriff did time for that offense and now is back in politics. Those of us in public office in Zavala County endured dozens of civil and criminal investigations and actual charges with trials to prove our innocence during the decade of the 1970s. I survived countless investigations by local, state, and federal police and accounting agencies, over 23 at last count. Federal agents from several agencies not only thought we were potential subversives but also petty criminals and drug dealers. There were, and perhaps still are, more investigations, not made public, by the FBI, IRS, CIA, DEA, and the like that were verified when files from these agencies were obtained through the Freedom of Information Act (FOIA). Personally, I was the named principal defendant in countless civil suits seeking money damages for alleged wrongdoing. I have placed these documents in the university libraries in Austin and San Antonio, Texas, as part of my archival contributions.

Our programs, operations, grants, and I personally, always emerged clean. Every penny in every budget that I or any other Raza Unida Party officeholder managed or had responsibility for as public officials was accounted for. I have never been a thief or a corrupt political leader. In the entire history of the partido's elected or appointed officeholders in Texas, other than Ramsey Muñiz, only Angel Noe Gonzalez and Amancio Cantu, the school superintendent of the Crystal City schools, were charged with crimes and tried. Juries exonerated both of them in separate trials. Others were simply charged, only to have the charges dropped later. It is the promotion of Chicano politics that prompts these allegations of corruption and crime.

Together with Armando Gutierrez, a professor of Government at the University of Texas in Austin, I began a systematic inquiry for documents revealing the extent of state and federal government surveillance and harassment of La Raza Unida. Requests to the Texas attorney general made under the Open Records Act were not successful. The requests were either denied, ignored, or filed to be researched. Requests made under the Freedom of Information Act of 1976, however, resulted in thousands of pages of documentation of that surveillance from more than a dozen agencies of the federal government. I have these documents and have contemplated publishing books solely on this surveillance.

The Party's Over

In the general election of 1978, Mario Compean, our candidate for governor, made a pitiful showing despite his efforts. The public character assassination carried on by the media since 1970 on Raza Unida Party activists, leaders, officeholders, and appointed officials and voters had taken its toll. He received under 15,000 votes, less than 2 percent of the total. Because of the low vote total the Raza Unida Party lost ballot status and state funding for any subsequent primary election. The party— La Raza Unida—was over, literally and figuratively.

Luz and I sought a way out of Cristal and the repression resulting from the death of the partido; nobody in Texas would hire me. The little money I earned was for work done outside of the state. Luz probably could have continued as director of the health center, but her life and mine would have been miserable since she would have to carry the entire financial burden of the family. We now had three children and another on the way, and we talked of my returning to law school. Several friends and former partido leaders had obtained licenses to practice law, one being my executive assistant throughout many of these years, Viviana Santiago. She and her husband, Abel Cavada, offered to pay my way through law school. I was not too interested in that career; teaching and research at a university attracted me. But I could never get my academic life started in Texas.

Luz and I decided to leave Texas altogether. We knew we would not be able to find jobs for ourselves in the state. Our friends and allies would consider us "hot potatoes." Activists and militants always find it hard to get employment. More importantly, allies and friends were afraid of hiring someone as political and vocal as ourselves for fear of not being able to control us.

Luz and I were very tired. We had been Chicano militant leaders for more than a dozen years. We had a mortgage. We had no savings. Certainly, we had suffered defeat plenty of times, but the thought of quitting the fight was painful. We would fight our enemies again another day. For now, Luz (with another baby on the way), the kids, and I would leave Cristal ten years after our first return in the summer of 1969. This decade had been a wonderful effort at building Aztlan. We had no regrets.

The scores of lawsuits filed by the attorneys Lupe Cortinas, Louis Segura, and Jesse Gamez on behalf of Anglos that named me as a party, individually, were increasing in number. These suits were threatening the financial well-being of my family. Friends and supporters who posted surety bonds on my behalf and on behalf of others were being sued and risked the loss of that money. Any judgment against me would have killed me economically and ruined my family for at least a generation, as well as ruining those who posted the surety bonds.

The people and my supporters in Zavala County would not benefit from my efforts to hang on to the public office. I had won re-election with a landslide; to get votes on the commissioners court for policies and programs, however, I would have to sell my soul. I turned instead to the option of resigning the office before the end of my term.

Luz and I agreed to offer the Democrat commissioners my resignation as county judge in exchange for all my back pay at full salary. The only questions remaining now were when and how to resign.

Luz was enamored of the Pacific Northwest. She had many contacts among the community health clinic programs of the region, and wanted to move there. I interviewed for a position with an area foundation in Seattle, but did not get the job. In 1979, I was hired as a consultant by David Hunter of the Stern Fund in Portland to put together technical assistance for community groups in the Northwest as they attempted redistricting, voting rights litigating, and lobbying. I began spending more time in the Northwest than in Zavala County.

As I went back and forth to Portland in the Northwest, leaving Luz behind with the kids and the political problems for longer and longer periods of time, family life became impossible. I decided to quit the fight as soon as possible. Luz and I agreed: we would move from Cristal. We decided on relocation to Oregon if I continued with funding from both the Stern Fund and Joint Support Foundation, by now another employer. I left with Olin, the youngest child at the time. Luz and the other two children joined me later, along with my mother.

The states of Oregon, Washington, and Idaho were slated to gain a congressional seat due to population increases from 1970 to 1980. With funds obtained from a consortium of foundations, I initiated the Northwest Communities Project and based myself out of Tualatin, a suburb of Portland, Oregon.

Soon after arriving in Tualatin, I volunteered for a dollar a year at the Colegio Cesar Chavez, a Chicano liberal arts college, located then in Mt. Angel, Oregon. This alternative institution of higher education was led by Salvador "El Huevo" Ramirez. The idea for this Chicano college had come from Celedonio "Sonny" Montes and José Romero, two students at Mt. Angel College, a private liberal arts college run by an order of nuns from the Catholic Church. They and other students had taken over the college administration building and demanded that it become a Chicano College. The nuns, facing a huge debt, declining student enrollment, and rising costs, accepted the idea after much debate and controversy. The students were able to get Cesar Chavez's help in renegotiating the debt with HUD. The Chicano militants put together a staff and recruited students. Together, they were making ends meet and had gotten past the first steps toward full accreditation. As a volunteer, I helped them in obtaining a Dean's Grant for bilingual education. I also began an international education course of study with Mexico at the Colegio.

My Resignation as County Judge

Back in Texas during Christmas of 1980, I maneuvered the negotiations for my resignation as county judge through the only Anglo officeholder, Ronnie Carr, the justice of the peace in Precinct 3, rather than through one of the existing county commissioners. The members of Ciudadanos Unidos, as well as other party officials, reasoned and counseled with me that it would be easier for them to defeat Ronnie Carr, in the upcoming election than to defeat one of the Mexican American Democrats who might gain favor by claiming credit for getting me to resign. Unfortunately, that prophesy did not turn out to be true. Ronnie Carr proved very effective in garnering support, not only among the Mexican American Democrats but also among La Raza Unida Party opponents of the Barrio Club. Carr's opponent in the Democratic primary was Rudy Palomo. He had been my childhood friend and later, my choice to succeed me on the school board. But Palomo, together with the members of the Barrio Club, had defected from the party and joined the Democratic Party. Carr easily defeated Palomo for the county judgeship in the 1982 Democratic primary election, as the Raza Unida party loyalists would not vote for a defector. Later, Carr was challenged in 1986 by Severita Lara, who actually did win the primary election. She was not able to sustain the litigation costs of an election contest, however, and forfeited the election to Ronnie Carr, who was able to continue into a second term in 1986. He then was succeeded by Pablo Avila, a former Raza Unida officeholder and county attorney. In the 1990s, Severita Lara was elected to the City Council of Cristal and became the third woman mayor of the city; the first had been Olivia Serna, mother of walkout leader Diana Serna. The Chicano political generations have come full circle: now, the activist children of the "Walkout of 1969" and the Chicano movement are replacing their parents in public office.

In Portland, the opportunity to head the Colegio Cesar Chavez opened, Huevo Ramirez having resigned as president, and I became a candidate for the presidency of the Colegio. There were two finalists, Reymundo Marin and myself. We both had agreed that in the event one of us got the job, the other would be his assistant. It seemed like a sure bet that either of us would be president, but I didn't get the job and neither did Reymundo. It went instead to Irma Flores Gonzales, a former secretary and member of the Colegio board. It seemed to us that she had rigged the election, coercing staff and student members. She had not even been an applicant, nor interviewed as the other candidates had done. In hindsight, perhaps we should have sued the Colegio or Irma Gonzales. While she was president, accreditation was not obtained from the regional higher education authority. Slowly, she sold off the assets of the Colegio, while continuing to pay her salary even as the college died. She used her position to become a member of the NCLR and, until recently, was chair of its board of directors. She is affiliated with a lackluster community-based organization in Oregon to maintain her status as an affiliate organization of NCLR to this day, but the only viable NCLR affiliate in Oregon is the Oregon Council for Hispanic Advancement (OCHA), which I founded in 1984.

NCLR, the successor to the Southwest Council of La Raza that we help formed in 1968, is the premier civil rights advocacy organization for Chicanos and other Latinos. It has among its members some three hundred community-based organizations across the country and represents some three million Chicanos and "Hispanics." But the leadership of NCLR is not accountable to its membership, and affiliate organizational members have very weak power within the governing structure. NCLR is a staff-led organization. Most officers on the board of directors of NCLR are Hispanics that represent corporate interests; they are not affiliated with any community-based organization. Some leaders, such as Irma, come from suspect community organizations. And, as is the case with many of our Chicano organizations, NCLR now also looks after the interests of other Latinos, not just Chicano interests. NCLR is not, however a pan-American organization interested in Latin American affairs, much less intercontinental unity. It just pretends that it is by accepting as organizational members other groups within the Latino community, such as Cubans.

In the foreclosure sale, the Colegio Cesar Chavez went back to the Catholic Church at a substantially lower price. That career opportunity over with, I ended up working part-time at Western Oregon State College (WOSC, then known as the Oregon College of Education) in Monmouth, Oregon, near Salem, the state capital. Later, I was hired on a full-time basis as an assistant professor of Social Science. Finally I was an academician!

I tendered my resignation as County Judge for Zavala County, Texas, in January of 1981. In exchange, the county commissioners agreed to restore all my back pay, as planned. As I suspected he would, Ron Carr maneuvered with my resignation and replaced me as the county judge at that time.

While in Oregon, I was not active electorally during the first few months. It was a very trying time for the family. By the time I collected the money owed to me from Zavala County, I was broke, and Luz could not find a job despite her many contacts in the region. The Oregon economy, heavily dependent on wood products, was in a downward spiral with no end in sight. Nationally, the economy was in bad shape, as well.

In addition to the part-time job at WOSC, I worked as a security guard on the graveyard shift at the local Dole Company mushroom plant. On weekends, I would cook and make Mexican *barbacoa* (barbecue) and tamales. My wife, Luz, and the older children, Adrian and Tozi, would sell the Mexican barbecue and tamales at the mushroom plant while Olin and I cared for the newborn baby girl, Avina Cristal. That's how we made ends meet during those first few months in Oregon after the Colegio debacle.

I also began volunteering for the Governor's Commission on Hispanic Affairs. A former schoolmate from Texas A & I University, Gilbert Anzaldua, had begun this effort a decade prior and not been very successful. Others now were trying to revive the initiative. I lobbied to get the agency legislatively created, and funded. The push for money paid

Gutiérrez family in front of their home in Independence, Oregon. *Top to bottom*, Adrian, Tozi Aide, Luz, Olin, and Avina Cristal.

off: This became my third part-time job, as executive director of the Oregon Commission on Hispanic Affairs. Later came a full-time opportunity at Western Oregon State College (WOSC).

By 1983, we had begun to live like a normal family again, tending to the needs of our growing children and making new friends. At the college, I buddied with Ken Jensen, an anthropologist, and with two couples, Raul and Nellie Vasquez and Hollis and Elaine Ferguson. The Marins, Reymundo and Maria, remained our friends and later *compadres* when they baptized Tozi Aide, my oldest daughter. These folks also were hurt by the politics at the Colegio Cesar Chavez and eventually relocated to the San Diego area.

We eventually bought a house in Independence, Oregon. The realtor at first steered us toward the cheaper homes in the Mexican section of Independence. Only upon learning that Luz ran a health clinic and I was a college teacher did he offer to show us homes in Monmouth. But Luz and I wanted to live among other Chicanos, for our children's sake. They had not been exposed to Anglos or blacks in Cristal to any degree, and they missed their culture. Independence was as close as we could get to recreating that type of atmosphere for them.

Into the Democratic Party Fold

Soon, we were in the thick of politics again. When our friend Maria Viramontes de Marin ran for county office in Portland, we helped out. Luz and Maria organized Mujeres de Oregon, a political organization for women. In the city of Independence we backed Chicano candidates for school board and city council and won.

We joined the Democratic Party in Polk County and worked for its various candidates in 1982. This decision was most difficult for Luz and me. Both of us had participated in Democratic Party precinct conventions in Zavala County, in the primary elections of 1980; we had, after La Raza Unida Party lost ballot status, returned to the very political party that historically had stolen our homeland in the Southwest and West, oppressed us with one-party rule in Texas for nearly a century, and taken our votes for granted. We believed, though, that the same brown tide of *raza* voters that had supported the candidates of the Raza Unida Party for a decade would inevitably take control of the Democratic Party in Texas, perhaps across the Southwest and Midwest by the year 2000. And in Oregon in 1984, the Democratic Party personnel seemed genuinely interested in the needs and social conditions affecting Mexican Americans.

In 1983, I began to organize the Rainbow Coalition for Jesse Jackson

in Oregon and in 1984 ran from Polk County as a Democrat for a legislative seat. In the race for state representative, I won the Democratic
Party nomination. The Republican ten-year incumbent, John Schoon,
became my opponent. Although 1984 was the year of the Reagan Republican landslide, I was nevertheless the top Democratic vote-getter in
the district, even outpolling influential and big name Democrats from
across the state on the local ballot, garnering 44 percent of the vote in
that race. Walking the entire district in search of the Democratic voters
on the precinct lists and asking them for their vote paid off. I probably
would have won the election had I been able to raise more campaign
money and not taken the summer off for a course of study on the presidency at the University of Texas at Austin, offered by Professor Robert
Divine, a noted authority on the subject.

Hindsight is always perfect vision. Perhaps I placed more emphasis
on improving my academic credentials than on an enlarged political ré-
sumé. Perhaps I simply missed Texas. Discussing this episode with
Rudy Acuña, a noted historian of Chicano history, he told me that I
could not cope without a role in the movimiento Chicano. He said, "You
are looking for a way back already. You cannot do without the movement, much less [deal] with the reality that the movement *can* do without you." I believe that there was another reason for going to Texas when
I could have had electoral victory in Oregon. I simply wanted to show
myself that I could seek office and conduct a credible campaign among
Anglo voters in the Democratic Party. The campaign was a catharsis: I
wanted to purge myself of any notion that I was merely an ethnic rural
leader from South Texas unable to compete in a setting void of Chicanos.

The Oregon experience taught me a great many lessons, the most important of which was working in a multiethnic setting. I had exposure
for the first time to organized groups of gays and lesbians; various tribes
of Native Americans; many different Asian subgroups; urban African
Americans; rich Jews; and, middle-class and poor whites. I never had
seen white poverty on this scale. In Cristal, Anglos had referred to the
poor of their kind as "white trash." We often repeated those words as a
slur toward gringos, but I never had seen as many poor white people as
I did in Oregon. In Cristal, the poorest gringo was still treated better
than the economically highest Chicano.

I was also in a unique position of being an ethnic minority and a numerical minority. That is to say, not only were Mexican Americans a minority among many others in Oregon, we were a very small population
in number, relatively speaking. Although between 1970 and 1980 persons of Mexican ancestry in Oregon surpassed the number of African
Americans in the state, black people remained the number one group in

Gutiérrez ran for the Oregon Legislature as a Democratic candidate in 1984. The state capitol in Salem is shown in the background.

the eyes of white Oregonians. They listened and responded to group demands made by blacks. I saw firsthand the beginning rivalries between blacks and browns for white patronage. Blacks seemed to enjoy, if it can be called that, the status of "Most-Favored Minority." We were ignored.

Most Oregonians believe us to be either illegal immigrants from Mexico or migrant farm laborers from other states who reside in Oregon for a few months in the summer. In either case, Oregonians take no responsibility for us. But every county in Oregon has Mexicans. There were Mexicans in Oregon before there were white or black people. The greatest concentration of our people were west of the Cascade mountain range, residing between Eugene and Portland, though another concentration of Mexican Americans is found in the eastern part of the state in Nyssa, Ontario, and Adrian, near the border with Idaho.

I learned how to coexist and work with others. This was a wonderful opportunity at learning crosscultural communication skills and how to build coalitions. To walk in someone else's shoes for a change was very different from working only with Chicanos against redneck gringos in South and West Texas. Yet during my campaign for state representative in Oregon, I recall meeting a man cutting firewood and approaching him to ask for his vote. He repeated my name over and over, searching in his mind for a connection. Finally, he asked me, "Are you that same 'Goo-Tea-Air-Ess' with that 'Rat-Sah' bunch in Texas?" When I answered affirmatively, he said, "I left Texas because of ya'll!" To which I replied, "Well, I guess you didn't move far enough."

Back to Organizing

Independence, Oregon, is a blue collar, poor, minority, and wet community of about 2,300 people. By "wet" I mean from alcohol and rain. When we bought our home, my wife and I got involved locally. Together, we assisted various candidates, and were able to get several Mexican Americans elected to the school board and the city council in Independence.

We also came to be very active within the local Catholic Church. I was selected by the bishop of Portland to serve as one of the Oregon representatives to the national board of directors for the Campaign for Human Development, the Catholic Church's grant-making, national foundation, which grants money to community groups, twelve to fifteen million dollars annually, divided by regions. During the three-year term I rose to become the Vice President for Economic Development. In that time, I got firsthand, inside knowledge of the workings of the campaign and its stranglehold over funding dollars by the Industrial Areas Foundation (IAF). The IAF network participates with active Catholic clergy in very safe projects and issues, and will not take a controversial stand on a political issue of importance to Chicanos. They often take on governmental entities and politicians over issues and projects that government ought to be supporting in the first place, such as better schools, a sewer project, water for *las colonias* (unincorporated neighborhoods along the border with Mexico), and other similar campaigns. But I have yet to see the IAF network of organizations demand redistribution of wealth; stand against the neoconservative ideology; propose minimum wage hikes; defend immigrant rights; or support the right of lawful residents to vote. In the Southwest, the IAF network is the Catholic Church's pacification program. They keep our people busy with less than substantive political work. They use our own money, contributed to the church as tithe at Sunday Mass, to fund others. Mexican Americans get less money from the Catholic Church's foundation than other Catholics, and yet, we are the majority of churchgoers for Catholic Mass across the country.

I also learned how, in absolute numbers, Anglos get more money than raza from the campaign, and African Americans obtain as much money from the campaign as raza. Anglos and African Americans work as key staff in all levels of the campaign and in higher numbers. Few Latinos work there. Anglos and African Americans are represented as directors of the fund in nearly all the regions. Others apply for grants even if they are not Catholic. Eligibility for campaign funds does not require the applicant to be Catholic, only that your local board be made up primarily of the poor. Yet, Latinos are about two-thirds of all the Catholics in the United States: there are more Catholic Masses said in Spanish in the country than in English. *We are* the Church in the Americas. The reciprocity and the reinvestment of our money into our communities and projects is just not there, and it makes no sense to me. It seems very short-sighted on the part of the Church for it not to recognize that an economically and politically healthy parishioner makes for a healthy parish, and therefore a vibrant church. They should be at the forefront of promoting social justice, championing the cause of the people of Mexican ancestry and other Latino immigrants because that is the makeup and grassroots membership of the Catholic church.

Dependent on lumber as the mainstay of its economy, Oregon went into a nose dive after the collapse of the home building industry across the country in the late 1970s and early 1980s. I survived four rounds of personnel cuts at WOSC in 1982–83 and 1983–84. But in 1985 the governor and chancellor finally declared financial exigency for the state system of higher education, and I was RIFted, one of the victims of a "reduction in force."

The only four Mexican American college professors at WOSC lost their jobs. We were all on tenure track, but only one was ever hired back. The provost, Billy Cowart, kept me on the payroll as a researcher and grant writer for another term while I desperately looked for employment, as we could not survive on Luz's salary alone. She finally had been able to work her way back into her field of health clinic administration, first in Salem and then at Salud de la Familia in Woodburn, as its director. She commuted from Independence daily to the job, an eighty-mile round-trip.

United Way of the Columbia-Willamette [Valleys] in Portland advertised for a contractor to provide outreach and innovative programs for "emerging populations." The agency wanted a person who could help them develop strategies on how to address these populations' needs. The euphemism "emerging populations" meant unwed teenage mothers, immigrants (particularly Latinos), Native Americans, and people with with AIDS. I got the job and proceeded to prioritize Latino immigrants as the number one target group, followed by people with AIDS and unwed teenage mothers. Programs were developed in conjunction with other agencies for the latter groups. I was able to convince the United Way leadership that what we needed was a broad-based, Hispanic, nonprofit, community-based organization in the Portland metropolitan area. In this capacity, I created and founded the aforementioned Oregon Council for Hispanic Advancement (OCHA) through United Way. First, I proposed that United Way adopt an advisory committee of Hispanics for the project. I identified, organized and nominated them. Then, the advisory committee and I met and, together, proposed a Hispanic Issues Conference at which we would learn of the needs firsthand. With United Way money and new financial assistance from the Fred Meyer Charitable Trust, I hired consultants to research and write papers on several important topics such as health, education, labor, transportation, and housing. With much publicity and working the various networks of Chicano organizations I knew across the Willamette Valley and the Portland area, we held an issues conference. The presentations were very good and the turnout was spectacular.

The presentations had been videotaped and were subsequently aired on cable access television repeatedly and published in book form in three volumes entitled *The State of Hispanics in Oregon*. This study was the first comprehensive look at Hispanics in the Portland area. The list of persons in attendance became my mailing list, my network to mobilize troops. Nothing is more effective at moving politicians and directors into action than personal presence at meetings where decisions on policy and budget are to be made. If you have the people present and vocal, you will probably get the vote. After the conference, everyone took credit for it and everyone, including United Way, was convinced that the committee should be the beginning of an organization. I agreed. It is always easier to organize people around an idea after they have made it their own.

I got more monies from United Way for OCHA and from the Campaign for Human Development for a Northwest Voter Registration and Education Project. Through funding from the Gannett Foundation that owns the Salem newspaper, I began a leadership institute for youth in the state. The issues conference soon evolved into an annual fundraising meeting for OCHA and enjoys significant corporate support, as does the youth program. Meanwhile, Luz was very active in organizing Mujeres de Oregon and was very instrumental in putting together a statewide network of influential women across the state. With her contacts, I met some exceptional Chicanas in Oregon—real pioneers. I did oral history video tapes on these Hispanic women through a grant from the Center for the Study of Women at the University of Oregon. Those tapes taught me a lot about history of our people in that region. Previously I thought, as did most Oregonians, that Mexican Americans in Oregon were primarily resettled migrants from Texas, but this is not so. The research and the interviews revealed that Spanish explorers were among the first to navigate the Pacific coastal waters and chart the course up to Alaska. Valdez, Alaska, is named after the Spanish Minister of the Navy, who preceded Lewis and Clark. Oregon was first Spanish and then Mexican territory before it became part of the United States. The Mexican Revolution of 1910 brought many more Mexicans to Oregon, along with the expansion of railroad lines to the West. These women related some stories from their ancestors dating to those earlier times. Today, these tapes are in the archives of the University of Oregon at Eugene.

I also developed a historical slide show for my classes at WOSC. Later, it was converted into a video format under the title *The Hispanic Presence in Oregon*. The slide show was widely used by the migrant programs and in the public schools in the state, and was the first of its kind.

At WOSC, I organized the first Cinco de Mayo party, which featured Governor Vic Atiyeh. I had a nasty fight with my compadre Gilberto Martinez over this fiesta. He had a collection of Agustin V. Casasola photographs of the Mexican Revolution, and promised to send me the photos for exhibition during the holiday. Casasola is a famous as Matthew

Brady for his photos of the Civil War. Gilbert had committed to helping me get those beautiful pictures, but Carlos Reyes, a former bodyguard of mine and his associate, canceled the shipment at the last minute. Without this central piece of the program, I was in trouble. Besides, I had requested funds for the exhibit rental and would have to return the money unspent! We assumed this was his way of paying Luz back for having terminated his mother-in-law from a job at the health clinic in Cristal.

Fortunately, I still had contacts with officials in Mexico. I was able to obtain several photographs by air shipment within days of the event, sweating bullets that week. I never forgave Carlos for his dirty deed or Gilberto for the lack of guts to override Carlos and make good on his promise. I could have lost my job over that fiasco, which would have hurt my family.

After OCHA was organized, additional funding was obtained during the second year. I hired new staff and began to expand operations and programs in the Portland metropolitan area. I developed a proposal for a youth leadership program and submitted it to the Gannett Foundation through its newspaper in Salem. The Commission on Hispanic Affairs in Salem was finally legislatively funded. I was paid to administer the program and had funds to hire a full-time office person. Several of us across the country, as executive directors of similar state commissions, sought to form a national association. The Cuban representatives from Florida opposed the idea and our entire agenda. Nevertheless, we met in St. Paul, Minnesota, in January, 1986, for an organizational meeting of the various state commissions. Over the course of two days we hammered out a structure, with representation and membership issues, drafted bylaws, and elected temporary directors and officers over the objections of the Cubans from Florida and Massachusetts. I invited the leaders and elected officers of the various commissions to come and incorporate a national association at the OCHA conference, to be held in March, 1986. We do not yet today have similar organizations at the state level, or serving as liaison between states and federal governments in all the states. Moreover, there are no Commissions on Hispanic Affairs or anything similar in the Southwest. They are only found to exist in the northern states, from west to east, with Florida being the exception.

The Puerto Rican representative of the Commission on Hispanic Affairs from the state of New York, Nestor Llamas, sided with the Chicanos at both the organizational meeting and the incorporation ceremony. He attended both; voting together we prevailed over the Cubans.

Interethnic Group Conflicts

I've learned that other Latinos will use the rhetoric of unity to obtain the use of numbers of Chicanos for their leverage in seeking jobs, positions, grants, and other power. Cubans seldom support our efforts, but always look for support from us. Their notion of inclusion is for *us* to *help* them *in* and *up,* but not the other way around. In addition, there are too many serious differences between the Chicano and Cuban communities to ever make cooperation, much less a community of interest, possible although an occasional alliance is workable. Let me list some fundamental differences.

Since 1960 Cubans have enjoyed a different set of standards regarding U.S. immigration policy. Cubans are literally paid to come to the United States. The U.S. government has brought them from the island and picked them up in the open sea of the Gulf of Mexico to safety. Once here, they are heavily subsidized and assisted in many ways to incorporate them into society. As favored immigrants they are provided with paid sponsors and mentors in this relocation and incorporation process. Cuban refugees are admitted into the United States on a fast track toward citizenship. The U.S. government has paid the early immigrant Cubans some $30 million dollars in subsidies from 1960 to 1980.

When the Marielitos—the criminal element Fidel Castro let out during President Carter's administration—came, the subsidy slowed down to a trickle. These Marielitos were mostly poor blacks. We now spend money to keep them in U.S. jails, in Panama, or on the Guantanamo Naval base within Cuba. In the case of Mexicanos who migrate north into the United States in search of work, there is a national police force that hunts them down, the Border Patrol. Today, federal troops also patrol the border with Mexico. In 1996 and by mid-July, 1997, U.S. soldiers had shot and killed two men, one an eighteen-year-old high school senior. The allegation against the latter was that he had shot his .22 caliber rifle at the Marines and they killed him in self-defense. What a stark contrast in U.S. immigration policy!

Another difference between Chicanos and Cubans is that the white, older Cubans think they are direct descendants of the Spanish Conquistadores. They deny that there is any African or indigenous genetic influence and mixture. These Cubans despise the Chicanos and Mexicanos among us who are *morenos,* dark skinned. Chicanos and Mexicanos are mostly dark skinned because we are *mestizos,* mixed bloods of Spanish with native Indios and Africans.

These white Cubans have also only one thought and one political

Gutiérrez and Luz hug their son, Adrian, celebrating his graduation from high school, 1986.

agenda on their minds, to get rid of Fidel Castro. Any person who is perceived to be liberal, socialist, supports the welfare state or is against the U.S. blockade of Cuba is deemed a pro-Castro communist sympathizer by these Cuban bigots. It is very hard to work with Cubans who have such a closed mindset and narrow view of the world; mostly you cannot. The younger generations of "born-here" Cubans are not as bigoted as their parents. Perhaps, the Latino youth can coalesce better than in my generation.

In the case of Puerto Ricans and immigration policy, they have no cause to worry. Since 1905 Puerto Ricans have had an open border between their island and the U.S. mainland. There are no Border Patrol agents checking documents of Puerto Ricans, and they were granted U.S. citizenship early in this century.

My Marriage Ends

By 1986, I had finished the organizing agenda that preoccupied me during 1985 and 1986. I was satisfied that I had helped create some institutions in the Northwest, particularly in Oregon. I could leave, happy with these accomplishments. It is always hard to know when to let go of positions of power and when to physically leave organizations. Organizers are not accountable to groups, only to ideas and strategies.

The problems caused by my layoff at WOSC in the spring of 1985, the daily hundred-mile commutes between Portland and Independence for the United Way job, and the job pressures for Luz at the health clinic in Woodburn, and me while organizing OCHA and the Commission on Hispanic Affairs steadily took their toll. Our nineteen years of marriage deteriorated to less than a friendly relationship. We discussed divorce. She and I had separated several times during our marriage and had made up. This time, it was not so. We each made an individual decision to divorce, and did.

I knew I could not stay in Oregon and be happy with this divorce, a broken family, and a fizzled academic career at age forty-one. In my heart I yearned to return to Texas and start anew. Perhaps, as Professor Acuña had observed, the Chicano movement could do without me, but I could not do without the Chicano environment. Oregon was lacking what I needed, political nourishment from other Chicanos. I began to look for a job in Texas.

I accepted an employment offer from David Hall, the board chair of the Texas Rural Legal Aid Foundation in Texas, to become the Foundation's executive director. I decided to return to the study of law but decided not to attend Willamette College of Law in Salem, Oregon, though I had been offered a full scholarship there. Instead, I chose Southern Methodist University (SMU) School of Law in Dallas, Texas, with a half scholarship.

Immediately after the second OCHA conference, I left Oregon for Dallas. I arrived in May, in time for the 1986 primary election. Many years back I had pledged to Severita Lara that whenever she sought public office I would be there to help her. She was a candidate in the Democratic primary for county judge of Zavala County. As well, Domingo Garcia, a former MAYO leader from the North Texas area and a Raza Unida party activist was a lawyer in Dallas. He was running for state representative in the democratic primary of Dallas County, and asked for my help. I was home again!

15

The Return to Texas

I arrived in Dallas in time to assist Domingo Garcia in his campaign to become the first Mexican American legislator elected in North Texas. Domingo was an interesting character. He drove a sporty car, had a mustache, walked with a swagger, talked with a high-pitched, squeaky voice, and acted real macho when others were around him. He had learned the basics of conducting a campaign during his years in North Texas as a youthful militant in La Raza Unida Party. Domingo, however, had a propensity for engaging in negative and dirty campaigning at a moment's notice. He seemed much too ambitious and greedy to suit me, but I figured he was simply too young and inexperienced, and I had already promised to help him, as he was the only Mexican American candidate in the May 1986 Democratic primary election in Dallas.

Discovering Cockrell Hill

In doing street canvassing one day, I made a mental note of a color change in the street signs for the area we were working. They were blue; and Dallas street signs were green. I figured we were in a different city. The young student volunteer working the streets with me couldn't believe my stupidity for asking if we were still in Dallas. Every time I would ask him he would shake his head in disbelief and kept telling me in a louder tone of voice that we were still in Dallas.

I realized just by the color change of the street signs that this area,

288

whatever city it was, had the potential to become the first Chicano-controlled city in North Texas. While walking house-to-house calling on potential voters, I noticed the large numbers of raza living in this area who were not registered to vote. The walking list of voters was outdated! Domingo was using someone's old list rather than buy a current one!

Back at the campaign office I finally figured out that the area I was in was the city of Cockrell Hill. It is an incorporated city, within Dallas, of nearly 5,000 residents—of whom I guessed 85 percent were Mexican Americans. After that afternoon of walking in the hot Texas sun I suggested to Domingo that we take over Cockrell Hill. He told me that Roberto Alonzo and his wife, Sylvana, young Chicanos from Cristal, lived there. I remembered them both well; they came from solid raza families in my hometown.

Over the next few days Domingo and Roberto both confirmed the large numbers of Chicanos in the little city surrounded by Dallas. I again suggested we organize and take over the community, but Domingo was focused on his race for state representative. He was not interested in a city council seat in an obscure little town. He couldn't see the potential.

Ramsey Muñiz was working with Domingo as his paralegal assistant at the time. Domingo, as attorney, had gotten Ramsey released from prison, though Ramsey had been incarcerated subsequently on charges of parole violations. I had not seen Ramsey in years. From our first meeting, he and I were tentative with one another. I didn't trust him anymore, and he probably didn't want to confess to me that he had been involved with drugs after the 1974 campaign. He sought to talk with me about his getting active in politics again, but I was not interested in discussing that subject with him.

One afternoon after more walking, Ramsey got a big laugh at my expense. There was no question that the distance I had traveled from Texas to Oregon was nothing compared to the distance between the early days of the movimiento Chicano and present day reality. Many things had changed radically. Some of the Garcia campaign volunteers and I had just opened a beer after another hot day of street canvassing. After a few hard pulls of the brew, I heard someone say, "Hey, the Rangers are in town! Let's go see them!" I shot straight up and shouted back "*¿Cuantos son y que es el pedo?*" (How many are they and what is the trouble?) The younger volunteers were startled at my instant reaction, while Ramsey doubled up in laughter. He said, between laughter and body shakes, "The Rangers are the baseball team!" I couldn't believe someone would name a baseball team the Texas Rangers! I couldn't believe Chicanos would support such a team! It seemed I was now a Chicano dinosaur.

That is not all that had changed. Henry Cisneros, the mayor of San

Antonio, was the object of hero worship, the likes of which I had never seen. In fact this Mexican American elected official was now held in greater esteem than the independent Chicano leaders of the recent past. Even Cesar Chavez did not carry the political clout of the politicos. The Four Horsemen of the Chicano Movement, as we were called by some historians—Cesar Chavez, Reies Lopez Tijerina, Rodolfo "Corky" Gonzales, and I—were eclipsed by the increasing political clout of Mexican American elected officials, overwhelmingly members of the Democratic Party.

The word "Chicano" was offensive to those who wished to be called Hispanic or Latino. To be pro-Chicano was equated with the politics of a bygone era and was not politically correct. Now we had to be inclusive and put the political interests of other related cultural groups on equal footing with our own—for unity, for greater Hispanic power. The local Hispanic Chamber of Commerce was the most visible nonprofit organization in the Dallas community. In the other major metropolitan areas of Texas, its counterparts enjoyed that same status. They now sought to do business with major Anglo-led and controlled multinational corporations. This was the wave of the future. The barrio-based, small business owner struggling to make ends meet and stay in business was ignored by the new generation of Hispanic leaders.

Severita Lara and Popeye

Just days prior to the primary election, I went down to Cristal in time to help Severita Lara during the last few days of the campaign. Another former Raza Unida Party officeholder, Rey Perez, was running for district judge. Rey had been the first Chicano chief of police in Cristal, under George Ozuna and Los Cinco Candidatos, and our county attorney under La Raza Unida. I made two speeches for Severita, then made the rounds of businesses and families asking them to vote for Severita and Rey.

It was great to be home! It was as if I had not left. The warmth with which I was again received by my people made me feel very good. I realized how much I missed Chicano politics. I had even missed the famous statue of Popeye in front of the city hall. That statue was cast in 1937 by Julian A. Sandoval, a Chicano from San Antonio, who also cast the famous Hertzberg elephant in front of the Public Library in San Antonio. Popeye was delivered to Cristal in March, 1937, and placed in the center of town in the orange grove across from the old city hall; the Cornejo administration later moved it to the front of the new city hall. During our first years in power back in the 1970s I attempted to move the statue to the Juan Garcia Park we built near Highway 83. My thought was that the children would love it there, but I was wrong. I got considerable protest from all quarters to not touch Popeye. I backed down, some things are not worth fighting for. But Severita's election was. City hall and the county courthouse were worth fighting for.

I watched the process of campaigning and electioneering. The methods used by both sides were still the same ones we had developed years earlier. The methods worked; it was now a matter of which candidates garnered more votes in the process. I did notice that the process had gotten more expensive. The volunteers were now paid to work the streets and get the vote out. I also noticed that voters waited to be taken to the polls rather than show personal initiative and interest by going to the polls on their own.

The raza voters in Zavala County voted for Severita, and she beat Ronnie Carr. In so doing, she became the first Mexican American woman to win that office in the state. Rey had beaten the incumbent Chicano district judge from Eagle Pass, and we celebrated Severita's and Rey's delicious victories. I particularly relished the revenge of sacking Ronnie Carr and the Democrat commissioners in this election. I knew that with Severita at the helm of the county, the raza would be in good hands. I left her victory party, went over to José O. Mata's house, and called Dallas.

Domingo had lost the election. This was the first of his many losses until he would become the first Chicano elected to the Dallas City Council from one of the newly drawn single-member districts in 1991. I helped finance the voting rights litigation that resulted in the City of Dallas adopting the "14–1" plan—fourteen districts and the mayor running at large for city council membership. Later in 1992, Roberto Alonzo would become the first Chicano state representative from North Texas.

I left Cristal for the Rio Grande Valley the next day to meet with David Hall, the board chair of the foundation I was to lead. He was in Weslaco. We reviewed the budget and discussed the work program of the foundation for a couple of days. I then packed up the records and supplies and headed to Dallas.

Later that summer, I learned that an election contests had been filed against Severita Lara and Rey Perez. They were going to court. I knew instantly that because of my own long experience with courtroom battles, she was going to lose the county judgeship. She did. Rey managed to hang in there with enough money to fight the other side and be declared the winner.

By now I was ready to try law school again, at SMU. SMU was a very white school, attended by rich students. They were also very young. I was in shock the first few days. Initially, I stayed with Domingo Garcia and his wife, Elba, until I found an apartment. The new law partner of Domingo Garcia and Roberto Alonzo was Alberto Garcia, and we decided to share an apartment. On the occasional evenings when all four of us would come together we would muse about forming the first Chicano full service law firm in Dallas. The idea was provocative. But, Domingo's boundless hunger for power made me wonder if he would actually settle for a quality law firm or use it as his power base.

My mother died the first month I was in law school, in September of 1986. Her death almost caused me to drop out of law school for the second time. I had no money with which to retrieve her body from Monterrey, Nuevo Leon, Mexico, where she died while visiting her brother, my uncle Jesus. I didn't have money to bury her in Cristal. For nearly a month, I missed classes. I begged for money from everyone I knew, and some dear friends loaned me what they could. Others, equally dear friends, turned me down cold. Only in times of tragedy do you really learn who your friends are. Somehow, I prevailed in these adverse times and survived that first year of law school, financially and emotionally. By January, 1987, just a mere semester into school, it was clear to me that the course of study at SMU was going to be too costly. The illegal recruiting of the football team by the athletic department at SMU had cost the students dearly, and SMU was prohibited from playing football for the next five years as a result. Facing huge losses for lack of a football season for the next five years, the school hiked tuition some 23 percent. It was already the highest tuition for law school in the state before the hike.

I was going heavily into debt trying to pay my child support, my mother's funeral expense loans, and my tuition. When Alberto married I invited Juan Jasso, another new lawyer at the Garcia law firm, to share my apartment. Dallas, SMU, and my situation were too expensive for me. The money I borrowed was not enough to bail me out, just to tide me over. I had to go to law school elsewhere.

I transferred to the University of Houston the summer of 1987. I was returning to the same school to study law that I had attended some twenty-one years earlier in the summer of 1966. Some professors were still there. When I had first attended the school, these same professors were not ready for me, and I was not ready for them. We argued about everything. Now, in 1987, I was reading cases with precedents that bore the very points I once argued for in class. For example, the Pancho Medrano case against the Texas Rangers was in my Remedies class textbook. La Raza Unida Party cases were in the readings for my Election Law seminar. I felt vindicated, but also, again, like a dinosaur.

While in Houston, telephone calls to and from Domingo and Roberto kept me abreast of events in Dallas. I learned that they finally had gotten interested in organizing in Cockrell Hill. From then on, I alternated between advising on how to organize Cockrell Hill and agonizing over a return to that political environment on a full-time basis. I wanted to be a lawyer; I wanted to make money; I was tired of poverty; I wanted to fight in courtrooms. I wanted to go up against the real powers in the state and nation that reside in Dallas. I had studied my options before returning to Texas and settled on Dallas as an ideal location. As much as I loved my friends and supporters in Cristal, I could never go back to that small community and survive as a lawyer. If I went to the Valley or anywhere in South Texas, including San Antonio, I would have other Mexican Americans as adversaries in the courtroom and bench. Houston was dominated by the remaining Castillo machine, built by the first Chicano elected as comptroller for the city of Houston, Lionel Castillo, who later became the first Chicano commissioner of the Immigration and Naturalization Service. His protege, Ben Reyes, formerly a state representative, was now on the city council and was very powerful. No changes in that leadership structure seemed obvious to me at the time although it did alter radically; it always does.

I made some of these changes happen with the threat to fund a redistricting lawsuit against the city of Houston. Unlike voter registration, which only increases the number of voters and the capacity of a group to elect someone of their choice, redistricting alters the structure and guarantees that group might elect someone of their choice. This is the work that Willie Velasquez had become enamored with after he left MAYO. Willie had opposed the creation of La Raza Unida Party. He insisted that we support completely the Democratic Party and seek to make change within the party structure. Not to do so, he argued, would be to help the Republican Party. I argued the opposite. We need to break away from the Democrats and build our own powerbase with which to obtain political leverage and power within and without the Democratic Party. I also argued for voting rights litigation over voter registration. What was the point of getting our people registered if they could not win in districts that deliberately diluted our collective power? The Democrats, after all, always break our community into as many districts as they can to create safe harbors for Democratic incumbents. Willie sought to register thousands of Mexican Americans to vote for the Democratic Party, and he did. Yet, one redistricting lawsuit could accomplish more in obtaining power than the thousands registered. Rolando Rios, George Korbel, Bill Garrett, and Joaquin Avila, among other attorneys, including some from MALDEF, have accomplished more by obtaining political seats for la raza than has the millions of dollars spent on voter

Gutiérrez, Gloria, and their baby daughter, Andrea, 1988.

registration. This is the area in which we still cannot get enough foundation dollars to litigate. And, today the political climate and the appellate court judges are not favorable for such litigation. Once we could have carried the day, but we didn't sue; and, now when we know better, the focus of the money, the law and the judges aren't on our side.

Dallas is a world-class city. The monied people and influential racists live and do business in Dallas. There was a leadership vacuum among Mexicans in Dallas when I arrived in the summer of 1986. There were few nonprofit organizations controlled by Mexican Americans. It was wide open. Domingo, Roberto, Alberto, and Juan were all eager to make things happen with a Chicano agenda. I committed to return to Dallas with my law degree and license, and to form the Garcia, Alonzo, Garcia, and Gutiérrez law firm.

I finally graduated from law school, the Bates College of Law at the University of Houston, in December, 1989. During this time, I had worked part-time at Apex Securities, an investment firm owned by Rodney Ellis and Richard Ramirez. They were just getting started and I interned there for a course and stayed to help build the business. Soon, I obtained my broker dealer license and began to call on elected officials on their behalf.

The Twenty-Five-Year Chicano Activist Reunion

During the 1988 Christmas season several of my former activist cronies from San Antonio and Austin and I held a reunion of Chicano activists from across the nation in San Antonio. It was a wonderful event. Other than looking older and worn, those who attended had the Chicano spirit and cause still etched in their psyche, although they were middle-aged and middle-class. Clearly, we were the past generation. Many of us at the reunion had grown children and grandchildren in tow. Many were divorced and had both new spouses and stepchildren in tow. We had those with original spouses, no spouse at all, same sex spouses, and those with the "other" person in the relationship attending our convention. We were the new American polygamists, introducing the children as "mine, hers, and ours." I was one of this group: I had all of my children from my marriage to Luz with me at the reunion, as well as my second wife, Gloria Garza—whom I'd married in Houston on July 17, 1988— and our two children. Gloria, a widow, had a daughter, Lina Maria Silva, from her previous marriage, and together we had had another girl, Andrea Lucia, born in 1988. (In 1990, our last child was born—another girl, Clavel Amariz.) Our children *truly were* mine, hers, and ours.

At the reunion, we had a session entitled "Mommy, what did you do

Gutiérrez and his second wife, Gloria, at his graduation from the University of Houston law school, 1988.

Gutiérrez and family at the Activist Reunion in San Antonio, December 27–30, 1989.

Activist Reunion: Gutiérrez, and *(seated left to right),* Maria Elena Martinez (former Texas party chairman for RUP), Maria Jimenez (former RUP candidate for state representative), Frank Shafer-Corona (school board member from Washington, D.C.).

in the Chicano Movement?" and a formal dinner as a tribute to Las Chicanas del Movimiento to drive home the point, lest we forget, that our leadership in MAYO, the Raza Unida Party, and the Chicano movement generally was built and led with the significant contributions of Chicanas. All of us had ample time to reminisce over champagne and tamales at breakfast or during an ice cream social and the *pachanga,* the long festive party of drinking and dancing, at Ruben Sandoval's Law Center. The anecdotes, stories, incidents, and exaggerations ran wild at these sessions. Our memories of Chicano movement days were crisp and gave no appearance of time gone by. Our wrinkles and gray hair were another matter. We definitely had aged. Twenty years had gone by. Many important issues and causes that we held dear had also faded or were cast aside for new causes and issues. We had made many babies in these twenty years and they had grown up. We had replaced ourselves and then some, for those who were into zero population growth. In retrospect our provocative slogan question of "Ballots or Bullets?" as ideological options for both the Chicanos and the gringo enemy should have included perhaps "Ballots, Bullets or Babies?"

Activist Reunion: Gutiérrez and his son, Olin, with Emma Tenayuca, the leader of the pecan shellers strike in San Antonio in the 1930s.

It was clear to me that while we may be the immediate past generation, the Chicano movement that we built and led was not a passing phase. Hispanics are quick to argue that Chicanos were a phase. These same Hispanics are willing to dismiss my generation of activists as peculiar, a passing political generation. In one simple twist of a few words, "phase" and "political generation," they erase the notion of commitment to the cause of uplifting our people. They also squash the ideological underpinnings of Aztlan by referring to our politics as merely generational.

We honored Emma Tenayuca, the former leader of the pecan shellers strike in San Antonio during the 1930s. Her dinner speech was motivational. She was the epitome of a fighter for social justice. Even though she was red-baited during the strike and emasculated by the press as a "pinko communist sympathizer" for seeking better wages for those shelling pecans, she never took a step back from her commitment.

Activist Reunion: Mario Compean, MAYO co-founder and the RUP candidate for governor in 1978, and Gutiérrez.

She didn't think protest was a passing phase nor that fighting for social justice was a generational phenomenon. She thought, back in the 1940s, as we did in the 1960s, 1970s, 1980s and now, that the fight for higher minimum wages, safe working conditions, and collective bargaining is timeless. The fight for our land and our dignity is timeless, until we prevail.

Reies Lopez Tijerina, the Chicano land recovery movement leader, told jokes during the midnight beer and jokes session. His speech on our claim to the land in the Southwest was impressive. Reies is a living hero, in my estimation greater than Malcolm X. There are many similarities between the two, and notable differences. Reies *did* what Malcolm X only talked about. Reies Lopez Tijerina, Virginia Muzquiz, Corky Gonzales, Cesar Chavez, Maria L. Hernandez, Emma Tenayuca, Dolores Huerta, and Baldemar Velasquez are leaders who have sought to empower our community. Today, politicians are more likely to use our community votes to empower themselves. Today, people revere the elected official, not the grass roots leader. The primacy of the politico among Hispanics is evident.

Ramsey Muñiz had a chance to bridge the gap between politico and

Activist Reunion: Gutiérrez and Reies Lopez Tijerina.

grass-roots leader as the gubernatorial candidate of the Raza Unida Party, but turned me down when I called him about being on the agenda of the reunion. He managed to arrive; he even attempted to give a speech, though that was a pathetic moment because few were interested in what he had to say. Many of us feel that he shamed us, *nos avergonzo*, with his drug deals. Chicanos have a fundamental sense of decency and integrity that reveals itself in a private and a public sense of shame. The phrase *no tiene verguenza* (has no shame) is the admonishment we hurl at the person who has publicly embarrassed la raza. The phrase *me da verguenza* (I am ashamed) is the private sense of shame and embarrassment.

Many of the Chicano leaders from across the country were in attendance, over eight hundred people from various states. The activists brought their photo albums and political buttons. The commemorative poster from the reunion is made up of these very same political buttons and bumper stickers from the earlier era. Of these activists, many were born-again Democrats. They had returned to the politics of the Democratic Party, and many were local leaders of that party. They were now the new brokers for our people.

Some in attendance were critical of the way the reunion was organized. They wanted more "inclusiveness" in the sessions. They meant two things: program space for gays and lesbians, and the presence of corporate America. They asked why we had no corporate sponsors. Some even suggested that Coors beer and Levis could have contributed to the events, though Coors and Levis had both been subject of Chicano consumer boycotts in the recent past.

We ignored many of the petty criticisms leveled at us about the reunion. A session entitled "1992: The Trip Back," for example, was singled out as being anti-Native American and pro-Columbus. I was involved with that session, inviting those interested to travel with me to Spain in 1992 as a celebration of our five-hundredth birthday as a people. My attempt was twofold: to free ourselves from part of that self-hate; and to end the Spain-bashing that had gone on for too long. Spain has a socialist democratic government. It is part of the European Economic Community and, more importantly, the father to many "Spains" in the Americas. That legacy is also ours. It is as much a crime for gringos and other racists to deny us our right to be Chicano as it is for us as Chicanos to deny our Spanish heritage and their contribution to our world. We do not have to choose between being *indio* or *español*. We are both at once, *mestizos*, mixed bloods, and because of this rich heritage, twice as good as monocultural xenophobic beings.

The real issues behind the criticisms of the reunion cannot be ignored. Corporations have become involved with our issues because their market approach is cause oriented. Corporations now can bless an organization or an event with funding and therefore can withhold financial support and doom that organization to minor success or limited impact. Corporations benefit from the public relations benefits inherent in cause marketing. Our organizations moderate their stand on issues and blunt their criticism of the corporate world by asking for necessary financial assistance. The current generation has forgotten that our two strengths as a people are labor and consumer power. While we do need jobs and must buy products to live, the employer and the corporation need us more than we need them. There are many jobs to be had. There are many competing corporate products to be bought. They need us to make their profits and obtain their market share. We should not sell out to employers or corporations.

Many gay and lesbian reunion attendees had come out of the closet during the time of the Chicano movement and were now seeking to make sexual orientation a civil right, as well as seeking greater recognition generally. In what was once the National Association of Chicano Studies, for instance, gays and lesbians successfully lobbied for a name change to include "Chicana" after "Chicano," arguing that the latter is

Texas Governor Ann Richards and Gutiérrez at the Justice Awards Dinner in Houston, 1989.

Gutiérrez speaking at Crystal City High School at the twentieth anniversary of the 1969 student walkout in December, 1989.

Gutiérrez poses after taking the oath admitting him to the Texas State Bar, May, 1990.

male. Within the Association a caucus was also formed, known as the National Association of Latino Gay Academics, or NALGA. (The acronym is intentionally amusing: *nalga* in Spanish means buttock.) The gay and lesbian community's criticism was that there was little inclusion provided for them at the reunion. Yet no one from their ranks had ever come forward to volunteer organizational efforts during the year I spent planning the event, and though several impromptu caucuses were called, not one was called by gays and lesbians. I am straight, but not narrow-minded: in organizing the reunion I strived for inclusiveness, and would have attempted to fit in any community or organization that desired inclusion.

Maria L. Hernandez, Ruben Sandoval, Ernesto Galarza, "Tiger" Perez, Elvirita de la Fuente, Chaca Ramirez, Gabe Tafolla, Willie Velasquez, and Cesar Chavez have all died, along with many other lesser-known activists. Those of us from the Chicano movement are all headed in that same direction: we are now in our fifties, well into middle age and considering membership in the American Association for Retired Persons. We are economically well off, from what I could tell of those in attendance at the reunion. The reunion's activities were fully funded by the participants and other Chicanos—mostly from San Antonio—and one Anglo, George Korbel, who paid for the champagne. Our children are not well versed in Chicano politics; some don't even speak Spanish or like Tejano music. It seems then that we have lost another biological generation to the white world. Like dinosaurs, those of us who called ourselves Chicanos and led the fight for our self-determination are on the verge of extinction. Perhaps another reunion is needed. Not one of pure revelry to celebrate the fact that we are still alive and kicking but a reunion to pass the torch to another generation of activists. The issues and actors may change, but the fundamentals do not. These fundamentals are commitment to our cause: the right of our people to exist in dignity, safety, and well being; the right to our homeland; the right to have our culture; and the right to a future.

Appendix
Index

Appendix: FBI Documents

UNITED STATES DEPARTMENT OF JUSTICE

FEDERAL BUREAU OF INVESTIGATION

San Antonio, Texas

In Reply, Please Refer to
File No.

February 29, 1968

LA RAZA UNIDA

On February 22, 1968, ▓▓▓▓▓▓▓▓▓▓▓▓▓▓▓▓▓▓▓▓▓▓▓▓ advised that Governor John Connally would be in Laredo, Texas, for the annual Washington's Birthday Celebration. He was scheduled to arrive in Laredo, Texas, approximately 3:30 p.m., February 23, 1968.

▓▓▓▓▓▓▓ advised ▓▓▓▓▓▓▓▓▓▓▓▓▓▓ that members of La Raza Unida organization planned to hold a demonstration against Governor Connally in Laredo, Texas, at the International Bridge ceremony and during the parade, both to be held on February 24, 1968. The purpose of the demonstration was to protest the Governor's stand on the minimum wage in Texas. The demonstration was to be peaceful.

According to "The Alamo Messenger", dated January 12, 1968, a weekly Catholic newspaper published at San Antonio, Texas, La Raza Unida is an organization devoted to uniting Mexican-Americans so they can better achieve their legitimate political and economic goals. Further, the organization wants to "live the American dream" of possessing the same equal opportunities as the next man.

An article appeared in the February 21, 1968, issue of the "Laredo Times", a daily newspaper published at Laredo, Texas, to the effect that President Lyndon B. Johnson might be an unannounced Laredo visitor for the Washington's Birthday Celebration. The article went on to say that Edward Jamison, U. S. Consul General, Monterrey, Mexico, would be the President's personal representative during the weekend festivities at Laredo, Texas.

157- 8887-1

ENCLOSURE

307

LA RAZA UNIDA

                    ▓▓▓▓▓▓▓▓▓▓▓▓▓▓▓▓▓▓ advised that La Raza
Unida did not plan to demonstrate against Governor Connally
during the festivities in Laredo, Texas, the weekend of
February 23, 1968. He stated that the organization had
entered a vehicle in the parade to be held Saturday, February 24,
1968. The organization planned to use this vehicle to carry
signs and placards while in the parade procession. This
was to let the Governor know that the Raza Unida is still
around. He stated that since Governor Connally is on "his
way out" as Governor, La Raza Unida did not feel that a
demonstration against the Governor at this time would be
effective and, therefore, they will only use the vehicle for
the above purpose.

        The following persons were advised of the foregoing
information on February 22, 1968:

                ▓▓▓▓▓▓▓▓▓▓▓▓ Texas Department of Public Safety,
                ▓▓▓▓▓▓▓▓▓▓▓▓ advised at 2:30 p.m.

        Sheriff P. L. Flores, Laredo, Texas,
        advised at 2:32 p.m.

        Bill Weeks, Chief of Police, Laredo, Texas,
        advised at 2:34 p.m.

        ▓▓▓▓▓▓▓▓▓▓▓▓ Special Agent, Secret Service,
        San Antonio, advised at 4:12 p.m.

        ▓▓▓▓▓▓▓▓▓▓▓▓ Special Agent, Secret Service,
        Austin, Texas, advised at 4:25 p.m.

        ▓▓▓▓▓▓▓▓▓▓▓▓▓▓▓▓▓▓▓▓▓▓▓▓▓▓▓▓▓▓
        Secret Service, LBJ Ranch, advised at 3:11 p.m.

                ▓▓▓▓▓▓ advised that Secret Service had received no
indication that President Johnson would travel to Laredo on
either February 23 or 24, 1968.

                On February 25, 1968, ▓▓▓▓▓▓▓▓▓▓▓▓▓▓▓▓▓▓▓▓
▓▓▓▓▓▓▓▓▓▓▓▓ advised that there was no demonstration in

                                -2-

LA RAZA UNIDA

Laredo, Texas, during the weekend activities and President
Johnson did not attend. He stated that the only display
against Governor Connally was during the parade on February 24,
1968. A truck officially entered in the parade carried placards
reading "Down with Connally", "Rangers, Gestapo" (meaning the
Texas Rangers), "Minimum Wage", "Remember New Braunfels"
(referring to the confrontation Governor Connally had with
a group of marchers protesting the lack of a minimum wage).
He stated there were no incidents during the parade or the
entire festival.

       On February 25, 1968, ▨▨▨▨▨▨▨▨▨▨▨▨▨▨▨▨
▨▨▨▨▨▨▨▨▨▨▨▨▨▨▨▨▨▨▨▨▨▨▨▨▨▨▨▨▨▨▨
▨▨▨▨▨ advised that Governor Connally returned to Austin, Texas,
that date, leaving Laredo approximately 9:00 a.m.

UNITED STATES GOVERNMENT

Memorandum

DIRECTOR, FBI (157-8887)   DATE: 5/31/68

SAC, SAN ANTONIO (157-858) (C)

LA RAZA UNIDA
RM

OO: SAN ANTONIO

Re San Antonio airtel to the Bureau dated 2/29/68.

AT LAREDO, TEXAS

advise that the group of
individuals using captioned name have had no further meetings
in Laredo. It is not an organization in the sense that it
has a membership list, officers, and the like. Sources
advise there are no officers in Laredo and the only meeting
held was that reported in referenced airtel.

It is noted that the same individuals who
participated in referenced meeting are now using the caption
"Barrios Unidos" and the activities of this group have been
reported under San Antonio file 62-3418 and will continue to
be followed and reported.

In view of the above, this matter is being closed
and the Bureau will be kept advised of all activities on the
part of Barrios Unidos.

2-Bureau
1-San Antonio
LEA:sdh
(3)

REC- 41 157- 8887 - 4

15 JUN 3 1968

5 9 JUN 6 1968

UNITED STATES DEPARTMENT OF JUSTICE

FEDERAL BUREAU OF INVESTIGATION

San Antonio, Texas

August 29, 1970

             JOSE ANGEL GUTIERREZ,
             ARTURO GONZALEZ,
    TE∧   MIGUEL (MIKE) PEREZ,
             EDWARD TREVINO
             Members, Crystal City Independent
             School District,
             Crystal City, Texas;
    TT∧   JOHN BRIGGS - VICTIM
             CIVIL RIGHTS

      By letter dated August 26, 1970, United States Attorney Seagal V. Wheatley, Western District of Texas, San Antonio, Texas, made available to the office of the Federal Bureau of Investigation, San Antonio, a letter from John Briggs. Mr. Wheatley requested an investigation to determine if there is a civil rights violation under Title 18, Section 241, U. S. Code.

      The letter from Mr. Briggs is set forth below:

UNITED STATES DEPARTMENT OF JUSTICE

FEDERAL BUREAU OF INVESTIGATION

In Reply, Please Refer to
File No.   EP. 100-C602

202 U. S. Court House
El Paso, Texas   79901
September 14, 1972

LA RAZA UNIDA NATIONAL CONVENTION
EL PASO, TEXAS
SEPTEMBER 1 - 4, 1972
INTERNAL SECURITY - SPANISH AMERICAN

The June 21, 1972, edition of the "El Paso
Herald-Post", a daily newspaper published in El Paso,
Texas, contained an article stating that earlier that
date, Ramsey Muniz, Texas gubernatorial candidate for
the "La Raza Unida Party," described as being a "Chicano"
(Mexican American) dominated third party, had announced
the Raza Unida Party (RUP) would hold its first national
convention in El Paso on September 1 - 5, 1972.

On September 5, 1972,   El Paso,
furnished the following information:

The first National Convention of the La Raza Unida
Party was held in El Paso on September 1 - 4, 1972. He
stated the entire convention was peaceful and conducted
in an orderly manner. According to   the
convention followed the following agenda:

CONVENTION AGENDA:

September 1:   Registration of party delegates
                                           and attenders began at 9:30 a.m.
                                           at the Paso del Norte Hotel. In
                                           the afternoon, state caucuses
                                           held separate meetings at the
                                           various El Paso hotels.

This document contains neither recommendations nor
conclusions of the FBI. It is the property of the FBI and
is loaned to your agency; it and its contents are not to be
distributed outside your agency, nor duplicated within your
agency.

LA RAZA UNIDA NATIONAL CONVENTION

September 2:   "National Strategy" was discussed
                               by delegates at Liberty Hall at the
                               El Paso City-County Building.

September 3:   "Chicano Priorities" were
                               discussed at the El Paso County
                               Coliseum.

September 4:   Guest speakers and a meeting of
                               the "Congreso de Aztlan"
                               (comparable to the Democratic
                               Party Executive Committee) met
                               at the El Paso County Coliseum

        The following prominent Mexican American political
leaders and guests were reported by local press as having
been present at the convention:

        Jose Angel Gutierrez, RUP founder from Crystal City,
          Texas

        Ramsey Muniz, RUP candidate for Governor of Texas

        Rodolfo "Corky" Gonzalez, leader of the RUP
          Colorado delegation from Denver, Colorado

        Reies Lopez Tijerina, known Mexican American
          activist and member of the RUP New Mexico
          delegation

        Patricio Flores, Catholic Church Bishop from
          San Antonio, Texas, also reportedly attended
          the convention but did not speak before the
          convention

        Jack Odell of the Southern Christian Leadership
          Conference (SCLC) also reportedly attended
          the convention as an "observer" and refused to be
          interviewed by members of the press

2

████████████████████

LA RAZA UNIDA NATIONAL CONVENTION

████████████████████████ approximately 500
party delegates and 2,500 spectators attended the four-day
convention. An estimated 500 party delegates were present
representing 16 states, including Texas, Arizona,
Colorado, California, Illinois, Indiana, Michigan, Nebraska,
New Mexico, Wyoming, Utah, Oregon, and Washington, New York,
Rhode Island, and Washington, D. C. sent representatives but
no delegates. The Colorado delegation was the largest with
approximately 300 members led by Chicano militant Rodolfo
"Corky" Gonzalez. Texas and California had delegations of
approximately 100 each. ████████████████ advised the convention
officially ended at approximately 4:30 p.m. on September 4,
1972.

████████████████ dvised that two reported members
of the Colorado delegation were killed in incidents not
related to the actual convention. Richard Lee Falcon, age
27, from Boulder, Colorado, was shot to death at Oro Grande,
New Mexico, on August 30, 1972, while enroute to El Paso, by
a service station owner during a personal argument. The
service station ████████████████ on,
████████████████████████████
████████████████████████████
████████████████████████████
████████████████

On September 6, 1972 ████ a ████████████████
who has furnished reliable information in the past, furnished
the following information concerning captioned convention.

The convention of the La Raza Unida Party was held
in El Paso over the weekend of September 1 - 4, 1972.

Approximately 3,000 delegates were in attendance.
Among the delegates were the following known Communist
Party, United States of America (CPUSA) members:

The CPUSA has been designated pursuant to
Executive Order 10450.

████████████

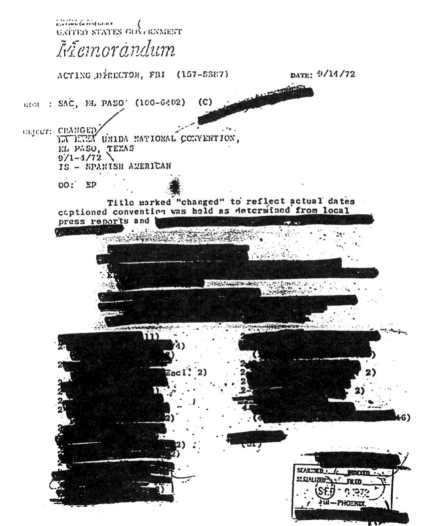

Index

Place names beginning with "El," "La," "Las," and "Los" can be found under those articles. Titles of books, newspapers, and organizations can be found under the first word *following* such articles.

Abernathy, Ralph, 224, 225
Acevedo, Juan, 70
Acosta, Oscar ("Zeta"), 8
Acuña, Rodolfo ("Rudy"), 16, 232, 233, 278, 287
Aeronaves de Mexico (airline), 102
African Americans, 9, 91, 113; autobiography among, 8, 10; and Chicanos, 93, 278, 280, 281; housing discrimination against, 91–92; lynching of, 17; as slaves in Texas, 15–16; stereotypes of, 90; in Texas schools, 123; voting power of, 219; and War on Poverty, 104, 112
agavachado, 22, 33, 47
Aguero, Bidal, 102
Aguilar, Fred, 217
AIM. *See* American Indian Movement
Alamo, 27, 49, 57–58, 124, 135
Alaniz, Johnny, 41, 69, 83, 155
Albuquerque (New Mexico), 103, 112, 217, 221, 223
Alejos, Candelario, 116
Aleman, Narciso, 159, 170, 178, 179
Alianza (Alliance of Free City States), 178, 217, 221, 227
Alice (Texas), 142
Alinsky, Saul, 93, 103
Allee, A. Y. (Texas Ranger), 42, 43–44, 51, 53–55, 57, 59, 185; son of, 168, 185–86
Allee, Tom (commissioner), 53–54
Allee, Tracy, 59
Allen, Susan, 192
Alliance of Free City States. *See* Alianza
Alonzo, Roberto, 289, 291, 292–93, 295
Alonzo, Sylvana, 289
Alpha Phi Omega fraternity, 81, 89, 94
"Alurista," 9
Alva, Hector, 51
Alvarado, Elvia, 10

Always Running: La Vida Loca (Rodriguez), 9
American Bandstand (TV show), 86
An American Dilemma (Myrdal), 113
American G.I. Forum, 28, 40, 70, 94, 99–100, 107–8, 114, 237
American Indian Movement (AIM), 225, 235
"americano," 22–23
American Party, 116
Americas Review (journal), 8
Among the Valiant (Morin), 103
Anaya, Rodolfo, 226
Andrade, Erasmo, 155, 205
Angiano, Lupe, 218, 228
Anglos: and Los Cinco Candidatos' victory, 65–66; as "discoverers" of Texas, 17–18; domination of Chicanos by, 23–24, 122–27; high school girls among, 46–47; privileges of, 33–35; settlement of, in Texas, 15–17; tactics used against Mexicans by, 13; teachers' strike among, 207; terms for, 22–23
Anglos and Mexicans in the Making of Texas, 1836–1986 (Montejano), 16
Anthony (Texas), 5
Apex Securities, 295
Appalachia, 112, 113
Arandas (Jalisco, Mexico), 230
Arizona, 217, 236–37
Arlington National Cemetery, 40
Asherton (Texas), 60, 61, 167, 187, 218
Atiyeh, Vic, 283
Atlanta (Georgia), 103
Austin (Texas), 103, 133–34. *See also* St. Edward's University; University of Texas (Austin)
Austin, Moses, 15
Austin, Stephen Fuller, 17

The Autobiography of a Brown Buffalo
(Acosta), 8
The Autobiography of Malcolm X, 10
Avalos, Diana, 153
Avena, Richard, 119, 170
Avila, Eddie, 51, 60, 61
Avila, Joaquin, 293
Avila, Pablo, 274
Avila, Richard, 162
Avila, Yolanda, 153
Aztlan (Chicano homeland concept), 11,
15–16, 110–11, 117, 223, 298; efforts to
build, 129, 141, 177–92, 215, 241; efforts
to reclaim Mexican lands associated
with, 217, 218, 221, 236–37, 253–54,
299; vs. New Mexico, 221

Baca, Herman, 217, 228
Balboa, Vasco Núñez de, 125
Baldenegro, Salomon, 217
Bancroft, Hubert Howard, 10
Baptists, 24
Barding, Ron G., 90, 94
Barker, Dale, 52
Barragan, Miguel, 112, 119
Barrera, Roy, 116
Barrera, Ruben, 170, 180
Barrio Betterment League, 116
Barrio Boy (Galarza), 8, 103
Barrio Club (Crystal City), 197, 199–200,
228, 240, 273–74
Bates College of Law (Houston Univer-
sity), 98, 123, 292, 295
Batesville (Texas), 76, 199, 248, 250, 252, 253
Bazan, Luz (Gutiérrez's first wife), 113,
114, 139, 169, 172, 247; as *Ciudadanos
Unidos* organizer, 193; courtship of, 79,
88, 98, 99; decision of, to leave Texas,
271–73; education of, 98, 99; employment of, 114, 131, 198, 258, 259, 271,
277, 282, 284, 287; in Europe, 263–64;
marriage and divorce of, 91, 105, 286–
87, 295; at MAYO national convention,
178; Oregon political activities of, 277,
280, 283; as poll watcher, 190, 191; and
school walkout organizing, 130–35,
137, 138, 141, 144, 146, 159, 162–66, 170,
171
Becerril de Brun, Maria de la Paz, 239
Bela, Rick, 267

Benavides, Irma, 149
Benjamin, Medea, 10
Bernal, Joe, 114, 155, 268
Bigger, Gary, 94
Bilbo, Theodore, 117
bilingual education, 33, 123, 124, 135,
205–7, 213
Billings, John, 143, 151–53, 174, 176, 203,
205
Bishop, Carrie Lee, 92
Bishop's Committee on the Spanish
Speaking, 99, 101, 103, 119
Bittinger, Stanley, 90, 94, 95
Black Berets, 217
Black Panther Party, 9
Black Power (Carmichael and Hamilton),
103
"blanco," 22
Bombace, Robert, 184–85
Bookout, Sylvia, 35
border patrol (U.S.), 23, 285, 286
Bowman Farms (Carrizo Springs), 71
Boy Scouts of America, 81
bracero program, 8, 17–22
Briggs, John, 205–7, 311
Briscoe, Dolph, 240, 254–57
Brown, Claude, 9
Brown, Elaine, 9
Brown Berets, 110, 217
Bullock, Bob, 219–21
Burgos-Debray, Elisabeth, 10
Burnet, Warren, 117, 267–68
Bustamante, Jorge, 110, 234
Bustamante, Juanita, 178
Byrd, Jim and Pat, 35

Cabello, Rufino, 188
Cabeza de Vaca, Alvar Núñez, 125
Cahill, Tom, 102
California: Mexicans in, 230; Raza Unida
Party in, 6, 7, 217; Viva Kennedy Clubs
in, 41. *See also* Mexican American Polit-
ical Association of California
California Packing Corporation, 20
Camarillo, Albert, 16
Campaign for Human Development, 256,
280–82
Camp Bullis (Texas), 115
Canales, Alma, 221, 250
Cantu, Amancio, 198, 200, 239, 271

CAP (Community Action Program) agencies, 104, 254
Cardenas, Antonio, 62, 63, 65
Carmichael, Stokely, 103
Carnegie Corporation, 211–13
Carr, Ronnie, 35, 273–75, 291
Carr, Vicki, 234
Carr Chemical Plant, 258–60
Carrizo Springs (Texas), 60, 167, 230, 259; Gutiérrez's work in, 71, 76; Raza Unida Party elections in, 187, 188; residents of, 35, 74, 99, 101, 131, 132
Carter, Jimmy, 254, 256–57, 285
CASAA (Citizens Association Serving All Americans), 139
Casa de las Americas, 239
Casado, Frank, 70
Casasola, Agustin V., 283–84
Casso, Henry, 112, 119, 155, 159
Castillo, Elva, 149
Castillo, Lionel, 293
Castro, Fidel, 239, 285, 286
Castro, Ramon, 239
Castro, Raul, 239
Castro, Sal, 119
Catholicism: among Anglos, 15, 24; among braceros, 21–22; and brown Madonna, 178; among Chicanos, 24, 112, 280–81; Gutiérrez's involvement with, 280–81; and Raza Unida party, 256. See also Bishop's Committee on the Spanish Speaking; Catholic Youth Organization; Colegio Cesar Chavez
Catholic Youth Organization (CYO), 100
Cavada, Abel, 271
CBS, 239
CDC (Community Development Corporation), 253–56
Center for the Study of Women (University of Oregon), 283
Central Intelligence Agency (CIA), 236, 270
Chacon, Ernesto, 217
The Changing Face of Texas (Sharp), 16
Chapa, Dario, 116
Chavez, Cesar, 234, 239; as Chicano labor leader, 103, 236, 290, 299; death of, 303; and Gutiérrez, 222, 224, 225, 235–36, 273
Chavez, Manuel, 116

Chicago (Illinois), 102, 103, 199, 217, 234; Gutiérrez's mother's employment in, 56, 69, 71, 74–76
Las Chicanas Del Movimiento, 295
Chicano (movie), 236
Chicano Del Año banquet, 195, 243
Chicano Narrative (Saldivar), 8
Chicano Press Association, 102
Chicano Revolt in a Texas Town (Shockley), 4
Chicanos: autobiography among, 8–11; domination of, by Anglos, 23–24, 122–27; governance by, 242–66; Hispanics contrasted with, 11–12, 28, 183, 298, 299; importance of women's organizing among, 5, 37, 38, 50, 63, 69, 81, 83, 144–46, 148, 297; importance of youth among, 7, 35–38, 50, 81, 82–83, 130; links of, with Mexico, 69–70, 110–11, 212, 224, 234–40, 251–52, 284; as majority in Texas school districts, 122–23, 125–26, 181; in Oregon, 278, 280; political motivations of, 11; "race" of, 30, 123, 301; reunion of activists among, 295–304; rivalries among, 66–67, 83–84, 178–80, 198–201, 221–36; scholarship on, 3–14; stereotypes of, 84–85, 90, 138; terms for, 22, 290; at Texas A & I, 79–96. See also Aztlan; specific organizations and leaders of
Chicanos in a Changing Society (Camarillo), 16
Chicano Studies programs, 109–10, 213, 301, 303
China, 240
Chiquita's Cocoon (Flores), 9
CIA, 236, 270
Los Cinco Candidatos, 4, 290; Anglo opposition to, 53–57, 244; campaign for, 36–45, 48–50, 57, 62–65, 132, 184, 230, 262; 1963 electoral victory of, 11, 62, 78, 82; press coverage of, 138; rivalry among, 66–67, 83–84; single term served by, 138–39
Cinco de Mayo celebrations, 42, 283–84
Cisneros, Henry, 117, 289–90
Citizens Association Serving All Americans (CASAA), 139
citizenship: of Chicanos, 130, 218–19; of Cubans, 285. See also illegal aliens; resident aliens; voting

City Public Service Board (San Antonio), 109

Ciudadanos Unidos (grassroots community organization), 187, 203, 212, 258, 259, 273; formation of, 11, 193–98; and school walkouts, 145, 158–60, 162, 166, 169; split in, 198–201

Ciudadanos Unidos II, 198, 200

civil rights movement, 93

class, 34–35, 80, 108, 135

Clayton, Lawrence, 192

Clinton, William Jefferson, 117

Coalson, George, 90

Colegio Cesar Chavez, 273, 274–75, 277

Colegio Jacino Treviño, 170, 178

Colombia, 240

Community Action Agencies. *See* CAP agencies

Community Development Block Grant (CDBG), 253

Community Development Corporation (CDC), 253–56

Community Services Administration, 254

Compean, Mario, 99–102, 106, 111, 115, 116–17, 170, 187; and MAYO national convention, 177–78; and Raza Unida Party, 219–21, 271; and school walkouts, 119, 159, 166

El Congreso de Aztlan, 223–24, 227, 228, 231, 232, 234, 313

Connally, John, 116, 255, 307–9

Conolly, Gilbert, 154

Contreras, Carmen, 34

Coors Company, 301

Cornejo, Juan, 116, 230; as Crystal City mayor, 66–67, 69, 290; mayoral campaign of, 64–65, 68; as one of Los Cinco Candidatos, 4, 54, 62, 140–41, 160; rivals of, 83–84

Corona, Bert, 9–10, 70, 217

Corpus Christi (Texas), 86, 218

Cortez, Hernan, 84–85

Cortina, Rodolfo, 123

Cortinas, Guadalupe ("Lupe"), 199–200, 263, 272

Cotrell, Charlie, 89–91, 95, 96, 103, 104

Cotrell, Glenda, 91

Cotulla (Texas), 5, 91, 144, 167, 187, 188, 218, 259

Council of Governments, 254

Cowart, Billy, 282

CPSB (San Antonio), 109

Crane, Bill, 90

Crawford, Gladys, 35

Cristal (Texas). *See* Crystal City (Texas)

The Cristal Experiment (Navarro), 4

Crockett, Davy, 27

Crusade for Justice, 180, 217, 224, 225, 227, 228, 230

Crystal City ("Cristal") (Texas): ammonia explosion in, 258–60; barrios in, 42, 48, 64, 67, 139, 252, 259, 260; charter of, 65–66; city hall in, 67–68; dual utility books in, 67–68; Japanese American internment camp in, 48, 209, 257; natural gas cutoff in, 250–52, 255, 260; PASO in, 41–42, 100; poll taxes in, 36–39, 49, 62, 76; Popeye statue in, 290–91; and Raza Unida Party, 91, 187, 188–89, 203, 218, 222; research on, 3–5, 7; school walkouts in, 129–39, 142–76, 178, 183, 203, 208, 274; segregation in, 24–25, 33–34, 42. *See also* Cinco Candidatos; Zavala County

Crystal City Chamber of Commerce, 38

Crystal City School District, 11

CU. *See* Ciudadanos Unidos

Cuba, 239–40, 256; exiles from, 284, 285

Cuevas, Betty, 217

Cumpian, Sra., 37

CYO (Catholic Youth Organization), 100

D'Aiello, Charon, 218

Dallas (Texas), 122, 231, 287, 291, 293, 295; Cockrell Hill section of, 288–90, 293

Davis, Stormy, 42, 53, 55

Days of Obligation (Rodriguez), 8

DEA. *See* Drug Enforcement Agency

DeBray, Regis, 103

The Decline of the Californios (Pitt), 16, 103

El Deguello (MAYO newspaper), 102, 107

de la Fuente, Elvirita, 83, 303

de la Fuente, Ramon, Jr., 170

de la Garza, Eulogio ("Kika"), 113

de la Garza, Rudolfo, 4

Delano: The Story of the California Grape Strike (Dunne), 103

de Leon, Arnoldo, 16

de Leon, Luis Diaz, 177

de Leon, Lupe, 217

Delgado, Gregoria, 184, 242
Delgado, Mike, 51
Del Monte Corporation, 20, 34, 54, 62, 184, 214, 254
Del Rio (Texas), 60, 142, 166, 218
Demarest, Sylvia, 212
Democratic Party: and Chicano issues, 113, 116, 138, 187, 255, 263, 277; Chicano supporters of, 198, 217, 232, 268–69, 274, 290, 293, 300; Gutiérrez as member of, 277–78; and investigation of Gutiérrez, 267–68; national and local versions of, 222; national conventions of, 229; and Raza Unida Party, 267–71; in Texas, 36, 80, 87, 100. See also Mexican American Democrats (MAD); PASO; Young Democrats
Denver (Colorado), 103, 129, 142, 167, 180, 217, 221, 223, 232
Detroit (Michigan), 74
Devine (Texas), 60, 76
D'Hanis (Texas), 76
Diaz, Elena, 184, 242, 248, 249, 253, 261, 264
Diaz, Richard, 190, 191
Diaz Ordaz, Gustavo, 70, 224, 236
Diez y Seis de Septiembre celebrations, 42
Dilley (Texas), 259
Dimmit County (Texas), 5, 131, 208
Divine, Robert, 278
Dole Company, 275
Domingo Peña Show (TV show), 86
Donecker, Frances, 16
Donna (Texas), 230
Don't Be Afraid, Gringo (Alvarado), 10
Dougherty, Ann, 71
Down These Mean Streets (Thomas), 9
Drug Enforcement Agency (DEA), 269, 271
Dunne, John Gregory, 103

Eagle gas station (Crystal City), 71
Eagle Pass (Texas), 13, 60, 70, 167, 187, 230, 259, 291
East Lansing (Michigan), 142, 154, 178, 230
East Los Angeles (California), 218
Echeverria Alvarez, Luis, 110, 224, 234–38
Economy Furniture, 133–34
Edcouch-Elsa (Texas), 142
Edgewood Technical High School (San Antonio), 119

El Editor (newspaper), 102
Edwards, Heather, 104
Edwards, Paul, 104
El Avispero en el Campo (Crystal City barrio), 48
El Campo Santo (Crystal City barrio), 67
El Congreso de Aztlan. See Congreso de Aztlan
Ellis, Rodney, 295
El Paso (Texas), 103, 117, 119, 218; hearings on Mexican American affairs in, 111–13; Raza Unida Party convention in, 7, 221–33, 235–36, 312–15; school walkouts in, 142
El Salvador, 231
"El Swiche" (Texas community), 74
English, J. P., 42, 66
English language: Chicano newsletter in, 51–52; newspapers in, 52; in schools, 33, 127, 135. See also bilingual education
Episcopalians, 256
Equal Employment Opportunity Commission, 111
Escalante, Jaime, 9
Escalante: The Best Teacher in America (Mathews), 9
Escobar, Eluterio, 128
Espinoza, Manuel, Jr., 243
Espinoza, Richard, 149, 162
Esquivel, Urbano, 147, 168, 169, 176
Estero Lake (Texas), 257
Estrada, Agustin, 114
Estrada's grocery store, 38
Exxon Corporation. See Humble Oil Company

Falcon, Ricardo, 225–26, 314
Falfurrias (Texas), 105, 135
family networks, 188–90, 197
Fanon, Franz, 103
Fargo (North Dakota), 230
farmworkers, 105, 116, 214, 222, 236. See also Chavez, Cesar
Faz, Andy, 153
FBI (Federal Bureau of Investigation), 171, 270; documents of, 268, 307–15
Ferguson, Hollis and Elaine, 277
Fernandez, Efrain, 101
Fierro, Manuel, 218, 228
Finch, Robert, 162

Findlay (Ohio), 230
Fisher, O. C., 121, 255
Fleming Corporation, 170
Flint (Michigan), 142
Flores, Bettina (Elizabeth) R., 8–9
Flores, Carmen, 246, 264
Flores, Patricio, 224, 313
Flores, Raul, 200
Florida, 125, 284
Fly, Sterling, 74
Foley, Douglas, 5–6
Ford Foundation, 113, 115, 117
Ford Motor Company, 73, 74
Forgotten People (Sanchez), 103
Fort Leonard Wood (Missouri), 115
Foundation of Solidarity between Mexicans and Americans, 239
Fox Technical High School (San Antonio), 111, 119
Fred Meyer Charitable Trust, 282
Freedom of Information Act (FOIA), 270, 271
Frio County (Texas), 5–6, 208, 268
From Peones to Politicos (Foley et al.), 5–6
Fuentes, Albert, 41, 69, 83
Fuentes, Carlo, 75
Fuentes, Carolina, 75
Fuentes, Ignacio (Gutiérrez's grandfather), 74
Fuentes, Ignacio (Gutiérrez's cousin), 75
Fuentes, Ignacio (Gutiérrez's uncle), 75
Fuentes, Jesus, 74, 75
Fuentes, Jesus, Jr., 75
Fuentes, Laura, 75
Fuentes, Lucia, 25
Fuentes, Refugio Casas, 25, 74, 75
Fuentes, Salvador, 74–75
Fuentes, Ulysis, 75
Fulbright and Jaworski law firm, 184

Galarza, Ernesto, 8, 13, 17, 103, 112, 303
Gallegos, Richard, 45
Galvan, Armandina, 20, 21, 48
Galvan, Pedro, 20, 48
Galvan, Pete, Jr., 34
Galvan, Roberto, 58, 123
Galvan Ballroom (Corpus Christi), 86
Gamez, Blanquita, 38
Gamez, Jesse, 90, 170, 183, 263, 272
Gamio, Manuel, 9

Gannett Foundation, 283, 284
Garcia, Alberto, 292, 295
Garcia, Diana Palacios, 264, 268
Garcia, Domingo, 287, 288–89, 291, 292–93, 295
Garcia, Elba, 292
Garcia, F. Chris, 4
Garcia, Ignacio, 4, 6–7, 231
Garcia, Mario T., 9–10
Garcia, Martin, 41, 83
Garfield High School (Los Angeles), 119
Garner, John Nance, 245
Garner State Park (Texas), 60
Garrett, Bill, 293
Gary (Indiana), 217
Garza, Eliseo, 115
Garza, Gloria (Gutiérrez's second wife), 95, 232–33, 295
Garza, Josue, 122
Garza, Ramon, 200
"gavacho," 22, 23
gays and lesbians, 301, 303
German, Light, 90
German language, 33
Germany, 264
GGL (Good Government League), 116–17
G.I. Forum. *See* American G.I. Forum
Gilroy (California), 230
Glendale (Arizona), 142
Goliad (Texas), 16, 237
Gomez Quiñones, Juan, 4
Gomez's grocery store, 38
Gonzales, Irma Flores, 274, 275
Gonzales, Margarita, 264
Gonzales, Mike, 117
Gonzales, Raul, 36
Gonzales, Rodolfo ("Corky"), 9, 112, 217, 221–35, 239, 290, 299, 313, 314
Gonzalez, Angel Noe, 195, 205, 206, 209–11, 271
Gonzalez, Arturo, 188, 199, 200, 203, 213, 311
Gonzalez, Diola, 206
Gonzalez, Henry B., 37, 83–84, 112–13, 116–18, 121
Gonzalez, Josue, 164, 165
Gonzalez, Ventura, 203
Good Government League (GGL), 116–17
Graduate Record Examination. *See* GRE

Gramsci, Antonio, 103
GRE (Graduate Record Examination), 93, 98
Greenwald, Robert, 171–73
"gringo," 22
Gringo Justice (Mirande), 23
A Gringo Manual on How to Handle Mexicans (Gutiérrez), 7, 13–14, 138
Guanajuato (Mexico), 231
Guerra, Carlos, 89, 101, 240
Guerrero, Cecilia, 153
Guerrero, Frank, 248, 249, 257–59, 261, 262
Guevara, Che, 103
Gutiérrez, Adrian, 114, 131–33, 137, 139, 258, 263, 275
Gutiérrez, Andrea Lucia, 295
Gutiérrez, Armando, 4, 271
Gutiérrez, Avina Cristal, 275
Gutiérrez, Clavel Amariz, 295
Gutiérrez, Concepcion (author's mother): Chicago employment of, 56, 69, 71, 74–76; childrearing by, 16, 44, 51, 127; death of, 13, 292; education of, 95; house of, 139, 258; in Oregon, 273; relatives of, 75; and voting, 36; as widow, 30–31, 33
Gutiérrez, Greg, 78
Gutiérrez, Horacio, 30
Gutierrez, John ("Top"), 115
Gutiérrez, José Angel: papers of, 7–8, 12–13, 270.
Gutiérrez, Luz Bazan. *See* Bazan, Luz
Gutiérrez, Olin, 258, 273, 275
Gutiérrez, Tozi Aide, 258, 263, 275, 277
Gutiérrez Crespo, Angel (author's father), 35, 48, 139; childrearing by, 16, 127; death of, 30–31, 33, 95; and Mexico, 75; as physician, 22, 27

Haley, Alex, 10
Hall, David, 287, 291
Hamilton, Charles, 103
Hamilton, Wayne, 203, 204
Hammerback, John, 14
Harbin (school principal), 175
Harper (teacher), 175
Harrison, Linda, 131–32, 144, 162, 166, 169, 170, 178
Head Start program, 177
Heldenfelds, Hugo, 115

"Hen House" (at Texas A & I), 87–89, 94
Hernandez, Maria, 128, 299, 303
Hernandez, Mario, 62, 63, 65, 69
Herrera, José, 200
Herrera, Saul, 200
HEW. *See* U.S. Health, Education, and Welfare Department
Hidalgo County (Texas), 187
Hill, Fred, 217
Hirsch, Herb, 4
Hispanic Chamber of Commerce (Dallas), 290
The Hispanic Condition (Stavans), 27
Hispanic Congressional Caucus, 113
Hispanic Issues Conference, 282
The Hispanic Presence in Oregon (slide show), 283
Hispanics: contrasted with Chicanos, 11–12, 28, 183, 298, 299; label of, 28, 30, 290
Hobbs, William, 86
Hogg Foundation, 256
Hondo (Texas), 60, 76, 142, 270
Hooks, Jackie, 246
Hoover, J. Edgar, 17
Houston (Texas), 103, 231, 293; schools in, 98, 122, 142, 293
Houston Post, 169
Houston University, 98
Howard, Dave, 31
Huelga (Nelson), 103
"huero," 22, 23
Huerta, Dolores, 299
Huitzilopotchtli (Aztec war god), 102
Humble Oil Company, 108–9
Hunger of Memory (Rodriguez), 8
Hunter, David, 272
Hutchison, Kay Bailey, 36

I, Rigoberta Menchu (Menchu), 10
IAF (Industrial Areas Foundation), 281
Ibarra, Juan, 154, 168
illegal aliens: Anglos as, in Texas, 15–17, 27; Chicanos portrayed as, 111, 131; U.S.'s encouragement of, 19; U.S.'s use of, 23–24
IMAGE (Involved Mexican American Government Employees), 101, 237
Independence (Oregon), 277, 280, 282
Indiana, 217–18

indio. See Native Americans
Industrial Areas Foundation (IAF), 281
Industrias Mexicanas, 170, 172
In Fact or Fiction (newsletter), 51–52, 102
Inferno (newspaper), 102
INS. *See* U.S. Immigration and Naturalization Services
Interagency Committee on Mexican American Affairs, 111–12
Internal Revenue Service (IRS), 269, 270
Involved Mexican American Government Employees. *See* IMAGE

Jackson, Jesse, 277
Jackson, Joaquin, 190–92, 270
"Jalisco" (tune), 207
Jalisco (Mexico), 230
Jamestown Colony, 125
Jamison, Edward, 307
Japanese Americans, 48, 209, 257
Jasso, Juan, 292, 295
The Javelin (school newspaper), 175
J.C. Penny store (Crystal City), 71
Jehovah's Witnesses, 24
Jensen, Ken, 277
Jensen, Richard, 14
Jernigan, James C., 94
Jews, 17
John F. Kennedy High School (San Antonio), 109, 110
Johnson, Lyndon Baines, 40, 103–4, 112, 307–9
Johnson, Wayne, 90
Joint Support Foundation, 273
Jordan, Barbara, 121
Jordan, Vernon, 167
Juan Garcia Park (Crystal City), 291
Juarez, Issac, 199
Juarez (Mexico), 224, 226

Kalamazoo (Michigan), 142, 178
Kansas, 217, 218
Kazen, Abraham, 255
Keller family, 65
Kelly Air Force Base (Texas), 109
Kennard, Joe, 37
Kennedy, David, 269
Kennedy, Edward M., 115, 155–56, 159
Kennedy, John F., 40, 50, 71–72
Kennedy, Robert F., 222

King, Martin Luther, Jr., 221
"King Antonio," 80
"King Citrus," 80
King Ranch, 108
Kingsville (Texas), 83, 92; Raza Unida Issues Conference at, 108–9; school walkouts in, 142, 164. *See also* Texas A & I
Kingsville Chamber of Commerce, 92
Korbel, George, 293, 303
Krueger, Robert, 121
KTSA radio, 105

labor union movement: at Del Monte plant, 184, 214; in early twentieth century, 17; for farmworkers, 214, 222, 236; and support for Chicanos, 41, 133; women in, 298–99
La Casita Farms (Rio Grande Valley), 105
Lair, John B., 143, 149, 151–53
La Lomita (Texas), 159, 161, 166, 169–70, 177–80, 187, 211
Lanier Technical High School (San Antonio), 111
Lantana Court, 89, 95
La Placita Park (Crystal City), 42, 43, 48, 49, 160
La Pryor (Texas), 60, 76, 185, 250, 252, 253, 259–62
La Pryor State Bank, 245
Lara, Linda, 162, 168, 186
Lara, Severita, 143, 147–49, 151–58, 160–65, 171; electoral campaign of, 274, 287, 290–91
La Raza Unida Party. *See* Raza Unida Party
Laredo (Texas), 79, 110, 307–10
Laredo Club (Texas A & I), 79–80
La Salle County (Texas), 5, 208, 268
Las Vegas (New Mexico), 217, 232, 270
"Latinos," 12, 27–28, 275, 281, 282, 290; interethnic conflicts among, 284–86
Lawrence, Pat, 89, 94
Law School Admissions Test. *See* LSAT
League of United Latin American Citizens. *See* LULAC
League of Women Voters, 167
Leakey (Texas), 60
Lebanon, 240
Legal Aid. *See* Legal Services Corporation;

Oficina de la Gente; Texas Rural Legal
  Aid Foundation
Legal Services Corporation, 104
Levi Strauss and Company, 301
Life magazine, 93
Lincoln, Abraham, 46
Lincoln High School (Los Angeles), 119
Lizcano, Elpidio, 207–8
Lizcano, Janette, 207
Llamas, Nestor, 284
Lone Star beer, 159
Long, James and Jane, 16
Longoria, Felix, 40
Look magazine, 93
Lopez (teacher), 175
Lopez, Cleto, 37
Lopez, Gerald ("Jerry"), 143
Lopez, Trini, 234
Los Angeles (California), 103; Gutiérrez
  in, 69–74, 78, 142; school walkouts in,
  119–20, 142. *See also* East Los Angeles;
  UCLA
Los Angeles City College, 73
Los Angeles County (California), 117–18
Los Angeles Times, 70
Los Cinco Candidatos. *See* Cinco Can-
  didatos
Louisiana Purchase, 125
Lo-Vaca Gas Gathering Company, 250–52
Lozano, Edgar, 240
LSAT (Law School Admissions Test), 93,
  98
Lubbock (Texas), 102, 142
Luera, Alberto ("Beto"), 170, 178, 180
Lujan, Manuel, 113
LULAC (League of United Latin Ameri-
  can Citizens), 30, 40, 70, 94, 99–100,
  107–8, 237
Luna, Ignacio ("Nacho"), 259
Luna Theater (Crystal City), 42, 194, 259
Lutherans, 33

McAllister, Walter, 116
McGovern, George, 159, 224–27
McHazlett, Matthew, 264
McWilliams, Carey, 16
MAD (Mexican American Democrats),
  268–69, 273
Madieros, Bishop, 178
Maedgen, "Buddy," 204

Magellan, Ferdinand, 125
Magon, Ricardo Flores, 103
Malcolm X, 10, 299
MALDEF (Mexican American Legal De-
  fense and Educational Fund), 84, 100,
  237, 293; and Crystal City school walk-
  out, 143, 168, 183; Gutiérrez's employ-
  ment by, 114–15, 117; and MAYO,
  117–19, 140, 141
Maldonado, Juan, 268
Maldonado, Manuel, 62–63, 65
Maldonado, Reynaldo, 150
La Malinche myth, 84–85
Manchild in the Promised Land (Brown), 9
MAPA. *See* Mexican American Political
  Association of California
Marielitos, 285
Marin, Maria Viramontes de, 277
Marin, Reymundo, 274, 277
Marinez family, 154
Martinez, David, 119
Martinez, Gilberto, 283–84
Maryland, 218
Mata, José O., 212, 246, 258, 259, 291
Mata, Paulino, 143, 149, 151, 152
Mathews, Jay, 9
Mathis (Texas), 5, 100, 116
Matta, Tom, 171–73
Maverick County (Texas), 208, 209
Mayer, Ed, 144, 147, 176, 204
MAYO (Mexican American Youth Orga-
  nization): demise of, 196; Gutiérrez's
  involvement with, 11, 99–121, 127–41,
  218; meetings of, with foreign officials,
  240–41; name of, 101–2; national confer-
  ence of, 159, 161, 166, 169–70, 177–
  80, 187, 211; opposition to, 84; research on,
  4, 5, 7; and school walkouts, 122,
  127–39, 203, 209. *See also* Raza Unida
  Party
Mayorga, Alicia ("Licha"), 106
MAYO Times (newsletter), 102
Medina County (Texas), 5, 76
Medrano, Pancho, 292
Melendez, Ambrosio, 90
Memories of Chicano History (Garcia), 9–10
men: and community organizing, 144–48;
  and electoral politics, 37, 50; employment of, 73; role of, in community organizing, 4–5.

Menchu, Rigoberta, 10
Mendoza, David, 259
Mendoza, Pura, 63, 149
Mendoza, Reynaldo, 62, 63, 65
Merchants of Labor (Galarza), 17
Methodists, 24, 256
Mexican American Democrats (MAD), 268–69, 273. *See also* PASO
Mexican American Legal Defense and Educational Fund. *See* MALDEF
The Mexican American People (UCLA study), 113
Mexican American Political Association of California (MAPA), 41, 70, 73, 78, 217
Mexican Americans. *See* Chicanos; Hispanics; "Latinos"
Mexican American Unity Council, 117, 155
Mexican American Youth Organization. *See* MAYO
Mexican American Youth Organization (Navarro), 7
The Mexican Immigrant (Gamio), 9
Mexicano Resistance in the Southwest (Rosenbaum), 16
Mexicanos Unidos, 268
Mexican Revolution of 1910, 75, 76, 218, 283
Mexicans: murder of, by Anglos, 17, 55; terms for, 22
Mexican Trade Fair, 234
Mexico: and *bracero* program, 17–19; burial of Mexican Americans in, 30, 75; Chicano links with, 69–70, 110–11, 212, 224, 234–40, 251–52, 284; invasion of, by Napoleon III, 22; migration from, 230–31; natural gas in, 251–52; 1910 revolution in, 75, 76, 218, 283; Texas's origins in, 15. *See also* Mexicans
Mexico Chico (Crystal City barrio), 42, 64, 139, 252, 259, 260
Mexico City (Mexico), 224
Michigan, 217
Middle Rio Grande Development Council, 254
Migrant Head Start Program, 177
Miller, Hubert, 166, 168
Milwaukee (Wisconsin), 102, 178, 188, 217, 230
Minor, Elena, 218
Mirande, Alfredo, 23

Mireles, Irma, 104–5
Mission (Texas), 80, 177. *See also* La Lomita
Mitchell, John, 162
Molina, Gloria, 118
Montejano, David, 4, 16
Montes, Celedonio ("Sonny"), 273
Montoya, Joseph, 113
Moore, Carlos, 41
Moore, Mr. (Crystal City school counselor), 152
Morales, Dan, 36, 166
Morales, Victor, 8
Moreno, Angel, 217, 234
Morin, Raul, 103
Mormons, 24
Moses Lake (Washington), 230
Mt. Angel College (Oregon), 273
Mujeres de Oregon, 277, 283
Muñiz, Ramsey: as gubernatorial candidate, 221, 225, 234, 242, 269, 312, 313; legal problems of, 13, 269–71, 289, 299–300
Muñoz, Carlos, 4
Muzquiz, Virginia, 63, 243, 246, 248, 299; and investigation into Gutiérrez as judge, 267; and PASO, 83; state legislative campaign of, 76–78, 230
My History, Not Yours (Padilla), 8
Myrdal, Gunnar, 113

Nacogdoches (Texas), 16
Najera, Esteban, 246, 248, 249, 253, 258–62, 264
NALEO (National Association of Latino Elected and Appointed Officials), 100
Napoleon III, 22
National Association of Chicano Studies, 301, 303
National Association of Latino Elected and Appointed Officials, 100
National Association of Latino Gay Academics (NALGA), 303
National Council of La Raza (NCLR), 118, 119, 237, 239, 274–75
National Labor Relations Board, 184
National Youth Liberation Conferences, 129, 180
Native Americans, 8, 15, 84–85, 301
Navarro, Armando, 4, 5, 7, 217, 228
NCLR. *See* National Council of La Raza

Nebraska, 217
Neighborhood Youth Corps (NYC), 104
Nelson, Eugene, 103
New Braunfels (Texas), 121
New Mexico, 217, 218, 221. *See also* People's Constitutional Party of New Mexico
New York City, 102, 103, 230
New York Commission on Hispanic Affairs, 284
New York Times, 165
Nicaragua, 240
Nixon, Richard, 209, 224–27, 253–55, 270
Noll, Jerry, 226–27
"norte americano," 22, 23
North from Mexico (McWilliams), 16
Northwest Communities Project, 273
Northwest Voter Registration and Education Project, 283
NYC. *See* Neighborhood Youth Corps

Obledo, Mario, 115
Obreros Unidos Independientes, 184, 214
OCHA. *See* Oregon Council for Hispanic Advancement
Ochoa, Abel, 117
Odell, Jack, 313
Odessa (Texas), 117
La Oficina de la Gente, 184, 212, 213
Ojeda, Irene, 246
Olguin, Ernesto, 212
Olivarez, Graciela, 254
Olympic Games, 224
Oregon, 11, 217, 267–87
Oregon Commission on Hispanic Affairs, 275, 277, 284, 287
Oregon Council on Hispanic Advancement (OCHA), 274, 282–84, 287
Oro Grande (New Mexico), 225–26, 314
Oswald, Lee Harvey, 72
Ozuna, George, 60, 66–67, 69, 83–84, 257, 290

Pacoima (California), 230
Padilla, Genaro M., 8
Palacios, Enriqueta, 63, 83
Palestine Liberation Organization (PLO), 240
Palmer, A. Mitchell, 17
Palmer, Dewey, 90

Palmer, Paul, 90
Palmer Raids, 17
Palomo, Rudy, 51, 60, 74, 200, 274
"pan blanco," 22–23
Papago Indians, 217
El Partido de La Raza Unida (Santillan), 6–7. *See also* Raza Unida Party
PASO (Political Association of Spanish Speaking Organizations), 37, 62, 70, 94, 99, 132, 138; and Cornejo, 64, 140–41; demise of, 69, 100; Gutiérrez's involvement with, 35–36, 38, 42–45, 49–51, 54–57, 78; opposition to, 84; press coverage of, 57, 100; rise of, 7, 40–42; student chapter of, 81–83, 89, 93, 101
Patlan, Elena, 106, 131, 132
Patlan, Juan, 51, 74, 99–101, 106, 111, 155–56, 187; and Mexican American Unity Council, 119; and school walkouts, 129, 131–34, 137, 159
Patlan family, 74
Peace Corps, 104
Pearsall (Texas), 5–6, 218, 268
Pegues, Aston, 46
Pegues, Bonita, 35
Pegues, Johnny, 35
Pegues, Lynn, 35
Peña, Albert, Jr., 222; and MAD, 268; and PASO, 41, 69, 81, 83; and school walkouts, 155, 156, 159, 160, 173–74
Peña, Amado, 94
Peña, Juan José, 217, 240
Peña, Roberto, 112, 119, 178
Peña's grocery store, 38
Pentecostals, 24
People's Constitutional Party of New Mexico, 218, 223, 227
Perales, Sra., 37
Perez, Alejandro, 264
Perez, Antonio, 260
Perez, Ben, 149
Perez, Ignacio ("Nacho"), 99–102, 106, 116, 187
Perez, Miguel ("Mike"), 188, 203–4, 213, 311
Perez, Orcilia, 106
Perez, Rebecca, 190
Perez, Rey, 190, 200, 246, 290, 291
Perez, "Tiger," 178, 303
Pharr (Texas), 240

Phoenix (Arizona), 103, 119
Piedras Negras (Mexico), 13, 30, 70
Pitt, Leonard, 16, 103
Plainview (Texas), 142
PLO (Palestine Liberation Organization), 240
Pochos, 22
Political Association of Spanish Speaking Organizations. *See* PASO
El Politico: The Mexican American Elected Official (Gutiérrez), 7
Polk, James K., 236
Polk County (Oregon), 277–78
poll taxes, 36–39, 49, 62, 76, 77, 100, 116
Pompa, Gilbert, 164
Poor People's Campaign, 221
Popeye statue (Crystal City), 290–91
Presbyterians, 256
Prestage, Joe, 31
Project SER, 101, 237
Puente, Pablo, 203
Puerto Rico, 9, 240, 286

Quebec (Canada), 240
Quevado, Eduardo, 70
Quijano, Rosa, 246

Rabel, Ed, 239
race, 30, 34–35, 80
RAG (underground newspaper at Texas A & I), 93, 94, 102
Rainbow Coalition, 277
Ramirez, Chaca, 303
Ramirez, Jesus ("Chuy"), 240, 255, 268
Ramirez, Juan, 250
Ramirez, Luis, 254
Ramirez, Richard, 295
Ramirez, Salvador ("El Huevo"), 273, 274
El Rancho (Texas A & I yearbook), 89, 95
Randall's grocery store chain, 231
Rather, Dan, 256
Rawlins, Braden, 89
Ray, Darrel, 205
La Raza Libre, 198
"La Raza Unida" (as possible name for MAYO), 101–2
La Raza Unida Issues Conferences, 107–10
La Raza Unida Party: convention of, 7, 221–33, 235–36, 312–15; demise of, 7, 232, 268–71, 277; electoral politics of,

203–44; expansion of, 7, 215–41; factions of, 198–99; federal surveillance of, 270–71; leaders of, 104; research on, 3–4, 6–7; and Richey, 91; rise of, 11, 187–90. *See also* Ciudadanos Unidos; MAYO
Reagan, Ronald, 278
Red Berets, 217
Renfro, Billie (Mrs. William E.), 90
Renfro, William E. ("Bill"), 90, 95
"rent-a-slave" operations, 17–19
Republican Party, 209, 233, 255, 269, 278, 293
resident aliens, 218
The Revolt of the Cockroach People (Acosta), 8
Reyes, Ben, 293
Reyes, Carlos, 284
Reyes, Lonnie, 119
Rich, Paul, 184, 212
Richards, Ann, 36
Richey, Linda. *See* Harrison, Linda
Richey, William Leon ("Bill"), 131–32, 167, 267; as Crystal City manager, 212; and Crystal City school walkouts, 144, 146–48, 155, 156, 162, 163, 166, 169, 170, 172; and farm cooperative, 253; at MAYO national convention, 178; as student, 90, 91, 94, 131
Rio Arriba courthouse raid, 221
Rio Grande City (Texas), 101, 270
Rio Grande Valley, 79–81, 99, 103, 124, 255; farmworkers' strike in, 105, 116
Rios, Rolando, 293
Rivera, Juan, 123
River Spur (Texas), 252
Robstown (Texas), 5
Rocha, Juan, 94
Rodriguez, Diamantina, 123
Rodriguez, Ernestina, 60
Rodriguez, Francisco, 51, 212
Rodriguez, Jesse, Jr., 34
Rodriguez, Jesus, 37, 38, 53, 55
Rodriguez, José, 190
Rodriguez, Luis J., 9
Rodriguez, Richard, 8
Rogers, Carole, 90
Rogers, Robert ("Bob"), 90, 96
Roggerson, Chris, 164, 167
Romero, Esequiel, 51, 60
Romero, José, 273

Roosevelt, Franklin Delano, 222
Rosenbaum, Robert J., 16
Roybal, Edward, 113
Ruby, Jack, 72
Ruiz, "Cha Chi," 200
Ruiz, Eugenio ("Gene"), 200
Ruiz, Mona, 9
Ruiz, Poncho, 178
Ruiz, Raul, 218, 229, 232, 233, 240
Ruiz's grocery store, 38
Rutledge (teacher), 175

Sabinal (Texas), 60, 76, 191
St. Augustine (Florida), 125
St. Edward's University (Austin), 101
St. Mary's University (San Antonio), 90,
    166, 199; Gutiérrez at, 11, 99–100, 102–4,
    113, 115, 123, 131
Salas, Jesus, 253–54
Salas, Julian, 145–46
Salazar, Suse, 46
Saldivar, Ramon, 8
Salem (Oregon), 282–84
Salon Compestre (Crystal City), 153, 168,
    172, 194
Salon Miguel Hidalgo (Crystal City), 193,
    194
Salud de la Family (Woodburn, Oregon),
    282, 287
San Angelo (Texas), 121
San Antonio (Texas), 60, 259; Chicano
    electoral campaigns in, 115–16, 218;
    City Public Service Board in, 251; Edge-
    wood area of, 5, 208; festivities in, 80,
    234; Gutiérrez's work in, 104–5; as
    MAYO headquarters, 133, 159, 162; and
    PASO, 35–36, 41, 49, 51, 54, 81–83; Raza
    Unida Issues Conference in, 109; school
    walkouts in, 111, 119–20, 128, 142. See
    also St. Mary's University; University of
    Texas (San Antonio)
San Antonio Neighborhood Youth Orga-
    nization (SANYO), 104
San Antonio River Authority, 104–5
San Benito (Texas), 230
San Bernardino (California), 217
Sanchez, Alfonso, 221
Sanchez, George I., 103
Sanchez, Rosaura, 10
San Diego (California), 217

Sandoval, Julian A., 290
Sandoval, Ruben, 295, 303
San Jose (California), 142, 218, 224–25
San Juan (Texas), 5, 230, 255
San Marcos (Texas), 142
San Miguel de Guadalupe, 125
Santa Ana, Antonio Lopez de, 27, 57–58,
    237
Santa Fe (New Mexico), 125
Santiago, Viviana, 170, 180, 211, 212, 253,
    271
Santillan, Richard, 4, 6
Santos, Juanita, 149
SANYO. See San Antonio Neighborhood
    Youth Organization
Schaefer, Ray, 41, 54
Schaief, Charles, 34
schools: certification of superintendents
    of, 209–13; Chicanos' problems with,
    104, 105, 122–27, 241; differences in
    Anglo and Chicano, 48–49; English
    language in, 33, 127, 135; segregation in,
    24–25, 74, 123, 128, 135, 166, 206; Span-
    ish language in, 33, 123, 124, 127, 135,
    205–7, 213; walkouts staged against, 7,
    11, 84, 111, 115, 119–20, 127–39, 142–76,
    180–81, 203, 274.
Schoon, John, 278
SCLC. See Southern Christian Leadership
    Conference
segregation: in Crystal City, 24–25, 33–34,
    42, 47–48, 61, 68, 135; in schools, 24–
    25, 74, 123, 128, 135, 166, 206; at Texas
    A & I, 81, 85–87, 91–93
Segura, Louis, 199, 262–63, 272
Selective Service Board, 97, 113–14
Serna, David, 247
Serna, Diana, 143, 149, 151, 152, 154–57,
    162–65, 193–94, 274
Serna, José, 162, 170, 193, 214, 242, 244, 247
Serna, Olivia, 193–94, 274
Serna, Victoriano ("Nano"), 141, 145–46,
    163
Serna's grocery store, 38
Serra, Junípero, 125
Shafer-Corona, Frank, 218, 228, 234, 240
Sharp, John, 16
Shockley, John, 4–6
Sigala, Homer, 166, 168
Silva, Lina Maria, 295

Sirica, John, 256–57
60 Minutes (TV show), 256
slavery (in Texas), 15–16. *See also* bracero
 program
Smith, Sherrill, 119
Socialist Workers Party (SWP), 223
South Chicago (Indiana), 232
Southern Christian Leadership Confer-
 ence (SLC), 221–22, 224, 235, 313
Southern Methodist University School of
 Law, 287, 291–92
South Texan (Texas A & I newspaper), 89
South Tucson (Arizona), 217
Southwest Council of La Raza. *See* Na-
 tional Council of La Raza
Southwest Texas Junior College (Uvalde),
 78, 104, 151, 245; Gutiérrez at, 51, 56–59,
 71, 74, 101, 123
Southwest Voter Registration and Educa-
 tion Project, 100
Spain, 15, 124–25, 240, 301
Spanish language: at Chicano rallies, 48,
 50–51; importance of, in diplomacy,
 237; at the polls, 39; on the radio, 39;
 in schools, 33, 123, 124, 127, 135, 205–7,
 213
Speer, J. L., 156–59, 167, 168, 170, 176, 183,
 186
Spiders in the House, Workers in the Field
 (Galarza), 17
Stand and Deliver (film), 9
The State of Hispanics in Oregon, 282
Stavans, Ilan, 27
Steen, Ralph W., 16, 17
Steinbaugh, Dimas, 90–91
Stern Fund, 272–73
Stewart, Belvin, 104
Supreme Court of Texas, 36
Sweeten, C. L., 42, 53–55, 57, 74–75, 183,
 190
SWP (Socialist Workers Party), 223

Tafolla, Gabe, 78, 81, 303
Tamez, Cleofas, 156–58, 186
Tapia, Raul, 52–53, 56–57, 71, 75
A Taste of Power (Brown), 9
Tate, R. C., 205
taxes: federal, 18–19; poll, 36–39, 49, 62,
 76, 77, 100, 116
Tax Reform Act of 1969, 118

Taylor, Irl, 243–46, 249, 250
Taylor, Joe, 34–35
Taylor, Jon, 35
Taylor, R. A., 66
TCTA (Texas Classroom Teachers' Associ-
 ation), 207
TEA. *See* Texas Education Agency
TEAM (Texans for the Educational Ad-
 vancement of Mexican Americans),
 164–69, 173, 174
Teamsters Union, 41, 54, 57, 184, 214;
 Cornejo's employment by, 62, 64
Teatro Luna. *See* Luna Theater
Telling Identities (Sanchez), 10
Tenayuca, Emma, 298–99
testimonios, 10
Texans for the Educational Advancement
 of Mexican Americans. *See* TEAM
Texas: Our Heritage (Steen and Donecker),
 16
Texas A & I University, 11, 78–96, 99, 101,
 123, 131
Texas A & M University System, 199
Texas Classroom Teachers' Association
 (TCTA), 207
Texas Education Agency (TEA), 154–57,
 160, 163, 164, 168
Texas Employment Commission, 114
Texas Institute for Educational Develop-
 ment (TIED), 159
Texas Journal, 192
Texas Observer, 51
Texas Rangers, 17, 23, 49, 76, 185, 259, 292;
 and Crystal City school walkout, 154,
 183; and electoral politics, 42–44, 49, 51,
 63, 190–92, 244–45; and farmworkers'
 strike, 105
Texas Rangers (baseball team), 289
*The Texas Rangers: A Century of Frontier
 Defense* (Webb), 17, 103
Texas Rural Legal Aid Foundation, 213,
 287, 291
The Texas Story (Steen), 17
They Called Them Greasers (de Leon), 16
Thomas, Piri, 9
Three Rivers (Texas), 40
TIED (Texas Institute for Educational De-
 velopment), 159
Tijerina, Pete, 114–15, 117
Tijerina, Ramon, 178

Tijerina, Reies Lopez, 178, 239, 313; as Chicano leader, 112, 217, 218, 221–28, 231, 290, 299; and Mexico, 236–37
Tlatelolco Plaza massacre, 224, 235
Tohono O'Odham, 217
Torres, Felipe, 248, 249, 257–62
Torres, Peter, 263
Tovar, Rafael, Jr., 60
Tower, John, 159
Tragedy at Chulamar (Galarza), 17
Treviño, Armando, 143, 147, 151, 154, 161, 163, 172
Treviño, Eddie, 147, 168, 171, 188, 203, 204, 311
Trevino, Lee, 234
Treviño, Mario, 143, 149–55, 157, 161–65, 169
Tualatin (Oregon), 273
Tucson (Arizona), 103
Tuggle, Emmett, 41
Tumlinson, Richard, 61
Turkel, Studs, 9
Turner, J. E., 92
Two Badges (Ruiz), 9
227th Engineering Company, 115

UCLA, 113
Underwood, Jerald, 58
U.S. Agriculture Department, 18
U.S. Army, 114, 115, 264
U.S. Census Bureau, 28, 30
U.S. Commission on Civil Rights, 103, 119, 170
U.S. Corps of Engineers, 257
U.S. Forest Service, 218
U.S. Health, Education, and Welfare Department (HEW), 164–68
U.S. Immigration and Naturalization Services (INS), 293; border patrol of, 23, 285, 286; and *bracero* program, 19, 22
U.S. Justice Department, 170, 171, 225
U.S. Labor Department, 18, 19
U.S. State Department, 234
United Way of the Columbia-Willamette Valleys (Portland), 282, 283, 287
United We Win (Garcia), 6–7, 231
University of California at Los Angeles, 113
University of Houston, 292, 295
University of Oregon, 283
University of Texas (Arlington), 11, 124

University of Texas (Austin), 123, 278; boycotts at, 109–10; Gutiérrez's application to, 71; Gutiérrez's doctoral program at, 98, 113–14; Gutiérrez's papers at, 7, 12–13, 270
University of Texas (San Antonio), 7, 12–13, 270
"Upland Empire" (California), 217
Urista, Al ("Alurista"), 9
USAEUR, 264
Uvalde (Texas), 51, 60, 61, 76, 117, 167, 187, 259; school protests in, 122, 142. *See also* Southwest Texas Junior College
Uvalde County (Texas), 5, 76, 208

Valdez (Alaska), 283
Vasquez, Raul and Nellie, 277
Vela, Carlos, 166
Vela, Romy, 104
Velasquez, Baldemar, 299
Velasquez, Felix ("La Llanta"), 247
Velasquez, Willie, 104, 187; as activist, 99–102, 106, 107, 111; death of, 303; and Democratic Party, 268, 293; and Southwest Council of La Raza, 119
La Verdad (Cristal newspaper), 141, 159, 161, 163, 170–72
Vietnam War, 82, 97, 114
Vigil, Ernesto ("Ernie"), 228
Villareal, Odilia, 74
Villegas, Pete, 153
VISTA (Volunteers in Service to America), 104
Viva Kennedy Clubs, 40, 41, 50, 70
Voter Education Project, 167
voting: by absentee ballot, 37, 63–64; age for, 130; by bloc, 58–59; Chicano attitudes toward, 130–31, 291; forbidden to resident aliens, 218; organizing for, 188–90, 243–44; and redistricting, 293, 295; registration for, in Oregon, 283; registration for, in Texas, 37–39, 41–43, 49, 54, 62, 63, 76–78, 116, 167, 169, 187; Texas law regarding, 219, 220, 243. *See also* poll taxes
Voting Rights Act, 84, 121, 124

Wallace, George, 116
A War of Words (Hammerback, Jensen, and Gutiérrez), 14

War on Poverty, 103–4, 111–13
Washington, D.C., 217, 218, 221–22, 231, 234
Washington, George, 17, 27, 80
Washington, Martha, 80
Washington State, 217, 230
Waterford (Wisconsin), 73–74, 78, 79
Webb, Ruth, 97, 113–14
Webb, Walter Prescott, 17, 103
Weslaco (Texas), 230
West, Mary Nan, 199
Western Oregon State College (WOSC), 275, 277, 281–83, 287
Wheatley, Seagal V., 311
White, W., 98
White House Cabinet Committee Hearings on Mexican American Affairs, 111–13
whites. *See* Anglos
Willamette College of Law (Salem, Oregon), 287
Williams, John, 104
Wimberly (Texas), 117
Winter Garden area (Texas), 5–7, 76, 103; Chicano plans for control of, 177–92, 203; Raza Unida Party in, 218; school walkouts in, 129–41
Winter Garden Cleaners, 169
women: Anglo, and Gutiérrez, 46–48, 59–61, 79; as Black Panther Party leaders, 9; as candidates for political office, 76–77, 246, 249–50; and community organizing, 5, 37, 38, 50, 63, 69, 81, 83, 144–46, 148, 297; discrimination against, 81, 100; employment of, 34, 56, 72–73; and MAYO, 105, 106; separation of, in mixed organizations, 193–94.

Women, Infants and Children program (WIC), 253
Woodburn (Oregon), 282, 287
Woodley (judge), 191
WOSC. *See* Western Oregon State College

X, Malcolm, 10, 299
Ximenes, Vicente, 111–12

Yanas, Antonio, 200
Yanas, Rita, 63
Yanta, John, 104
Yarborough, Ralph, 159, 162, 164, 167
YDs. *See* Young Democrats
Ynosencio, Ester, 149, 162, 168, 186
Yo Soy Joaquin (Gonzales), 9
Young Democrats (YDs), 80, 81, 94
youth (in Chicano movement), 7, 35–38, 50, 81, 82–83, 130
Youth Association, 153–54

Zaragoza, Ignacio, 237
Zavala, Lorenzo de, 27, 48, 116
Zavala County (Texas), 5, 7, 35, 38, 76, 131, 208–9; candidates for sheriff of, 116, 242, 244; governing of, 11, 213–14, 242–68, 272, 275, 287; Raza Unida Party organized in, 187, 277. *See also* Crystal City (Texas)
Zavala County Bank, 244–45
Zavala County Centro de Salud, 252, 253, 257, 284
Zavala County Economic Development Corporation, 253–56
Zavala County Road and Bridge Department, 243, 245–46, 248, 252, 260
Zavala County Sentinel, 52, 154, 255

Wisconsin Studies in Autobiography

Williams L. Andrews
General Editor

Robert F. Sayre
The Examined Self: Benjamin Franklin, Henry Adams, Henry James

Daniel B. Shea
Spiritual Autobiography in Early America

Lois Mark Stalvey
The Education of a WASP

Margaret Sams
Forbidden Family: A Wartime Memoir of the Philippines, 1941–1945
Edited, with an introduction, by Lynn Z. Bloom

Journeys in New Worlds: Early American Women's Narratives
Edited by William L. Andrews

Mark Twain
Mark Twain's Own Autobiography:
The Chapters from the "North American Review"
Edited, with an introduction, by Michael J. Kiskis

American Autobiography: Retrospect and Prospect
Edited by Paul John Eakin

Charlotte Perkins Gilman
The Living of Charlotte Perkins Gilman: An Autobiography
Introduction by Ann J. Lane

Caroline Seabury
The Diary of Caroline Seabury: 1854–1863
Edited, with an introduction, by Suzanne L. Bunkers

Cornelia Peake McDonald
A Woman's Civil War: A Diary with Reminiscences of the War, from March 1862
Edited, with an introduction, by Minrose G. Gwin

Marian Anderson
My Lord, What a Morning
Introduction by Nellie Y. McKay

American Women's Autobiography: Fea(s)ts of Memory
Edited, with an introduction, by Margo Culley

Frank Marshall Davis
Livin' the Blues: Memoirs of a Black Journalist and Poet
Edited, with an introduction, by John Edgar Tidwell

Joanne Jacobson
Authority and Alliance in the Letters of Henry Adams

Kamau Brathwaite
The Zea Mexican Diary
Foreword by Sandra Pouchet Paquet

Genaro M. Padilla
My History, Not Yours:
The Formation of Mexican American Autobiography

Frances Smith Foster
Witnessing Slavery: The Development of Ante-bellum Slave Narratives

Native American Autobiography: An Anthology
Edited, with an introduction, by Arnold Krupat

American Lives: An Anthology of Autobiographical Writing
Edited, with an introduction, by Robert F. Sayre

Carol Holly
Intensely Family: The Inheritance of Family Shame and the
Autobiographies of Henry James

People of the Book: Thirty Scholars
Reflect on Their Jewish Identity
Edited by Jeffrey Rubin-Dorsky and Shelley Fisher Fishkin

William Herrick
Jumping the Line: The Adventures and Misadventures of an American Radical

John Downton Hazlett
My Generation: Collective Autobiography and Identity Politics

Women, Autobiography, Theory: A Reader
Edited by Sidonie Smith and Julia Watson

José Angel Gutiérrez
The Making of a Chicano Militant: Lessons from Cristal